A Handbook for the First-Year Writing Program
at the University of Central Florida

SIXTH EDITION

EasyWriter

Andrea A. Lunsford
STANFORD UNIVERSITY

Coverage for multilingual writers with

Paul Kei Matsuda   **Christine M. Tardy**
ARIZONA STATE UNIVERSITY   UNIVERSITY OF ARIZONA

macmillan learning
curriculum solutions

bedford/st.martin's • hayden-mcneil • w.h.freeman • worth publishers

FOR BEDFORD/ST. MARTIN'S

Vice President, Editorial, Macmillan Learning Humanities: Edwin Hill
Editorial Director, English: Karen S. Henry
Senior Publisher for Composition, Business and Technical Writing, Developmental Writing: Leasa Burton
Executive Editor: Carolyn Lengel
Associate Editor: Jonathan Douglas
Senior Production Editor: Ryan Sullivan
Senior Media Producer: Allison Hart
Senior Production Supervisor: Jennifer Wetzel
Marketing Manager: Emily Rowin
Copy Editor: Wendy Polhemus-Annibell
Indexer: Kirsten Kite
Senior Photo Editor: Martha Friedman
Senior Art Director: Anna Palchik
Text Design: Claire Seng-Niemoeller
Composition: Jouve
Printing and Binding: King Printing

4 5 6 7 8 9 10   23 22 21 20 19 18

For information, write: Macmillan Learning Curriculum Solutions, 14903 Pilot Drive, Plymouth, MI 48170   (macmillanlearning.com)

ISBN 978-1-319-21516-3

ACKNOWLEDGMENTS

Art acknowledgments and copyrights appear on the same page as the art selections they cover.

How to Use This Book

Chances are that you're called on to write and do research often, maybe even every day. Whenever you have questions about writing and research, *EasyWriter* offers quick and reliable answers.

Finding Help in the Book

Brief Contents. Under the front cover flap is a brief table of contents. If you're looking for advice on a specific topic, just flip to the chapter. The tabs at the top of each page tell you where you are.

Model Student Projects. If you're looking for examples of different writing projects, the guide inside the front cover lists models of real student writing in the print book and digital resources.

The Top Twenty. On page 1 is advice on the twenty most common problems teachers are likely to identify in academic writing by first-year students. The Top Twenty provides examples and brief explanations to guide you toward recognizing, understanding, and editing these common errors. Cross-references point to other places in the book where you'll find more detailed information.

Media References. Turn to the back cover for information on all the digital resources — online videos of student writers, exercises, adaptive quizzing, student writing models, and more. Cross-references at the bottom of a page direct you to media content related to that section of the book.

Documentation Navigation. Each documentation section has its own color-tabbed pages; look for directories within each section to find models for citing your sources. Color-coded source maps walk you through the process of citing sources.

Glossary/Index. The index lists everything that's covered in the book. You can find information by looking up a topic, or, if you're not sure what your topic is called, by looking up the word you need help with. The index doubles as a glossary that defines important terms. Any **boldface term** you see in the print book is defined in the index.

Revision Symbols. The list of symbols on the last book page can help you learn more about any markings an instructor or a reviewer may make on your draft.

Glossary of Usage. This glossary, which appears right before the index, gives help with commonly confused words.

Page Navigation Help

The descriptions below correspond to the numbered elements on the sample pages on the next page.

① Guides at the top of every page. Headers tell you what **chapter** or **section** you're in, the **chapter number** and **section letter**, and the **page number**. **Icons** that indicate the name of the section (building blocks for Grammar, for example) also appear at the top of the page.

② "Multilingual" icons. Help for speakers of all kinds of English, and from all educational backgrounds, is identified with a "Multilingual" icon. A directory to all content for multilingual writers appears on p. 389.

③ Hand-edited examples. **Example sentences** are hand-edited in orange, allowing you to see an error or nonstandard usage and its revision at a glance. Orange pointers and boldface type make examples easy to spot on the page.

④ Cross-references to digital resources. Cross-references at the bottom of a page point you to video, quizzing, student writing models, and more.

⑤ Boxed tips. Many chapters include quick-reference **Checklist** boxes with an overview of important information, and **For Multilingual Writers** boxes appear throughout the book.

Grammar

Writing
Processes

Writing
That Works

Research

Grammar

Punctuation/
Mechanics

---

146 25 Modifier Placement

don't make sense. However, many seeming
multiple meanings, all of which are widely
example, *unique* may mean *one of a kind or u*
simply mean *distinctive* or *unusual*.

If you think your readers will object to
more perfect (which appears in the U.S. Co
such uses.

25 Modifier Placement

To be effective, **modifiers** should clearly
modify and should be positioned close to
this command:

DO NOT USE THE ELEVATORS IN CASE O

Should we avoid the elevators altogether,
a fire? Repositioning the modifier *in case*
confusion—and makes clear that we are to
if there is a fire: IN CASE OF FIRE, DO NOT

25a Revising misplaced modifie

Modifiers can cause confusion or ambiguit
enough to the words they modify or if they
than one word in the sentence.

▷ She teaches a seminar this term **on voodo**
The voodoo is not at the college; the seminar

▷ **Billowing from the window, he** saw clouds of smoke;
People cannot billow from windows.

▷ Nixon told reporters that he planned to get out of politics, **after
he lost the 1962 race.**
Nixon did not predict that he would lose the race.

Grammar: Parts of Speech > LearningCurve (4)

Using conditional sentences appropriately **21i** 131

THAT CLAUSES EXPRESSING A REQUEST OR DEMAND

▷ The plant inspector insists that a supervisor *is* on site at all times.

IF CLAUSES EXPRESSING A CONDITION THAT DOES NOT EXIST

▷ If public transportation *was* widely available, fewer Americans
would commute by car.

One common error is to use *would* in both clauses. Use the subjunc-
tive in the *if* clause and *would* in the other clause.

▷ If I *would have* played harder, I would have won.

21i Using conditional sentences
appropriately

English distinguishes among many different types of conditional sen-
tences: sentences that focus on questions and that are introduced by *if* (or
its equivalent). Each of the following examples makes different assump-
tions about the likelihood that what is stated in the *if* clause is true.

▷ **If you *practice* (or *have practiced*) writing often, you *learn* (or *have
learned*) what your main problems are.**

This sentence assumes that what is stated in the *if* clause may be true;
any verb tense that is appropriate in a simple sentence may be used in
both the *if* clause and the main clause.

▷ **If you *practice* writing for the rest of this term, you *will* (or *may*)
understand the process better.**

This sentence makes a prediction about what is
stated may turn out to be true. Only the main clause uses the future
tense (*will understand*) or a modal that can indicate future time (*may
understand*). The *if* clause must use the present tense.

▷ **If you *practiced* (or *were to practice*) writing every day, it *would*
eventually seem easier.**

This sentence indicates doubt that what is stated will happen. In the
if clause, the verb is either past—actually, past subjunctive (21h)—or

---

Preparing a list of sources **16c** 99

For almost all research projects, drafting should begin well before
the deadline in case you need to gather more information or do
more drafting. Begin drafting wherever you feel most confident. If
you have an idea for an introduction, begin there.

Working title and introduction. The title and introduction set
the stage for what is to come. Ideally, the title announces the sub-
ject in an intriguing or memorable way. The introduction should
draw readers in and provide any background they will need to un-
derstand your discussion.

Conclusion. A good conclusion helps readers know what they have
learned. One effective strategy is to begin with a reference to your
thesis and then expand to a more general conclusion that reminds
readers why your discussion is significant. Try to conclude with
something that will have an impact—but avoid sounding preachy.

16b Reviewing and revising a research project

Once you've completed your draft, reread it slowly and carefully.
As you do so, reconsider the project's purpose and audience, your
stance and thesis, and the evidence you have gathered. Then, ask
others to read and respond to your draft. (For more on reviewing
and revising, see Chapter 4.)

16c Preparing a list of sources

Once you have a final draft with your source materials in place, you
are ready to prepare your list of sources. Create an entry for each
source used in your final draft, consulting your notes and working

For Multilingual Writers

Asking Experienced Writers to Review a Thesis

You might find it helpful to ask one or two classmates who have
more experience with the particular type of academic writing to
look at your explicit thesis. Ask if the thesis is as direct and clear as
it can be, and revise accordingly.

Developing paragraphs **2e** 25

▶ *Checklist*

Drafting

▷ Set up a computer folder or file for your essay. Give the file
a clear and relevant name, and save to it often. Number your
drafts if you decide to try a new direction, save the file as a
new draft—you can always pick up with a previous one if the
new version doesn't work out.

▷ Have all your information close at hand and arranged according
to your organizational plan. Stopping to search for a piece of
information can break your concentration or distract you.

▷ Try to write in stretches of at least thirty minutes. Writing can
provide momentum, and once you get going, the task becomes
easier.

▷ Don't let small questions bog you down. Just make a note of
them in brackets—or in all caps—or make a tentative decision
and move on.

▷ Remember that first drafts aren't perfect. Concentrate on
getting your ideas down, and don't worry about anything else.

▷ Stop writing at a place where you know exactly what will
come next. Doing so will help you start easily when you return
to the draft.

you see that your plan is not working, don't hesitate to alter it. If
some information now seems irrelevant, leave it out. You may learn
that you need to do more research, that your whole thesis must be
reshaped, or that your topic is still too broad and should be nar-
rowed further. Very often you will continue planning, investigating,
and organizing throughout the writing process.

2e Developing paragraphs

Three qualities essential to most academic paragraphs are unity,
development, and coherence.

Writing Processes: Planning & Drafting > Student Writing
Writing Processes: Developing Paragraphs > LearningCurve

Welcome to the First-Year Writing Program and your Composition Course! Whether you are taking ENC 1101 or ENC 1102, we hope the course will help you to not only fulfill the University of Central Florida's composition requirements but also to help you develop the reading, thinking, researching, and writing skills that will help you succeed as a writer at UCF and beyond.

In offering a gateway to your writing as a student, a citizen, and a professional, our First-Year courses are designed around a set of shared principles held by writing instructors here at UCF and across the country. These principles have been carefully developed from the best of what research knows about learning to write. All of our courses have been systematically developed from these principles and affirm our dedication to helping you gain firmer footing with your knowledge of writing and your development of writing skills.

ENC 1101 and 1102 at UCF are based on these guiding principles:

- **Writers need both declarative and procedural knowledge about writing.** That is, they need to know how to use language effectively and how to adjust their writing processes to be most effective given the rhetorical situation in which they are writing. But they also benefit from a deep understanding of writing-related concepts such as rhetorical situation, genre, plagiarism, error, incubation, discourse community, and so on. Thus, the UCF composition courses include instruction in drafting and revising, but also have a clear content drawn from writing studies research and theory about composing.

- **Writers need to engage in sustained drafting and revision in order to write most effectively.** Student writers respond best to comments about their writing when they have time and opportunities to incorporate suggestions into revised drafts. Thus, the UCF composition courses are based on a process approach to writing instruction that requires students to engage in substantive global revision over time, in addition to careful editing at the sentence level, to produce thoughtful and polished final drafts.

- **Writers write most effectively when their writing is purposeful, transactional, communicative, contributive, and rhetorical.** Thus, the UCF composition courses encourage students to understand and write for specific audiences to achieve clear purposes that are meaningful to the student.

- **Writing instruction should strive to teach transferable practices and concepts.** Thus, the UCF composition curriculum is rooted in research on knowledge transfer that suggests students should learn flexible concepts about writing rather than rigid rules, and they should engage in continual reflection on their writing practices to encourage mindfulness.

- **Particular genres are best learned in the contexts where they mediate activity.** Thus, the UCF composition curriculum focuses on purpose and content first in the belief that form follows function. Students in ENC 1101 and ENC 1102 will write in a variety of genres appropriate to their rhetorical purposes and learning goals. Genres specific to various disciplinary activity systems (for example, lab reports or philosophy essays) should be taught within the classrooms where those genres mediate meaningful work and learning. Genres or "modes" will not be taught a-contextually in ENC 1101 and ENC 1102.

We know that these principles may differ from how you have been taught to think about writing. In fact, much of your First-Year Writing experience here at UCF may be new to you. But we encourage you to embrace these challenges as adventures in becoming lifelong effective writers across the many writing situations you hope to respond to. All of us, students, teachers, and professionals of all stripes, write more today than in any time in human history. We hope that our Program can give you agency and authority for this new reality.

Angela Rounsaville
Director of First-Year Composition

What Is First-Year Composition at UCF?

The principles that guide First-Year Composition at UCF have been translated for you as a student into learning outcomes, which indicate the practices, skills, and habits of mind that support gaining an expertise in real world writing across a variety of contexts, and especially academic contexts. These learning outcomes also indicate how you might attain those practices, skills, and habits of mind, and are thus fundamental to the assignments you will be asked to complete. These outcomes, as writing actions derived from our principles, will guide not only your assignments but also your instructor's lessons and your assessment. Writing research tells us that it is extremely important for students to know explicitly the skills they are expected to master. Please take time to look over these learning outcomes because they articulate to you what you will learn, how you will learn, and how you will be assessed.

Outcomes for ENC 1101

OUTCOME 1. Students will be able to read and use scholarly texts to support their writing goals.

Possible pathways for demonstrating this outcome include:

- The writer demonstrating an understanding of key readings by using terms, concepts, and arguments from scholarly texts correctly.
- The writer referencing scholarly texts in strategic ways to support writing goals. This might include summarizing, paraphrasing, or quoting.
- The writer applying concepts from scholarly texts in order to consider, analyze, and learn more about their own experiences and examples.
- The writer reflecting on useful strategies for reading difficult texts.
- The writer identifying and explaining the rhetorical moves common to academic, scholarly texts (e.g. creation of a research space, references to prior research, explanation of methodology).

OUTCOME 2. **Students will be able to describe and analyze writing processes in order to flexibly adapt them to support their goals.**

Possible pathways for demonstrating this outcome include:

- The writer using acquired vocabulary to talk about writing processes, including terms like incubation, recursiveness, invention, and revision.
- The writer describing and evaluating their own writing processes.
- The writer investigating and evaluating the writing process of at least one other individual.
- The writer demonstrating substantial and successful revision by creating successive drafts that show global improvement and/ or respond to substantive issues raised by instructor and peer feedback.
- The writer reflecting on their writing processes over time to making claims about learning.

OUTCOME 3. **Students will learn how to adapt to different writing contexts they need to address.**

Possible pathways for demonstrating this outcome include:

- The writer using acquired vocabulary to discuss writing contexts, including terms like rhetorical situation, discourse community, exigence, and lexis.
- The writer analyzing at least one writing context.
- The writer employing style, tone, conventions, and technologies appropriate to the demands of at least one particular genre and situation.
- The writer articulating and assessing the effects of their writing choices on their audiences.
- The writer making claims about their ability to adapt to specific writing contexts by reflecting on their own writing products.

OUTCOME 4: Students will consider how social, rhetorical, and technological contexts shape writing conceptions, processes, rules, and learning.

Possible pathways for demonstrating this outcome include:

- The writer employing acquired vocabulary to discuss how language mediates a community's actions and people's identities, including terms like genre, authority, and literacy.
- The writer identifying and analyzing at least one specific genre and how it is shaped by the particular social and rhetorical context in which it operates.
- The writer analyzing the constructedness of writing conceptions and rules in light of the varying social and rhetorical contexts of academic, professional, civic, and/or personal writing situations.
- The writer evaluating their own conceptions of writing in light of learning in the course.

Outcomes for ENC 1102

OUTCOME 1: Students will be able to analyze and synthesize complex texts in ways that demonstrate an understanding of the situated and intertextual nature of writing and research.

Possible pathways for demonstrating this outcome include:

- The writer using complex texts in strategic, focused ways to both enter into and respond to ongoing inquiry. This might include summarizing, citing, applying, challenging, re-contextualizing, and/or synthesizing relevant background texts.
- The writing is intertextual, meaning that a "conversation" between texts and ideas is created in support of the writer's goals.
- The writer assessing the inquiry and writing choices of other writers to inform their own inquiry and writing decisions.
- The writer responsibly using community-appropriate conventions for citation (e.g., MLA or APA).

OUTCOME 2: Students will engage in a recursive, inquiry-based writing and research process that is meaningful for a specific community.

Possible pathways for demonstrating this outcome include:

- The writer developing and framing a research question or problem that matters to a specific community.
- The writer researching, developing, and employing community-appropriate research and analytical methods.

- The writer working flexibly and iteratively with primary and secondary research, including designing, adapting, and where necessary revising research questions and methods given emergent discoveries.
- The writer using and synthesizing multiple kinds of evidence gathered from various sources and genres (e.g., library research, interviews, surveys, observations, textual analysis, cultural artifacts) in order to support writing goals.
- The writer demonstrating substantial and successful revision by creating successive drafts that show global improvement and/ or respond to substantive issues raised by instructor and peer feedback.

OUTCOME 3: Students will be able to interpret their research findings in order to produce arguments that matter to specific communities by addressing real-world exigencies.

Possible pathways for demonstrating this outcome include:

- The writer producing at least one argument that involves analysis, which is the close scrutiny and examination of evidence, assumptions, and counterarguments in support of a larger set of ideas.
- The writer persuasively articulating the stakes of at least one argument (why what is being argued matters).
- The writer demonstrating a clear understanding of their audience and why their argument matters to that audience, with various aspects of the writing (mode of inquiry, content, structure, appeals, tone, sentences, and word choice) being addressed and strategically oriented to that audience.

OUTCOME 4: Students will examine their own conceptions of writing and research in response to their inquiry, reading, and writing throughout the course.

Possible pathways for demonstrating this outcome include:

- The writer employing acquired vocabulary for discussing the roles that writing and research play in a given community.

- The writer considering the technologies and research methods that mediate writing, research, and the construction of knowledge.
- The writer using acquired vocabulary for discussing their writing and research practices, including reflecting on their own writing situations using terms such as genre, discourse conventions, and rhetorical situation.
- The writer demonstrating a meta-awareness of their growth as a writer and researcher over time by reflecting on their writing and research practices and products and making claims about their learning.

What Do These Learning Outcomes Mean for You?

There are several aspects of these learning outcomes that should be further emphasized. First, you might notice right away their emphasis on the study of writing generally and on your writing, in particular. ENC 1101 and ENC 1102 are not simply classes in which you will write. You will do plenty of that, but you will also learn about writing. We believe that writing and writing about writing are the best combination to support your development as a writer. Thus, in our classes, students act as writing researchers, investigating writings' role for themselves, their families, their friends, and their communities. Students investigate social media writing, writing in the disciplines, writing in popular culture, and more. Students take ownership of concepts and theories about writing from the field of writing studies and use those for their own ends. As writing researchers, students ask questions about writing and how writing works such as: Where do writers get their ideas? How do different writers compose? How do writers know their work is "good"? Why do the expectations for writing seem to change so much from situation to situation, sometimes frustratingly so? Asking and answering questions like professional writing researchers can be profoundly empowering. When writers understand how writing works in their world, they gain valuable insight into how best to use writing to make a difference in those worlds.

The second aspect of these learning outcomes that we would like to emphasize is the role they play in your assessment. Throughout your composition course, you will do a variety of types of writing, in many genres, and for many different purposes. This writing will be

What Do Students Say?

"The First-Year Composition Program at UCF has empowered me as both a writer and a person, enabling me not only to find my voice but to know how to express it in writing. Being capable of employing critical self-examination, unpacking horrifyingly dense academic texts, and constructively utilizing feedback and audience awareness is invaluable in academic writing in any discipline and beyond."

—Gabrielle Casey, Interdisciplinary Studies, Class of 2016

"These classes not only prepare you to conduct your own research, but they also prepare you for what a college course is really like. They say writing a research paper is like running a marathon. It's a long road, but once it's completed you'll feel like a champion crossing the finish line."

—Christina Coffee, Radio-Television, Class of 2016

"At UCF, your composition should be messy. Writing mistakes are good— they're learning opportunities that'll hopefully transform your conceptions of composition."

—Mikael R., Writing and Rhetoric, Class of 2015

"Reading and obtaining information from scholarly articles became much easier for me. I have read academic writing in other classes since then and it was not intimidating or confusing at all."

—Jacob Vogelbacher, Digital Media, Class of 2017

"The first-year composition classes at UCF are some of the most excellent programs I have ever been involved in. The pedagogical benefits of allowing students to incorporate their own disciplinary interests into the field of rhetoric and composition has insurmountable value that is sure to help students in whichever field they choose to pursue. Students gain a proficiency in building upon areas of their own disciplinary fields that provides both academic and social relevance."

—Daniel Huang, Biomedical Sciences, Class of 2017

"The writing program is really a journey into the art and science of communication. I thought I knew what to expect, but I was utterly and pleasantly surprised. This isn't your mother's comp program.... This is 'take it to the real world stuff.'"

— Komysha Hassan, Political Science Pre-Law, Class of 2017

assessed on an individual basis throughout the semester as well as in a final portfolio that you create for your end of semester assessment. While you are likely very used to being assigned and graded on individual writing tasks throughout a school year or school semester, you may be less familiar with final writing portfolios. Like our use of learning outcomes, our use of portfolios derives from our principles statement, which itself comes directly from in-depth writing research. We believe in using portfolios because they showcase both the writing processes and products from a variety of genres and can demonstrate writing development throughout the semester. They are important for helping you synthesize and reflect on your learning and let you be graded on your best work rather than your first work. As we've mentioned, your portfolios are assessed based on your demonstration of the learning outcomes.

Finally, the First-Year Writing Program's main aim is to support your development as a writer. As we hope you can see through the voices of prior ENC 1101 and ENC 1102 students in this section, students in our classes have felt affirmed in this goal.

How Student Scholars Research and Write about Writing

In this section, we include sample student writing from ENC 1101 and ENC 1102 that have been published in *Stylus: A Journal of First Year Writing*, UCF's own journal of first-year student writing. We hope that these selections can both inspire you in your own writing and thinking as well as present you with sample types of writing that may be assigned in your courses. Both ENC 1101 and ENC 1102 are unique courses as they empower student writers to take ownership over writing-related concepts and processes and make them meaningful for their own lives. With writing as the content and the activity of ENC 1101 and ENC 1102, student writers become writing studies experts in their own right. As each example showcases, writers gain knowledge, habits of mind, strategies, skills, and confidence to transfer what they have learned into future writing situations.

In ENC 1101, students encounter and grapple with writing-related concepts such as rhetorical situation, genre, literacy sponsors,

code-meshing, and writing process, and investigate how those concepts matter to and have manifested in their lives. We are honored to showcase the following exemplary student essays from ENC 1101:

Wan, Julie. "Chinks in My Armor: Reclaiming One's Voice." *Stylus: A Journal of First-Year Writing*, vol. 9, no. 1, 2018.

Yandra, Shravan. "Note-Taking Involving Native and Modern Languages: A Detailed Analysis of My Code-Meshing." *Stylus: A Journal of First-Year Writing*, vol. 7, no. 2, 2016, pp. 7–11.

Celestine, Jaydelle. "Did I Create the Process? Or Did the Process Create Me?." *Stylus: A Journal of First-Year Writing*, vol. 8, no. 2, 2017, pp. 1–12.

In ENC 1102, students embark on a semester-long research project into some aspect of writing, rhetoric, literacy, or language. Through semester-long inquiry projects, students in ENC 1102 work hard to ask meaningful questions about writing, research those questions using multiple methods, and then present their findings to real audiences in authentic, disciplinary genres. We are honored to showcase the following exemplary student essays from ENC 1102:

Halvey, Madeline. "Simple Forms of Dance and Movement Literacy." *Stylus: A Journal of First-Year Writing*, vol, 3, no. 1, 2015, pp. 28–36.

Halvey, Madeline. "Annotated Bibliography: Simple Forms of Dance and Movement Literacy."

Samayoa, Priscilla. "The Extent of Influence That Genre Conventions Have on TED Talks." *Stylus: A Journal of First-Year Writing*, vol. 8, no. 2, 2017, pp. 46–59.

Following each work, you will find discussion and reflection questions to push your thinking about how writing—when treated as both the content and the activity of a composition course—can expand our conceptions about itself, help us develop deliberate and empowered relationships to our writing lives, and put us on the path to writing success in future academic, professional, and civic situations.

Showcasing Student Writing in ENC 1101

Chinks in My Armor: Reclaiming One's Voice

Wan, Julie. "Chinks in My Armor: Reclaiming One's Voice." *Stylus: A Journal of First-Year Writing*, vol. 9, no. 1, 2018.

Though I was too young to grasp shame in all its shades and magnitude, my early English transactions can only be described as humiliating, isolating, and fraught with cultural dissimilitude. At a tender three years of age, I was transplanted from rural China to the more urban United States and my nascent literacy was abruptly, vertiginously redefined. After twenty years of persistently conditioning my English writing and speaking, I developed an armor around my person to facilitate my integration and educational advancement. Though restrictive and unnatural at first, it became more fitted and authentic with time. But there remain chinks in the armor even now: eccentricities in my speech that I can't iron out, or certain idioms and pronunciations that continue to elude me because they were unheard-of in my ethnic household. Though unapparent, the chinks glare egregiously once noticed. When I bumble, it isn't absolved as a momentary slip or attributed to mild illiteracy. Rather, it's tantamount to being *un-American*. Even after forfeiting my mother tongue and spending two decades ostensibly assimilating in English, I still can't assume the American psyche of being an unequivocal, unified whole. My early Chinese socialization continues to frame and disrupt my literacy.

When learning English, I had studiously emulated how *White* people spoke because I'd wanted to sound impeccable. But I've since encountered many great orators that collectively broadened the faces and terms I associate with "native" English speaker. Code-meshing advocate Vershawn Young refuted the notion of a standardized English, performed invariably by White Americans, by exhibiting the dismaying illiteracy of even the most affluent, purportedly educated, public officials (164-5). As it stands, White

Americans benefit from inflated perceptions of their literacy while non-Whites are linguistically marginalized and devalued.

I've had the distinct impression throughout my life that my literacy was held to a separate, lower standard. Not uncommonly, it won't be initially assumed or even tacitly acknowledged that I'm fluent in, let alone speak, English. If I delay to respond within nanoseconds of appropriate timing, or am a few decibels shy of hearability, it'll be tersely deduced that I "don't speak English." Within my radius, presumptions take precedence and my tenuous self-identity can be revoked. I've startled people in many parts of the world when I spoke a common phrase in English without a perceptible accent. I recall an incident in Johannesburg, South Africa, where I aroused a woman's sudden fascination in my singular upbringing. Forgetting that *I* approached her, she bypassed my inquiry and demanded, "Where are you from?" She might've been alarmed that I, an outsider, had breached her Western-born stronghold. Conversely, I've discovered that I can set people at ease with a Chinese affectation. I have a White, Asian Studies friend that always laughs, red and breathlessly, when I reproduce my mother's accent. Even though I capably speak it, English is still regarded as a White language and, owed to how others perceive me, I have to constantly re-negotiate and defend against lower estimations of my literacy.

From thirteen months until the age of three, I'd lived in a purely Chinese vacuum under my grandmother's care in Guilin, China. Though the city is touted for its picturesque caves, mountains and rivers, my baby photos depict squalor and filth. In one of my earliest photos, I am squatting beside sewage and litter on a dirt road, with smudged cheeks, inflamed mosquito bites and half of a rice flour biscuit in my hand. I spoke my first words unabashedly and uninhibitedly, in an accepting, shared language fabric of close family and friends. Though affectionately monikered "Guilinese" by my mother and its people, the Guilin dialect is unbearably doltish. The mouth is kept agape and elongated, syllables are rhythmically pitched and unceremoniously dropped, and sudden volume spikes at sentences' end are characteristic. The people

who speak it are unflinchingly uncouth. As an example, if my grandmother half-heartedly tried to discipline me, I'd squawk (in Chinese), "I'll throw uh cawck atcha!" And out of love or ignorance, my grandparents didn't wish or teach me differently.

Across the world in New York City, my parents had completed advanced degrees and were industriously, financially situating themselves, wanting their only child to have a formal, first-world education. They calculated that geographical proximity to esteemed American powerhouses like Yale and Princeton would ensure my ascension, but a grand metamorphosis seemed unlikely. I was a scrawny, unrefined kid in an intimidating, new world. As ghetto as Queens was during the '90s, it remained utterly unrelatable from provincial Guilin. We were comparably much poorer, and it never felt like there was room for us. Our one bedroom apartment was confining and nightmarish. The walls teemed with the ghostly pitter patter of mice and roaches. The summer months sweltered without the costly indulgence of air conditioning. I was disoriented by and unaccustomed to the thick fat crowds, the ear-numbing roar of the LIRR and tall seated toilets. When people spoke to me, they might have well just spoken *at* me. I would press a nervous finger against my lips in ponderance. My father was rarely present during this tumultuous transition. It felt that I'd only see him every few weekends. As English was one of his weaker languages, he had to take a job in another city. I orbited around the only remaining constant, my mother, who served as my de facto translator and literacy sponsor.

When first familiarizing myself with English, my mother and I were already busied with converting my Guilinese to Mandarin, so my mispronunciations and malapropisms of English were enabled and concretized. My parents spoke the bougie, standard Mandarin of prodigious Beijing. They'd met while attending Peking University (China's Harvard). Because my provincial dialect wasn't dissimilar, I could organically decode and mimic them. English, on the other hand, was irreconcilable. When contoured around my tongue, the sounds were graceless, either too drawled or blunted.

Any word I became acquainted with would be reproduced incongruously. I used "sweetheart" often, even though it was very mid-century and sounded incredulous and mismatched for a small, brutish child. Rather, the terminology befitted someone more charming, perhaps a fuller, rosy-cheeked Southern woman; a Western ideal of a deep and capable resource of love. In actuality, and completely opposite my adult reticence, I was once an incredibly loving and effusive child that always gravitated towards my mother. Despite its myriad of hybridizations, my most spoken words retained one message: "妈妈 I love you," or " 我爱你 mama!"

My English vocabulary inherited meanings through comparable Chinese precedents and were initially given minor or supplementary roles. If I wasn't confident that my English sample alone would successfully convey what I wanted to say, I'd resort to a select arsenal of Mandarin with designated meanings. The McDonald's golden arches looked like pigtails to me (ours was beside a Wendy's, so I might've associated both logos with hairstyles). Whenever we walked by I would ask, "Can we go My Donna 辫子的地方 (pigtail place)?" I was decipherable if my mother only circumvented the obtusely accented English and focused on my Mandarin. She alone understood me without question so we failed to address my corrupt language use. I'd pulled heavily from Chinese to draw associations and comparable meanings, so my English was, at its bones, an impure derivative that flailed without context. Linguists have studied the language learning processes of young children and concluded that it's impossible to remove one's first language from the target language (Young 160). Because my English was birthed ancillary to and reliant on my mother tongue, they were intertwined in spite of them being two strikingly different languages.

For a few reluctant weeks, I was placed in day-care even though my mother wasn't working. The experience may have served to gently prod my immersion, but it proved distressing and intolerable. Allegedly, I lacked commonalities with the other children and fundamental, preschool level intelligence. I truly can't remember any friends but can vaguely recall the

impatience and insensitivity of the teachers. I was untranslatable and boring, my reality too austere when compared to the grandiose fictions the children worshipped. My unrushed, lifelike drawings of bowls of rice and squat toilets starkly contrasted with other kids' castles, princesses, and heroes. And somehow, even though I'd practically lived on a farm in China, I wasn't at all advantaged when it came to animals. I didn't know that cows incontrovertibly "mooed" or that pigs could never be the color green. And most offensively, I couldn't use seated toilets. I had to be lifted onto the ivory perch, where I'd ritually squat and splatter pee everywhere.

Though I was hastily removed, I was already knocked out of the safety of my mother's orbit during those lonely, debasing weeks. Exposed to the world, I was suddenly made aware of the edges of my inherent otherness, a deformity and depreciation of my being. My revelation was a kind of double consciousness—a constant duality and tension between my living self and the outward perception that was stigmatized and made inferior—that propelled me to furiously learn English and abate my differences (Young 151). The very next year, I entered Kindergarten with same age peers. Because English wasn't my first language and America didn't feel like "home," I nursed a habit of overcompensating in order to obtain my literacy and some semblance of normalcy.

I was extremely self-conscious of my dictation and how I enunciated. Owed to my anxieties about my speech and general lack of friends, I rarely socialized and turned inward, honing my writing as a means to assimilate. I was never taught how to read or write in Chinese, so the act of putting pen to paper served as immaculate soil for cultivating my English literacy. At our first parent-teacher conference, my mother felt a momentary wave of disbelief followed by immense pride when my teacher declared that I was *good* at writing. After briefly showcasing the notebook to prove that it was indeed my handwriting (my lettering identifiable by its tidy assembly and modelesque stature), she commended my heavily borrowed retelling of the *Three Little Pigs*. I'd apparently absorbed the tale from somewhere and regurgitated the

main plot points during free writing. The lack of ingenuity was obvious, and excused, by my command of sentence structure, paragraphing, and overall grammar. But I question that teacher's judgment because I never considered it a triumphant piece. I knew in my heart that the story was not mine, and that my writing was not good when compared to the enthralling storytelling of the original.

Though that was meant to be a pivotal moment in my life where my literacy first and finally garnered approval and notice from someone with am educative purview, it felt undeserved. She was likely swayed by my mediocre piece because I wore the same clothes day to day, had a fresh off the boat bob cut and an Asiatic monosyllabic surname. Her being impressed was contingent on my being a Chinese immigrant from an impoverished background. The public school was in a multicultural blue-collar sect and I don't believe that the literacy standard would be up to par with those of a more expensive, privileged curriculum. In "Sponsors of Literacy," Deborah Brandt discusses the systemic distribution of literacy and its impacts: as education is democratized and made accessible, its requirements are increasingly stratified and escalated (89). My teacher's expectations were adjusted according to our collectively lower proficiency. In addition to my own vacillation between English and Mandarin, the classroom was filled with the varied dialects of Black, Muslim, and Hispanic students. Most likely, none of us had access to reliable sources of "standard" English.

I improved my faculty of English by emphasizing my reading and writing throughout grade school and was affirmed when my appealing, formulaic essays tested me into challenging, specialized programs in more affluent districts. When I was accepted into a high school for the intellectually gifted on the Upper East Side, my mother became complacent with matters regarding my education and intervened less. We ceased our private, intimate exchanges and gradually drifted further apart with every passing school year. As my performance in English served as precious currency for advancement, it became my predominant, then *only* language. In the mornings, I'd take the

Manhattan-bound train to new English speaking territories, while my mother remained in ethnic Queens. All these years, she's kept biased towards her native tongue while working at the same Citibank in Chinese-concentrated "Falasheng" (Flushing). And yet she coddled my bumbling Mandarin by conversing with me in her lesser English to help me along.

When I'd stopped using bilingual options to convey exclusive nuances with my mother, a monumental portion of my literacy became void. Alarmingly, my writing began deteriorating. It scattered with misdirection, bloated with redundancy, and read jarringly. I fixated on my sentences, composing, re-arranging, and protracting until they lost direction. And though I strained for the right words, they always proved lofty or inaccurate. I grew frustrated with writing and became reluctant towards papers. Teachers' comments felt abrasive, like lashes on tender flesh, but the failure resided in my own work. I couldn't produce clear expressions to explain myself because my thought processes were fundamentally rooted in Chinese, my faculty of which was so lost by then that the memories could've been a remnant from another lifetime. I've yet to develop adequate English equivalents to fill or transition over the vacancies. Without my native speech saturating, supporting, and connecting my ideas, my writing became dissociated, tedious, and ineffectual.

As someone who code-switched and converted, rather than code-meshed and integrated, I lost the raw, expressive quality in my communication (Young 162). I compromised my literacy by letting my Chinese go out of practice and evaporate. I can only manage forced, short exchanges in a language I should naturally, competently speak. I have disappointed expectant relatives and visitors by failing to confidently address them in our once shared dialogue. My parents and grandparents are disheartened by my negligent, vaporous Mandarin. Though they'd wanted me to have an American education, they hadn't expected the brunt of cultural divide. I've attempted to re-learn Mandarin with flashcards, beginner's books, and Chinese dramas, but the characters are unfamiliar and rebound from memory. Having obtusely

abandoned the only language tethering me, I became estranged from my heritage and lost a sense of belonging and clarity.

When I ascribe idiosyncrasies or lapses in my speech to the fact that I am Chinese, I receive an impatient dismissal: "You are Asian *American* and you don't have an accent." Perhaps I've conveniently and too often used my ethnicity as a crutch to allow myself some cultural leeway whenever I rubbed off as abnormal. But it truly is the reason why I speak and write the way that I do. If anyone has a prolonged conversation with me, they'll discern my unusual vocabulary and locutions, my pre-mediated evasions of certain pronunciations, and the underlying tremors that exacerbate my inarticulateness. Nancy Sommers, with her own displaced heritage, aptly describes in "I Stand Here Writing" that "...only children of immigrant parents can understand the embarrassing moments of inarticulateness, the missed connections that come from learning to speak a language from parents who claim a different mother tongue" (217). I began intentionally collecting my mother's peculiarities of speech over the years, as mementos, hoping that I might also inherit her resilience. English is her fourth language. She's managed through two widely disparate continents and marriages. Despite our distinct histories—hers by comparison so weighted with strife—we're united and alike. We both suffer from our respective neuroses (I'm bipolar) but my hypercritical approach, where I overthink and over-strive, also stems from the double consciousness surrounding my incurable otherness.

And yet, all this time, I've been envisioning a perfect, American English that doesn't exist. The threshold concept of writing is that text and language aren't static. Any transmission, regardless of its form, is an attempt in flux and never assured. Its interpretation is based on the audience and the totality of *their* experiences. On the last day of ENC 1101, first year Composition, we watched Jamila Lyiscott's TED performance on her three languages, all beautiful flavors of *English*. After someone implied that they hadn't, on account of her race, expected her to be "articulate," she rebuffed, "I may not come always before you with excellency of speech, but do not

judge me by my language" (Lyiscott). Even if the delivery deviates from what's considered "standard" according to the dominant ideology imposed by those that speak only a single variant, there's a rich, gorgeous quality inherent in the wording of the marginalized (Young 164). Sommers, who argued that every person is a capable source of information, encouraged a more receptive audience, "to be open to other voices, untranslatable as they might be" (220). Even if the conveyance is hard to understand or relate to, there is still something worth a modicum of patience and reflection. Within every transaction, every written or spoken word, is a dynamic, evolving reconvergence of meaning. Just as Young advocated a multi-dialectical society that would benefit from the contributions of everyone's native intelligence by embracing and empowering their multitudes of self-expression, I've begun to appreciate aspects of my literacy that are far adrift from the norm and make my voice inimitable (161). Successful or not, my obsessive method, with its immeasurable layers of wandering, analysis and devotion, produces and contributes my own poetic wisdom.

When a kid summarily hissed "chink" in my direction in 2nd grade, it came into place that being Chinese was a permanent, irrevocable condition—no matter if I didn't speak any Chinese at all. He'd employed its negative connotation, but I've since reexamined and reassigned its meaning. Wardle and Downs preface their reasons for studying writing by reporting that most people have painful literacy beginnings that permeate into their later lives as writers, and that while those initial feelings can adjust over time, we remain "an accumulation of everything we have experienced" (9). My own process of learning English wasn't without difficulty and sacrifice. Adapting and functioning in a social capacity in order to further my education required building an armor around my person. I relied so heavily on the armor that I forgot to take it off and converse with my grandmother on the phone from time to time. I didn't reclaim and secure my heritage, so the armor became hollow, fragile, and developed chinks. But the chinks in my armor are intrinsic and meaningful. My literacy is the culmination of my singular life experiences,

and my chinks are the acquired, distinctive scars that allow the light from within to shine through.

Works Cited

Brandt, Deborah. "Sponsors of Literacy." Wardle and Downs, pp. 68-99.

Lyiscott, Jamila. "What Does It Mean to Be 'Articulate'?" *TED Radio Hour*, 14 Nov. 2014, npr.org/templates/transcript/transcript. php?storyId=362372282.

Sommers, Nancy. "I Stand Here Writing." Wardle and Downs, pp. 212-22.

Wardle, Elizabeth, and Doug Downs, editors. *Writing about Writing: A College Reader*. 3rd ed., Bedford/St. Martin's, 2017.

Young, Vershawn Ashanti. "'Nah, We Straight': An Argument Against Code Switching." Wardle and Downs, pp. 148-71.

Responding to "Chinks in My Armor"

QUESTIONS FOR DISCUSSION

1. Wan spends time in her literacy narrative fleshing out ideas related to literacy from her own experiences and from other sources, such as Vershawn Young, Deborah Brandt, and Nancy Sommers. What new or familiar ideas did you find in Wan's narrative related to literacy? What is new or familiar about them? How does this help you add to or reinforce your prior understanding of literacy?

2. Make a list of the literacy sponsors and experiences Wan includes in her literacy narrative. How did each of these play a role in her literacy development? What is significant about these sponsors or experiences?

QUESTIONS FOR REFLECTION

3. In her final paragraph, Wan cites Wardle and Downs to discuss how our beliefs, practices, and attitudes toward reading, writing, and language are the culmination of all of our literacy experiences over time. Considering your own literacy history, what literacy sponsors and experiences stand out to you, and why? What are

some of your beliefs, practices, and attitudes toward reading, writing, and language, and how have they been shaped over time?

4. How does motivation play a role in Wan's literacy development? How do you think motivation has played a role in your own literacy development, and what has impacted that motivation?

5. Many of Wan's literacy experiences revolve around her desire to perfect her speaking and writing in American English. What do you consider to be "good" writing, and how have your literacy experiences shaped that definition?

ACTIVITIES FOR FURTHER EXPLORATION

6. Threshold concepts are those constructs or new sets of knowledges that, once known, transform how we understand the world. For studies of writing and literacy, threshold concepts include ideas and realizations about how writing works that often fly in the face of prior misconceptions. Once we internalize these concepts, though, we move to a new place of understanding and see the world of writing in a whole new and clearer light. Wan's analysis of her literacy history leads her to realize that she has "been envisioning a perfect, American English that doesn't exist." What threshold concept of writing underlies this realization, and what does it mean to you? Extending Wan's essay and line of thinking, how has this threshold concept impacted your life? What can you know or do differently after having realized what this concept is and how it works?

Note-Taking Involving Native and Modern Languages: A Detailed Analysis of My Code-Meshing

Yandra, Shravan. "Note-Taking Involving Native and Modern Languages: A Detailed Analysis of My Code-Meshing." *Stylus: A Journal of First-Year Writing*, vol. 7, no. 2, 2016, pp. 7–11.

In the present world, where there is so much exchange of information, people cannot remember everything heard in speeches, lectures, and conversations. The mind of the receiver cannot retain every piece of important information provided by the source with one hundred percent

accuracy. This is common for everyone from a first grader to a professor with a doctorate degree. Even though the audience might be very keen observers, they might not remember what they hear over a considerable amount of time. So, there is a need to practice an activity to remember and keep track of the ideas projected by the speaker. People engage in a number of writing activities; however, from my personal experiences, I think that note-taking activities play a significant role in the retention of ideas in a systematic and efficient manner. Using multiple languages such as Hindi, Sanskrit, and English increases the speed of this activity and helps me retain knowledge of these languages for a long time. I mainly use Hindi to present my ideas briefly and Sanskrit to describe the actions of the subject. Suresh Canagarajah, in his chapter, "World Englishes as Code-Meshing," explains that code-meshing is a process of combining different languages to communicate an idea in a more efficient manner (273). When I do code-meshing, I use multiple languages because it helps me save time during note-taking, as well as retain knowledge about Hindi and Sanskrit languages. Code-meshing helps me communicate my ideas to myself in a concise manner, understand multiple features of how languages work together, and maintain relationships with other people who speak the same languages.

I started taking notes in classes when I was in the eleventh grade. In the beginning of the year, my friend, Vinay Gupta, helped me inculcate the habit of note-taking in class using English. He constantly reminded me of the importance of taking notes as a tool to focus in class and revise in the future for examinations. After regular reminders from him, I started getting habituated to this writing activity. I continue to use pencil and paper to note the ideas in class so that I can make necessary corrections in case of errors. I start my note-taking by writing a date on the left-hand side of the page. I generally take notes only in History, Politics, Geography, and other subjective classes because I cannot memorize the facts presented in these subjects. Since facts were not always explained with logic and theory, I forgot them as time passed. Therefore, using a note-taking strategy during the lectures

helped me pay attention in classes as well as study for the examinations. My notes are concise and easy to review, so I did not have to read entire chapters in the textbook to prepare for the examination. On the other hand, writing notes in the class is challenging, as I have to write very fast in order to follow with the professor.

Although I wrote the notes in English from the beginning of the eleventh grade, I started incorporating two different languages into my note-taking as my friend, Neha Singh, advised me to do so at the beginning of twelfth grade. Sanskrit is one of the most commonly used languages of India. I learned Sanskrit as my third language from fifth grade to eighth grade. The main reason for the inclusion of Sanskrit into my note-taking is my passion for becoming more proficient in using verbs in Sanskrit. In Sanskrit, there are about thirty different forms of words representing a particular verb, determined by the tense and the number of people involved in a particular action. Since learning all the verbs by just reading them from books and using them is a tedious process, I thought of including the verbs in my daily writing activities. As my note-taking activity does not require a second person reading my text, I could include Sanskrit in my writing. I made notes only for myself and made them in such a manner that only I could understand. This gave me the freedom to use any language that I wanted.

Figure 1: Sample of my note-taking activity taking during my Florida History class

Along with Sanskrit, I started using English and Hindi in my note-taking activity. I am proficient in English and Hindi as they were my first and second languages respectively in the curriculum followed by my school. So, I started learning these languages from second grade onwards. Among all languages, I use English more often as I am more skilled in this language over the others. My school emphasized learning English and this prompted me to learn English more effectively than any other language. I mainly use English for noting the nouns in the sentences as I was exposed to various different types of nouns from my childhood. Hindi is one language that, used at appropriate places, conveys a large meaning in short phrases or words. I use Hindi in certain places as it uses a limited number of words to convey a greater number of ideas. The note- taking writing activity including code-meshing is so efficient that I still continue to do this even in my present classes. For example, the figure above illustrates my note-taking activity in my Florida History class. This was one of the classes that I was enrolled in during my first semester as a freshman at the University of Central Florida. I felt that this class included a lot of facts that could not be learned through a reasoning approach. So, I extensively used note-taking in this class to successfully gain knowledge about the history of Florida.

The title of my note-taking activity involves two different languages—Hindi and English. The first word depicts that this chapter is a concise history. Then I included "Florida" in English that shows the main subject of discussion. In total, the title implies that this is a chapter that provides a brief historical description of Florida. Under the title, I stated two Sanskrit words that mean "first came" and a single English word that states the main subject of discussion in the point—Spanish. In the second point, I used English to describe that Florida, also known as the Sunshine State, is the main port of entry for the invaders. In this sentence, I lacked the knowledge of conversion of verbs into Sanskrit. Also, I could not find a way to shorten this sentence by conversion into Hindi. In the sentence below, I used Hindi words that mean that the weather is generally very hot and the air contains

a lot of water vapor. This results in a hot and humid climate. I used an arrow to connect the details to the subject. In total, the two sentences describe the weather of Florida and the importance of Florida for the United States. The next two sentences are in English, as they are comprised of nouns which include the names of tribes and which country ruled the United States at a particular time. So, I could not write them in any language other than English. The dots after the word "Seminoles" indicate that there were various other tribes pertaining to the same locality, but the ones listed are the most significant ones. However, the fifth point in the figure states a Hindi word meaning there was a significant transfer of infectious diseases. So, the fifth point states that with the invasion of Europeans into the United States, infectious diseases were transferred to the Americans on a large scale. In the last sentence, the Sanskrit word represents that something was eaten in large quantities. When I combine the English words with the Sanskrit word in the sentence, I understand that corn was a major part of the diet of Seminole community. Therefore, I understand that code-meshing helps me save time during note- taking and also helps me retain knowledge about Hindi and Sanskrit languages.

Code-meshing directly influences me and indirectly plays an important role in my social life. Using two languages apart from English in my daily life that are related to my home country, India, helps me remember these languages in a more apt manner. Also, I gain more fluency in these languages, which supports me better during communication in these languages. For example, I always have a conversation in Hindi with most of my friends in India as they speak this language. If I did not code-mesh different languages in my writing, I would gradually lose command over the languages and might not be able to make proper conversation with friends. Eventually, this might also create rifts in friendship due to lack of proper conversation with them. Also, having a conversation in another language would not allow me to share my emotions comfortably. So, I think code-meshing different languages helps me retain the knowledge about various languages that I learned in my home

country before high school. Also, I can continue to speak to my parents in Hindi, which is given primary importance in my family. So code-meshing enables me to communicate and think in Hindi. As a result, I can continue communicating fluently in the language that has been given high importance in my family for generations.

Apart from retaining knowledge about languages, I save a lot of time by using a code-meshing process while taking notes in the classes. This writing activity helped me as it made my work easier and faster. For example, in the image of my note-taking for my Florida History class, I included three Hindi words below the second point that explained the weather conditions as hot and moist air. However, if I would have written in English then I would have written, "Weather – Very hot, air consists of the intense amount of water vapor." This shows that using code-meshing helps to reduce the word count that results in less time taken to complete my note-taking. On the other hand, some people feel that using code-meshing requires more effort and consumes more time. In "From Journals to Journalism: Tracing Trajectories of Literate Development" by Kevin Roozen, Angelica Herrera explains how code-meshing makes her put more effort into her writing. She states, "It took me a long time to come up with it" (Roozen 557). This was her reaction when she got a comment on her essay that was submitted in her English 100 class. While trying to incorporate her voice in her writing, she took a huge amount of time to produce creative opening sentences in her first paper. This shows that different methods of code-meshing take different amounts of time to complete.

Besides serving as a force in my world, integrating code-meshing into my note-taking has helped me realize the important features of using languages. Like Suresh Canagarajah, who asserted, "The languages of multilinguals are not necessarily at war with one another; they complement one another in communication" (274), I learned from my writing activity how languages are dependent on each other to convey the main idea clearly. In the example I provided about note-taking, the words in Hindi and Sanskrit

provide specific details for the words in English that helped me understand the main idea of the sentences in an intelligible manner. The absence of any one of the languages in my writing activity would have created difficulty for me in understanding precisely about Florida and its history. Contrary to my experience, Angelica faced a situation where she was told that her mixtures of codes did not work really well. In the English 100 class, the professor did not value the Spanish method of writing descriptive introductions in the assignments. In addition, the professor was inclined towards writing specifically about the topic rather than providing an imaginary description in the beginning of the essay.

Another crucial feature I learned about language is that multiple languages cannot be used in public writings. In my method of code-meshing, I cannot employ languages such as Hindi and Sanskrit in my examinations and other assignments that require submission to professors. The main reason is because English is the primary language that is highly valued by the educational system in my school. So, my strategy of code-meshing is limited to private forms of writing in which a second person is not involved in reading the way I code-mesh. My situation is profoundly different from the situation encountered by Angelica in her Journalism 150 class. In Angelica's method of code-meshing, she was successfully accepted by her professor. In his analysis, Roozen writes, "The instructor recognized this paper as a successful performance, praising Angelica for the drama she created in the closing portion" (560). The instructor not only found that Angelica's strategy was valuable, but encouraged her to continue this method.

Therefore, code-meshing helps in learning different aspects of languages. In general, code- meshing is a term that is not commonly known by a lot of people around the world. In fact, many people use code-meshing in their daily lives without the knowledge of it. Each person code-meshes in different techniques to achieve certain objectives. Some methods of code-meshing are more efficient than others in conveying the main idea. So, people should choose whatever method they intend to apply in an activity to achieve

success. They might face difficulties during the application of code-meshing strategies; however, they should have determination and confidence when completing that activity.

Works Cited

Canagarajah, Suresh. "World English as Code-Meshing." Code-Meshing as World English: Pedagogy, Policy, and Performance, edited by Vershawn Young and Aja Martinez, 2011, pp. 273- 81.

Roozen, Kevin. "From Journals to Journalism: Tracing Trajectories of Literate Development." *College Composition and Communication*, vol. 60, no. 3, 2009, pp. 541-572.

Responding to "Note-Taking Involving Native and Modern Languages"

QUESTIONS FOR DISCUSSION

1. What is code-meshing, and what are the reasons Yandra finds it to be beneficial? Provide specific examples from his analysis to explain these advantages.

2. In "Chinks in My Armor: Reclaiming One's Voice," Julie Wan says that she code-switched rather than code-meshed. Now that you've read Yandra's work, consider the differences between code-switching and code-meshing. Discuss examples from these authors' experiences navigating multiple languages, and compare the outcomes of Wan's code-switching approach with Yandra's code-meshing approach.

3. What are some rhetorical choices that Yandra analyzes in his code-meshing? Provide an example or two of your own writing and discuss how different audiences, exigencies, contexts, and constraints have impacted the ways you use language(s).

QUESTIONS FOR REFLECTION

4. One of the learning outcomes of ENC 1101 is that "students will be able to describe and analyze writing processes in order to flexibly

adapt them to support their goals." How had Yandra adapted the creativity afforded through code-meshing to support specific goals he has as a student? What about code-meshing encourages this kind of flexibility for writers, and how have or might you use code-meshing to support your writing goals?

5. Yandra's essay reveals a richly literate life and wealth of writing-related knowledge that he already possesses. For instance, he shows us how he developed for himself code-meshing strategies to make note-taking more efficient. Think of some literacy practices where you are your sole audience. What are some of the ways that you use language(s) to benefit yourself as the writer and reader?

6. Yandra notes that there is freedom to his code-meshing approach because he only writes for himself. Can you think of any situations in which you felt you had more freedom as the speaker or writer? If so, what do you think contributed to that sense of freedom? If not, why do you think you've never felt a sense of freedom while speaking or writing?

ACTIVITIES FOR FURTHER EXPLORATION

7. Yandra uses the writing theory of code-meshing to investigate and analyze his own writing activity, and he argues, after having done his self-analysis, that code-meshing is a rhetorical act. He states that "Each person code-meshes in different techniques to achieve certain objectives. Some methods of code-meshing are more efficient than others in conveying the main idea. So, people should choose whatever method they intend to apply in an activity to achieve success." Use Yandra's article and argument as a model for your own reflection on a text or series of texts you've composed recently. Think of examples where you might have included multiple languages or codes, multiple registers (formal and informal), or multiple modes (textual, visual, gestural). How did the interaction of each language, code, register, or mode enhance or interact with the other? What strategic decisions were behind using certain languages, codes, registers, or modes over another? How did the circumstance for which you wrote affect these rhetorical choices?

"Did I Create the Process? or Did the Process Create Me?"

Celestine, Jaydelle. "Did I Create the Process? Or Did the Process Create Me?" *Stylus: A Journal of First-Year Writing*, vol. 8, no. 2, 2017, pp. 1–12.

I'm at my desk in my dorm finishing breakfast and I don't really know where to start. It is a beautiful Friday morning, and navigating my thoughts as to the best way to proceed with this essay proves much more difficult than I anticipated. I never gave much thought to the habits and factors that influenced my writing process, and now I've been challenged to do so. My approach needs to be specific, different to what I've already been taught. As I get lost in my thoughts and explore the patterns of my earliest pieces of literary work from the earliest parts of my childhood, slowly, each piece falls into place. I surprise myself as to the memories that I uncover, the emotions I felt and the breakthroughs I've made. What is happening, I soon realize, is the beginning of a beautiful story that culminates at this stage in my life and reveals the factors of which make me the writer I am today.

At this moment I have the entire dorm to myself. This is the ideal setting for me. Over the years I have definitely been able to produce most of my best work this way, in seclusion. I raise my hands to type, and a truck pulls up rumbling loudly outside for what seems like forever. I could *never* focus in uproar, especially when I remember how my process started as a child and the role my mother had in that process.

I believe my mom is the primary catalyst as to the affinity I've developed when it comes to both reading and writing. At that point in time, she worked at our local library, which was very close to our school. Once classes ended, I'd make my way straight to the library to wait on her to finish work so we could go home.

In the earlier stages, she would sit me down in a room at the back, give me a book to make my company until she was ready, and close the door. It was always just me in that room, and reading without any distraction was

amazing. I was my own company; I could concentrate and disappear into my own little world of wild imagination until 4 o'clock. I really enjoyed that space she created for me, and it definitely stayed with me more than I thought throughout my life as well.

As I got older, I chose my books while I waited in that same room and my imagination slowly broadened. You would think it stopped there, but it didn't. Most of my gifts as a young boy growing up included toys, but it mainly consisted of books. A book then became my favorite gift. I preferred it above all else (well, not counting the occasional twenty-dollar bill that would fall out of my birthday and Christmas cards). As time progressed, it was books like *Goosebumps*, *Robin Hood*, *Frankenstein*, *Dr. Jekyll and Mr. Hyde*, *The Time Machine* and countless others that inspired me to become a storyteller of my own one day. Those books had me writing all sorts of idle short stories whenever I could as a result.

The Profound Effect of My Facebook Story

It was a warm Thursday morning in May 2014, and I was on the computer in our study room at home. Our study room was very cozy. A dark green carpet that lined the floor, a thick, sturdy mahogany desk near the window, as well as a huge shelf on the left that climbed upwards of four levels, housing books, board games and VHS cassettes of my early childhood.

I literally had nothing to do on the computer that day: I opened and closed browsers, googled all sorts of nonsense that came to mind, found nothing interesting on YouTube. And so I made my way to Facebook. Well that was initially an effort in futility as well; there was nothing fascinating happening there either. Generally, it was just people complaining about life and asking questions to engage comments, such as, "Who'd you rather, Rihanna or Beyoncé?" and a couple of interesting pictures sprinkled in between the timeline to break up the monotony.

I remember hearing cheesy music playing, looking around at the TV, and saw that it was a rerun on one of our local channels of the soap opera, *The*

Young & the Restless. I watched for a bit, intrigued as this lady was crying hysterically begging this old guy not to leave her and him telling her rather directly that he couldn't do *this* anymore (whatever *this* was). After snapping myself out of watching that tragedy, I was gazing at our airport out of the study window at the lone British Airways flight that remained the night prior, and my mind ran on my family in England.

Turning around at the TV once more, there was an advertisement now of a new *Beauty & the Beast* DVD in HD or something like that. I told myself that women always needed saving, that they were always perceived as "damsels in distress" and someone needs to do something about that. Men are not always the bad guys, or the "beasts" they're most times made out to be.

That was all it took. I closed the study door to rid myself of distractions, opened up the note portion of my Facebook page, and started writing the ideas that came to my mind. This consisted of a prince and a princess, dancing at a ball after their marriage ceremony in their English palace. This story would be different, the woman would be the bad guy and no one would be the wiser. I set it all up so that it all it appeared to be her dream come true after growing up poor and marrying into royalty, but included a mass murder at said ball with her trying to escape for her life, only to reveal that she orchestrated the entire thing. It took me a while to really get it all together. I knew what I wanted to do, but I had never done a written piece in that format and especially on a forum like Facebook.

I would usually try to isolate myself away from any distraction, give myself a time frame to work with, draft my thoughts via pen and paper, proofread, type out my final product, review and do whatever necessary after. This was different, and a new turning point happened that would slightly alter how I approached writing. I just typed as the words came, paused occasionally, read it over and made slight changes. What eventually continued happening in that moment was I tried to type so fast as the ideas came. It was like I didn't want to stop for fear of losing the ideas through the momentum.

Inevitably I stopped, and stopped a lot, because I ran out of ideas. I found myself stretching, staring at my screen, playing with our dog or going outside, and walking around idly and finding stuff to do in the kitchen that I wouldn't normally do. I was trying to find some sort of inspiration, or unconsciously giving myself a break. The longer I stayed away, the more I heard my secondary school English teacher, Ms. Patrick, in my head saying, "Paint their minds with your creativity, Jaydelle. Be descriptive, reel them in."

Ms. Patrick is always in my head now, anytime I write something, always coaching and constantly criticizing. I always try to live up to her expectations because she always believed and fed my potential. However, I would then head back to the computer and find myself googling stuff again, trying to listen to music (which helped, but later on in life would just become a distraction), and then heading back in an attempt to finish the piece. I did finish. I started around 9 am and was able to post it a little before noon. That has always affected me in my writing going forward, as that ritualistic fashion of starting and then straying or procrastinating has stayed with me to this day, a process that was nowhere near the habits I had in secondary school.

After all was said and done, I was able to hit the post button of my short story, and received much more feedback than I anticipated. People actually read it and I felt pretty good. They didn't just hit the "like" button, but some commented too, on my seven-paragraph story born out of idleness. Ms. Patrick would be proud. It felt much longer after having read the finished product, but the feedback encouraged me to do a second piece in July of that same year. All because of my imagination from those damn books as a child, with a little nudge from a soap opera, a *Beauty & the Beast* commercial, and some time on my hands. It made me continue writing more short stories after that, but what was even stranger was that whereas before I would have written drafts down with pen and paper, I now begun typing it via Microsoft Word. My primary and secondary school processes were somewhat abandoned and this new one now formed. It still remains a huge part of who I am in my writing, to this day.

The Woman Who Changed the Process

Here enters this professionally clad lady on a sunny morning in January of 2001. She was about 5'7", walking slowly but proudly, holding the edges of her black jacket. She wore a hairstyle reminiscent of Scary Spice from the Spice Girls, and had way too much makeup on. She chewed her gum vigorously as though anxiously awaiting something to happen and wore a smile that accentuated how badly she had lined her lips. Her mouth opened and surprised everyone with a deep and boisterous, "Good Morning, boys!" and received the echoes of us all in the room as we stood and greeted her back. "I am Angela Patrick, your English A Teacher. Please have your seats."

Ms. Patrick was both the *worst* and the *best* English teacher I've ever had. She pushed you to your limit, especially as far as being creative was concerned. Not only did she love a good piece of writing, she spoke and breathed it as well. Anyone from the class of '06 could tell you that she could beat a metaphor to death. She encouraged us differently than any other teacher I had up until that point: write a draft, read and make corrections, produce the final piece, but verify one last time. Having to do all that and be timed in 40-minute class sessions helped make us some of the most efficient writers of the 2006 graduating class. It became so natural after the initial stress of it passed, and a lot of us had her to thank as it helped us in time management as well. Her grading scheme was particularly rigid, even for the simplest of assignments. If any student got as much as an 18/25, it was cause for mass celebration. Her main gripe was never punctuation; rather, it was pulling out of us the potential she knew was there. She emphasized content, helping the audience live vicariously through our work. She expected nothing less.

There was one instance I remember her coming to class in her usual mid-morning slot and spontaneously giving us one of her infamous "Short Story" assignments. However, this experience was different, because generally what accompanied those assignments were at least five topics to choose from. This time, we were on our own to choose whatever we wanted, and

have it completed by the end of our 40-minute class session. Knowing what Ms. Patrick expected, the pressure was on. Everything had to be perfect, from introduction through the body and wrapping it up at the end.

This was a bit difficult to do. As a 15- or 16-year-old student, you were already accustomed to having been spoon-fed your creative direction, and now you felt like a fish out of water when it was left up to you. I had no topic and no idea what I wanted to write about. Plus, attending an all boy school was the worst as far as distraction was concerned; it made it so difficult to focus at times. I always wanted to escape and gather my thoughts as I usually do, but I couldn't. Here it was again, this pesky noise issue following me, and I had no control over it. I couldn't come up with anything.

Before we knew it, the bell rung and students started fussing about who wasn't finished, who had nothing and if we could complete it for homework. Unknown to everyone, the joke was on us and Ms. Patrick was going to have the last laugh. She told us that this wasn't a graded assignment, and we all stared in shock. Her response in turn was this: "You boys have to learn that there would be times when you're asked to pull from you, not have someone pull from yourselves, for you." In hindsight it made sense, but back then it felt like the worst thing ever. She asked something very simple of us, yet none of could do it effectively (and, at 16, that's a bit embarrassing. I bet it made for a good staffroom joke though). We had to learn to expect the unexpected and be prepared for anything, and that didn't apply only for her class, but for life in general.

Putting the Pieces Together

I've realized while typing this that what it means for me to produce an effective written piece has changed over time and has been heavily tied in part to my environment, which in turn affects my writing habits. From writing short stories as a child in a primary school of over three hundred, that lacked partitions between classes and having no sense of strict time for the assignments. To essays and assessments of varying degrees in a more

organized secondary school, but with three times the students, a stricter time rule and set revision pattern. To now, an actually structured research essay, rigid citation guidelines and projects while at the mammoth of a school that is UCF, but where you as the student have more control as to what your environment is and how it affects your output. I honestly don't know the exact reason why those habits changed, but I'm sure it has something to do with what each of my teachers required at those various stages of my life. However, back then, each stage would have served me as some sort of guide as to how I should go about writing each required piece of text, thus culminating into what my writing habits and preferred environment are at this point in my life.

In primary school we didn't know better, but we had more freedom to express ourselves with just a tad bit of guidance into associating with the norm. I was never as productive as I could be surrounded by distraction, though, as I remember my mom clearly telling me that my teachers back then said. I would rip my paper up and put my hand over my ears when I wrote something; noise and I just weren't the best of friends. My teachers would, however (with the best of intentions I'm sure), tell me how it's supposed to be done and make sure I did so accordingly.

In secondary school, a defined structure was given, and we had to navigate how to produce our best piece of work within a more firm time frame and very formal setting. That period of time in particular was annoying because there wasn't only chaos to worry about in an all boy school; you had to satisfy what your teacher wanted and still inject a part of you into that work.

My two years at the T.A. Marryshow Community College were also very revealing to me; the game changed drastically. No teacher paid you the time of day, like they did back in secondary school. Nobody had time to run after students begging them to turn in work, or give them pep talks. You were in charge of you, and the environment was much different now as you returned to a mix of co-ed students, who were free to skip class at their choosing and a host of other unproductive choices to choose from. As spacious as the

campus was, noise was still everywhere. By now you would think I'd be able to navigate through the distraction of others given I've been prepped for it all of my life, but I still wasn't. You would also think that being from a culture whereby the people naturally talk at more elevated levels, I could deal with that too, but it proved challenging.

As a culture in the Caribbean, we tend to be loud, dramatic and very descriptive with how we communicate, and it rolled over into teachings at home and in the classroom. To give you a better idea, we don't just say, "Take a left and around the corner there's a red building, that's your destination." We might say, "Take a left and look for a tall tree that's bent slightly as though it has scoliosis, then around the corner you would find a bright red building, made completely of bricks, and you usually have to enter where there's an exit sign." Both ways are effective, but one more memorable than the other. This innate trait of who we are as a people, coupled with my imagination and love of film, always resulted in me writing short stories.

How My Culture Impacted the Process

My island itself—Grenada—is rather small. We're about 133 square miles and our population is approximately 106,000. We have sparkling blue waters, clear skies, sunny days and friendly people. We are but one of the many gems the Caribbean has to offer. Coming from a small island, you tend to either run the risk of (1) not being heard of, (2) mistaken for somewhere else, or (3) having to find some trait that stands out so you can inject yourself into a conversation to let people know that they may in fact know who you are.

Our families and communities are tight-knit. Everyone knows everyone (both a gift and a curse) and in the rare instances you don't know someone, they know you (generally by parentage). Coming from a smaller island in the Caribbean also affords a loose version of the "Napoleon Complex." We feel the need to overcompensate, as we aren't recognized on the same level as everyone else. Growing up in this environment instilled a sense of pride whenever an islander received positive international recognition, and

reinforced that no matter how small we might be that we should always be especially proud of our heritage.

My life changed when I got accepted to one of the largest universities in Florida, for the fall semester of 2016. The University of Central Florida boasts a student population of approximately 60,000. This in itself was overwhelming. On my first official day of school, I saw so many different people of all shapes and sizes, colors and creeds from various walks of life that it left me in awe. I've been to New York and I've traveled to many other Caribbean islands, but obviously nothing compares to the institution that is UCF. As Dorothy would tell me, I was definitely not in Kansas anymore.

Walking through the Student Union was the best feeling for me; I saw the flags of countries that represented the nationalities of UCF's student population. Anxiously looking for mine (I couldn't be the only Grenadian here); I was left with the disappointment that my flag wasn't there. I probably looked like a madman pacing back and forth looking through each row just to be certain, and taking pictures on top of that too. After confirming what was inevitably true, I walked away and decided I would fix that. But how would I? I would fix it through one of my most favorite mediums: writing.

In January 2017, I spoke to a polite young lady at the Guest Services Desk at the Student Union, and asked her who the best person was to speak to regarding the issue of my flag. She pointed me in the direction of Jamie Morales (the Associate Director in charge of Maintenance and Operations for the Student Union). So, in transit to my next class, I crafted a formal inquiry that praised the diversity of UCF, how happy I was to be there, and its efficiency that was displayed to me in any aspect when I needed it. Ms. Patrick taught me back home that to be successful in conveying an effective message one must know how to appeal to the senses of whom they are speaking to. This allowed me through my email, to further confirm the good work that UCF has been doing over the years by touching on its efficiency, as well as acknowledging how large and diverse a school it indeed is and the

people that continue to make it that way by how helpful they are. However, I also conveyed the absence I felt from that diversity when I noticed my flag wasn't there, and that I felt my culture wasn't recognized on the level it should be with everyone else. Being able to speak up helped serve as a catalyst to effect this change I wanted, through a written piece.

Maybe if I wasn't literate enough, or didn't have the experience of writing so many essays in the past, I would not have known what was alright to say or not in this circumstance, but my experience taught me better. Mr. Morales messaged me back within minutes, thanking me for my email and explaining why I may not have seen it there, as well as a link of the flag to ensure that had the correct one for when they had to place the order. He assured me my flag would be there very soon, and I felt that he understood my message and was going to do his best to address it.

Imagine my surprise and the happiness I felt a week or two later, when, while walking through the Student Union, I found my country's flag. I immediately felt a sense of accomplishment. *I* did that. I texted my mom and then my best friends back home, and I posted it on my social media to overwhelmingly positive, private and public feedback. This was a writing success for me, one that I would never forget; I automatically look up every time I pass through the Student Union at my flag, smiling every time. Had it not been for the way I was taught to write growing up, or the pride I grew up with, I may have been less likely to care and make a difference. Now here is my flag, proudly hanging with the others, a part of that international community that makes up the bulk of UCF. This is simply amazing!

The process of that experience, however, was different than what I was used to. When I wrote about my country's flag being missing from the display of flags in the Student Union, that wasn't in a formal environment. I was actually typing that email in transit to my next class, timing myself as I typed and I still produced an effective piece that got me what I wanted. Before, I needed absolute quiet to focus and produce my best work. Now that didn't even apply for me to effectively get what I wanted. I was surrounded

by students and chatter, but what made that situation different than the rest? Maybe this was Ms. Patrick at work again, taking lessons learned from her class about time management and efficiency. At this university, most correspondence is sent via email during the day. One may not have the time to get to a library or a controlled environment, sit, and gather their thoughts and type. One has to be flexible enough to do it on the go sometimes, maximizing both time and efficiency, especially to effectively attain the result they want.

I don't know why I prefer being in complete solitude when it isn't needed to necessarily produce my best work. In university, being in total quiet is a huge challenge and distractions are everywhere. It still seems unfortunate that I can't read textbooks or accomplish anything that requires real thought in the main campus library (so if you ever see me there with a book open, you know it's a ruse of some sort). People, chatter, and movement distract me. At the Rosen campus, the library on the right day is all mine, but I would always prefer my dorm room's privacy.

However, if not in isolation, just like the day I created my short story on Facebook, I find myself easily sidetracked, getting up ever so often and looking for excuses to procrastinate. Does that help? Sometimes it does and I focus much better, but other times I can't and I don't really know why. Now I understand it to a degree. Presently, I am adjusting to working in varied noise levels and am making progress. I won't always find absolute seclusion as experienced in the past, so that habit may not be the best for maximizing efficiency. I don't like the fact that I completely abandon whatever I'm doing whenever I get stuck creatively in general either, but I've been doing it for so long that it's become part of who I am. It just feels like I waste so much time when I do so, and I must improve that before it consumes me.

* * *

Why am I so easily distracted? I still can't give a concrete answer for that no matter how many times I ask it, and you know what? That's okay. I've

come to the realization that, regardless of how I went about the many writing experiences I've had over the years and how I've been taught, that I can efficiently produce content that is meant to be understood though my desired mode of communication. Typing this now, I know that back then I was trying to please someone specific at that point in time regarding my content. It was about what *they* wanted, how *they* thought they could get the best out of me, and not how *I* could get the best out of *me* but still satisfy them. There is an ideal situation for my writing processes, but I've found that I adapt to suit. Do I have a preference? Of course I do, and as I'm learning right now as there are people chatting in the living room and listening to music, I modify, but won't forsake the quality of my work because of it.

It's phenomenal coming to the realization that the seed for me preferring the silence of my environment may have been planted from the days of when I visited my mom after primary school. That helped cultivate my reading, thinking, and writing habits. It has apparently been a common denominator throughout various aspects of my writing life as well. It played a huge part in my Facebook short story's success, but it made me struggle in my secondary school life because the environment wasn't in my control. When I wrote my short story, it also helped add another layer to my habit, which was typing my thoughts instead of jotting by pen, and allowing me to free my thought process by abandoning the desk whenever I chose.

What secondary school helped incorporate in my process, to some extent, was time management and efficiency. It has helped me at every point from then until now. That has allowed me to hone my own methods even further by doing things on my own time and knowing how to take breaks. As I've matured, I've learned how long those breaks should be, and allow myself to be rejuvenated creatively; so, I am in control.

In primary school and college, I was still constrained by my environment. I was even more frustrated with the latter, because here I was in a situation where I should be able to change it, but couldn't. In a funny way, it's as though I was trying to rebel. I've been doing things by

the standard of others for too long, even if it has helped me to some extent create my own process and become a better writer.

At UCF, I've discovered I can be effective without being tied to a chair, or with what I identified as a distraction for the majority of my life: noise. I can write effectively on the go and not in the ideal surroundings, because I choose to. Where I am also influences how I write and my thought process. With my Facebook story I had no one in authority judging me. I did it according to my own standards and was successful at it because in part my audience was different. I may still hear Ms. Patrick from time to time, but that's alright. Her influence will forever be etched in my life. She is a big part of the reason that I am who I am today.

Learning how to bring both my environment as well as how I've been taught together works better for me than against me. I am at that stage in life where responsibility sneaks itself into almost anything I do. Writing and my environment is no exception. It's interesting looking back at my growth process to see what it means in the grander scheme of things for me as a young adult. As much as the demands of my process can hold me back, it has made me better, and as much as it frustrates me, it relieves me. I am a bit more conscious of it now than I was then. It will never stay stagnant. I know that as I continue to grow, it will continue to change. It is undoubtedly part of who I am as a writer today, and now instead of fearing the journey, I embrace it and what it's done for me.

I have many more questions than answers right now. When will I see new writing habits form? Have they already started and I don't know? Will it be more challenging now than before? How much of it will affect what I've learned up until now? Is my environment going to help me or hold me back as a result? Not knowing what the answers are for these questions puts the fear of God in me, yet excites me at the same time. It makes me more cognizant of my current habits and behavioral patterns every time I'm about to engage in a piece of writing. What fascinates me even more is that I may have started to form new habits and probably don't even know. This has birthed one of

the most important lessons I've probably taken away from any composition class: understanding the process is just as important as anything else when it comes to crafting an effective written piece. I need to understand who I am as a writer and what influences me during that process, and then use that to my advantage to take my work to the next level.

Responding to "Did I Create the Process? or Did the Process Create Me?"

QUESTIONS FOR DISCUSSION

1. Celestine begins his essay by discussing how he'd never really thought about his writing as a process before. What are your experiences with writing as a process? What are you already aware of within your own writing processes? Drawing upon your own experiences and prior knowledge, explain your understanding of writing as a process.

2. In analyzing his writing processes, Celestine makes note of key literacy sponsors and experiences. Make a list of all of the people, institutions, materials, and motivations he includes in his article. How did each of these play a role in influencing his writing process and approach to rhetorical situations? What is significant about each of these literacy sponsors and experiences?

QUESTIONS FOR REFLECTION

3. One of the learning objectives of the ENC 1101 curriculum is that "students will learn how to adapt to different writing contexts they need to address." Consider some of the various writing situations you are likely to encounter in your undergraduate studies, such as writing a research paper for your ENC 1102 course, preparing a visual presentation for a club meeting, and requesting a letter of recommendation from a professor. How can you use rhetorical knowledge to be successful in composing these documents? How might thinking about the conventions of the genre aid you in adapting to these writing situations?

4. If you have also read Julie Wan's and Shravan Yandra's work, think about what you have learned from each of them. While the essay have different focuses, on literacy development, literacy practices, and writing processes, what kinds of common themes can you trace across them? What insights have the authors offered that are shaping your understanding of literacy, writing, and rhetoric?

ACTIVITIES FOR FURTHER EXPLORATION

5. Think about a recent writing task you completed (e.g., a homework assignment, a social media post, a résumé, an email) and the process that was involved. Try to draw out your process without using any words. Make note of any significant factors, challenges, or aides that were part of the process.

6. Choose another recent writing task, different than the one you sketched out for the previous activity, and draw out your process again. Then, compare the two. What is different, and what is the same? Can you find anything that worked better or hindered your process between these examples? What do you think accounts for similarities or differences?

7. One takeaway from Celestine's analysis is that his writing process was developed over time. How do you think your writing processes have been influenced and shaped over the years? If you've done a literacy narrative or literacy history analysis, think about how those sponsors and experiences influenced your actual process of writing. Using Celestine's essay as a model, develop your own timeline of literacy transformation, noting also where you think you may go, given where you've been.

Showcasing Student Writing in ENC 1102

Simple Forms of Dance and Movement Literacy

Halvey, Madeline. "Simple Forms of Dance and Movement Literacy." *Stylus: A Journal of First-Year Writing*, vol, 3, no. 1, 2015, pp. 28–36.

"Okay, that was a good run. Now go grab your notebooks and come sit over here for corrections." These directions are nothing new to dancers at the Cambridge School of Ballet—in fact, this scene happens at almost every rehearsal, especially during the few weeks before a performance. What the students are about to do is not what most expect out of a dance class: they are going to write down what they did wrong and what they need to improve.

For centuries, dance forms such as ballet have been studied through imitation and visual learning techniques. Thus, reading and writing are not often readily associated with this type of physical movement. However, as established above, there are small, yet important forms of literate activity within the dance realm that profoundly impact the learning processes of dance instruction. Such evidence of dance literacy has been studied over the past thirty years through debates over what is considered proper dance pedagogy (Cooper, 2011; Davenport and Forbes, 1997; Forbes, 2000) and how movement literacy is applied in specific, real-life situations (Perry, 2012; Phillips, 2009). Over the past two years, this debate has focused on digitizing dance education (Alvarez, 2013; Lehoux, 2013; Skjulstad and Morrison, 2005; Sutil, 2012).

Intriguingly, the complex forms of dance literacy have been studied to a greater extent than its simpler counterparts. Cooper (2011) argues that analyzing and describing dance movement through the use of essays and extended literary works benefits a dancer's literacy of movement. She concludes from her studies as a college-level dance instructor that together, dancing and writing can enhance a dancer but only when that writing is fully "embodied," or has much depth and analysis (Cooper, 2011, p. 53). Davenport and Forbes (1997) similarly discuss the "use of dance to teach grammar, punctuation, phrasing, and shape in written language" (p. 292). Cheryl Forbes, a language professor who enrolled in Donna Davenport's dance class, was especially intrigued by the connection between body movement and literacy, claiming that "most of us need to be instructed to connect with our bodies as we write" (1997, p. 302). In this case, both scholars put to

practice the "embodied" writing Cooper (2011) advocates—they use feelings of body movement from dance as their foundation to connect themselves to the writing experience (Davenport and Forbes, 1997).

Lehoux (2012) claims that the best understanding of dance movement is through notation systems, which describe the movement of the body through symbols on a staff, and act as a form of documentation for choreography. The significance of these systems is their adaptability to the digital times, as well as their ability to "contribute to a richer dance heritage" (Lehoux, 2012, p. 154). Sutil (2002), too, argues that a specific notation system, Labanotation, is particularly beneficial as a form of dance literacy in that it molds thinking and dance analysis together. However, notation systems are learned solely through years of training—exemplifying the complexity of this form of dance literacy.

What most dance and literacy scholars have not discussed is the technique of documenting dance corrections and choreography pertaining to specific dance instruction. In fact, all leading dance literacy scholars previously mentioned have lacked incorporation of the simplest forms of dance literacy into their studies. One scholar has come close. Newkirk (1989/2014) broke ground in studies of children's artwork, claiming that they were fully functioning forms of literacy, despite the lack of actual text. Though it doesn't pertain to dance specifically, Newkirk's studies of pictorial literacy complement the findings from one of the cases in my following study, which incorporates child-like drawings and symbols as a form of her dance literacy.

The purpose of this study is to explore the literacy techniques found in a specific case study where literate dance activity revolves primarily around writing choreography and corrections, and to compare this case study to the pedagogy of a lower-level college dance class. As a foundation for my research in this area of study, I would like to look further into the literate form of dance movement, and pose the following questions: do literate forms of dance have to be fully comprehensive in order to serve a purpose in the

dance realm? Can simpler forms of movement literacy be those that are most beneficial for dance pedagogy?

Methods

In this data analysis, I focused on two case studies: one of a dance instructor named Briana and another of a college-level ballet class. My data from Briana is compiled from her answers to a twelve-question e-mail interview I sent her, which asked general questions about her literate activities for any movement-based part of her life. I've known Briana since she first started teaching dance, and I have been a student in her Jazz class for the past three years. Over the past few months, I've had the privilege of observing her Jazz class and used this time to assess her teaching methods, incorporate what Prior (2004/2014) calls "participant observation" (p. 519). For instance, in the beginning of the dance year (August-September), I was a participant in the Jazz class, learning with the rest of the students; once she began to teach choreography for the studio's Nutcracker performance in November, I took on more of an observer's role. More recently, I spent my time in her Jazz class writing corrections for the dance her students are practicing to perform; this is something Briana asked me to do, as she needed another "set of eyes" to watch for mistakes in the choreography of her piece. To fully integrate "data from multiple sources," I've supplemented the interview and observations with pictures of Briana's literate activity in dance (Prior, 2004/2014, p. 519).

Other data I have collected is from a college-level ballet class I enrolled in during the Fall 2014 semester. This class provided sufficient data from many sources. First, I e-mailed this course's instructor, Kris, the same twelve-question interview that I sent to Briana. This gave me a general understanding of the movement-based literacy activities Kris' practices. Next, I compiled the class syllabus, assignments, and required texts that make up most of the literate activities within the class. By doing this, I was able to implement the process of "tracing a series of texts" (Prior, 2004/2014, 500).

Finally, my data analysis includes my personal experience in Kris' class and how her incorporation of literate activity affected my role as a student.

From their interviews, my observations, and my experiences in both Briana's and Kris' dance classes, I will compare the movement-based literate activities of each class.

Case Study: Briana

Now in her early twenties, Briana Hofer has been dancing since she was seven. She is a recent graduate of the University of Central Florida, where she studied Sports and Exercise Science. Since becoming a jazz, pointe, and ballet instructor at Cambridge School of Ballet (CSO) in Orlando, Florida four years ago, Briana added a literate form of dance to her movement studies. In part, this is due to CSO's policy of requiring upper-level dance students to write in a notebook the dance corrections that they were given verbally. Although Briana's role as a dance instructor requires her to incorporate forms of dance movement literacy, she also chooses to incorporate literate activity into other kinesthetic activities in her life (namely, workouts). In this case study, I look specifically at Briana's literacy as a dance instructor.

Role of Dance Instructor: Choreography and Corrections

Briana's main dance literate activity as an instructor is her written choreography and corrections. Briana writes choreography about three times a year and brings her written choreography texts in a binder to every class she teaches. Most of her pages are filled with text from top to bottom. Briana writes cast lists, movement words, positions, and "other things [she] wants to emphasize"—all of which are supplemented by small "drawings" to visually supplement her text (personal communication, September 14, 2014). Figure 1 is an example of these drawings. In this picture, the dots represent dancers and the arrows establish the dancers' movements across the stage. Briana tends to write in different colored inks to separate sections of choreography. As seen in Figure 2, her "chunks" of choreography are similar to paragraphs

of an essay—they mark when movement pauses or changes slightly in style or movement. Briana's writing style helps her define parts of the piece where the dancers are in new spots or where the actual choreography differs from the previous choreography (on this specific page the "chunks" differentiate between the "fighting" and "dancing" parts of the piece).

During rehearsal of her choreography, Briana watches her class perform the piece and takes note of the dancers' movements on a scrap piece of paper. These notes are called "corrections," or movements the dancers can specifically improve upon. When the performance is finished, Briana verbalizes the corrections she wrote out, often timesexemplifying certain steps or styles of the choreography that she wants her dancers to emphasize in the piece. Briana mentioned in her interview that she only rereads her written corrections aloud one time before crossing them off and never looking at them again. She goes through this whole process each time the piece is rehearsed.

Figure 1: A page from Briana's dance binder showing some of her drawings.

Uses of Digital (or Technology-Based) Dance Literacy

Though she did not mention it in her interview, Briana uses technology as she writes choreography. Most ballet variations are age-old: choreography for specific pieces has been set years ago and remains virtually intact to this day (this is called Petipa, after French choreographer Marius Petipa). CSO Ballet uses similar theories for their performances. That is, Briana watches videos of past performances of "The Nutcracker," which is the choreography she is currently teaching and writes down the movements of the dancers. She then adds her own "flair" of movements to the choreography without vastly changing what was already set. Briana writes down past choreography and changes it only in ways that benefit her dancers' physical abilities. For instance, Briana changed a set of eight count movement in the middle of her "fight scene" Nutcracker piece (Figure 2) because her dancers had improved since they last performed this piece and they needed to be challenged with more difficult choreography.

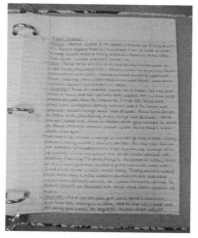

Figure 2: A page from Briana's dance binder showing some of her written choreography for her piece "Fight Scene."

Not only does Briana watch dance videos to learn ballet choreography, but she also shows her class the videos she takes choreography from so that they can understand how the movement works. She points out what she likes in the video, what she is going to change about the video's choreography, and how the dancers can improve their own performance of this particular choreography. In doing this, Briana teaches her students how to learn from other dancers.

Briana reported that she keeps herself up-to-date about the dance world by reading what she refers to as "random articles" online pertaining to dance or working out. When she needs fresh ideas for teaching a ballet class, Briana refers to *100 Lessons in Classical Ballet* by Vera S. Kostrovitskaya. For instance, if Briana is having a difficult time creating a combination for her ballet class to do at barre, she might refer to one of these texts for inspiration.

As an additional literate activity, Briana started a workout journal around the same time she began documenting dance. Briana's workout journals are not related to dance, but they do document literate activity in her other high-priority kinesthetic activity: exercising. Briana writes in her workout journal about five times a week, documenting what workout movements she's done that day and which ones she has deemed "especially good" or "most beneficial" (personal communication, September 14, 2014). Unlike her dance corrections, Briana reads back over her workout journal multiple times. Even though she writes in her workout journal at home, Briana brings it wherever and whenever she works out. She has filled many workout journals throughout the past four years.

Summary

Briana has taught herself to use reading, writing, and drawing as forms of literate dance activity for her occupation as a dance instructor. She has learned to apply each type of activity to her students, her job, and her personal reflection. From this, I can conclude that Briana has fully integrated

the two worlds of literate and kinesthetic activities into one interrelated set of processes.

Case Study: Kris

Kristina "Kris" Stevens is a ballet instructor at both Valencia College in Orlando, Florida and Rollins College in Winter Park, Florida. She has been a part of many dance companies, worked as a dancer/actor for Disney and received a degree in Dance from Valencia College. Kris's literate movement activity revolves solely around dance. In this case study, I will analyze all forms of Kris' literate dance activity.

Role of Dance Instructor: Assignments and Exams

As a college professor of dance, Kris writes lesson plans and choreography for students a couple of times each week. A visual learner, Kris says writing down her choreography or lessons helps her remember and clarify information, particularly which teaching methods and choreography work best or are most enjoyable. She keeps all of her class lessons and past choreography in both notebooks and computer files, and she will often reread her writings to reuse the information in future classes.

Figure 3: One of the notecards cards I made for Kris's "notecard card assignment."

As her Ballet 1class is a college course, Kris has also written a class syllabus that explains expectations, grading policies, assignments, required materials, and the "Valencia Department of Dance Writing Principles." The syllabus requires two textbooks for student use: *The Technical Manual and Dictionary of Classical Ballet* by Gail Grant and *Ballet Basics* by Sandra Noll Hammond. Both of these include written descriptions of ballet terms, forms, and movements, as well as pictures and figures that demonstrate the movement. Care of the body and proper dance etiquette also make up a few chapters in the Hammond textbook. During class, focus is on the five basic ballet positions and the eight positions of the body. Kris has her students first look at the picture of a certain form or movement, then read the text describing the movement, and then do the movement themselves.

The syllabus also outlines the dates and explanations for exams and assignments throughout the semester, which includes a written midterm, seventy-six note cards for studying, an essay reviewing a dance performance that her students must attend, and a dance presentation final.

Kris's pedagogy puts heavy emphasis on writing correct ballet terms. One assignment we did before the midterm, for example, encompassed memorization of seventy-six fundamental ballet terms by writing their definition and pronunciation on the front and back of a note card (Figure 3). In this way, my fellow classmates and I were able to really learn the ballet tenns, which I found helpful for both the midterm and barre exercises in class.

As another literate dance activity, Kris writes difficult or certain barre exercises on the whiteboard in the dance room at the end of class. Her students are required to write these combinations down, work on them at home using the written form for reference, and then perform the same exercise with improvement during the next class. To provide some guided study, Kris has her students read certain chapters of the textbooks that demonstrate specific movements. Figure 4 includes a few of my combination entries and notes from the months of August and September.

Figure 4: A page from my dance notebook for Kris's class showing certain combinations we learned and homework she assigned.

Finally, all dance classes at Valencia require students to write a four- to five-page essay about the Choreographers' Showcase Dance Performance, which all dance students are required to attend. The essay analyzes and critiques a minimum of four dance pieces that were part of the Choreographers' Showcase. The essay has specific requirements (e.g. MLA formatting) that are listed on the assignment page in BlackBoard. Different from all of her other assignments, this activity is Kris's most complex.

Uses of Digital (or Technology-Based) Dance Literacy

This ballet course also includes an online component called BlackBoard. Blackboard is a website used by Valencia College where Kris can post files, assignments, and messages for her students. Currently, she posts the syllabus, a list of ballet terms and definitions, music from a dance piece the class is performing, the essay assignment guidelines, and a few miscellaneous documents about dance and the body.

Kris allows her students to use cell phones, laptops, and/or other devices to record her teaching of new barre combinations or choreography during class time. She then has the students post their recordings on BlackBoard so that all the students in the class may see them.

Kris reads many pieces of literature regarding dance (biographies, programs for concerts, "how-to" articles, pedagogy essays and books, and reviews) mainly for her own enjoyment in learning about the topic (personal communication, September 17, 2014). Recently, she had her class read a blog from another dance instructor that was written to motivate students to work harder.

Summary

Kris learned to be literate in dance from both her degree in dance as well as her many years teaching the subject at the college-level (which requires texts, grades, and policies to qualify as a credit course). Kris applies many different forms of dance literacy to her course, involving both simple and complex literate activity. In my own experience, I found the simpler forms to be most helpful in my navigation through the course. That being said, I have yet to reach the most complex literate activity of the course— the essay.

Like Briana, Kris has integrated the two worlds of dance and literacy.

Comparison: Briana and Kris

Upon enrolling in Kris's Ballet 1 class at Valencia College, I found that the way Kris teaches is similar to Briana in some aspects but includes more structure and maintains a different focus. Similarities occur in the way both instructors write choreography in a binder that they bring with them and look over during class. Both seem to find inspiration for their dance classes by reading recent dance literature, such as news articles about dance and books entailing proper dance technique. Kris recently had her students read a blog post from a dance instructor talking about motivation in ballet; this is much

like the articles about dance Briana reads on the Internet. Both use textbooks about ballet fundamentals to help with their barre combinations for ballet class: Kris reads from *sby* Sandra Noll Hammond while Briana chooses *100 Lessons in Classical Ballet* by Vera S. Kostrovitskaya.

Despite these parallels, Kris's dance pedagogy is much more structured than Briana's. Whereas Briana has her students write their dance corrections in their own personal styles, Kris has her students write the movement combination they are doing in correct French. This may have to do more with the mental and physical level of dance students each instructor has contact with: Kris works with students primarily new to the dance realm, while Briana has been working with most of the same girls since her first year teaching. Thus, Kris' form of dance literacy requiring text is most beneficial for her beginner students, while Briana's lack thereof still effectively incorporates a form of dance literacy that is best for her more advanced dancers.

Discussion

In her studies of dance, Cooper (2011) found that "the creative and compositional processes involved in dance-making and writing are complementary" (p. 53). This concept coincides with what many literacy scholars have to say about literacy across two or more discourse communities. For example, Newkirk's (1989/2014) study focuses on the literacy of children's drawings. He analyzed students' artwork and found that "drawing can help develop perceptual ability—the ability to make refined observations, which is useful for more than artwork" (p. 104). While Briana's dance literacy (specifically her written choreography and corrections) may not be anything like the literate activity that Newkirk (1989/2014) examined, it exemplifies his idea that these simple forms of literacy are useful in multiple genres and situations. This can be seen in Briana's beginning to write her workout journals around the same time her new occupation as a dance instructor required her to be literate in dance. Briana is not only improving her ability

to be literate, but she is building her ability to observe and analyze her own processes and performance in dance and exercise.

Dance literacy studies like Cooper's (2011), however, fail to discuss the simple forms of dance literacy that we see in Briana's work. Cooper (2011) tells us that dancing and writing can together enhance a dancer, but only when that writing is fully "embodied" (p. 54). That is, based on her successful student analyses of dance movement, Cooper (2011) believes deep explanation of movement that gives "a real sense of dance as a sensual and corporeal experience" is the best way to experience dance literacy (p. 59). I disagree, noting that Briana's simple system of dance literacy invokes personal growth and reflects her maturity in the dance realm. She has not only learned to be effective with her literacy techniques in regards to her work as a dance instructor, but she also applies these reflection techniques to her personal workout experience. Likewise, Briana provides an example for her dance students to be equally literate in the art of dance.

Similar to Cooper (2011), Davenport and Forbes' (1997) campaign for extended analysis of dance literacy fails to explain Briana's literate dance activities. According to Davenport and Forbes (1997), both writers and dancers can benefit from experiencing the mind-body connection. Specifically, dancers would do well to think of their movement as grammar: colons, semicolons, and punctuation that put "flow" in their "kinesthetic experience" (p. 300). Davenport incorporated literacy in her dance classes by having the students do an activity that Forbes fashioned for her writing students: to rewrite (or, in this case, re-choreograph) different endings to a movement piece in order to find the best one possible (Davenport and Forbes, 1997, p. 300). While this form of dance literacy is arguably beneficial to dance pedagogy, it doesn't encompass all beneficial techniques in the dance instruction practice. Briana teaches her students to write down the choreography they learn as well as the corrections they are given. My own college-level ballet class also includes writing specific choreography or combinations. Both instances provide a foundation to grow as a dancer. These

simple forms of dance literacy improve students' "synthesis of knowledge, and retention of new information" as they learn to understand the basics of their movement (Davenport and Forbes, 1997, p. 300).

In a wholly disparate form of dance literacy, Lehoux (2013) affirms that "notation systems are essential to the description of movement" (p. 154). Sutil (2012) agrees, specifying that Labanotation "has found a new readership in digital dance contexts" of this century (p. 161). In simpler terms, both scholars make the claim that these complex forms of movement documentation (similar to music scores) are advantageous to dance literacy. While intrigued by the idea of using staff and symbols as representations of body movement and pieces of choreography, I can't help but disagree as I find these systems unnecessarily complex. Briana cohesively documents her choreography using language she understands best and is effectively able to teach her movements this way. More than that, Briana develops most of her choreography from past performances that she and her dancers watch on video. I argue that learning from choreography documented this way (video and written) is much more effective in helping dancers develop specific style or flair to their dance. As she shows her dancers a video of choreography, Briana points out certain parts that can be improved, changed, or incorporated into her dancers' movement of the piece. While notation systems may contribute to "richer dance heritage" in the long run, they only apply to students who are trained in the system (Lehoux, 2013, p. 154). Primitive forms of dance literacy, however, can be universally understood and applied.

Over the years, dance has become more of a literate activity than ever before, even though I argue that the most beneficial dance movement literate activities are those in the simple form. From this perspective, the understanding we might want to more readily incorporate into dance pedagogy is simply the ways students learn and are taught to do movement pieces—as well as the way choreographers or dance instructors develop, teach, and improve those pieces—by simple forms of writing and watching other dancers. From my observations during this study, there are many ways

dancers learn choreography and take corrections; perhaps applications of many different pedagogical practices of dance instruction (a mix of simple and complex forms) could result in a more approachable and comprehensive design of dance instruction.

Works Cited

Alvarez, I. (2013). High aspirations: Transforming dance students from print consumers to digital producers. *Journal of Interactive Media in Education*, 1-16. Retrieved from jime.open.ac.uk

Cooper, B. (2011). Embodied writing: A tool for teaching and writing in dance. *Journal of Dance Education*, 11(2), 53-7. Retrieved from http://ndeo.org/jode

Davenport, D. R. & Forbes, C. A. (1997). Writing movement/dancing words: A collaborative pedagogy. *Education, 118*(2), 293-302. Retrieved from http://projectinnovation.com/education.html

Forbes, C. (2000). Writing the body: An experiment in material rhetoric. *Rhetoric Review, 19*(1/2), 60-72. Retrieved from www.tandfonline.com/loi/hrhr20

Lehoux, N. (2013). Dance literacy and digital media: Negotiating past, present, and future representations of movement. *International Journal of Performance Arts & Digital Media, 9*(1), 153-174. doi: 10.1386/padm.9.1.153_1

Newkirk, T. (2014). Draw me a word, write me a picture. In E. Wardle & D. Downs (Eds.), *Writing about writing: A college reader*, (2nd Ed.) (pp. 76-106). Boston, MA: Bedford/St. Martin's. (Reprinted from *More than stories: The range of children's writing*, pp. 35-66, by T. Newkirk, 1989, Portsmouth, NH: Heinemann)

Perry, K. (2012, June). The movement of composition: Dance and writing [Video File]. Retrieved from technorhetoric.net

Phillips, S.A. (2009). Crip walk, villain dance, pueblo stroll: The embodiment of writing in African American gang dance. *Anthropological Quarterly*, 82(1), 69-97. Retrieved from aq.gwu.edu

Prior, P. (2014). Tracing process: How texts come into being. In E. Wardle & D. Downs (Eds.), *Writing about writing: A college reader*. (2nd Ed.) (pp. 492-526). Boston, MA: Bedford/St. Martin's. (Reprinted from *What writing does and how it does it*, pp. 167-200, by C. Bazerman and P. Prior, Eds., 2004, Mahwah, NJ: Lawrence Erlbaum)

Skjulstad, S. & Morrison, A. (2005). Movement in the interface. *Computers and Composition*, 22(4), 413-33. doi: 10.1016/j.compcom.2005.08.006

Stevens, K. (2014). "MW Ballet Syllabus." [Class Handout]. Department of Dance, Valencia College, Orlando, FL.

Sutil, N. (2012). Laban's choreosophical model: Movement visualisation analysis and the graphic media approach to dance studies. *Dance Research*, 30(2), 147-168. doi: 10.3366/drs.2012.0044

Responding to "Simple Forms of Dance and Movement Literacy"

QUESTIONS FOR DISCUSSION

1. What does Halvey seem to mean by "literate activity"? Can you think of examples of literate activities in your own life?

2. What methods did Halvey employ here? How did she investigate the connection between writing and dance classes? Why do you think these methods were appropriate given what she set out to learn? (To learn more about the methods available to writing researchers— including you—see pages R-4–R-15 in the section on "Researching Writing and Literacy at UCF," following Part Three, of this handbook.)

3. How does Halvey use secondary research (i.e., sources) in her essay? Where do they appear? What ideas does she seem to get from these sources? How does she contrast her study with previous

research? In other words, what does Halvey see herself as adding to the ongoing conversation about her subjects?

4. Halvey references researcher Thomas Newkirk to make the point that "Newkirk broke ground in studies of children's artwork, claiming that they were fully functioning forms of literacy, despite the lack of actual text." What do you think of this claim? What might be the implications of considering literacy as more than just reading or writing text with letters (what writing researchers sometimes call "alphabetic" text)?

QUESTIONS FOR REFLECTION

5. One of the learning objectives of the ENC 1101 curriculum is that "students will be able to read and use scholarly texts to support their writing goals." Halvey successfully uses a variety of sources in her writing. Name some of the writing you have done that uses sources effectively to support your argument. What are some of the rhetorical strategies you had to consider to accomplish this? When did you learn these?

6. A learning objective of ENC 1102 courses is that "students will engage in a recursive, inquiry-based writing and research process that is meaningful for a specifi community." Halvey lists her research questions in paragraph 6. How do you think she arrived at these literate-activity focused questions? List some of the possible initial, broader interests that you think could have guided her research. What are some interests of yours that could possibly lead to research you do in 1102?

ACTIVITIES FOR FURTHER EXPLORATION

8. One of the things we like about Halvey's article is how she is able to find and examine the literate activity in a context (dance class) where we might not expect there to be much reading and writing. Try this out for yourself. Make a list of some of the different endeavors (think school, work, hobbies, and so forth) in which you participate on a daily or weekly basis. Then, jot down some of the literate activities associated with these endeavors. Finally, pick one literate activity that seems interesting or important to you, and write a few paragraphs explaining that activity to someone

unfamiliar with it. What goes into the literate activity? What do people engaging in that activity need to know? What might surprise an outsider to the activity? What might a researcher like Fishman or Halvey have to say about it? If you can, try to incorporate visuals to help explain your literate activity, like Halvey does in her article.

9. Now, take your research a step further. Talk to someone else who participates in that same literate activity. What is their perception of the activity? How do they engage in it in ways that are similar to or different from you? Again, try to collect some data you can use (e.g., pictures, examples of texts) to help explain what your findings to someone else. If you need some ideas for the sorts of questions to ask when interviewing someone, see pages R-12–R-15.

Annotated Bibliography:
Simple Forms of Dance and Movement Literacy

Halvey, Madeline. "Annotated Bibliography: Simple Forms of Dance and Movement Literacy."

Dance forms, such as ballet, have been studied for centuries through imitation and visual learning techniques. Thus, reading and writing are not usually activities associated with this type of physical movement. However, there has been recent evidence of literacy within the dance realm. Within the past thirty years, there have been arguments of what is considered proper dance pedagogy (Cooper; Davenport and Forbes) and how movement literacy is applied in specific, real-life situations (Phillips); over the past two years, these arguments have turned to digitalizing dance education (Alvarez; Lehoux). What has not been discussed, though, is the technique of documenting dance corrections and choreography pertaining to specific dance instruction.

The purpose of this annotated bibliography is to provide background information on studies relating to dance and literacy while also exploring the lives, first-hand, of those who incorporate literacy into their dance studies. I would like to look further into the literate form of dance movement, and pose the following questions: does incorporating this type of writing technique

into dance students' pedagogy at beginning levels of dance help in the development of a dancer? Can personal reflection in one type of movement be beneficial to other movement activities? Is personal reflection an effective way to improve group dance movement? Could learning proper dance movement language be key to improving the utilization of dance literature?

Primary Research

Hofer, Briana. Email Interview. 14 Sept. 2014. Briana is a ballet, Pointe, and jazz dance teacher at Cambridge School of Ballet in Orlando, Florida. She has been dancing competitively since she was seven, and received all of her dance training in the Orlando area. Briana is a UCF graduate of Sports and Exercise Science Strengthening and Conditioning track. I asked her twelve interview questions about her writing and reading activities that pertain to dance. In her interview, Briana states she did not start writing or reading in dance until she became a dance instructor four years ago. Since then, she has come to read and write in her other kinesthetic activities. For instance, she has many filled workout journals and writes in her current workout journal about five times a week. Briana taught herself how to write about dance; however, she does refer to 100 Lesson's in Classical Ballet by Vera S. Kostrovitskaya, as well as online articles about workout or dance, as inspiration for new teaching methods or dance combination ideas. Finally, Briana writes choreography and corrections as part of her job as a dance instructor. She writes choreography three times a year, and she writes corrections every dance rehearsal (though once she has expressed a correction verbally to a dancer, she doesn't look back at her written correction). This interview with Briana poses the questions of whether teaching literate techniques in beginning dance classes will help in both dance movement and other kinesthetic activities in the future or as the activities progress to higher levels.

Judy, Chandra. Email Interview. 14 Sept. 2014. Judy is a ballet teacher at Cambridge School of Ballet in Orlando, Florida. She has a B.F.A with

Honors in Choreography from Wright State University and has been a part of over five dance companies across the Eastern U.S. I asked her twelve interview questions about her writing and reading activities that pertain to dance. Judy's main literacies in dance include writing choreography and lesson plans for the classes she teaches. She writes her plans once a week and has been participating in these literate activities for over thirty years now. Judy keeps all her written materials regarding dance either in a binder that she takes with her to teach or in "easily assessable" files at her home. She writes strictly at home and always in English. Most importantly, Judy writes for many reasons: improvement of dancers, "edification of self-education," "artistic expression and beauty of movement through choreography," "time saving when referring back to choreography," and, what she deems most important, "Glory to God." This interview really shed light on writing corrections and choreography for interpersonal reasons—she doesn't just write for herself, but for a greater being, which she put much emphasis on in the interview.

Stevens, Kristina. Email Interview. 15 Sept. 2014. Kristina is a ballet instructor at both Valencia College in Orlando, Florida and Rollins College in Winter Park, Florida. She has been a part of many dance companies, worked as a dancer/actor for Disney, and finally received a degree in Dance from Valencia College. As a college professor of dance, Kristina writes a syllabus every semester as well as lesson plans, choreography, and corrections for students a couple times a week. She writes mainly at her workplace and does so in a combination of English and French language. A visual learner, Kristina says writing down her choreography or lessons helps her remember and clarify information—especially what teaching methods work best and choreography she particularly enjoyed. She keeps all of her class lessons and past choreography in both notebooks and computer files, and she will often reread her writings to reuse the information in future classes.

Kristina reads many pieces of literature regarding dance (biographies, programs for concerts, "how-to" articles, "pedagogy essay/books", and reviews) mainly for her own enjoyment of learning about the topic. This interview brought up the concept of college-level pedagogy of dance movement and how effective its use of literate activity is for beginning-level dancers.

Stevens, Kristina. "DAA 1200/1201 Syllabus." Print. 17 Sept. 2014. In this syllabus for her ballet one and two class at Valencia College in Orlando, Florida, Kristina emphasizes her classroom objectives and purpose. This syllabus documents the requirement of two texts: *The Technical Manual and Dictionary of Classical Ballet* by Gail Grant as well as Ballet Basics by Sandra Noll Hammond. Students are informed within the syllabus that they will be evaluated on not only their physical dance technique improvement over the course of the semester, but also on their final essay which is a critical writing assignment about a dance performance that students are required to attend. Other important aspects of this syllabus include: "Valencia Department of Dance [Writing] Principles," "Internet Research Statement," and "Grading Policy and Standards." This document is a vital piece of information for my study in that it is first-hand evidence of required literacy about dance movement.

Secondary Sources

Alvarez, Inma. "High Aspirations: Transforming Dance Students from Print Consumers to Digital Producers." *Nottingham OER* 2013. Spec. issue of *Journal of Interactive Media in Education* (2013): n. pag. Web. 12 Sept. 2014. In this article, Inma reports findings from a study in which a digital-based curriculum was incorporated into a Bachelor's of Dance program at a university. The technology created for this curriculum focused on e-learning materials for five classes as well as other numerous digital materials to assist in audio-visual learning. Inma found that, at first, students did not take to the digitalized

version of dance education—they did not understand its connection to physical movement and they began to resist it. However, as the Dance Department became more technology-based, students began to see how using e-learning and other technologies bridged the gap between dance movement and dance literature, providing them with a more professional and experienced outlook on dance as a whole. This article is interesting in that it considers online learning as a supplement to face-to-face learning within dance pedagogy, thus broadening my scope of dance-related literacy.

Cooper, Debra. "Embodied Writing: A Tool for Teaching and Writing in Dance." *Journal of Dance Education* 11.2 (2011): 53-59. *SPORTDiscus*. Web. 12 Sept. 2014. This scholarly article focuses on incorporating vigorous writing activities into the curriculum of dance education. In her studies, Cooper created an introductory level undergraduate course where she designed a curriculum focused on compositional process of analyzing and describing dance movement—an activity she calls "embodied writing." Her method of research was to have students participate in classroom free-writes as well as an extensive writing assignment that acted as the final exam for the class. Using a thorough review and peer-editing process for this last and most important assignment, the author concluded that students successfully integrated her methods of dance composition in such a way that they were able to detail complete dance movement in descriptive prose (third person point of view) while also providing explanations for how it felt to complete dance movement (first person point of view). The author felt she had successfully completed her goal to bring awareness to student's complete compositional process, not only in dance, but in other discourse communities, as well. This focus of compositional processes about dance movement can be included in my study as an example of literate activity pertaining to dance movement that crosses two discourse communities.

Davenport, Donna R., and Cheryl A. Forbes. "Writing Movement/Dancing Words: A Collaborative Pedagogy." *Education* 118.2 (1997): 292-302. *Professional Development Collection*. Web. 11 Sept. 2014. In this collaborative journal article, Davenport and Forbes explore each other's departments and find pedagogical connections between the two. Both authors provide their own initial take on the exploration of the other's department— Davenport, a dancer, explores writing about dance; while Forbes, a writer, enrolls in a dance class to learn about movement. After their initial anecdotes, each author goes into detail about the connections they have made between dance movement and writing. They conclude that there are many similarities between the two departments. Davenport emphasized similarities in punctuation, vocabulary, and voice of dancers and writers, claiming that fusing the two pedagogies of dance and movement makes for a developed and experienced dancer. Likewise, Forbes articulates that her experience in dance has broadened her perspective about writing, particularly in regards to space, weight, and time. Together, these two authors conclude that while dance and writing are separate entities, they connect the mind and body in ways that promote an overall enhanced learning experience. I can include this unique collaboration in my article as a way to introduce the initial concept of writing about dance movement from both dancer and writer perspectives.

Lehoux, Natalie. "Dance Literacy and Digital Media: Negotiating Past, Present, and Future Representations of Movement." *International Journal of Performance Arts & Digital Media* 9.1 (2013): 153-74. *International Bibliography of Theatre & Dance*. Web. 11 Sept. 2014. This article takes a closer look at a historical notation system movement process that has been developing over the past thirty years. Lehoux defines the notation system as a symbolic representation of dance movement similar to recording music notes on a staff. She argues for a more developed use of notation systems in dance literature, emphasizing the need for notation system movement to be recorded digitally as a means to provide

better access of dance records (such as choreography) for the dance community. In regards to my research on the topic of dance movement literacy, notation systems are a unique concept that provide more insight about recording techniques of dance movement.

Phillips, Susan A. "Crip Walk, Villain Dance, Pueblo Stroll: The Embodiment of Writing in African American Gang Dance." *Anthropological Quarterly* 82.1 (2009): 69-97. *JSTOR*. Web. 10 Sept. 2014. In this article, Phillips explores gang dance ceremonies involving double Dutch, dance movement, hand signals, and writing as a form of socially accepted expression. In her observations, this author found that gang- related literate activities were expressed in a form of movement called Crip Walk—a game in which members would skip rope and, at the same time, throw up hand signals or write memorials for loved ones in the dirt. Phillips also describes gang dances in which members of the African American communities will use specific dance step patterns as a way to sign, signal, or initial their gang affiliation. Phillips concludes that dance movement and writing make up an important part of gang-related communication. She infers that the body and the mind are never completely separable in these instances—they are incorporated in the distinction of gang literacy. This article is helpful to my research in that it exemplifies dance movement literacy across a discourse community that would otherwise not be related to what I had originally considered "dance movement."

Responding to Madeline Halvey's Annotated Bibliography

QUESTIONS FOR DISCUSSION

1. What purpose does each annotation seem to serve? If you are a reader unfamiliar with Halvey's research, what sort of information does each annotation offer? What does an annotation tell you about the source? Try to link your discussion to one or two specific examples.

2. What purpose does Halvey's brief introduction (i.e., the two paragraphs before her source lists) seem to serve? What does it do for you as a reader?

QUESTION FOR REFLECTION

3. One of the learning objectives of the ENC 1102 curriculum is that "students will be able to analyze and synthesize complex texts in ways that demonstrate an understanding of the situated and intertextual nature of writing and research." The annotated bibliography is akin to "listening" to the research conversation before entering it. Why is this step essential in the research process? Refer to Halvey's final research presented earlier in this introduction: Where do these sources appear in her writing? How does she use them?

ACTIVITIES FOR FURTHER EXPLORATION

4. Look back at Halvey's finished work—it starts on p. li—and search for two or three of the sources she writes about in the annotated bibliography. How are they used? How is Halvey's writing in her finished article similar to or different from what the writing used for her annotations?

5. Look at the sources Halvey chose to include in her final essay (see pp. lxvi–lxvii) that are not in this annotated bibliography. Why do you think she chose to add them? What do they seem to do for her article?

6. Find one of Halvey's secondary sources (they're all available electronically, either online or via the UCF Libraries website) and skim through it. How does the source compare to Halvey's annotation of it? What did Halvey choose to focus on in her annotation, and why do you think she chose to do so? Conversely, what did Halvey leave out, and why do you think she did so?

Priscilla Samayoa, "The Extent of Influence that Genre Conventions Have on TED Talks"

Samayoa, Priscilla. "The Extent of Influence that Genre Conventions Have on TED Talks." *Stylus: A Journal of First-Year Writing*, vol. 8, no. 2, 2017, pp. 46–59.

Introduction

Communication has evolved greatly in recent times, especially when it refers to sharing information. Sending messages directly and indirectly has come a long way from what are now considered antiquated methods such as the fax machine and the handwritten letter. The internet, for example, has digitized and taken over almost every single method of intercommunication between human beings. The digital spreading of useful information has become second nature, as we have access to a seemingly endless source of information through the web. Over the years, audio-visual content has also evolved into a significant form of communication. Videos provide a different, more innovative way of presenting a topic to an audience: instead of reading about it and coming up with their own conclusions about a certain topic of interest, people who view these videos are exposed to a more interactive method of communication.

One of the most influential sites that offers new information delivered in video form is the TED Talk site, a database of videos that offers a wide variety of information, for free, on the internet. TED Talks—whose acronym stands for Technology, Entertainment and Design—are some of the most recognized new forms of communication of innovative ideas that exist in the world. They are presented at conferences held throughout the year that feature a variety of speakers that regularly break barriers of knowledge by transmitting their thoughts and projects to a live audience, as well as on the internet. TED is a non-profit organization dedicated to the spreading of new and relevant information via conferences and free, accessible videos published on the institution's webpage. According to the webpage, "TED Talks are videos that present a great idea in 18 minutes or less. They're filmed at flagship TED conferences, independent TEDx events, and other programs. Their goal is to share Ideas Worth Spreading—in fields like science, technology, business, culture, art and design—around the world" (TED). The speakers at TED conferences are experts in their fields, and often have innovative and refreshing takes on several of today's world practices.

Because of their increased popularity and success in sharing knowledge and ideas on a vast amount of fields and topics, many people have dedicated studies to find out more about the way TED Talks work. These studies, however, are usually focused toward the talks' rhetorical structure, and often focus on identifying factors that would be of use in imparting knowledge to students in today's school classrooms. Keith Grant-Davie defines rhetoric and rhetorical situation as "a set of related factors whose interaction creates and controls a discourse" (350). This suggests that any activity that needs to be answered with some kind of discourse or communicative interaction to accomplish a specific goal is a rhetorical situation. Chang and Huang, in their research, identified "the rhetorical and linguistic nature of TED talks... to explore their pedagogical potential in the training of oral presentation skills" (31) by generating a rhetorical prototype of 58 different TED Talks (29). Their results suggest that all or most TED Talks use seven main rhetorical moves to present their idea to an audience: "Listener orientation, topic introduction, speaker presentation, topic development, closure, and concluding messages" (Chang and Huang 38). During each one of these moves, the TED Talk speaker would accomplish a milestone that would have a different impact on the audience's perception of the speaker, the presentation, and the quality of the information being delivered. These rhetorical moves play a crucial role in imparting the desired message correctly and effectively. For that reason, the decision of how to approach these moves in relation to sequence or style of presentation was personalized by each speaker to adapt to his or her particular topic.

One of the rhetorical moves that is commonly featured in TED Talks is identified by researcher Giuseppina Scotto di Carlo. In her research, she argues that "pathos is established [in TED Talks] in this relatively new form of popularisation that breaches the typical 'scientist- mediator-audiences' triangularisation, bringing scientists directly into contact with their audiences" (23). Pathos, defined by Braziller and Kelinfeld as "an appeal to an audience's emotions or values" (11), is used as a tool to be able to relate

with the audience that the presenter is talking to, and it is commonly used alongside logical appeals to create a sense of credibility for the speaker. This is accomplished through the communication of a balance of knowledge and personal vulnerability, which creates a connection with the audience. The use of this and many other rhetorical moves, however, is optional, and limited only to a circumstance called for by the context of the talk.

Chang and Huang developed a quantitative genre prototype of TED Talks based on the rhetorical moves used while imparting it. Amy Devitt explains that "genres develop... because they respond appropriately to [rhetorical] situations that writers encounter repeatedly" (qtd. in Dirk 252). These situations often ask for a response and, since the situations are recurring, the responses are going to be similar, as is the case for the TED Talk. All TED Talks, no matter how different their topics of interest are, aim to reach an audience of people to make an impact on their lives and help create a global network to share important information.

Even though several TED Talks have been deeply analyzed before, the qualitative information regarding the genre of the TED Talk, and the genre conventions—rules and characteristics that all pieces of writing have in common to be able to be considered as part of that genre (Braziller and Kleinfeld 18), and which define the genre—are lacking. More specifically, there has been insufficient research that addresses the individual differences between each TED Talk. Identifying these differences would demonstrate the amount of flexibility that each author is allowed, in each TED Talk, to modify and personalize their own presentation to fit the context and situation that the talk requires, while still falling into the category of a TED Talk. This discovery would lead to a better understanding of the genre conventions of TED Talks, and the expectations that the genre of TED Talks holds to be able to communicate information effectively.

This paper searches for the extent of the influence of genre conventions present in TED Talks, as well as the rhetorical moves that presenters make when allowed certain flexibility in their talks, while still participating and

creating a piece for a single genre. My research will focus on the following questions:

How do the different genre conventions and characteristics of a TED Talk work and have worked, individually and collectively, to provide appropriate answers to the specific rhetorical situation that TED addresses?

How does each TED Talk presenter personalize the answer to a very similar, recurring rhetorical situation to produce drastically different video results that are still considered to be one single genre?

I answer these questions by analyzing interviews and podcasts with presenters and members of the TED non-profit, performing a case study on different successful TED Talks, and engaging in observation and genre analysis of the structure of TED Talks.

The results of my research show that TED Talks are formatted as a presentation that aims to be innovative and different for every presenter. Genre conventions vary based on whether the focus is on the collective TED Talk movement or on the individual formulation of a TED Talk. The TED Talk, if viewed from an individual perspective, can be analyzed as having set boundaries and rigid genre conventions that must absolutely be followed for the TED Talk to be successful, and the presenters then provide flexibility and diversity to their own talks as an adaptation to the set format of the talk. On the other hand, the collection of talks that TED represents offers a complementary, but slightly different set of genre conventions, which affect the general composition of a TED Talk. From this point of view, TED Talks' genre conventions include the flexibility, difference, and innovation that were just an extra, or an addition to each individual TED Talk. In the more general scope of TED Talks, the genre conventions require the speaker to be unique, when in the more specific, individual scope of TED Talks, speakers followed a pattern, and chose to break the rigid convention to mold it to their own unique topic.

Methodology

Data Collection

Chris Anderson, the owner and curator of TED Talks, offers, in the TED website, vast amounts of information on TED Talks such as interviews, comments, information about the non-profit, instructions to organize an independent (TEDx) event or conference, as well as the collection of TED Talks themselves. To collect data on the genre conventions of TED Talks, I first analyzed several interviews with Anderson, in which he discusses his opinions on the success and history of the TED non-profit. Once I understood the purpose behind the conferences and the talks, I observed and searched new information on what characteristics are crucial to make an effective TED Talk. I analyzed more interviews, now focused on how TED Talks are structured and delivered.

The observation of a small documentary, "Behind The TED Talk 2009," allowed insight into the performance of the talks, and the final preparation that the speakers undergo before taking the stage, as well as the use of tools that help the speakers time and pace their own rehearsed presentations. From the TED Talk website, I analyzed the information provided on how to prepare future TEDx speakers at an independent conference.

Finally, I performed a case study on four different, very successful TED Talks: Jill Bolte Taylor's "My Stroke of Insight," James Veitch's "This is What Happens When You Reply to Scam Emails," Dan Lok's "The Invisible Force— Self-image—Enables You to Achieve Great Goals," and Roman Mars's "Why City Flags May Be The Worst-Designed Thing You've Never Noticed." I first gathered insight in each of the speakers' preparation and editing processes by watching interview videos and podcasts. Then, I analyzed these four videos by identifying the factors they had in common regarding the structure of the talk and the method of presentation as well as their differences and personal modifications to the standard model provided by the TED Talks preparation website, and interviews with Chris Anderson.

Data Analysis

To analyze the data collected, I employed the concept of genre conventions, which affect how a genre is structured. Kain and Wardle argue that genre conventions can include set elements such as style, tone or voice, design, sources, etc., with the genre conventions provide guidelines on what a piece of writing should accomplish in answering the recurring rhetorical situation that the genre is faced with (19). From the interviews and podcasts collected, I derived these genre elements that allowed me to identify most of the genre conventions of a TED Talk. These genre conventions, along with the responses to rhetorical situations that arise, compose a genre. (Dirk; Braziller and Kleinfeld). Dirk also mentions that, apart from the previous information, "a rhetorically sound definition of genre must be centered... on the action it is used to accomplish" (qtd. in Dirk 252). This means that genres are essential to being able to accomplish certain actions.

These actions, or reactions from the audience who is hearing the talk, can be accomplished by the strategic use of mediums and modes.

Braziller and Kleinfeld argue that the mode is the way that the information is being communicated to the audience. This can be through visual, audible, and written aids and tools (21). The modes influence how the audience will interpret the information, as they are responsible for the audience's interaction (21). When a rhetor chooses a mode, he or she has to identify the appropriate medium to communicate the information. The medium is the specific tool used for the communication. Depending on the context of the situation and the purpose of the rhetor, different modes and media are chosen to cause different reactions from the audience.

With the case study, I was able to point out the different modes and media used for each talk, and analyze how these decisions impacted the audience. A further focus on the delivery techniques of TED Talks allowed me to identify the use of different tools, physical and abstract, to produce a unique effect on the audience and their new understanding of an innovative topic. I was also able to analyze the aspects of flexibility and inflexibility in

delivering a talk when compared to the conventions provided by TED, as well as the different outcomes and rhetorical moves that each speaker performed to answer to the TED rhetorical situation.

After analyzing the four individual TED Talks, along with the interviews, documentary, and podcasts, I discovered a new way of analyzing TED Talks from two different points of view. This prompted me to connect TED Talks to a system of genres, which consists of the analysis of genre sets and genre systems within TED Talks. A system of genres, according to Bazerman, is "a framework which organizes work, attention, and accomplishment" (375) of an activity. Genre systems, which Bazerman explains are "several genre sets of people working together in an organized way, plus the patterned relations in the production, flow, and use of documents," describes the relationships between genre sets, which are "the collection of types of texts someone in a particular role is likely to produce" (Bazerman 374). A genre system works in a more collective way than a genre set, and usually people working within a genre system have a common goal in mind, or goals that all relate to one another. It includes all the types of writing involved in accomplishing a common social activity. This final analysis of TED Talks allowed me to identify the genre conventions that are active in the TED scope and differentiate the necessary flexibility allowed to each speaker to respond to their specific rhetorical situation effectively.

Results

TED Talks Emerge as a Genre

The origin of TED Talks can be traced back to 1984, in Monterey, California. Architect and graphic designer Richard Saul Wurman organized a conference focused on the topics of technology, entertainment and design in the hopes of commemorating the recent advances that top scientists had accomplished in those three fields. Wurman's hope was to host an annual conference with the brightest minds in various scientific fields, and have "the ultimate dinner party" (qtd. in Bryant). In February of 1984, Wurman

hosted his first conference in the Monterey Conference Center in California. Among the 300 attendees, there were representatives of several innovative companies such as Pixar and Sony. Speakers included Mickey Schulhof, at the time president of Sony, and Nicholas Negroponte, founder of the MIT Media Lab (Moran). These characters demoed improvements and inventions that would later be considered the newest devices and technologies in the world. Some of the products featured in the conference were the compact disk, the beginnings of voice-recognition technology, and the introduction of the early Macintosh 128k by Steve Jobs (Moran).

Despite having some of the best thinkers and innovators present, the event was not as successful as Wurman would have liked it to be, and the conference lost money. Reflecting back on it, Wurman remembers, "I lost money on the first TED conference, but people talked about it long after the event was over. What transpired at TED went viral—and this was before the days of the Internet, texting and smartphones" (Moran). The lasting effect of the first conference, and the impact it had on the audience, inspired Wurman to try again in 1990, even though he ran the risk of failure a second time. The turnout for the second TED event was, financially, very much unlike the first one. The conference made a profit, and Wurman was able to establish TED as an annual conference for the advancement of technology, entertainment, and design for the world.

By that time, Wurman had introduced the rule of the eighteen-minute talk. This rule was based on the idea that the average human attention span lasts about eighteen minutes; hence a speaker will only be listened to with utmost attention if the message that he or she is trying to communicate does not take more than eighteen minutes to deliver (Bryant). This new way of approaching speeches was one of the characteristics that set TED Talks apart from other conferences.

In 2001, after eleven years of yearly conferences organized by Wurman, media entrepreneur Chris Anderson decided to acquire the rights to the TED conferences and start an organization. Anderson also made the key decision

of turning TED into a non-profit. This decision allowed Anderson to "stand by the principles that made TED great: the inspired format, the breadth of content, the commitment to seek out the most interesting people on Earth and let them communicate their passion" ("History of TED"). The TED non-profit expanded tremendously after Anderson's modifications, and the recognition that the annual conferences received called for an even bigger expansion of the TED conferences. Anderson, talking about the expansion of TED in the early 2000s, mentions that the non-profit "tried and failed to get TED onto television. But in 2006, with the arrival of online video, we started 'TED Talks' as an experimental video podcast" ("The History of TED Talks"). A year after the birth of YouTube, TED posted six "talks" that had been featured in that year's conference as an experiment to globalize the non-profit. The videos were released for free onto the internet. Within days of publication, the TED Talks had received a million views, marking the beginning of TED Talks' online success.

TED Talks as a Genre Today

In 2017, the TED Talk is considered one of the best-known educational, inspirational, and inventive videos on the internet. The non-profit organization has added numerous features, activities, and requirements for TED Talks, conferences, and independent events. Some of these additions include the implementation of a TED prize, a TED Global conference for international ideas, and the ability to franchise the TED concept by creating independent, regional conferences called TEDx Talks, among many more events. The growth of TED has also created a common goal that inspires and drives the non-profit, which is the desire to communicate "Ideas Worth Spreading" to the world. The TED philosophy changed into encouraging any and all people that have something meaningful to share to come forward and speak. Because of this concept, TED Talks now feature hundreds of topics and different ideas.

The diversity and variety of ideas that are found within TED Talks are difficult to place into one category, or even a single rhetorical situation. Every single talk answers to a personal issue, story, or experience of the featured speaker. This led many to believe that perhaps TED Talks was starting to lose its focus. Chris Anderson, in an interview, talked about this issue and provided insight into the rhetorical situation that occurs in every single TED Talk that exists: "Even though these speakers and their topics all seem completely different, they actually do have one key common ingredient. And it's this: your number one task as a speaker is to transfer into your listeners' minds an extraordinary gift: an idea" (Anderson "TED's Secret" 0:57-1:14). This concept allowed TED Talks to encompass a limitless amount of information and speeches. One speaker at a TED conference commented, "One of the interesting things of a TED Talk is that they've actually evolved into a new unit of information. You have things like a formulated song, a ninety-minute movie, a five-page article, and then you have an eighteen minute talk" (qtd. in "Behind the TED Talk" 5:26-5:36). Ideas communicated via an impacting eighteen-minute talk became the recurring reason why TED Talks existed, thus, what made it a genre, regardless of the topic chosen by the speaker.

Genre Conventions of The Modern TED Talk

The genre of the TED Talk has evolved and expanded throughout time according to the new technologies available to the world. The activities of the non-profit have in fact been so recognized in the modern world that the representatives have created a sort of brand name for TED Talks. This means that the videos uploaded to the internet all share specific characteristics that are proprietary and crucial for all TED Talks. These characteristics have been set aside as factors that separate a TED Talk from a common speech. In an interview, Chris Anderson states, "If communicated properly, ideas are capable of changing, forever, how someone thinks about the world and shaping their actions both now and well into the future" ("TED's Secret" 4:40-4:47). In TED conferences, communicating an idea in a proper manner has

been standardized to a certain extent to preserve the brand name that TED has constructed. This standardization takes place in all stages of the TED Talk preparation process, as well as the presentation of the speech.

Speech Preparation

TED speakers are invited to the annual TED conference, or to independent TEDx events. They are carefully chosen among scientists and experts in various fields to deliver the best idea they have, in the best way possible. To do this, speakers go through a lengthy and meticulously formulated pre-talk writing, editing, and rehearsing process to make sure that the talk is structured and delivered according to the TED Talk standards.

The process begins six-to-nine months before the speaker's TED Talk. "A speaker will start working with the staff and producers and editors to craft your story along with you" (qtd. in Bryant). The preparation starts with an outline and the proposal for the idea that the speaker wants to communicate to the audience. The TED website provides guidelines for scheduling each draft and stage of the talk (See Appendix A). The deadlines proposed in the schedule ensure that the speaker will be familiarized and confident with the talk so that the presentation goes smoothly.

While writing drafts for the TED Talk, the TED non-profit has very specific conventions that every speaker should follow in order to be approved and deemed worthy to be part of the brand format of the TED Talk. These are structure, brevity, and purpose. The structure of a TED Talk needs to have a "clear introduction, middle, and end" (TED). This means that there cannot be any ambiguous finales or a speech that starts out talking about the main issue without providing context to it. The talk needs to be written in a conversational tone, and the speaker needs to speak as if the script was never written, and the speaker is just having a conversation with the audience. To connect with the audience, the talk should include a pathos approach that contains honest, captivating emotion (TED). In addition to this, every speaker should avoid political agendas, religious or racial profiling, talking

about their own TED Talk, trying to sell the idea to the audience instead of communicating and spreading it, or making TED puns at any time during their talk. Speakers should also be aware of copyright laws, and make sure to not violate them.

Brevity is one of the most important genre conventions of a TED Talk, as it was established before the online talk itself. Every speaker needs to make sure that the talk takes eighteen minutes or less to deliver. The speaker should also be able to express their idea effectively in the allotted time. Editors "make sure their script is an appropriate length for their time slot, or else their content may seem cramped" (TED). To do this, speakers have to limit themselves to communicating only one idea to the audience. They have to focus on that idea and develop it so that speakers can easily relay their talk by sharing simply organized, yet powerful information about their topic.

Purpose is the third convention that a TED Talk must possess. Every idea that is delivered in TED should matter to the general audience. If the idea does not have any importance the talk is rendered useless, and its purpose of spreading a useful idea is defeated. Anderson comments that to give a successful TED Talk, the speaker ought to "give your listeners a reason to care... stir your audience's curiosity. Use intriguing, provocative questions to identify why something doesn't make sense and needs explaining" (Anderson "TED's Secret" 5:33-5:55). When delivering a speech with purpose, the audience is supposed to be interested, and care about the speaker's words. Only that way will the idea be successfully spread among people throughout the world.

Speech Presentation

Genre conventions and TED regulations do not stop at the time of performance at the conference. Rather, speakers are faced with a new set of rules that they must abide by for a successful TED Talk. The documentary "Behind the TED Talk 2009" revealed that TED representatives, and in some cases Anderson himself, will coach the speakers in the venue where the

conference will take place. Coaching helps speakers get accustomed to the TED stage, the cameras, and the presentation style that the TED Talk must follow.

The first thing that speakers are introduced to is the countdown clock. In every TED Talk, there is a digital clock that tracks the amount of time that the speaker has left. This clock is equipped with an LED light that serves as a tracking system for speakers: "At two minutes the light, it turns yellow. Okay? When it gets down to zero—which it shouldn't do—it will stay on zero and flash red at you, and you really must wrap up" (Anderson "TED's Secret" 0:50-1:00). This is one of the most important conventions of the TED Talk conference, and it links directly to the speaker's preparation for the brevity of the talk.

Stage presence is also an important convention that needs to meet TED standards. Before the conference, speakers perform a dress rehearsal where they are coached on the correct ways to behave onstage. The critiques range from posture and movement around the stage to voice intonation and demonstration of confidence. Anderson argues, "It's much more powerful to just stand there on the stage. If you're going to move, move deliberately and confidently, perhaps from one spot to another" ("TED's Secret" 1:02-1:09). The presentation of the TED Talk is set to be of high calibre, so that the image of TED continues to soar above the average speech. Speakers achieve these standards by following the guidelines given by TED, and adding tools, activities, jokes, and confident moves.

TED Talks are presentations more than they are speeches. The dialogue has already been set and rehearsed, and is often repeated line by line at the stage. Speakers are expected to be familiar with their speeches, which is why there are no teleprompters allowed at the conferences. Speakers can, however, use notecards, power point slides, or any other tool that helps them finish their speech. TED Talk conferences are arranged in such a way that there are never going to be two TED Talks happening simultaneously. This means that the entire conference is gathered to listen to a single speaker at a time. This adds pressure to the speaker's performance, which is why TED insists on thorough memorization of the talk.

The technology that captures the TED Talk has a significant role in the conventions of a TED Talk. The way that a TED Talk is filmed contributes to the overall TED Talk feel. To make sure that the talks, the speakers, and the audience are captured in the eighteen-minute video, TED has implemented a set of cameras. A crewmember commented on this factor of TED Talks. He states, "Right away we wanted to raise the production values, and that has to do with how we light everything, how we shoot everything, how we rehearse with the performers... we have 5 cameras circling around the speakers, two looking back on the audience, we've got one camera that is on a crane so it can just swoop in over the audience straight up to the speaker" (qtd in Behind the TED Talk 2:02-2:23). With state of the art technology, TED can create videos that are simple but captivating, focusing on the speaker, the audience, and the delivery of the speaker's idea.

Case Study: Analysis of Four Successful TED Talks

Successful TED Talks have demonstrated the ability to share an idea in a more straightforward, entertaining way than other speeches. These TED Talks communicate this idea in many different ways, using different tools, rhetorical appeals, and structures of narration. Yet these talks are considered by many as belonging to the same category as other successful TED Talks. For that to be the case, these talks have to fulfill all of the previously mentioned genre conventions, and communicate an idea to the audience. The differences between each talk, and the way that it is delivered is personalized by each speaker, who molds the genre conventions of a TED Talk to adapt to their own situation.

"The Invisible Force—Self Image—Enables You to Accomplish Great Goals"
by Dan Lok

Dan Lok, entrepreneur and successful businessman, focuses his TED Talk on the idea that the way that people look at themselves is the key to success. In his talk, Lok shares his awareness about the importance of self-image.

He uses quotes, statistical facts, and personal experiences to establish credibility with the audience. His pathos rhetorical move is directed toward the audience, as he makes examples about several situations that could be affected by a change in self-image. Lok uses the concept of self-image to establish a situational example that he shares with the audience. Meanwhile, the camera angles shift between the audience and the speaker, as Lok also incorporates several audience participation opportunities into his talk. He proposes "setting the room at seventy degrees. This is a metaphor for your comfort zone. It is also known as your self-image" (Lok "Invisible Force" 04:33). He then argues that people's goals tend to be higher than what each person can accomplish in the comfort zone. This, according to Lok, makes people face a difficult decision: either lower their goals and self-image, or raise them ("Invisible Force"). This metaphor is an example that Lok uses to connect with the audience and transmit his message in such a way that it is easy and entertaining for the audience.

The tools that Lok uses are limited to only his body language and stage presence. His tone is thoughtful and encouraging. He uses no PowerPoint, and is entirely alone at the stage. He demonstrates authority over the audience by sharing wisdom that he claims most people never learn in their entire lives (Lok "Invisible Force" 01:30). After explaining his topic, he demonstrates closure by inviting the audience to ask themselves questions about their self-image, and encouraging them to improve it. The talk is 16:38 minutes long, which fits into the convention that TED Talk stands by.

"This Is What Happens When You Reply to Spam Emails" by James Veitch

This TED Talk is retelling the story of comedian James Veitch's experience when he replied to a spam email that appeared in his email's inbox section. Veitch starts out talking about the odd situation of finding an email in the inbox section that did not belong there. He then proceeds to show the audience the conversation between himself and the spammer through PowerPoint slides that contain the contents of said emails. The outcome of

this exchange makes for a hilarious story, and shares the idea that by amusing yourself with spam email replies, you are wasting the spammers' time that they would use to scam other people out of their savings (Veitch).

The talk has a light and funny tone, and it consists of reading several PowerPoint slides that make up the emailed conversation. Body language and voice intonation are very important while reading the PowerPoint slides, as it aids the audience's reaction to laugh. During the video, there are some instances in which the camera focuses on the audience's reaction to the information that is being provided by Veitch, who are mostly laughing. Despite being a long and elaborated joke, as the scammer was tricked into writing an email in which code words such as "lawyer" and "legal" were replaced with candy and sweets, names such as "gummy bear" and "peanut M&M's" (Veitch), the talk was structured as a story, told in under eighteen minutes, and delivered with confidence.

"Why City Flags May Be the Worst Designed Thing You've Never Noticed" by Roman Mars

Roman Mars is a podcaster, and a radio show host, which meant that his most comfortable place was behind a desk, talking as if he were in his podcast setting. In his TED Talk, he breaks convention completely by actually using this mode of communication while he is sitting down. He also makes use of a new multimedia tool that uses technology that is not normally used in speeches: computerized sounds, or rather, voices. Mars presents his talk as having some sort of conversation with these voices, which all talk about how city flags are so poorly designed. The use of this tool keeps the audience engaged at all times, as it is a new tool that they had not seen before used in such a way. Mars also incorporates slight moments of comedic dialogue in his speech to lighten the tone, or simply to make the talk more interesting.

The talk is about the poorly designed city flags across the United States, and how we can improve them to symbolize patriotism for the city,

instead of a despicable work of art. With the help of PowerPoints that show the flags, and audio-visual aids to define key terms and provide commentary, Mars considers himself to be an "information DJ" (qtd. in Bryant). His tone is light and informative, as well as slightly emotional at the end. He first uses humor to make fun of poorly designed flags, and then closes his argument by explaining what flags should mean to the people that are represented by them, and makes an emotional connection to patriotism and pride for one's home. This video is what could be said to be a "traditional" TED Talk when it comes to length, as it is almost exactly eighteen minutes long, and shares a personal idea that is, according to Mars, worth spreading.

"My Stroke of Insight" by Jill Bolte Taylor

This TED Talk is probably one of the most watched ones on the internet. Bolte Taylor shares a personal anecdote about having a stroke, and, being a neuroanatomist, her stroke and what biologically happened inside her brain allowed her to discover a state of mind that all people should engage in. In her talk, she explains how a brain works, and states that the left hemisphere is usually in charge of controlling the logical, planned side of life, while the right hemisphere focuses on the here and now, and craves life's immediate pleasures. To establish credibility and engage her audience, she brought a human brain to the TED Talk as a tool to communicate her idea, and show the audience what happened in her own brain as she experienced the stroke.

She shared her experience as her stroke made the left hemisphere of her brain go dormant, which made her experience an inability to think logically and about her own safety. Instead, she was caught up in the moment, and she felt as if everything on Earth was beautiful, colorful, and happy (Bolte Taylor). She masks the terror of having experienced a stroke by adding a comical note or two as she explains her actions on that day. She wraps up her talk slightly over the eighteen- minute mark. Nevertheless, it communicated an idea that has spread to millions of people. During her talk, camera

angles change to show the human brain, as well as the reactions from the audience, as Bolte Taylor reaches certain key points in her speech. Her tone is emotional and informative. When thinking about her talk, she mentioned, "It was the last six minutes [that were hard]. Do I teach or do I hold the space of what I had created with the morning of the stroke?... In the end it was that willing to go out on a limb and the fruit was truly there" (Bolte Taylor qtd. in "Behind the TED Talk" 4:23-4:45). This shows that Bolte Taylor could have approached her TED Talk in one of many different ways. She decided to adapt the genre conventions of TED Talks and make the experience extremely intimate and personal, which made a huge impact on the audience and their response to the talk.1

TED Talks as a System of Genres

The four individual TED Talks analyzed in the case study have several factors in common, which can be attributed to the genre conventions that TED has specifically set for every presenter. They all use the same audio-visual mode to communicate an idea, they all possess a clear introduction, middle, and closing statement, and they focus on a single idea, delivered within eighteen minutes, to make an impact. Some of these conventions, however, seem to be bent, modified, or even completely dismissed in certain TED Talks, such as Roman Mars's radio show setup in a conference environment. Even though the fundamental rules were broken, Mars was able to share and spread an idea in an innovative way. As a result, his TED Talk is considered to be one of the best ones ever recorded. This suggests that TED takes pride and purposefully searches for people that alter their rules; as Roman Mars put it, "They want you to break convention" (qtd. in Bryant).

This desire to be original and unconventional is ever-present at the back of speakers' and editors' minds during the entire preparation process of a TED Talk. However, the specific TED Talk that the speaker will later present does have to follow a set amount of rules or conventions to be considered a TED Talk. This seemingly contradictory idea led me to the concept of TED Talks

as a system of genres. The individual TED Talk ought to follow a fairly strict structure and purpose. The drafts and speeches that the speaker prepares form a genre set, which has to answer to the recurring rhetorical situation of producing a final draft that fits within the TED guidelines. Each individual TED Talk provides a certain level of flexibility in the genre conventions of a TED Talk; in other words, each speaker personalizes his or her TED Talk according to what the speaker is trying to communicate. This is a genre system, which includes and follows the TED Talk conventions closely, yet each speaker adds diversity and uniqueness to the talk as an extra. This extra factor is what usually makes TED Talks so successful. The originality of the communication of TED Talks is one of the reasons why TED Talks are not placed in the same category as speeches. TED Talks in general, then, have a different goal and rhetorical situation than individual TED Talks, such that the collective group of TED Talks includes the extra uniqueness of individual TED Talks in its genre conventions. TED Talks, viewed as a collection of individual talks, consists of a system of genres, and it includes all the talks, topics, and ways to communicate ideas that TED stands behind. All of these talks are unique and different from one another, which makes communicating a unique and innovative TED Talk a requirement, or convention, to be able to form a part of the general scope of TED.

Discussion

From the performed research, it is clear that the TED Talk genre has evolved and expanded greatly since it was first introduced in 1984. Richard Saul Wurman's idea of hosting a yearly "ultimate dinner party" (qtd. in Bryant) for the brightest minds in the world to share ideas quickly advanced and propagated through the world thanks to modern technologies such as social media, internet, and audio-visual technology. The genre of TED Talks nowadays includes over two thousand videos shared and viewed by millions of people every day. The amount of topic and speaker diversity is huge, yet TED

Talks still fall under the category of a single genre by satisfying the response to the recurring rhetorical situation of spreading ideas throughout the world.

Despite being all part of one genre, TED Talks can be separated and categorized as a system of genres. Within this system, there are genre conventions for each TED Talk to fulfill to be considered as worthy, or as part of TED. These conventions are rigid and are shared by all the TED Talks that exist, such as being 18 minutes long, sharing an idea, memorizing the speech to perform it, and behaving in a confident and professional manner. In these individual TED Talks, the speakers have to mould, alter, or add on to these genre conventions to provide a unique, personal talk that adapts to the topic and context of the situation. Diversity and flexibility can be considered add-ons to an individual talk.

When multiple, or all the TED Talks in existence, are considered in the research, however, the conventions of the genre system of TED Talks change. The purpose of TED Talks is to share a personal idea that is worth sharing. The TED non-profit prides itself in having an innovative and unique repertoire of information on many different fields of study, presented in many different ways. This suggests that the more general system of genres of TED Talks' genre conventions include the aspect of flexibility, diversity and uniqueness to their genre conventions, as all TED Talks are required to have these characteristics. The genre conventions of an individual TED Talk presentation, and the collective TED Talk scope, are different, but they complement each other.

The combination of these genre conventions and collaboration between the individual and collective TED Talks show how TED Talks are effective in communicating ideas by implementing a non-conventional way of delivering a talk. Further research could focus on the impact that the talk has on the audience and the effect that the audience has on the TED speaker as well as a deeper exploration of what encompasses the different genre sets and systems that the TED system of genres possesses.

Works Cited

Anderson, Chris. "TED's Secret to Great Public Speaking." *YouTube*, uploaded by TED, 19 Apr. 2016, www.youtube.com/watch?v=-FOCpMAww28.

Anderson, Chris. "The History of TED Talks." *HuffPost*, 10 Jun. 2016, www.huffingtonpost.com/quora/the-history-of-ted-talks_b_10399406.html.

"Behind the TED Talk 2009." *YouTube*, uploaded by TED Blog Video, 23 Dec. 2011, www.youtube.com/watch?v=aASvyfFUMdk.

Bazerman, Charles. "Speech Acts, Genres, and Activity Systems: How Texts Organize Activity and People." Wardle and Downs, pp. 365-394.

Bolte Taylor, Jill. "My Stroke of Insight." *TED*, Feb. 2008, www.ted.com/talks/jill_bolte_taylor_s_powerful_stroke_of_insight/transcript?language=en.

Braziller, Amy and Elizabeth Kleinfeld. "Understanding Genres." *The Bedford Book of Genres: A Guide & Reader*, Bedford/St. Martins, 2014, pp. 4-37.

Bryant, Charles W. "How TED Talks Work: Featuring Roman Mars." *Stuff You Should Know* from *HowStuffWorks.com*, 24 Mar. 2017, www.stuffyoushouldknow.com/podcasts/how-ted- talks-work.htm.

Chang, Yu-jung, and Huang Hung-Tzu. "Exploring TED Talks as a Pedagogical Resource for Oral Presentations: A Corpus-Based Move Analysis." *English Teaching & Learning*, vol. 39, no. 4, 2015, pp. 29-62. *Education Source*, doi: 10.6330/ETL.2015.39.4.02.

di Carlo, Giuseppina Scotto. "Pathos as a Communicative Strategy for Online Knowledge Dissemination: The Case of TED Talks." *Southeast Asian Journal of English Language Studies*, vol. 21, no. 1, 2015, pp. 23-34. *Education Source*, doi: 10.17576/3L-2015-2101-03.

Dirk, Kerry. "Navigating Genres." *Writing Spaces: Readings on Writing*, vol. 1, edited by Charles Lowe and Pavel Zemliansky, Parlor Press, 2010, pp. 249-62, writingspaces.org/sites/default/files/dirk--navigating-genres.pdf.

Grant-Davie, Keith. "Rhetorical Situations and Their Constituents." Wardle and Downs, pp. 347-63.

"History of TED." *TED*, www.ted.com/about/our-organization/history-of-ted.

Kain, Donna, and Elizabeth Wardle. "Activity Theory: An Introduction for the Writing Classroom." Wardle and Downs, pp. 284-301.

Lok, Dan. "Behind The Scenes of a TEDx Speaker." *YouTube*, uploaded by Dan Lok, 10 Nov. 2016, www.youtube.com/watch?v=eMEO2-KH5Fg.

Lok, Dan. "The Invisible Force—Self-image—Enables You to Achieve Great Goals." *YouTube*, uploaded by TEDx Talks, 16 June 2016, www.youtube .com/watch?v=C5dyGh3oMVQ.

Mars, Roman. "Why City Flags May Be the Worst-Designed Thing You've Never Noticed." *TED*, Mar. 2015, www.ted.com/talks/roman_mars_why_city _flags_may_be_the_worst_designed_thing_you_ve_never _noticed#t-931896.

Moran, Bryan. "Richard Saul Wurman: TED's Founder Discusses How It All Began." *American Express*, 18 Mar. 2014, www.americanexpress.com/us/ small-business/openforum/articles/richard-saul-wurman-teds-founder -discusses-how-it-all-began/.

"Prepare Your Speakers + Performers." *TED*, www.ted.com/participate /organize-a-local-tedx-event/tedx-organizer-guide/speakers-program /prepare-your-speaker.

Veitch, James. "This is What Happens When You Reply to Spam Email." *TED*, Dec. 2015, www.ted.com/talks/james_veitch_this _is_what_happens_when_you_reply_to_spam_email.

Wardle, Elizabeth, and Doug Downs, editors. *Writing about Writing: A College Reader*. 2nd ed., Bedford/St. Martin's, 2014.

Responding to "The Extent of Influence That Genre Conventions Have on TED Talks"

QUESTIONS FOR DISCUSSION

Research in ENC 1102 is geared toward the discourse community of writing studies, which focuses on questions and arguments about how writing works in the world. Samayoa's essay enters into conversations in writing studies to advance our collective knowledge

of the field. To successfully enter into scholarly conversations and make contributions, writers need areas of research, objects of analysis, scholarly literature, and lines of argument that matter to and are recognizable within that field of study. With all of that in mind, consider the following:

1. What research area does Samayoa choose to study and what were the research questions that guided her research?

2. What did she seem to want to learn more about during this project? What do you find interesting about this?

3. What scholarly conversation does Samayoa seem to be joining with her research? How does she frame her project as adding to this conversation?

4. What primary research does Samayoa collect to gain insight into her line of inquiry? What seems useful (or not) about each piece of data? How does she analyze each piece of data in her paper?

5. How does Samayoa answer the "so what" question? What do you think is significant about her findings? Does she have any suggestions for further research?

QUESTIONS FOR REFLECTION

6. One of the learning outcomes for ENC 1102 is that "students will examine their own conceptions of writing and research in response to their inquiry, reading, and writing throughout the course." What did you learn about writing, rhetoric, and research from Samayoa's study? How has reading Samayoa's piece enhanced your understanding of how academic writing is targeted to specific communities, which carry their own expectations, values, and rhetorical approaches to writing? What ideas does this give you for conducting your own investigation into the ways writing and rhetoric work in the world?

ACTIVITIES FOR FURTHER EXPLORATION

7. One of the best ways to understand how a piece of writing (discourse) works within a discourse community (like writing studies, biology, or engineering) is to investigate the genres that

writers produce. Just as Samayoa examined the conventions of TED Talks, this activity asks that you examine the conventions of academic researched articles from the field of writing studies. When entering new writing situations, savvy writers often do a genre analysis to learn what's acceptable and help them adhere to conventions. Write a 2–3 page reading response that answers the following: What are the key elements of the rhetorical situation, and why are they important factors in determining how to best produce rhetorical discourse? What conventions or moves appear in Samayoa's text (think structure, organization, formal/informal language, types of evidence used, types of analysis presented)? Bring in other researched reports from *Stylus* to develop your analysis and support your claims about what is a genre convention versus an innovation or idiosyncrasy of the writer.

Where Can You Get Support for Your Writing at UCF?

There are many resources at UCF you can take advantage of to support your writing, both during your time in composition classes and beyond. We've provided some information on these resources below.

University Writing Center
uwc.cah.ucf.edu

The University Writing Center (UWC) is for confident and struggling writers alike. The UWC offers individual writing support for students at all levels, from first-year to graduate, in all majors. The UWC is much more than a grammar lab.

Instead, trained peer tutors assist at every stage of the writing process, from understanding an assignment, to drafting and organizing, to revision. Consultations are available face-to-face, online, and in small groups.

The UWC also provides a wealth of writing resources on the web, from style guides to handouts on professional writing, grammar, and punctuation.

The UWC has offices on the main UCF campus in Orlando, as well as branches at the Rosen Library, Eastern Florida State College,

and Daytona State College. Drop in, schedule online, or phone for an appointment. Information about hours, locations, and scheduling an appointment with the UWC can be found at **uwc.cah.ucf .edu.**

WHAT ARE SOME THINGS UWC TUTORS CAN HELP YOU DO?

- Understand assignment requirements
- Develop ideas
- Plan and organize your writing
- Identify and address some key aspects of your writing for you to revise
- Learn to cite and document sources
- Practice strategies for proofreading and editing
- Learn to correct errors in grammar, punctuation, and mechanics

WHAT CAN YOU DO TO THE GET THE MOST OUT OF A UWC CONSULTATION?

- Visit the UWC well before your assignment is due.
- Allow enough time to have multiple consultations (on different days) for big writing projects. You probably won't be able to discuss all aspects of your writing in just thirty to forty-five minutes.
- You don't need to have a completed draft. Working with the UWC earlier in your writing process—even before you get started—can be just as useful.
- For long-term help, arrange a recurring weekly appointment to meet with the same tutor at the same time throughout the semester.
- If you're not sure how to handle a complicated assignment, or if you've got writer's block, those are good times to visit the UWC!

WHAT SHOULD YOU BRING TO A UWC CONSULTATION?

- Your assignment requirements or guidelines for writing
- Your work—everything you've done so far
- Your notes, outline, sources—everything you've used to help you write

- Ideas, questions, and specific learning goals you'd like to accomplish

UCF Libraries
library.ucf.edu

Did you know that UCF has fourteen libraries on multiple campuses? You may be familiar with the John C. Hitt Library in the center of the Orlando campus, but there are branch and regional libraries in many locations, including at the Rosen College, College of Medicine, Cocoa, Daytona Beach, and nine other regional campuses. The UCF Libraries house almost two million items, including online books and journals accessible from anywhere in the world.

You can use the Libraries web page to search for items in any of the collections, and also search hundreds of databases for access to hundreds of thousands of articles, ebooks, and historical documents. Students simply log in to the Libraries web page with their NID, and all available information is at their fingertips.

Reference librarians are available at the Research & Information Desk and using the Ask Us service.

Following are some useful Library services for Composition students.

ASK US

library.ucf.edu/ask

The Ask Us service offers research assistance in person or via live chat, text message, email, or telephone. Reach a librarian when you really need one!

INTERLIBRARY LOAN (ILL)

library.ucf.edu/services/borrowing-from-other-libraries

If there's an article or book that you need for your research, and the UCF Libraries don't have access, the Interlibrary Loan & Document Delivery Services (ILL/DDS) Department will get it for you! Interlibrary Loan borrows items from other libraries, and its services are free. Students can request books, articles, and other materials through ILL by logging into their ILLiad account (which new users

can create in a matter of minutes). Books are typically available in 7–10 business days, and articles are typically available to download within 3–5 business days.

SUBJECT LIBRARIANS AND UCF RESEARCH GUIDES

guides.ucf.edu

Did you know there is a subject librarian for your major? John Venecek is the librarian for writing and rhetoric, and there are librarians for each academic discipline at UCF—from accounting to tourism.

The UCF Research Guides are subject-specific guides created by subject librarians in their area. Each guide contains resources and collections that are important in a given discipline, and can serve as a useful entry point into your research, no matter the field.

RESEARCH CONSULTATIONS

library.ucf.edu/help/schedule-an-appointment

A research consultation is a one-on-one appointment with a librarian for extensive, in-depth research assistance. If you need extra help finding sources on a tough topic, you can schedule a session with your subject librarian.

Additional Online Resources

STYLUS: A JOURNAL OF FIRST-YEAR WRITING

writingandrhetoric.cah.ucf.edu/stylus

Since 2010, *Stylus: A Journal of First-Year Writing* has published two issues a year of outstanding writing from UCF's own first-year composition students. These articles can be all be found online at the journal's website, and might serve as inspiration for the writing and research you are doing in your own composition class. Look to what these past students have written for another perspective on a concept you've been talking about in class, ideas for how to investigate some aspect of your own writing, and models of how you might organize and present your own thinking.

arc.lib.montana.edu/ojs/index.php/Young-Scholars-In-Writing

As with *Stylus*, *Young Scholars in Writing: Undergraduate Research in Writing and Rhetoric* (*YSW*), a peer-reviewed journal for undergraduates, can provide inspiration and models for your own writing and research. The journal publishes research and theoretical articles from undergraduates on writing, writers, rhetoric, discourse, language, and related topics, so you should find the articles presented there highly relevant to the work you are doing in your composition class. There is also a "Spotlight on First-Year Writing" section in each issue that publishes work from students in first-year composition courses. All articles are accessible online. Visit the YSW website for details on submitting work for consideration.

COMPPILE

comppile.org

CompPile is a database of publication information for books and articles relevant to writing studies. CompPile does not contain the texts themselves (though you can sometimes find a direct link), but many of the publications you discover in CompPile can be found in the UCF Libraries. This makes CompPile a useful first stop when researching subjects related to writing or rhetoric. Additionally, the WPA-CompPile research bibliographies (**comppile.org/wpa /bibliographies**) provide quick overviews of a variety of writing- and literacy-related topics.

PURDUE OWL

owl.english.purdue.edu/owl

The Online Writing Lab (OWL) at Purdue University is home to many resources that you might find helpful at all stages of the writing process, including information and advice about getting started, overcoming writer's block, grammar and mechanics, and citation. It's easy to use, reliable, and free, so take advantage of it if you have a question not answered in this handbook.

How Can You Stay Involved with Writing at UCF?

Your first-year composition course represents only the first step in a larger writing experience at the university. Below, we've outlined some of the ways you might stay involved with writing after your composition course has ended.

Stylus: A Journal of First-Year Writing
writingandrhetoric.cah.ucf.edu/stylus

The UCF Department of Writing and Rhetoric's First-Year Composition Program publishes *Stylus: A Journal of First-Year Writing* to provide a forum for the exemplary writing and research produced by students enrolled in Composition I and II at the university. Bringing together work from across a program of some four thousand students, *Stylus* celebrates writing that demonstrates an inquiring mind, compelling prose, and original thought.

Published online biannually in the fall and spring, the journal accepts work produced in composition classes by all students who are currently enrolled in the first-year writing program, or who were enrolled the previous semester. All submissions go through an intensive peer review and selection process. Submission guidelines and procedure can be found on the *Stylus* website. Additionally, students interested in gaining editorial experience after completing their composition courses should contact the journal's editor for details.

President John C. Hitt Prize for Excellence in First-Year Writing
writingandrhetoric.cah.ucf.edu/stylus/hittprize.php

If *Stylus* represents the best of UCF's First-Year Composition Program, the President John C. Hitt Prize for Excellence in First-Year Writing is for the best of the best.

Awarded yearly, the Hitt Prize recognizes the talent and hard work of one student published in either of the preceding fall or spring issues. This $500 award includes a $250 book scholarship from the President. More than money, however, the Hitt Prize is a

prestigious honor recognized by UCF faculty and administration as well as the larger academic community.

The Hitt Prize is named for UCF President John C. Hitt, whose commitment to undergraduate success has included using tuition differential money to lower class size in composition courses, hire additional full-time faculty to teach composition, and fully fund the University Writing Center.

Knights Write Showcase
writingandrhetoric.cah.ucf.edu/showcase.php

The Knights Write Showcase is an annual event held in the Pegasus Ballroom that provides a chance for students and faculty from across campus to get a glimpse of the exciting work currently going on in UCF's first-year composition classes. Activities include student displays, student and faculty panels, and the *Stylus* Awards Ceremony. The Hitt Prize is awarded at the Showcase, and awards are also given for the best student displays.

To learn about previous Showcases and watch presentations by student panelists, visit the Knights Write Showcase website. Check with your professor for details on when the next Knights Write Showcase will be held and how to submit work for consideration.

The UCF Undergraduate Research Journal
urj.ucf.edu

The mission of the UCF *Undergraduate Research Journal* (URJ) is to showcase articles of exemplary works from a wide range of student scholarship in all fields. The journal seeks outstanding research submitted by undergraduate students who have been involved in faculty-mentored research projects and activities related to scholarship. Issues are published online, so check out their previous issues to get a sense of the broad scope of research opportunities at UCF. Students interested in pursuing some of these opportunities should visit the Office of Undergraduate Research website at **our.ucf.edu**.

Peer Tutoring at the University Writing Center
uwc.cah.ucf.edu/become-a-consultant

To assist writers across the disciplines, the University Writing Center (UWC) hires undergraduate and graduate tutors from a wide variety of majors. Tutors provide individual and small-group writing support to students, faculty, and staff from first-year to graduate in every discipline, while studying writing center research and theory. As they teach and learn in collaboration with others, tutors develop their own writing abilities, interpersonal skills, and leadership potential. Visit the UWC website to learn more about how to become a writing consultant.

Department of Writing and Rhetoric Undergraduate Programs
writingandrhetoric.cah.ucf.edu

The UCF Department of Writing and Rhetoric offers three programs for undergraduate students: a B.A. in Writing and Rhetoric, a minor in Writing and Rhetoric, and an undergraduate certificate in professional writing. Students in these programs improve their writing and rhetorical knowledge and competencies, preparing them to be successful communicators in disciplinary, professional, and public contexts. Students undertake rigorous intellectual work to increase their effectiveness as writers, develop their facility with language, and deepen their engagement with writing as a form of social action. More information about these programs can be found on the Department of Writing and Rhetoric website.

Bachelor of Arts in Writing and Rhetoric

The Bachelor of Arts in Writing and Rhetoric provides students with in-depth training in writing, rhetorical, and literacy studies, preparing them for a range of writing-focused jobs that involve the analysis, creation, editing, and coordination of texts, including digital and multimedia ones. In addition to preparing students for graduate/professional study and jobs across a variety of sectors (e.g., publishing and media, education, healthcare, marketing and public relations, entertainment and hospitality, civic organizations), the major prepares students to be more effective and ethical citizen-communicators.

Minor in Writing and Rhetoric

The Minor in Writing and Rhetoric is best suited for students planning to enter writing-intensive professions such as law, publishing or editing, journalism, public relations, marketing, communications management, and new media development. The minor prepares students to rhetorically analyze, effectively participate in, and critically reflect about writing experiences in their disciplines, professional workplaces, and community and civic environments. Students in the minor gain and apply historical and theoretical knowledge about rhetoric and writing. They also develop rhetorical and writing-related competencies and habits of mind that support effective and ethical communication in the twenty-first century. The minor is only 18 credit hours, which makes it convenient to add to a variety of majors.

Certificate in Public and Professional Writing

The 12-hour Certificate in Public and Professional Writing is appropriate for students in any major, including technical ones, as it can enhance their credentials for employment. The certificate provides students with additional training and experience in disciplinary, workplace, and public (e.g., civic, community-based) writing, preparing them to be effective, flexible professional communicators.

Sentence Guides for Academic Writers (SG)

If you're a college student, then you're a writer, someone who makes sense of what you are learning through writing and who responds to a variety of writing assignments in any field of study. In most of these assignments, you'll be doing academic writing.

But just what do we mean by academic writing? The answer to this question can vary from field to field, but we can point to several features that almost all academic writing shares:

- Conventional grammar, spelling, punctuation, and mechanics
- Organization that links ideas explicitly
- Easy to read type size and typeface, conventional margins and spacing
- Explicitly stated claims supported by evidence
- Careful documentation of sources
- Use of conventional academic formats, such as research essays, lab reports, or literature reviews

Writing academically also means thinking academically—asking a lot of questions, exploring the ideas of others, and entering into scholarly debates and academic conversations. As a college writer, you will be asked to read different kinds of texts; understand and evaluate authors' ideas, arguments, and methods; and contribute your own ideas. In this way, you present yourself as a participant in an academic conversation. As an example, suppose you and your friends have an ongoing debate

about the best film trilogy of all time. During your conversations with one another, you analyze the details of the films, introduce points you want your friends to consider, listen to their ideas, perhaps cite what the critics have said about a particular trilogy. This is the same way conversations work in academic fields—except that scholars might be debating the best public policy for a social problem or the most promising new theory in treating disease rather than film trilogies.

If you are uncertain about what academic writing *sounds like* or if you're not sure you're any good at it, this booklet offers guidance for you at the sentence level. It helps answer questions such as these:

> How can I present the ideas of others in a way that demonstrates my understanding of the debate?
>
> How can I agree with someone, but add a new idea?
>
> How can I disagree with a scholar without seeming, well, rude?
>
> How can I make it clear which ideas are mine and which ideas are someone else's?

The following sections offer sentence guides you can use and adapt to your own writing situations. As in all writing that you do, you will have to think about your purpose (reason for writing), your audience (readers), and the context for your writing before knowing which guides will be most appropriate for a particular piece of writing or for a certain part of your essay.

The guides are organized to help you present background information, the views and claims of others, and your own views and claims—all in the context of your purpose and audience.

Academic Writers Present Information and Others' Views

Some academic writing will call on you to provide some background information or set a context for your main idea or argument. Doing so often requires you to present or summarize what is known or what has already been said in relation to the topic you are exploring in your writing.

SG1 Presenting what is known or assumed

Here are some structures that may be helpful when you are providing background information about your topic or subject:

As history tells us, _____.

X has shown that _____.

Research by X and Y suggests that _____.

According to X, _____ % of _____ are/favor
_____.

In other situations, you may have the need to present information that is assumed to be conventional wisdom:

Children often believe that _____.

Conventional wisdom suggests that _____.

Many Americans share the idea that _____.

_____ is a widely held belief.

In order to challenge an assumption or a widely held belief, you have to acknowledge it first. Doing so shows your readers that you are placing your ideas in an appropriate context.

Although many people tend to believe X, there is significant benefit to considering the merits of Y.

College students tend to believe that _____ when, in fact, the opposite is much more likely the case.

SG2   Presenting others' views

As a writer, you build your own ethos, or credibility, by being able to represent the views of others accurately and fairly. As an academic writer, you will often be expected to demonstrate your understanding of a text by summarizing the views or arguments of its author(s). To do so, you may use sentences with these phrases in them:

X argues that _____.

X emphasizes the need for _____.

In this groundbreaking article, X and Y claim _____.

X endorses _____ because _____.

X and Y have recently criticized the idea that _____.

_____, according to X, is the most critical cause of _____.

Although you will create your own variations of these sentences as you draft and revise, such sentence guides can help you think through how best to present another writer's claim, or finding, clearly, concisely, and accurately.

SG3   Presenting direct quotations

When the exact words of a source are important for accuracy, authority, emphasis, or tone, you will probably want to use a direct quotation. Ordinarily, you will introduce direct quotations with a signal verb.

In her essay on global warming, X *characterizes* the problem this way: ". . ."

According to X, _____ *is defined as* "..."

"...," *explains* X.

X *argues* strongly in favor of the policy, pointing out that "..."

The signal verbs you use can reflect your attitude toward the person you are quoting. If you write that "X characterizes the problem," you are taking a neutral stance. If you write "X mischaracterizes the problem," however, you are signaling that you do not agree with X.

NOTE: You will generally cite direct quotations according to the documentation style your readers expect. MLA style, used in English and in other humanities courses, recommends using the author name paired with a page number, if there is one. APA style, used in most social sciences, requires the year of publication generally after the mention of the source, with page numbers after the quoted material. In *Chicago* style, used in history and in some humanities courses, writers use superscript numbers (like this[6]) to refer readers to footnotes or endnotes. In-text citations, like the ones shown below, refer readers to entries in the works cited or reference list.

MLA   Lazarín argues that our overreliance on testing in K-12 schools "does not put students first" (20).

APA   Lazarín (2014) argues that our overreliance on testing in K-12 schools "does not put students first" (p. 20).

Chicago   Lazarín argues that our overreliance on testing in K-12 schools "does not put students first."[6]

As an academic writer, you may often use direct quotations to advance an argument of your own:

> Standardized testing makes it easier for administrators to measure student performance, but it may not be the best way to do so. Too much testing wears students out and suggests that recall is the most important skill we want them to develop. Even education policy advisor Melissa Lazarín argues that our overreliance on testing in K-12 schools "does not put students first" (20).

Student writer's idea

Source's idea

SG4   Presenting alternative views

Most debates, whether they are scholarly or popular, are complex—often with more than two sides to an issue. Sometimes you will want to synthesize the views of multiple participants in the debate before you introduce your own ideas.

> While X reports that _____, Y insists that _____.
>
> Even though X endorses the policy, Y refers to it as ". . ."
>
> X, however, isn't convinced and instead argues _____.
>
> X and Y have supported the theory in the past, but new research by Z suggests that _____.

Academic Writers Present Their Own Views

When you write for an academic audience, you will want to demonstrate that you've done your homework and are familiar with the views of others who are thinking and writing about your topic or subject. In addition, you will usually want to put your own argument in the context of what others have said about the topic.

When you write a summary of what someone else has written or when you are reporting information, your own views and arguments are generally not called for. However, much of the writing you will be assigned to do in college asks you to take a persuasive stance and present a reasoned argument—at times in response to a single text, and at other times in response to multiple texts.

SG5 Presenting your own views: agreement and extension

You can signal that you agree with the author of a source:

X's argument is convincing because _____.

Most respected scientists agree with X that _____.

X makes a compelling point when she says _____.

Other times you may find that you agree with the author of a source, but that you want to extend the point or go a bit deeper in your own investigation. So you acknowledge the source for its helpfulness but then go on to build on what the source has said with contributions of your own.

X's proposal for _____ is indeed worth considering. Going one step further, _____.

X makes the claim that _____. By extension, isn't it also true, then, that _____?

_____ has been adequately explained by X. Now, let's move beyond that idea and ask whether _____.

SG6 Presenting your own views: queries and skepticism

While good academic writers pay careful attention to their sources, they also question them, making sure that they are credible and ethical. You can raise such questions or challenge your sources, then, while still being respectful.

Couldn't it also be argued that _____?

But is it reasonable to agree that X is always the case?

While X insists that _____ is so, he is perhaps asking the wrong question to begin with.

The claims that X and Y have made, while intelligent and well-meaning, leave many unconvinced because they have failed to consider _____.

SG7 Presenting your own views: disagreement or correction

You may find that at times the only response you have to a text or to an author is disagreement.

X's claims about _____ are misguided.

The best scientific evidence suggests that X's claims are false.

X presents a long analogy comparing _____ to _____; in the end, the comparison is unconvincing because _____.

It can be tempting to disregard a source completely if you detect a piece of information that strikes you as false or that you know to be untrue.

Although X reports that _____, recent studies indicate that is not the case.

While X and Y insist that _____ is so, an examination of their figures show that they have made an important miscalculation.

A note about using first person "I"

Writers in most disciplines use the first person (I), though they do so differently and some disciplines are more inclined to use "I" than others, preferring to stick to the third person. The huge Corpus of Contemporary American English (COCA), which includes academic writing from 100 peer reviewed sources across all disciplines indicates that writers in the humanities use "I" more than those in other disciplines, while writers in the sciences, technology, and history use "I" least often. If you are unsure about whether or not to use first person, bring the issue up in class: other students probably have the same question!

First person (I, me, my, we, us, our)

I question Heddinger's methods and small sample size.

Harnessing children's technology obsession in the classroom is, I argue, the key to improving learning.

Lanza's interpretation focuses on circle imagery as symbolic of the family; my analysis leads in a different direction entirely.

We would, in fact, benefit from looser laws about farming on our personal property.

Third person (names and other nouns)

Heddinger's methods and small sample size are questionable.

Harnessing children's technology obsession in the classroom is the key to improving learning.

Lanza's interpretation focuses on circle imagery as symbolic of the family; other readers' analyses may point in a different direction entirely.

Many Americans would, in fact, benefit from looser laws about farming on personal property.

Both first and third person can work well in academic writing, as these examples suggest.

SG8 Presenting and countering objections to your argument

Effective college writers know that their arguments are stronger when they anticipate objections that others might make and consider alternative points of view.

> Some will object to this proposal on the grounds that _____.

> Not everyone will embrace _____; they may argue instead that _____.

Countering, or responding to, opposing voices fairly and respectfully strengthens your writing and your ethos, or credibility.

> X and Y might contend that this interpretation is faulty; however, _____.

> Most _____ believe that there is too much risk in this approach. But what they have failed to take into consideration is _____.

Academic Writers Persuade by Putting It All Together

Readers of academic writing often want to know what's at stake in a particular debate or text. They want to know why they should care about the topic at hand, why they should keep reading. In addition to crafting effective individual sentences, then, you must keep the bigger picture in mind as you attempt to inform or persuade your audience.

SG9 Presenting stakeholders

When you write, you may be doing so as a member of a group affected by the research conversation you have entered. For example, you may be among the thousands of students in your state whose level of debt may change as a result of new laws about financing a college education. In this case, you are a *stakeholder* in the matter. In other words, you have an interest in the matter as a person who could be impacted by the outcome of a decision. On the other hand, you may be writing as an investigator of a topic that interests you but that you aren't directly connected with. You may be persuading your audience on behalf of a group of interested stakeholders—a group of which you yourself are not a member.

You can often make your argument more effective if you show clearly who is affected by the discussion of the issue and decisions that will be made about it. Doing so will demonstrate what is at stake in the issue and who will be most affected. The groups of stakeholders are highlighted in the following sentences.

Those whose jobs have been eliminated may not agree with X that _____.

The most recent research will come as a surprise to parents of children with Type 1 diabetes.

X's proposals have the power to raise the tuition of every college student in the state.

Marathoners might want to reconsider their training regimen if stories such as those told by X and Y are validated by the medical community.

SG10   Presenting the "so what"

Getting and keeping the attention of your readers is easier if you can show them that the topic you're addressing is of importance to them. So good academic writing often hooks readers with a sense of urgency—a serious response to a reader's "So what?"

Having a frank discussion about _____ now will put us in a far better position to deal with _____ in the future. If we are unwilling or unable to do so, we risk _____.

Such a breakthrough will affect _____ in three significant ways.

Some argue that the stakes aren't high enough to be alarming; in fact, _____ will be affected by _____.

Widespread disapproval of and censorship of such fiction/films/art will mean _____ for us in the future. Culture should represent _____.

_____ could bring about unprecedented opportunities for _____ to participate in _____, something never seen before.

New experimentation in _____ could allow scientists to investigate _____ in ways they couldn't have imagined _____ years ago.

SG11   Presenting the players and positions in a debate

Some disciplines ask writers to compose a review of the literature as a part of a larger project—or sometimes as a freestanding assignment.

In a review of the literature, the writer sets forth a research question, summarizes the key sources that have addressed the question, puts the current research in the context of other voices in the research conversation, and identifies any gaps in the research.

Writing that presents a debate, its players, and their positions can often be lengthy. What follows, however, can give you the sense of the flow of ideas and turns in such a piece of writing.

_____ affects more than 30% of children in America, and signs point to a worsening situation in years to come because of A, B, and C. Solutions to the problem have eluded even the sharpest policy minds and brightest researchers. In an important 2015 study, W found that _____ _____, which pointed to more problems than solutions. [. . .] Research by X and Y made strides in our understanding of _____ but still didn't offer specific strategies for children and families struggling to _____. [. . .] When Z rejected both the methods and the findings of X and Y, arguing that _____, policymakers and health care experts were optimistic. [. . .] Too much discussion of _____, however, and too little discussion of _____, may lead us to solutions that are ultimately too expensive to sustain.

Student writer states the problem

Student writer summarizes the views of others on the topic

Student writer presents her view in the context of current research

Appendix

Verbs matter   Using a variety of verbs in your sentences can add strength and clarity as you present others' views and your own views.

WHEN YOU WANT TO PRESENT A VIEW FAIRLY NEUTRALLY

acknowledges	observes
adds	points out
comments	reports
contends	suggests
notes	writes

X points out that the plan had unintended outcomes.

WHEN YOU WANT TO PRESENT A STRONGER VIEW

argues	emphasizes
asserts	insists
declares	

Y argues in favor of a ban on _____; but Z insists the plan is misguided.

WHEN YOU WANT TO SHOW AGREEMENT

agrees

confirms

endorses

An endorsement of X's position is smart for a number of reasons.

WHEN YOU WANT TO SHOW CONTRAST OR DISAGREEMENT

compares

denies

disputes

refutes

rejects

The town must come together and reject X's claims that _____ is in the best interest of the citizens.

WHEN YOU WANT TO ANTICIPATE AN OBJECTION

> admits
>
> acknowledges
>
> concedes

Y admits that closer study of _____, with a much larger sample size, is necessary for _____.

Notes

Strengthening Academic Writing Skills (ESL)

Marcy Carbajal Van Horn

Kimberli Huster   *Robert Morris University*

Strengthening your academic writing skills will benefit you both during college and after college. Writing clearly, using appropriate vocabulary, understanding the ideas of others, and seeking feedback about your ideas are all good habits that can be developed over time. This section will help you improve your academic skills whether you're the first in your family to attend college, you speak a language other than English at home or with friends, or you started college a little less prepared than your peers.

AW1 Participate actively in class and in groups.

As odd as it may seem, writing is a social activity. Academic writing requires that you think about and respond to the ideas of others and that you compose your own writing with your audience in mind and with feedback from peers, tutors, and instructors. Participating in class discussions and in group activities will help you to be a better thinker, which will help you to become a better academic writer.

Class participation   To increase your chances of success, take an active part in class discussions. Remember that your instructors will not always expect you to recall or restate an idea from the text or a previous class. More often, they will ask you to show critical thinking. If you do

not participate, your instructor might assume that you don't know the material or that you have come to class unprepared.

If you feel intimidated by class discussions, or by sharing your ideas you can often overcome your fears by preparing well before class. Here are some strategies you can use to get ready for class discussions:

- **Read actively** and annotate the assigned textbook pages or articles before class. Highlight or underline major ideas, and write notes or questions in the margins of the page.
- **Anticipate** some of the questions your instructor might ask in class. Many instructors provide discussion topics or reading questions in the syllabus or in assignments.
- **Record** some thoughts about the text after you read by writing brief notes in your journal or notebook. Using just a few sentences, try to summarize the main points of the passage.
- **Reflect** on the importance of these main ideas. How do they relate to other topics you have discussed in class?
- **Review** you notes just before class so that you can share your ideas when the discussion begins.

Working in groups　　Group work, or collaborative activity, gives students the chance to learn about the assigned course work while building communication, academic writing, and leadership skills.

A group project for an environmental studies course, for example, might require students to learn about and report on the levels of chemicals in the local water supply. To complete the project, the team will need to take several steps:

- Determine what tasks need to be completed to find answers to team members' questions.
- Divide the work among the team members.
- Choose a leader (or leaders) to coordinate the team's actions.
- Work together to write, compile, and edit the final report.

The group's final report on the water supply will include contributions from all group members, much more information than a person working alone could gather.

You might find it difficult to adjust to collaborative work if you come from a culture that emphasizes individual learning or if your high school teachers did not assign group projects. But be prepared to encounter group work in college. Most instructors feel that it creates an atmosphere in which new ideas can emerge. Group work also serves as preparation for the professional world, where many jobs require some form of collaborative activity.

Speaking in English The ability to speak two or more languages is an asset that you should take pride in, but it is also important to be sensitive to your instructor and classmates in a shared learning environment. Whenever possible, use the language that all participants in the class can understand easily. In US academic settings, this language is English. However, occasionally during class you may feel the need to discuss or clarify an idea with a friend in your native language. It is best to discuss this possibility ahead of time with your instructor.

AW2 Visit the writing center often.

Most colleges have writing centers (sometimes called *writing labs*) staffed with instructors or experienced students, often called *writing tutors* or *consultants*. They can assist you at various stages of the writing process. The tutors are typically trained to help in the following areas:

- brainstorming ideas for a writing assignment
- suggesting ways to revise a draft
- identifying areas of a draft that need clarification
- pointing out places in a draft where more development is needed
- diagnosing recurring mistakes in a paper or patterns of error in your writing

It is important to remember that writing center tutors provide guidance, not proofreading services. With their help, you can learn to analyze assignments and evaluate your own writing. They are not

there just to "fix" your mistakes. The more prepared you are for your visit and the more willing you are to discuss your writing problems, the more productive your time with the tutor will be.

Visiting the writing center

Before your visit

- Know the center's location and hours, and make an appointment if one is required.
- Gather the materials needed for the visit:

    the assignment provided by the instructor

    a printout of your essay draft

    copies of any sources you have cited in your paper previous papers with instructor comments and grades
- If you have any questions about the assignment, contact your instructor before your appointment.
- Look at your previous papers for the class and determine whether your instructor's comments can help with your current paper.
- Prepare questions for the tutor about specific parts of your draft.

During your visit

Understand the limitations of the visit. Tutors can make suggestions to improve your paper, but they will not rewrite it. Also be aware that, because of time limitations, your tutor may not have time to review your entire paper.

- Discuss the assignment description and the draft of your paper with your tutor.
- Participate actively by asking specific questions (*Do you understand my main point? Can you help me review my use of verbs? What do you mean by "audience"?*).
- Listen to your tutor's suggestions; take notes.

After your visit

- Go over your notes, clarify anything you don't understand, and write down any notes you didn't have time to make during the visit.

- Use your notes to review your entire paper for problems you discussed with the tutor. As you revise, try not to focus only on the parts of the paper that you specifically looked at in the session.

AW3 Become familiar with academic vocabulary.

Although it is possible—and often preferable—to learn academic vocabulary in the context of your readings and class discussions, you can get a head start by becoming familiar with the words in the Academic Word List. The Academic Word List, compiled by a linguist, contains almost six hundred of the most frequently used academic English words as well as words that are derived from them. The full Academic Word List appears online at this URL: www.victoria.ac.nz/lals/resources/academicwordlist. The following words are just a small fraction of the full list:

analyze	debate	indicate	respond
approach	economy	justify	significant
benefit	evident	method	structure
commit	function	modify	symbol
concept	hypothesis	policy	vary
context			

Because you will encounter these words regularly in textbooks and in class, it's a good idea to familiarize yourself with them early in your college experience.

AW4 Paraphrase sources effectively.

Effective paraphrasing is an important skill for writing in college. You will frequently paraphrase information from your textbooks to answer homework and exam questions, and you will especially need this skill when you are writing essays that incorporate information from other writers. However, learning how to paraphrase can be challenging, especially for multilingual writers.

The purpose of paraphrasing is to restate an author's ideas in your own words. Most writers find the following process for paraphrasing useful:

1. Read and understand the text.
2. Put the text aside.
3. Express the information in your own words.
4. Compare your paraphrase to the original text to check that you have used different words and different sentence structures but have kept the author's meaning.

This is an effective way to paraphrase; it requires that the writer have a large vocabulary and well-developed sentence-writing abilities. Sometimes it's hard to find the right words to paraphrase a sentence or to know whether a paraphrase has the same meaning as the original source.

The following sections provide several rules of thumb that can help you develop skill with paraphrasing.

Avoid replacing a source's words with synonyms. Learning to paraphrase will help you communicate the ideas of authors effectively and avoid plagiarism—using another person's ideas or words without giving credit to that person. However, even if you tell your reader that information comes from another author, you can still commit plagiarism if you change only the words but do not make the presentation of the information your own.

The following examples illustrate some of the problems that can arise with word-by-word paraphrasing.

Here is a short passage from Rebecca Webber's article "Make Your Own Luck."

ORIGINAL SOURCE

> People who spot and seize opportunity are different. They are more open to life's forking paths, so they see possibilities others miss. And if things don't work out the way they'd hoped, they brush off disappointment and launch themselves headlong toward the next fortunate circumstance. As a result, they're happier and more likely to achieve their goals.
>
> —Rebecca Webber, "Make Your Own Luck," p. 64

The following is a word-by-word paraphrase of the sentences highlighted in light grey.

UNACCEPTABLE PARAPHRASE: MEANING CHANGED

Persons who see and grab chances are diverse. They are further exposed to life's dividing trails, and they view prospects others ignore.

The first problem with this paraphrase is that the student who wrote it used the same sentence structure as in the original passage. Because she did not use her own sentence structure, this paraphrase is plagiarized. Second, the words that the student substituted are not exact synonyms, so the paraphrase has lost some of the meaning of the original passage.

- The word *grab* is an informal synonym of the word *seize* and may not be acceptable in a formal paper.

- *Diverse* and *different* have similar, but not identical, meanings. The word *different* in the original passage implies that people who are open to opportunities are different from people who are not open to opportunities. using *diverse* in this context implies that people who welcome opportunity are different from one another. using *diverse* distorts the meaning of the sentence.

- Using *exposed* instead of *open* changes the meaning. *Exposed* implies that something negative has happened to these people, while *open* is a positive character trait.

As you paraphrase, it might help to keep this in mind: simply substituting synonyms into the original passage does not guarantee an accurate paraphrase.

Determine the meaning of the original source. Rather than trying to paraphrase word-for-word within each sentence, a better approach is to look at an entire passage and try to understand the meaning of the passage as well as how the information is organized before you try to present it in your own words.

Here is the original passage as the student writer annotated it. She worked through the original passage, repeatedly asking herself, "What is the author's point here?"

ORIGINAL SOURCE WITH STUDENT ANNOTATIONS

⤶ Lucky people?
People who spot and seize opportunity are different. They are

⤶ More willing to take risks?
more open to life's forking paths, so they see possibilities others

miss. And if things don't work out the way they'd hoped, they

⤶ Don't get discouraged/upset   ⤶ Keep looking?
brush off disappointment and launch themselves headlong toward the

                    More positive personalities overall ⤷
next fortunate circumstance. As a result, they're happier and more

likely to achieve their goals.

Present the author's meaning in your own words. If you analyze a paragraph in its entirety rather than look at each word individually, you should be able to organize your information differently from the way the original author did and write a better paraphrase. Here is one student's paraphrase of Rebecca Webber's work using her annotations of the text.

ACCEPTABLE PARAPHRASE

Individuals notice and respond to life's chances in different ways. Some people notice opportunities that other people might not notice, they are more willing to take risks, and they do not get discouraged if their decisions do not work out. Because they do not get discouraged easily, they are able to stay positive and content and to continue to search enthusiastically for the next opportunity (Webber 64).

This paraphrase presents the student's understanding of the author's meaning—without using words or sentence structure from the original. Notice that the paraphrase includes a citation. The idea is still Webber's idea, so a citation is needed, but the student uses her own words to communicate the information.

Writing a summary:
Excerpt from a student paper

Writing a summary gives you an opportunity to capture a writer's main ideas but offer a shorter version of the original text for your reader. Succesful summary writers break a text down into sections and zero in on understanding the main idea for each section.

Student writer HwaSoo Ryoo was assigned to summarize an article. Included here is HwaSoo's first paragraph. A draft with instructor comments appears first, and then HwaSoo's revision follows.

ROUGH DRAFT (EXCERPT), WITH INSTRUCTOR'S COMMENTS

RYOO 1

HwaSoo Ryoo

Dr. Kim Huster

ENG 101 College Writing

27 February 2013

Summary of "You, the Language Learner"

According to linguists Joan Rubin and Irene Thompson, language learner's success or failure is not from outside but mostly from learner's own. People have a different characteristic and different ways to acquire a language. Rubin and Thompson identify individual characteristic and ways for language learners to analyze their own predispositions. They report the factors as age, aptitude, psychological predispositions, and past experience.

Instructor's comments:

What do you mean by "learner's own"?

Pay attention to singular and plural of count nouns.

This language comes from the chapter. What do you think it means?

Use quotation marks around words from the source.

FINAL DRAFT (EXCERPT)

RYOO 1

HwaSoo Ryoo

Dr. Kim Huster

ENG 101 College Writing

10 March 2013

Summary of "You, the Language Learner"

According to linguists Joan Rubin and Irene
Thompson, a language learner's success or failure comes
not from the outside but mostly from within the learner.

Ryoo borrows language from the article, but she uses quotation marks and an in-text citation.

People have different characteristics and different ways to
acquire a language. Rubin and Thompson identify individual
characteristics and ways for language learners to examine
their own strengths and weaknesses. The authors report that
the factors affecting success are age, aptitude, "psychological
predispositions," and past experience (Rubin and Thompson
3-8).

AW6 In persuasive writing, assert your claim before providing the evidence.

Readers in most academic situations will expect to see your claim—your thesis or main idea—before seeing your evidence or support for the claim. This is quite different from academic styles in some other languages, which leave the main point open to readers' interpretations or which conclude rather than begin the essay with the main idea.

If you're not accustomed to stating a thesis before providing support, you might find it useful to outline your essays carefully before beginning to write.

1. Outline your ideas in the method with which you are familiar (for example, with the main idea or claim at the end).
2. Read your outline and highlight the main idea and the supporting points in your outline.
3. Rearrange your outline so that the main idea is at the beginning.
4. Use your rearranged outline as a guide when you draft your essay.

Don't be concerned if this planning stage takes time. Remember that the planning stage of writing often takes longer than the writing stage does.

ORIGINAL OUTLINE: MAIN IDEA LAST

1. In the United States, teenagers often move out of their parents' homes when they turn eighteen.
2. The parents' money is considered only the parents' money—not the money of their adult children.
3. Without their parents' financial help, young adults in the United States often struggle to find affordable housing, transportation, and jobs to pay for all their needs.
4. The fast pace of their daily activities and their lack of job security can be very stressful.
5. Even after they finish school, young adults in the United States may need their parents' support to achieve lasting independence.

REVISED OUTLINE: MAIN IDEA FIRST

1. Even after they finish school, young adults in the United States may need their parents' support to achieve lasting independence.
2. In the United States, teenagers often move out of their parents' homes when they turn eighteen.
3. The parents' money is considered only the parents' money — not the money of their adult children.
4. Without their parents' financial help, young adults in the United States often struggle to find affordable housing, transportation, and jobs to pay for all their needs.
5. The fast pace of their daily activities and their lack of job security can be very stressful.

AW7   Take a stand on an issue.

As an academic writer, you often need to take a stand to convince readers of your position in a debate. Although you must present opposing views fairly, you should clearly state your own position (claim) and the evidence to support that position. Your readers will expect you to take one side and to argue reasonably that your position is better or stronger than other positions. Here is an example of a paragraph that was revised to stay focused on one side of an issue.

ORIGINAL: DOES NOT TAKE A STAND

Most experts in the United States agree that spanking is not an appropriate form of discipline for children. Some people, however, feel that spanking is acceptable because it can correct rude behavior. Spanking may lead to larger problems of fear and anxiety. Many children experience no lasting emotional problems from it. Opinions differ on this controversial topic.

REVISED: TAKES A STAND

Most experts in the United States agree that spanking is not an appropriate form of discipline for children. Spanking may temporarily correct rude behavior, but it may lead to larger problems such as increased aggression, and it may teach children that violence is an acceptable means of getting what they want ("Guidance" 726). Spanking should be used sparingly as a discipline option.

The original version does not take a stand on the issue of spanking. It only points out that there are differing views on the subject. In the revision, the writer takes a position and uses expert opinion (an article from the Journal of the American Academy of Pediatrics) for support.

EasyWriter

The Top Twenty

Surface errors—grammar, punctuation, word choice, and other small-scale matters—don't always disturb readers. Whether your instructor marks an error in any particular assignment will depend on personal judgments about how serious and distracting it is and about what you should be focusing on in the draft. In addition, not all surface errors are consistently viewed as errors: some of the patterns identified in research for this book are considered errors by some instructors but stylistic options by others. Such differing opinions don't mean that there is no such thing as correctness in writing—only that *correctness always depends on some context*, on whether the choices a writer makes seem appropriate to readers.

Research reveals a number of changes that have occurred in student writing over the past thirty years. First, writing assignments in first-year composition classes now focus less on personal narrative and much more on research essays and argument. As a result, students are now writing longer essays than they did in the 1980s and working much more often with sources, both print and nonprint. Thus it's no surprise that students today are struggling with the conventions for using and citing sources.

What else has changed? For starters, wrong-word errors are *by far the most common* errors among first-year student writers today. Thirty years ago, spelling errors were most common by a factor of more than three to one. The use of spell checkers has reduced the number of spelling errors in student writing—but spell checkers' suggestions may also be responsible for some (or many) of the wrong words students are using.

All writers want to be considered competent and careful. You know that your instructors usually judge you by your control of the conventions you have agreed to use, although the conventions change from time to time. To help you in producing academic writing that is conventionally correct, you should become familiar with the twenty most common error patterns among U.S. college students today, listed here in order of frequency. A brief explanation and examples of each error are provided in the following sections, and each error pattern is cross-referenced to other places in this book where you can find more detailed information and examples.

> ▶ *Checklist*

The Top Twenty

1. Wrong word
2. Missing comma after an introductory element
3. Incomplete or missing documentation
4. Vague pronoun reference
5. Spelling (including homonyms)
6. Mechanical error with a quotation
7. Unnecessary comma
8. Unnecessary or missing capitalization
9. Missing word
10. Faulty sentence structure
11. Missing comma with a nonrestrictive element
12. Unnecessary shift in verb tense
13. Missing comma in a compound sentence
14. Unnecessary or missing apostrophe (including *its/it's*)
15. Fused (run-on) sentence
16. Comma splice
17. Lack of pronoun-antecedent agreement
18. Poorly integrated quotation
19. Unnecessary or missing hyphen
20. Sentence fragment

1   Wrong word

> ▶ Religious texts, for them, take ~~prescience~~ *precedence* over other kinds of
>
> sources.

Prescience means "foresight," and *precedence* means "priority."

▶ The child suffered from a severe ~~allegory~~ *allergy* to peanuts.

Allegory is a spell checker's replacement for a misspelling of *allergy*.

▶ The panel discussed the ethical implications ~~on~~ *of* the situation.

Wrong-word errors can involve using a word with the wrong shade of meaning, using a word with a completely wrong meaning, or using a wrong **preposition** or another wrong word in an idiom. Selecting a word from a thesaurus without knowing its meaning or allowing a spell checker to correct spelling automatically can lead to wrong-word errors, so use these tools with care. If you have trouble with prepositions and idioms, memorize the standard usage. (See Chapter 20 on word choice and Chapter 27 on prepositions and idioms.)

2 Missing comma after an introductory element

▶ Determined to get the job done, we worked all weekend.

▶ Although the research study was flawed, the results may still be useful.

Readers usually need a small pause—signaled by a comma—between an introductory word, **phrase**, or **clause** and the main part of the **sentence**. Use a comma after every introductory element. When the introductory element is very short, you don't always need a comma, but including it is never wrong. (See 35a.)

3 Incomplete or missing documentation

▶ Satrapi says, "When we're afraid, we lose all sense of analysis and reflection" (263).

The page number of the print source for this quotation must be included.

> According to one source, James Joyce wrote two of the five best
>
> ("100 Best").
>
> novels of all time./
>
> The source mentioned should be identified (this online source has no
> author or page numbers).

Cite each source you refer to in the text, following the guidelines of the documentation style you are using. (The preceding examples follow MLA style—see Chapter 45; for other styles, see Chapters 46–48.) Omitting documentation can result in charges of plagiarism. (See Chapter 15.)

4 Vague pronoun reference

POSSIBLE REFERENCE TO MORE THAN ONE WORD

> Transmitting radio signals by satellite is a way of overcoming the
>
> the airwaves
>
> problem of scarce airwaves and limiting how ~~they~~ are used.
>
> In the original sentence, *they* could refer to the signals or to the
> airwaves.

REFERENCE IMPLIED BUT NOT STATED

> a policy
>
> The company prohibited smoking, ~~which~~ many employees
>
> appreciated.
>
> What does *which* refer to? The editing clarifies what employees
> appreciated.

A **pronoun** should refer clearly to the word or words it replaces (called the *antecedent*) elsewhere in the sentence or in a previous sentence. If more than one word could be the antecedent, or if no specific antecedent is present, edit to make the meaning clear. (See Chapter 26.)

5 Spelling (including homonyms)

> Reagan
>
> Ronald ~~Regan~~ won the election in a landslide.
>
> Everywhere
>
> ~~Every where~~ we went, we saw crowds of tourists.

The most common misspellings today are those that spell checkers cannot identify. The categories that spell checkers are most likely to miss include homonyms, compound words incorrectly spelled as separate words, and proper **nouns**, particularly names. After you run the spell checker, proofread carefully for errors such as these—and be sure to run the spell checker to catch other kinds of spelling mistakes.

6 Mechanical error with a quotation

▶ "I grew up the victim of a disconcerting confusion,"/

Rodriguez says (249).

The comma should be placed *inside* the quotation marks.

Follow conventions when using quotation marks with commas (35h), colons, and other punctuation. Always use quotation marks in pairs, and follow the guidelines of your documentation style for block quotations. Use quotation marks for titles of short works (39b), but use italics for titles of long works (43a).

7 Unnecessary comma

BEFORE CONJUNCTIONS IN COMPOUND CONSTRUCTIONS THAT ARE NOT COMPOUND SENTENCES

▶ This conclusion applies to the United States/ and to the rest of

the world.

No comma is needed before *and* because it is joining two phrases that modify the same verb, *applies*.

WITH RESTRICTIVE ELEMENTS

▶ Many parents/ of gifted children/ do not want them to skip

a grade.

No comma is needed to set off the restrictive phrase *of gifted children*, which is necessary to indicate which parents the sentence is talking about.

Do not use commas to set off **restrictive elements** that are necessary to the meaning of the words they modify. Do not use a comma before a **coordinating conjunction** (*and, but, for, nor, or, so, yet*) when the conjunction does not join parts of a compound sentence (error 13). Do not use a comma before the first or after the last item in a series, between a **subject** and **verb**, between a verb and its **object** or object/complement, or between a **preposition** and its object. (See 35i.)

8 Unnecessary or missing capitalization

▶ Some ~~Traditional~~ Chinese ~~Medicines~~ containing ~~Ephedra~~ traditional medicines ephedra

remain legal.

Capitalize proper nouns and proper adjectives, the first words of sentences, and important words in titles, along with certain words indicating directions and family relationships. Do not capitalize most other words. When in doubt, check a dictionary. (See Chapter 41.)

9 Missing word

▶ The site foreman discriminated women and promoted men with against

less experience.

Proofread carefully for omitted words, including prepositions (27a), parts of two-part verbs (27b), and correlative **conjunctions**. Be particularly careful not to omit words from quotations.

10 Faulty sentence structure

▶ ~~The information which high~~ school athletes are presented with High

~~mainly includes~~ information on what credits ~~needed~~ to graduate, they need

~~and thinking about the college~~ which ~~athletes are trying~~ to play *colleges to try* *how to* for, and apply. ^

A sentence that starts with one kind of structure and then changes to another kind can confuse readers. Make sure that each sentence contains a subject and a verb, that subjects and **predicates** make sense together (30b), and that comparisons have clear meanings (30d). When you join elements (such as subjects or verb phrases) with a coordinating conjunction, make sure that the elements have parallel structures (see Chapter 33).

11 Missing comma with a nonrestrictive element

▸ Marina, who was the president of the club, was first to speak.

The clause *who was the president of the club* does not affect the basic meaning of the sentence: Marina was first to speak.

A **nonrestrictive element** gives information not essential to the basic meaning of the sentence. Use commas to set off a nonrestrictive element (35c).

12 Unnecessary shift in verb tense

▸ Priya was watching the great blue heron. Then she ~~slips~~ and ~~falls~~ *slipped* *fell* into the swamp.

Verbs that shift from one **tense** to another with no clear reason can confuse readers (34a).

13 Missing comma in a compound sentence

▸ Meredith waited for Samir, and her sister grew impatient.

Without the comma, a reader may think at first that Meredith waited for both Samir and her sister.

A compound sentence consists of two or more parts that could each stand alone as a sentence. When the parts are joined by a coordinating conjunction, use a comma before the conjunction to indicate a pause between the two thoughts (35b).

14   Unnecessary or missing apostrophe (including *its/it's*)

▶ Overambitious parents can be very harmful to a ~~childs~~ *child's* well-being.

▶ The library is having ~~it's~~ *its* annual fund-raiser. ~~Its~~ *It's* for a good cause.

To make a noun **possessive**, add an apostrophe and an *-s* (*Ed's book*) or an apostrophe alone (*the boys' gym*). Do *not* use an apostrophe in the possessive **pronouns** *ours*, *yours*, and *hers*. Use *its* to mean *belonging to it*; use *it's* to mean *it is* or *it has*. (See Chapter 38.)

15   Fused (run-on) sentence

▶ Klee's paintings seem simple, *but* they are very sophisticated.

▶ *Although she* ~~She~~ doubted the value of meditation, she decided to try it once.

A **fused sentence** (also called a *run-on*) joins clauses that could each stand alone as a sentence with no punctuation or words to link them. Fused sentences must either be divided into separate sentences or joined by adding words or punctuation. (See Chapter 28.)

16   Comma splice

▶ I was strongly attracted to her, *for* she was beautiful and funny.

▶ We hated the meat loaf, *that* the cafeteria served ~~it~~ every Friday.

A **comma splice** occurs when only a comma separates clauses that could each stand alone as a sentence. To correct a comma splice,

you can insert a semicolon or period, connect the clauses with a word such as *and* or *because*, or restructure the sentence. (See Chapter 28.)

17 Lack of pronoun-antecedent agreement

> ~~Every student~~ All students must provide their own ~~uniform.~~ uniforms.

> Each of the puppies thrived in ~~their~~ its new home.

Pronouns must agree with their antecedents in gender (male or female) and in number (singular or plural). Many **indefinite pronouns,** such as *everyone* and *each*, are always singular. When a singular antecedent can refer to a man or a woman, either rewrite the sentence to make the antecedent plural or to eliminate the pronoun, or use *his or her, he or she*, and so on. When antecedents are joined by *or* or *nor*, the pronoun must agree with the closer antecedent. A collective **noun** such as *team* can be either singular or plural, depending on whether the members are seen as a group or as individuals. (See 26b.)

18 Poorly integrated quotation

> A 1970s study of what makes food appetizing showed how color affects taste: "Once it became apparent that the steak was actually blue and the fries were green, some people became ill" (Schlosser 565).

> According to Lars Eighner, "Dumpster diving has serious drawbacks as a way of life" (~~Eighner~~ 383). Finding edible food is especially tricky.

Quotations should all fit smoothly into the surrounding sentence structure. They should be linked clearly to the writing around them

(usually with a signal phrase) rather than dropped abruptly into the writing. (See 15a.)

19 Unnecessary or missing hyphen

▶ This paper looks at fictional and real-life examples.

A compound adjective modifying a noun that follows it requires a hyphen.

▶ The buyers want to fix-up the house and resell it.

A two-word verb should not be hyphenated.

A compound **adjective** that appears before a noun needs a hyphen. However, be careful not to hyphenate two-word verbs or word groups that serve as subject complements. (See Chapter 44.)

20 Sentence fragment

NO SUBJECT

▶ Marie Antoinette spent huge sums of money on herself and her favorites. And helped bring on the French Revolution.

Her extravagance

NO COMPLETE VERB

▶ The old aluminum boat sitting on its trailer.

was

BEGINNING WITH A SUBORDINATING WORD

▶ We returned to the drugstore, Where we waited for our buddies.

where

A **sentence fragment** is part of a sentence that is written as if it were a complete sentence. Reading your draft out loud, backwards, sentence by sentence, will help you spot sentence fragments. (See Chapter 29.)

▶ Checklist

Taking a Writing Inventory

One way to learn from your mistakes is to take a writing inventory. It can help you think critically and analytically about how to improve your writing skills.

1. Collect two or three pieces of your writing to which either your instructor or other students have responded.

2. Read through these writings, adding your own comments about their strengths and weaknesses. How do your comments compare with those of others?

3. Group all the comments into three categories—*broad content issues* (use of evidence and sources, attention to purpose and audience, and overall impression), *organization and presentation* (overall and paragraph-level organization, sentence structure and style, and design and formatting), and *surface errors* (problems with spelling, grammar, punctuation, and mechanics).

4. Make an inventory of your own strengths in each category.

5. Study your errors. Mark every instructor and peer comment that suggests or calls for an improvement, and put all these comments in a list. Consult the relevant part of this book or speak with your instructor if you don't understand a comment.

6. Make a list of the top problem areas you need to work on. How can you make improvements? Then note at least two strengths that you can build on in your writing. Record your findings in a writing log that you can add to as the class proceeds.

Writing
Processes

**Writing
Processes**

Writing That
Works

Research

Language

Grammar

Style

Punctuation/
Mechanics

Documentation

1 A Writer's Choices

You send a text message to your best friend confirming weekend plans. Later on, you put together an analysis of cost-cutting possibilities for the manager of the company you're interning for. And later still, just before calling it a day, you pull out the notes you took on your biology experiment and write up the lab report that is due tomorrow. In between, you do a lot of other writing as well—notes, lists, blog entries, Facebook status updates, tweets, and so on.

These are the kinds of writing most of us do every day, more or less easily, yet each demands that we make various important choices. In your text message, you probably use a kind of shorthand, not bothering to write complete sentences or even entire words. For your boss, however, you probably choose to be more formal, writing complete sentences and appropriate punctuation. And for your lab report, you probably choose to follow the format your instructor has demonstrated. In each case, the choices you make are based on your **rhetorical situation**—the entire context in which your writing takes place.

1a Moving between informal and formal writing

Students are doing more writing and reading today than ever before, and much of it is online—on Facebook, Twitter, Tumblr, Snapchat, and other social media sites. Writing on social networking sites is generally informal and allows almost instant feedback; anticipating audience responses can make online writers very savvy about analyzing audiences and about using an appropriate style and tone for the occasion.

Student Stephanie Parker tweeted:

Rain's over, going to Trader Joe's for some healthy stuff to fight this cold . . . suggestions?

Student Erin McLaughlin posted on Facebook:

Help send one of my Ghanian friends to college. The smallest contribution helps! http://www.indiegogo.com/teachaman

In these two short messages, Stephanie and Erin show a keen aware-ness of audience and two common purposes for social writing—to ask for information (healthy food suggestions for Stephanie) and to give information (about a cause Erin supports). Erin is asking her audience to help a friend from Ghana go to college, and since most of her friends are also college students, she assures them that they don't need to have a lot of money to make a difference. The link goes to a site about a group effort to raise enough funds to send a young man, Jey, to the University of Ghana.

Like Stephanie and Erin, you are probably adept at informal social writing across a range of genres and media. You may not think very hard about your audience for a tweet or Facebook post, or about your purpose for writing in such spaces, but you are probably more skilled than you give yourself credit for when it comes to making appropriate choices for varying kinds of infor-mal writing.

Because social media writing is so common, it's easy to fall into the habit of writing very informally. But remember the importance of a writer's choices: don't forget to adjust style and voice for differ-ent occasions and readers.

In the writing you do from now on, you'll need to be able to move easily back and forth between informal and formal situations. So take time to look closely at some of your informal social media writing: What do you assume about your audience? What is your purpose? How do you represent yourself online? What do the pho-tos you post and your likes and dislikes say about you? Do you come across as the person you want others to see you as? How do you establish your credibility? Why do you write the way you do in these situations? Analyzing the choices you make in an informal writing context will help you develop the ability to make good choices in other contexts as well.

1b   Email and other "in-between" writing

When writing some academic and professional messages, includ-ing emails to instructors, you may find yourself somewhere in the middle of the spectrum between "informal" and "formal" writ-ing. On these occasions, lean toward following the conventions

of academic English, and be careful not to offend or irritate your audience. For email especially, this will mean stating your purpose clearly and succinctly in the subject line and using a formal greeting (*Dear Professor Banks* rather than *Hey!*).

In addition, you will want to keep your messages as clear and concise as possible and sign off with your name. Make sure you have proofread the message and that you've addressed your intended audience. Finally, make sure that the username on the account you use for formal messages does not present a poor impression. If your username is Party2Nite, consider changing it, or use your school account for academic and professional communication. And remember: such messages are permanent and always findable.

1c Meeting expectations for academic writing

Expectations about academic writing vary considerably from field to field (see Chapter 10), but becoming familiar with widespread conventions will prepare you well for writing in most academic contexts.

Authority.   Most instructors expect you to begin to establish your own authority—to become a constructive critic who can analyze and interpret the works of others.

To establish authority, assume that your opinions count (as long as they are informed rather than tossed out with little thought) and that your audience expects you to present them in a fair, well-reasoned manner. Show your familiarity with the ideas and works of others, both from the assigned course reading and from good points your instructor and classmates have made.

Directness and clarity.   Research for this book confirms that readers depend on writers to organize and present their material—using sections, paragraphs, sentences, arguments, details, and source citations—to aid understanding. Good academic writing offers a clear **thesis**, prepares readers for what is coming next, provides definitions, and includes topic sentences.

To achieve directness in your writing, try the following strategies:

- State your main point early and clearly. Academic writing may call for an explicit **claim** or thesis (2b and 8d).

- Avoid overqualifying your statements. Instead of writing *I think the facts reveal*, come right out and say *The facts reveal*.

- Avoid unnecessary digressions. If you use an anecdote or example from personal experience, be sure it relates directly to the point you are making.

- Use appropriate evidence and authorities of various kinds to support each point you make (2c). Carefully document all of your sources, including visuals and media.

- Make explicit links between ideas (2e). The first sentence of a new paragraph should reach back to the paragraph before and then look forward to what comes next.

- Follow clear, easy-to-follow organizational patterns.

▶ Checklist

U.S. Academic Style

▶ Consider your purpose and audience carefully, making sure that your topic is appropriate to both. (1d–f)

▶ State your **claim** or **thesis** explicitly, and support it with evidence and authorities of various kinds. (2b)

▶ Carefully document all of your sources, including visual ones. (Chapters 45–48)

▶ Make explicit links between ideas. (2e)

▶ Use the appropriate level of formality. (20a)

▶ Use conventional formats for academic genres. (Chapter 10)

▶ Use conventional grammar, spelling, punctuation, and mechanics. (Chapters 21–44)

▶ Use an easy-to-read type size and typeface and conventional margins. For print projects, double-space text. (3a)

1d   Considering the assignment and purpose

For the writing you do that isn't connected to a class or work assignment, you may have a clear purpose in mind. Even so, analyzing exactly what you want to accomplish and why can help you communicate more effectively.

An academic assignment may explain why, for whom, and about what you are supposed to write, or it may seem to come out of the blue. Comprehending the assignment is crucial to your success, so make every effort to understand what your instructor expects.

- What is the primary purpose of your writing—to persuade? to explain? to entertain? something else?
- What purpose did the person who gave you the assignment want to achieve—to test your understanding? to evaluate your thinking and writing abilities? to encourage you to think outside the box?
- What, exactly, does the assignment ask you to do? Look for words such as *analyze*, *explain*, *prove*, and *survey*. Remember that these words may differ in meaning from discipline to discipline and from job to job.

1e   Choosing a topic

Experienced writers say that the best way to choose a topic is to let it choose you. Look to topics that compel, puzzle, or pose a problem for you: these are likely to engage your interests and hence produce your best writing.

- Can you focus the topic enough to write about it effectively in the time and space available?
- What do you know about the topic? What else do you need to learn?
- What seems most important about it?
- What do you expect to conclude about the topic? (Remember, you may change your mind.)

For information on exploring a topic, see 2a.

Writing Processes: Rhetorical Situations > Storyboards

1f Reaching appropriate audiences

Every communicator can benefit from thinking carefully about who the audience is, what the audience already knows or thinks, and what the audience needs and expects to find out. One of the characteristics of an effective communicator is the ability to write for a variety of audiences, using language, style, and evidence appropriate to particular readers, listeners, or viewers. Even if your text can theoretically reach people all over the world, focus your analysis on those you most want or need to reach and those who are likely to take an interest.

- What audience do you most want to reach—people who are already sympathetic to your views? people who disagree with you? members of a group you belong to? members of a group you don't belong to?

- In what ways are the members of your audience different from you? from one another?

- What assumptions can you legitimately make about your audience? What might they value—brevity, originality, deference, honesty, wit? How can you appeal to their values?

- What sorts of information and evidence will your audience find most compelling—quotations from experts? personal experiences? statistics? images?

- What responses do you want as a result of what you write? How can you make clear what you want to happen? (For more on audience, see 17c.)

1g Considering stance and tone

Knowing your own stance—where you are coming from—can help you think about ways to get your readers to understand and perhaps share your views. What is your overall attitude toward the topic—approval? disapproval? curiosity? What social, political, religious, or other factors account for your attitude? You should also be aware of any preconceptions about your topic that may affect your stance.

Your purpose, audience, and stance will help to determine the tone your writing should take. Should it be humorous? serious?

impassioned? Think about ways to show that you are knowledgeable and trustworthy. Remember, too, that visual and audio elements can influence the tone of your writing as much as the words you choose.

1h   Considering time, genre, medium, and format

Many other elements of your context for a particular writing project will shape the final outcome.

- How much time will you have for the project? Do you need to do research or learn unfamiliar technology? Allow time for revision and editing.
- What genre does your text call for—a report? a review? an argument essay? a lab report? a blog post? Study examples if you are unfamiliar with the conventions of the genre.
- In what medium will the text appear—on the open Internet? on a password-protected website? in a print essay? in a presentation? Will you use images, video, or audio?
- What kind of organization should you use?
- How will you document your sources? Will your audience expect a particular documentation style (see Chapters 45–48)? Should you embed links?

1i   Collaborating

Writers often work together to come up with ideas, to respond to one another's drafts, or to coauthor texts. Here are some strategies for working with others:

- Establish ground rules for the collaboration. Be sure every writer has an equal opportunity—and responsibility—to contribute.
- Exchange contact information, and plan face-to-face meetings (if any).
- Pay close attention to each writer's views. Expect disagreement, and remember that the goal is to argue through all possibilities.
- If you are preparing a document collaboratively, divide up the drafting duties and set reasonable deadlines. Work together to iron out

Writing Processes: Working with Others > Tutorial
Writing Processes: Working with Others > Video Prompt

the final draft, aiming for consistency of tone. Proofread together, and have one person make corrections.

- Give credit where credit is due. In team projects, acknowledge all members' contributions as well as any help you receive from outsiders.

2 Exploring, Planning, and Drafting

One student defines drafting as the time in a writing project "when the rubber meets the road." As you explore your topic, decide on a thesis, organize materials to support that central idea, and sketch out a plan, you have already begun the drafting process.

2a Exploring a topic

Among the most important parts of the writing process are choosing a topic (1e), exploring what you know about it, and determining what you need to find out. The following strategies can help you explore your topic:

- Brainstorm. Try out ideas, alone or with another person. Jot down key words and phrases about the topic, and see what they prompt you to think about next.
- Freewrite without stopping for ten minutes or so to see what insights or ideas you come up with. You can also "freespeak" by recording your thoughts on your phone or other device.
- Draw or make word pictures about your topic.
- Try clustering—writing your topic on a sheet of paper, then writing related thoughts near the topic idea. Circle each idea or phrase, and draw lines to show how ideas are connected.
- Ask questions about the topic: *What is it? What caused it? What is it like or unlike? What larger system is the topic a part of? What do people say about it?* Or choose the journalist's questions: *Who? What? When? Where? Why? How?*
- Browse sources to find out what others say about the topic.

Writing Processes: Prewriting > Video Prompts (3)

2b Developing a working thesis

Academic and professional writing in the United States often contains an explicit **thesis statement**. You should establish a working thesis early in your writing process. Your final thesis may be very different from the working thesis you begin with. Even so, a working thesis focuses your thinking and research, and helps keep you on track.

A working thesis should have two parts: a topic, which indicates the subject matter the writing is about, and a comment, which makes an important point about the topic.

▶ In the graphic novel *Fun Home*, images and words combine to make meanings that are more subtle than either words alone or images alone could convey.

A successful working thesis has three characteristics:

1. It is potentially *interesting* to the intended audience.
2. It is as *specific* as possible.
3. It limits the topic enough to make it *manageable*.

You can evaluate a working thesis by checking it against each of these characteristics, as in the following examples:

▶ Graphic novels combine words and images.

INTERESTING?   The topic of graphic novels could be interesting, but this draft of a working thesis has no real comment attached to it—instead, it states a bare fact, and the only place to go from here is to more bare facts.

▶ In graphic novels, words and images convey interesting meanings.

SPECIFIC?   This thesis is not specific. What are "interesting meanings," exactly? How are they conveyed?

For Multilingual Writers

Stating a Thesis

In some cultures, it is considered rude to state an opinion outright. In the United States, however, academic and business practices require writers to make key positions explicitly clear.

▶ Graphic novels have evolved in recent decades to become an important literary genre.

MANAGEABLE? This thesis would not be manageable for a short-term project because it would require research on several decades of history and on hundreds of texts from all over the world.

2c Gathering evidence and doing research

What kinds of evidence will be most persuasive to your audience and most effective in the field you are working in—historical precedents? expert testimony? statistical data? experimental results? personal anecdotes? Knowing what kinds of evidence count most in a particular field or with particular audiences will help you make appropriate choices.

If the evidence you need calls for research, determine what research you need to do:

- Make a list of what you already know about your topic.
- Keep track of where information comes from so you can return to your sources later.
- What else do you need to know, and where are you likely to find good sources of information? Consider library resources, authoritative online sources, field research, and so on.

(For more on research, see Chapters 13–16.)

2d   Planning and drafting

Sketch out a rough plan for organizing your writing. You can simply begin with your thesis; review your notes, research materials, and media; and list all the evidence you have to support the thesis. An informal way to organize your ideas is to figure out what belongs in your introduction, body paragraphs, and conclusion. You may also want—or be required—to make a formal outline, which can help you see exactly how the parts of your writing fit together.

Thesis statement

I.   First main idea
   A.   First subordinate idea
      1.   First supporting detail or point
      2.   Second supporting detail
      3.   Third supporting detail
   B.   Second subordinate idea
      1.   First supporting detail
      2.   Second supporting detail

II.   Second main idea
   A.   First subordinate idea
      1.   First supporting detail
      2.   Second supporting detail
   B.   Second subordinate idea
      1.   First supporting detail
      2.   Second supporting detail
         a.   First supporting detail
         b.   Second supporting detail

The technique of storyboarding—working out a narrative or argument in visual form—can also be a good way to come up with an organizational plan. You can create your own storyboard by using note cards or sticky notes, taking advantage of different colors to keep track of threads of argument, subtopics, and so on. Move the cards and notes around, trying out different arrangements, until you find an organization that works well for your writing situation.

No matter how good your planning, investigating, and organizing have been, chances are you will need to do more work as you draft. The first principle of successful drafting is to be flexible. If

 Checklist

Drafting

▶ **Set up a computer folder or file for your essay.** Give the file a clear and relevant name, and save to it often. Number your drafts. If you decide to try a new direction, save the file as a new draft—you can always pick up with a previous one if the new version doesn't work out.

▶ **Have all your information close at hand and arranged according to your organizational plan.** Stopping to search for a piece of information can break your concentration or distract you.

▶ **Try to write in stretches of at least thirty minutes.** Writing can provide momentum, and once you get going, the task becomes easier.

▶ **Don't let small questions bog you down.** Just make a note of them in brackets—or in all caps—or make a tentative decision and move on.

▶ **Remember that first drafts aren't perfect.** Concentrate on getting your ideas down, and don't worry about anything else.

▶ **Stop writing at a place where you know exactly what will come next.** Doing so will help you start easily when you return to the draft.

you see that your plan is not working, don't hesitate to alter it. If some information now seems irrelevant, leave it out. You may learn that you need to do more research, that your whole thesis must be reshaped, or that your topic is still too broad and should be narrowed further. Very often you will continue planning, investigating, and organizing throughout the writing process.

2e Developing paragraphs

Three qualities essential to most academic paragraphs are unity, development, and coherence.

Unity. An effective paragraph focuses on one main idea. You can achieve unity by stating the main idea clearly in one sentence—the **topic sentence**—and relating all other sentences in the paragraph to that idea. Like a thesis (see 2b), the topic sentence includes a topic and a comment on that topic. A topic sentence often begins a paragraph, but it may come at the end—or be implied rather than stated directly.

Development. In addition to being unified, a good paragraph holds readers' interest and explores its topic fully, using whatever details, evidence, and examples are necessary. Without such development, a paragraph may seem lifeless and abstract.

Most good academic writing backs up general ideas with specifics. Shifting between the general and the specific is especially important at the paragraph level. If a paragraph contains nothing but specific details, its meaning may not be clear to readers—but if a paragraph makes only general statements, it may seem boring or unconvincing.

Coherence. A paragraph has coherence—or flows—if its details fit together in a way that readers can easily follow. The following methods can help you achieve paragraph coherence:

- A general-to-specific or specific-to-general *organization* helps readers move from one point to another.
- Repetition of key words or phrases links sentences and suggests that the words or phrases are important.
- Parallel structures help make writing more coherent (see Chapter 33).
- **Transitions** such as *for example* and *however* help readers follow the progression of one idea to the next.

The same methods that you use to create coherent paragraphs can be used to link paragraphs so that a whole piece of writing flows smoothly. You can create links to previous paragraphs by repeating or paraphrasing key words and phrases and by using parallelism and transitions.

The following sample paragraph from David Craig's research project (45e), which identifies a topic and a comment on the topic and then offers detailed evidence in support of the point, achieves

 Checklist

Strong Paragraphs

Most readers of English have certain expectations about how paragraphs work:

▶ Paragraphs begin and end with information that is important for the reader.

▶ The opening sentence is often the topic sentence that tells what the paragraph is about.

▶ The middle of the paragraph develops the idea.

▶ The end may sum up the paragraph's contents, closing the discussion of an idea and anticipating the paragraph that follows.

▶ A paragraph makes sense as a whole; the words and sentences are clearly related.

▶ A paragraph relates to other paragraphs around it.

coherence with a general-to-specific organization, repetition of key content related to digital communication and teenagers, and transitions that relate this paragraph to the preceding one and relate sentences to one another.

Based on the preceding statistics, parents and educators appear to be right about the decline in youth literacy. And this trend coincides with another phenomenon: digital communication is rising among the young. According to the Pew Internet & American Life Project, 85 percent of those aged twelve to seventeen at least occasionally write text messages, instant messages, or comments on social networking sites (Lenhart et al.). In 2001, the most conservative estimate based on Pew numbers showed that American youths spent, at a minimum, nearly three million hours per day on messaging services (Lenhart and Lewis 20). These numbers are now exploding thanks to texting, which was "the dominant daily mode of

Transition from preceding paragraph

Topic sentence

Supporting evidence

Sentence-to-sentence transition

communication" for teens in 2012 (Lenhart), and messaging on popular social networking sites such as Facebook and Tumblr.

3 Making Design Decisions

In a time when millions of messages are vying for attention, effective design is especially important: the strongest message may not get through to its audience if it is presented and designed in an ineffective, bland way. You will want to understand and use effective design to make sure you get—and keep—your audience's attention.

3a Design principles

In designer Robin Williams's *Non-Designer's Design Book*, she identifies four simple principles that are a good starting point for making any print or digital text more effective.

Contrast. Begin with a focal point—a dominant visual or text that readers should look at first—and structure the flow of other information from that point. Use color, boldface or large type, white space, and so on to set off the focal point.

Alignment. Horizontal or vertical alignment of words and visuals gives a text a cleaner, more organized look. In general, wherever you begin aligning elements—on the top or bottom, on the right or left, or in the center—stick with it throughout the text.

Repetition. Readers are guided in large part by the repetition of key words or design elements. Use color, type, style, and other visual elements consistently throughout a document.

Proximity. Parts of a text that are related should be physically close together (*proximate* to each other).

3b Appropriate formats

Think about the most appropriate way to format a document to make it inviting and readable for your intended audience.

White space. Empty space, called "white space," guides the reader's eyes to parts of a page or screen. Consider white space at the page level (margins), paragraph level (spacing between paragraphs or sections), and sentence level (space between lines and between sentences). You can also use white space around particular content, such as a graphic or list, to make it stand out.

Color. Choose colors that relate to the purpose(s) of your text and its intended audience.

- Use color to draw attention to elements you want to emphasize—such as headings, bullets, boxes, or visuals—and be consistent in using color throughout your text.
- For academic work, keep the number of colors fairly small to avoid a jumbled or confused look.
- Make sure the colors you choose are readable in the format you're using. A color that looks clear onscreen may be less legible in print or projected on a screen.

Paper. For print documents, choose paper that is an appropriate size and color for your purpose. A printed essay, poster, and brochure will probably call for different sizes and types of paper. For academic papers, put your last name and the page number in the upper-right-hand corner of each page unless your instructor requires a different formatting style.

Type. Choose an easy-to-read type size and typeface, and be consistent in the styles and sizes of type used throughout your project. For most college writing, 11- or 12-point type is standard. And although unusual fonts may seem attractive at first glance, readers may find them distracting and hard to read over long stretches of material.

Spacing. Final drafts of any printed academic writing should be double-spaced, with the first line of paragraphs indented one-half inch. Other documents, such as memos, letters, and web texts, are usually single-spaced, with a blank line between paragraphs and no paragraph indentation. Some kinds of documents, such as newsletters, may call for multiple columns of text.

Headings. Consider organizing your text with headings that will aid comprehension. Some kinds of reports have standard headings (such as *Abstract*) that readers expect.

- Distinguish levels of headings using indents along with type. For example, you might center main headings and align lower-level headings at the left margin.
- Look for the most succinct and informative way to word your headings. You can state the topic in a single word (*Toxicity*); in a noun phrase (*Levels of Toxicity*) or gerund phrase (*Measuring Toxicity*); in a question to be answered in the text (*How Can Toxicity Be Measured?*); or in an imperative that tells readers what to do (*Measure the Toxicity*). Use the structure consistently for all headings of the same level.

3c Visuals and media

Choose visuals and media that will help make a point more vividly and succinctly than words alone. In some cases, visuals may even be your primary text. Consider carefully what you want visuals, audio, or video to do for your writing. What will your audience want or need you to show? Choose visuals and media that will enhance your credibility, allow you to make your points more emphatically, and clarify your overall text. (See the series of figures on pp. 31–32 for advice on which visuals to use in particular situations.)

Effective media content can come from many sources—your own drawings or recordings you make, as well as audio or video materials created by others. If your document will be on the web, you can insert clips that readers can watch and listen to as they read your text. Such inserts can make powerful appeals: if you are writing about the ongoing migrant crisis in Europe, for example, a link to

a video clip of people barely surviving in border "camps" may make the point better than you can do in words. Include such links as you would other visuals, making sure to provide a caption as well as a lead-in to the clip and a commentary after it if appropriate. And remember: if you are using media created by someone else, be sure to give appropriate credit and to get permission before making it available to the public as part of your work.

Position and identification of visuals and media. Position visuals alongside or after the text that refers to them. In academic and other formal writing, number your visuals (number tables separately from other visuals), and provide informative captions. In some instances, you may need to give readers additional data such as source information in the caption.

Fig. 1. College Enrollment for Men and Women by Age, 2015 (in millions)

Table 1. Refugee Population by Country or Territory of Origin: 2011-2015, UNHCR, 2016

Use *pie charts* to compare parts to the whole.

Use *bar graphs* and *line graphs* to compare one element with another, to compare elements over time, or to show correlations and frequency.

Use *tables* to draw attention to detailed numerical information.

Use *diagrams* to illustrate textual information or to point out details of objects or places described.

Use *maps* to show geographical locations and to emphasize spatial relationships.

Use *cartoons* to illustrate a point dramatically or comically.

Use *photographs* or *illustrations* to show particular people, places, objects, and situations described in the text or to help readers find or understand types of content.

Use *links to audio or video material* to help readers see and hear the point you are making.

3d Manipulation of visuals and media

Technical tools available today make it relatively easy to manipulate media. As you would with any source material, carefully assess any visuals and video or audio files you find for effectiveness, appropriateness, and validity.

- Check the context in which the content appears. Is it part of an official government, school, or library site?
- Is the information you find about the visual or media source believable?
- If the visual is a chart, graph, or diagram, are the numbers and labels in it explained? Are the sources of the data given? Will the visual representation help readers make sense of the information, or could it mislead them?
- Is biographical and contact information for the designer, artist, or photographer given?

> ▶ *Checklist*

Using Visuals and Media Effectively

▶ Use visuals and media files as a part of your text, not just as decoration.

▶ Tell the audience explicitly what the visual or media file demonstrates, especially if it presents complex information. Do not assume readers will "read" the material the way you do; your commentary on it is important.

▶ Number and title all visuals. Number tables and figures separately.

▶ Refer to each visual or media file before it actually appears in your text.

▶ Follow established conventions for documenting sources, and ask permission for use if someone else controls the rights. (15b)

▶ Get responses to your visuals and media in an early draft. If readers can't follow them or are distracted by them, revise accordingly.

▶ If you alter a visual or media file, be sure to do so ethically.

At times, you may make certain changes to visuals and media that you use, such as cropping an image to show the most important detail, enhancing sound quality, or brightening a dark image. To ensure that your alterations to images are ethical, follow these guidelines:

- Never mislead readers. Show things as accurately as possible.
- Tell your audience what changes you have made.
- Include all relevant information about the original visual or media file, including the source.
- Make sure you have identified the sources of all still and moving images, audio files, and so on.

4   Reviewing, Revising, and Editing

After giving yourself—and your draft—a rest, make time to review your work (by yourself or with others) and to revise and edit. Becoming an astute critic of your own writing will pay off as you get better and better at taking a hard look at your drafts, revising them thoughtfully, and editing them with care.

4a   Reviewing

Reviewing calls for reading your draft with a critical eye and asking others to look over your work. Ask classmates or your instructor to respond to your draft, answering questions like these:

- What do you see as the major point, claim, or thesis?
- How convincing is the evidence? What can I do to support my thesis more fully?
- What points are unclear? How can I clarify them?
- How easy is it to follow my organization? How can I improve?
- What can I do to make my draft more interesting?

Writing Processes: Reviewing & Revising > Storyboards (3)
Writing Processes: Reviewing & Revising > Practice
Writing Processes: Reviewing & Revising > Video Prompts (3)

4b Revising

Revising means using others' comments along with your own analysis of the draft to make sure it is as complete, clear, and effective as possible. These questions can help you revise:

- How does the draft accomplish its purpose?
- Does the title tell what the draft is about?
- Is the thesis clearly stated, and does it contain a topic and a comment?
- How does the introduction catch readers' attention?
- Will the draft interest and appeal to its audience?
- How does the draft indicate your stance on the topic?
- What are the main points that illustrate or support the thesis? Are they clear? Do you need to add material to the points or add new points?
- Are the ideas presented in an order that will make sense to readers?
- Are the points clearly linked by logical transitions?
- Have you documented your research appropriately?
- How are visuals, media, and research sources (if any) integrated into your draft? Have you commented on their significance?
- How does the draft conclude? Is the conclusion memorable?

4c Editing

Once you are satisfied with your revised draft's big picture, edit your writing to make sure that every detail is as correct as you can make it for the readers you plan to share it with (5a).

- Read your draft aloud to make sure it flows smoothly and to find typos or other mistakes.
- Are your sentences varied in length and in pattern or type?
- Have you used active verbs and effective language?
- Are all sentences complete and correct?
- Have you used the spell checker—and double-checked its recommendations?

- Have you chosen an effective design and used white space, headings, and color appropriately?
- Have you proofread one last time, going word for word?

(For more on troubleshooting your writing, see "The Top Twenty" on pp. 1–11.)

5 Sharing and Reflecting on Your Writing

Once you have completed a piece of writing, think about sharing it. You've worked hard on a topic that's important to you, and there's a good chance others will care about it, too. Sharing and talking about a piece of writing that you've finished is also a good step toward reflecting back over the entire writing experience and assessing what you learned from it.

5a Sharing with audiences

Chances are, you have already shared some of your writing with family, friends, and others online (1a). So why not go ahead and share what you've written with others you think will be interested? You might just hear back from them. Making your work more available to readers can engage other audiences and start a conversation.

- Can you find other interested readers through social media sites like Facebook or Twitter?
- Should you keep a blog to share your writing, using a free site such as Blogger?
- Would your work find audiences on YouTube, Instagram, or other visual platforms?
- Could you submit your writing to student publications or organizations on your campus?

You can also share your ideas by joining conversations started by others. You might contribute to Wikipedia or other wikis; comment

on online newspaper or magazine articles, editorials, or videos; write reviews for books and other products on Amazon; post to fan fiction sites; or find other public sites where you can participate in producing content and responding to work others have written. As a writer today, you have nearly limitless possibilities for interaction with other readers and writers.

5b Reflecting on your own work

Thinking back on what you've learned helps make that learning stick. Whether or not your instructor requires you to write a formal reflection on a writing course or piece of writing, make time to think about what you have learned from the experience.

Your development as a writer. The following questions can help you think critically about your writing:

- What lessons have you learned from the writing? How will they help you with future writing projects?
- What aspects of your writing give you the most confidence? What needs additional work, and what can you do to improve?
- What confused you during this writing? How did you resolve your questions?
- How has this piece of writing helped you clarify your thinking or extend your understanding?
- Identify a favorite passage of your writing. What pleases you about it? Can you apply what you learn from this analysis to other writing situations?
- How would you describe your development as a writer?

Writing Processes: Reflecting to Learn > Student Writing
Academic, Professional, and Public Writing: Portfolios > Student Writing

Writing That Works

Writing Processes

Writing That Works

Research

Language

Grammar

Style

Punctuation/ Mechanics

Documentation

6 Learning from Low-Stakes Writing

Professor Peter Elbow differentiates between "high-stakes writing"—which you do for formal graded assignments and examinations—and "low-stakes writing"—informal writing that is often ungraded but that helps you think about, learn, and remember course material and stay engaged with your classes. So one very good way to put your writing to work is to use it as a way to learn!

6a The value of low-stakes writing

Sometimes referred to as "writing to learn," low-stakes writing is powerful because it gives you a chance to figure out what you know and don't know about a topic, and can help you watch your own mind at work—all without having to be judged or graded. Research shows that reflecting on your own thinking, writing, and learning style can contribute significantly to your development as a knowledgeable and critical thinker. Your instructor may assign such low-stakes writing throughout the term; if so, take advantage of it. If not, do some informal writing yourself and see how it helps improve your understanding of course material—and your grades!

6b Types of low-stakes assignments

Quickwrites. A good way to get mental gears going, quickwrites are prompts—usually open-ended questions about a topic of study—to which writers respond in short bursts of two to eight minutes. Instructors often use quickwrites to get class discussion started and focused, but you can use them on your own to get your thinking about a subject down on paper (or screen).

Freewrites. Like quickwrites, freewrites ask you to write about a topic without stopping, usually for ten minutes. Freewrites let you explore your thinking without worrying about correctness, grades, and so on.

Thought pieces. Some instructors assign thought pieces—pieces of writing that sum up background information and your own opinions

and analyses of a subject. They can help you see how much you know—and how much more you need to know—about your topic.

Reading responses. These may be the most frequently assigned type of low-stakes writing. In reading responses, you sum up your understanding of an assigned reading and evaluate its effectiveness. Whether or not your instructor assigns such responses, you will profit by setting up a reading log and recording your responses and critical evaluations there.

Class discussion forums. Many instructors set up forums online—on a local course management system, a class blog or wiki, or a class page on Facebook or other social media site—as a space to continue dialogues from the classroom. Active participation in these forums will allow you to get your views out there for others to respond to and help you understand the viewpoints of others.

▶ **Checklist**

Participating in Class Blogs, Wikis, and Other Forums

▶ Take seriously these opportunities to put your writing to work. Engaging with others about the course material and summing up your views in writing will help you internalize the information.

▶ Be polite and professional when writing to a class blog, wiki, or other forum.

▶ Avoid unnecessary criticism of others; the point of these activities is to have productive exchanges about what you are learning. Rather than criticize, simply ask for clarification or offer what you take to be correct information.

▶ If others seem to be criticizing you, give them the benefit of the doubt and reply with courtesy and patience.

▶ For email threads, decide whether to reply off-list to the sender of a message or to the whole group, and be careful to use REPLY or REPLY ALL accordingly to avoid potential confusion.

▶ Remember that many class forums, blogs, wikis, and email lists are archived, so more people than you think may be reading your messages.

7 Analyzing and Reading Critically

Reading critically is an important aspect of putting your writing to work because what you write will always be in response to what others have said. Critical reading is crucial today, when information is coming at you so fast that it's tempting to skim. Although skimming is an important tool, high-stakes reading requires you to read carefully, asking questions about the meaning of the text, the author's purpose, and why the text is convincing (or not).

7a Previewing

Find out all you can about a text before beginning to look closely at it, considering its context, author, subject, genre, and design.

- Where have you encountered the work? Are you encountering it in its original context? What can you infer from the original or current context of the work about its intended audience and purpose?
- What information can you find about the author, creator, or sponsor of the text? What purpose, expertise, and possible agenda might you expect this person to have?
- What do you know about the subject of the text? What opinions do you have about it, and why? What more do you want to learn about it?
- What does the title (or caption or other heading) indicate?
- What role does the medium play in achieving the purpose and connecting to the audience?
- What is the genre of the text—and what can it tell you about the intended audience or purpose?
- How is the text presented? What do you notice about its design and general appearance?

7b Annotating

As you read a text for the first time, mark it up or take notes, highlighting the author's main ideas and key terms. Consider the text's content, author, intended audience, genre, and design.

- What do you find confusing or unclear about the text? Where can you look for more information?
- What key terms and ideas—or key patterns—do you see? What key images stick in your mind?
- What sources or other works does this text refer to?
- Which points do you agree with? Which do you disagree with? Why?
- Do the authors or creators present themselves as you anticipated?
- For what audience was this text created? Are you part of its intended audience?
- What underlying assumptions can you identify in the text?
- Are the medium and genre appropriate for the topic, audience, and purpose?
- Is the design appropriate for the subject and genre?
- Does the composition serve a purpose—for instance, does the layout help you see what is more and less important in the text?
- How effectively do words, images, sound, and other media work together?
- How would you describe the style of the text? What contributes to this impression—word choice? references to research or popular culture? formatting? color? something else?
- Talk back to the text throughout, noting where you agree and disagree—and why. Jot down questions you'd like to ask the writer.

7c Summarizing

Try to summarize the contents of the text in your own words. A summary *briefly* captures the main ideas of a text and omits information that is less important for the reader. Try to identify the key points in the text, find the essential evidence supporting those points, and then explain the contents concisely and fairly, so that a reader unfamiliar with the original text can make sense of it all. Deciding what to leave out can make summarizing a tricky task. To test your understanding—and to avoid unintentional plagiarism—put the text aside while you write your summary.

7d Analyzing

You can learn many good lessons about how to make appropriate and effective choices in your own writing by studying the choices other writers have made. You may want to begin the process of analysis by asking additional questions about the text.

- What are the main points in this text? Are they implied or explicitly stated? What major claim is made?
- Which points do you agree with? Which do you disagree with? Why?

 Checklist

Analyzing a Text

▸ What cultural contexts—the time and place the argument was written; the economic, social, and political events surrounding the argument; and so on—inform the text? What do they tell about where the writer, creator, or sponsor is coming from and what choices he or she has had to make?

▸ What is the main issue of the text?

▸ What emotional, ethical, or logical appeals has the writer chosen to use in the text? Are the appeals reasonable and fair?

▸ What strategies has the writer chosen to establish credibility?

▸ What sources does the author use to inform the text? How current and reliable are they? Are some perspectives left out, and if so, how does this exclusion affect the argument?

▸ What claim does the text make, and how solid is the supporting evidence?

▸ How has the writer or creator chosen visuals and design to support the main ideas of the text? How well do words and images work together to make a point?

▸ What overall impression does the text create? Are you favorably impressed—or not?

Critical Thinking & Argument: Reading Critically > Student Writing (6)
Critical Thinking & Argument: Analyzing Arguments > LearningCurve (2)

- Does anything in the text surprise you? Why, or why not?
- What kinds of examples does the text use? What other kinds of evidence does the text offer to support its claims? What other examples or evidence should have been included?
- Are opposing viewpoints included and treated fairly?
- How trustworthy are the sources the text cites or refers to?
- What assumptions does the text make? Are those assumptions valid? Why, or why not?
- Do the authors or creators achieve their purpose? Why, or why not?
- What intrigues, puzzles, or irritates you about the text? Why?
- What else would you like to know?

7e Student rhetorical analysis

For a class assignment, Milena Ateyea was asked to analyze the choices former Harvard president Derek Bok made in a brief text arguing that colleges should seek to persuade rather than censor students who use speech or symbols that offend others. In analyzing "Protecting Freedom of Expression on the Campus," Milena focuses on Bok's choice of particular emotional, ethical, and logical appeals.

Critical Thinking & Argument: Analyzing Arguments > Student Writing
Critical Thinking & Argument: Reading Critically > Tutorial
Critical Thinking & Argument: Analyzing Arguments > Tutorials (2)

Title suggests
mixed response
to Bok

Connects
article to her
own experience
to build
credibility
(ethical
appeal)

Brief overview
of Bok's
argument

Identifies Bok's
central claim

Links Bok's
claim to strate-
gies he uses to
support it

Direct
quotations
show appeals
to emotion
through vivid
description

Bok establishes
common
ground between
two positions

Emphasizes
Bok's credibility
(ethical appeal)

A Curse and a Blessing

When Derek Bok's essay "Protecting Freedom of Expression on the Campus" was first published in the *Boston Globe*, I had just come to America to escape the oppressive Communist regime in Bulgaria. Perhaps my background explains why I support Bok's argument that we should not put arbitrary limits on freedom of expression. Bok wrote the essay in response to a public display of Confederate flags and a swastika at Harvard, a situation that created a heated controversy among the students. As Bok notes, universities have struggled to achieve a balance between maintaining students' right of free speech and avoiding racist attacks. When choices must be made, however, Bok argues for preserving freedom of expression.

In order to support his claim and bridge the controversy, Bok chooses a variety of rhetorical strategies. The author first immerses the reader in the controversy by vividly describing the incident: two Harvard students had hung Confederate flags in public view, thereby "upsetting students who equate the Confederacy with slavery" (69). Another student, protesting the flags, decided to display an even more offensive symbol—the swastika. These actions provoked heated discussions among students. Some students believed that school officials should remove the offensive symbols, whereas others suggested that the symbols "are a form of free speech and should be protected" (69). Bok chooses ways to establish common ground between the factions: he regrets the actions of the offenders but does not believe we should prohibit such actions just because we disagree with them.

The author earns the reader's respect because of his knowledge and through his logical presentation of the issue. In partial support of his position, Bok chooses a U.S. Supreme Court ruling, which reminds us that "the display of swastikas or Confederate flags clearly falls within the protection of the free-speech clause of the First Amendment" (70). The author also emphasizes the danger of

the slippery slope of censorship when he warns the reader, "If we begin to forbid flags, it is only a short step to prohibiting offensive speakers" (70). Overall, however, Bok's choice of appeals lacks the kinds of evidence that statistics, interviews with students, and other representative examples of controversial conduct could provide. Thus, his essay may not be strong enough to persuade all readers to make the leap from this specific situation to his general conclusion.

Links Bok's credibility to use of logical appeals

Comments critically on kinds of evidence Bok's argument lacks

Throughout, Bok chooses to imply his personal feelings rather than state them directly. As a lawyer who was president of Harvard for twenty years, Bok knows how to present his opinions respectfully without offending the feelings of the students. However, qualifying phrases like "I suspect that" and "Under the Supreme Court's rulings, as I read them" could weaken the effectiveness of his position. Furthermore, Bok's attempt to be fair to all seems to dilute the strength of his proposed solution. He suggests that one should either ignore the insensitive deeds in the hope that students might change their behavior, or talk to the offending students to help them comprehend how their behavior is affecting other students.

Reiterates Bok's credibility

Identifies qualifying phrases that may weaken claim

Analyzes weaknesses of Bok's proposed solution

Nevertheless, although Bok's proposed solution to the controversy does not appear at first reading to be very strong, it may ultimately be effective. His rhetorical choices leave enough flexibility to withstand various tests, and Bok's solution is general enough that it can change with the times and adapt to community standards.

Raises possibility that Bok's imperfect solution may work

In writing this essay, Bok faced a challenging task: to write a short response to a specific situation that represents a very broad and controversial issue. Some people may find that freedom of expression is both a curse and a blessing because of the difficulties it creates. As one who has lived under a regime that permitted very limited, censored expression, I am all too aware that I could not have written this response when I lived in Bulgaria. As a result, like Derek Bok, I believe that freedom of expression is a blessing, in spite of any temporary problems associated with it.

Summarizes Bok's task

Ties conclusion back to title

Returns to own experience, which argues for accepting Bok's solution

Work Cited

Bok, Derek. "Protecting Freedom of Expression on the Campus."
Current Issues and Enduring Questions, edited by Sylvan Barnet
and Hugo Bedau, 10th ed., Bedford/St. Martin's, 2014, pp. 69-71.
Originally published in *The Boston Globe*, 25 May 1991.

8 Building Arguments

Research conducted for this book shows that argument is the most
frequently assigned genre in first- and second-year writing classes.
Learning how to respond successfully to such assignments and com-
pose your own arguments will serve you well in college and beyond.

8a Identifying basic appeals in an argument

Emotional appeals. Emotional appeals stir our emotions and
remind us of deeply held values. In analyzing any text, look care-
fully to see how the writer has chosen to use emotional appeals to
rouse the audience's emotions.

Ethical appeals. Ethical appeals support the credibility, moral
character, and goodwill of the argument's creator. To identify these
appeals, ask what the writer or creator has chosen in order to show
the audience that he or she has done homework on the subject and
is knowledgeable about it. In addition, ask what the writer does to
suggest or show that he or she is trustworthy and fair. What word
choice or examples show that the writer is honest and credible?

Logical appeals. Even though recent research demonstrates that
most people make decisions based on emotion more than anything

else, logical appeals are still often thought to be the most persuasive for Western audiences. As some say, "The facts don't lie" (though facts can certainly be manipulated). In addition to checking the facts of any text, then, look for firsthand evidence drawn from observations, interviews, surveys or questionnaires, experiments, and personal experience, as well as secondhand evidence from authorities, precedents, the testimony of others, statistics, and other research sources. As you evaluate these sources, ask how trustworthy they are and whether all terms are clearly defined.

8b Analyzing the elements of an argument

According to philosopher Stephen Toulmin's framework for analyzing arguments, most arguments contain common features: a **claim** (or claims); reasons for the claim; stated or unstated assumptions that underlie the argument (Toulmin calls these **warrants**); **evidence** such as facts, authoritative opinion, examples, and statistics; and **qualifiers** that limit the claim in some way.

Suppose you read a brief argument about abolishing the Electoral College. The diagram below shows how you can use the elements of argument for analysis.

Elements of a Toulmin Argument

8c Arguing for a purpose

Since all language is in some sense argumentative, the purposes of argument vary widely.

Arguing to win.   In the most traditional purpose of academic argument, arguing to win, you aim to present a position that prevails over or defeats the positions of others.

Arguing to convince.   A frequent goal of argument is to convince others to change their minds about an issue. To convince, you must provide reasons so compelling that the audience willingly agrees with your conclusion.

Arguing to understand.   Rogerian argument (named for psychologist Carl Rogers) and invitational argument (named by researchers Sonja Foss and Cindy Griffin) both call for understanding as a major goal of arguing. Your purpose in many situations will be to share information and perspectives in order to make informed political, professional, and personal choices.

8d Making an argument

Chances are you've been making convincing arguments since early childhood. But if family members and friends are not always easy to convince, then making effective arguments to those unfamiliar with you presents even more challenges, especially when such audiences are anonymous and in cyberspace. To get started, you'll need an arguable statement.

Arguable statements.   An arguable statement must meet three criteria:

1. It should seek to convince readers of something, to change their minds, or to urge them to do something.
2. It should address a problem that has no obvious or absolute solution or answer.
3. It should present a position that readers can have varying perspectives on.

ARGUABLE STATEMENT	Violent video games lead to violent behavior.
UNARGUABLE STATEMENT	Video games earn millions of dollars every year.

Argumentative thesis or claim. To make the move from an arguable statement to an argumentative thesis, begin with an arguable statement:

ARGUABLE STATEMENT	Pesticides should be banned.

Attach at least one good reason.

REASON	Pesticides endanger the lives of farmworkers.

You now have a working argumentative thesis.

ARGUMENTATIVE THESIS	Because they endanger the lives of farmworkers, pesticides should be banned.

Develop the underlying assumption that supports your argument.

ASSUMPTION	Farmworkers have a right to a safe working environment.

Identifying this assumption will help you gather evidence in support of your argument. Finally, consider whether you need to qualify your claim in any way.

Ethical appeals. To make any argument effective, you need to establish your credibility. Here are some good ways to do so:

- Demonstrate that you are knowledgeable about the issues and topic.
- Show that you respect the views of your audience and have their best interests at heart.
- Demonstrate that you are fair and evenhanded by showing that you understand opposing viewpoints and can make a reasonable counterargument.

Visuals can also make ethical appeals. Just as you consider the impression your Facebook profile photo makes on your audience, you should think about what kind of case you're making when you choose images and design elements for your argument.

Logical appeals. Audiences almost always want proof—logical reasons that back up your argument. You can create good logical appeals in the following ways:

- Provide strong examples that are representative and that clearly support your point.
- Introduce precedents—particular examples from the past—that support your point.
- Use narratives or stories in support of your point.
- Cite authorities and their testimony, as long as each authority is timely and is genuinely qualified to speak on the topic.
- Establish that one event is the cause—or the effect—of another.

A Visual That Makes a Logical Appeal

Visuals that make logical appeals can be useful in arguments, since they present factual information that can be taken in at a glance. Consider how long it would take to explain all the information in the chart on p. 52 by using words alone.

Emotional appeals. Audiences can feel manipulated when an argument tries too hard to appeal to emotions like pity, anger, or fear. Nevertheless, you can appeal to the hearts as well as to the minds of your audience with the ethical use of strong emotional appeals:

- Introduce a powerful text that supports your point.
- Use concrete language and details to make your points more vivid.
- Use figurative language—metaphors, similes, analogies, and so on—to make your point both lively and memorable.

Visuals that make emotional appeals can add substance to your argument as long as you test them with potential readers to check whether they interpret the visual the same way you do.

8e Organizing an argument

Although there is no universally "ideal" organizational framework for an argument, the following pattern (often referred to as the classical system) has been used throughout the history of the Western world:

INTRODUCTION

- Gets readers' attention and interest
- Establishes your qualifications to write about your topic
- Establishes common ground with readers
- Demonstrates fairness
- States or implies your argumentative thesis

BACKGROUND

- Presents any necessary background data or information, including pertinent personal narratives or stories

LINES OF ARGUMENT

- Present good reasons and evidence (including logical and emotional appeals) in support of your thesis, usually in order of importance
- Demonstrate ways your argument is in readers' best interest

CONSIDERATION OF ALTERNATIVE ARGUMENTS

- Examines alternative or opposing points of view fairly
- Notes advantages and disadvantages of alternative views
- Explains why one view is better than other(s)

CONCLUSION

- May summarize the argument briefly
- Elaborates on the implication of your thesis
- Makes clear what you want readers to think and do
- Makes a strong ethical or emotional appeal in a memorable way

8f   A student's argument essay

The digital resources for this book include an essay by Benjy Mercer-Golden, which argues that sustainability and capitalism can and must work together for an effective response to environmental degradation. (See the inside back cover for more details.)

9   Creating Portfolios

One especially good way to put your writing to work is by developing a portfolio that showcases your abilities and experiences. Your instructor may require you to assemble a portfolio of work in your course, but you may also want to keep a portfolio throughout your college career, adding outstanding examples of your work from year to year.

9a Creating a portfolio for your course

Most instructors who assign portfolios as a culmination of the course will give you advice about what to include: a cover letter introducing the portfolio and pointing out its contents; a personal reflection on what you have learned about writing and improving your writing, with examples from your work; several polished pieces of your writing; an early draft accompanied by the final draft; examples of your work as a peer responder or as a participant in class forums or online discussion groups; and so on.

9b Assembling your portfolio

As you assemble your portfolio, keep these tips in mind:

- If the portfolio is assigned by your instructor, make sure you understand exactly what is to go into the portfolio and how it is to be organized.

- Decide, with your instructor's guidance, whether your portfolio will be print or digital.

- Consider audience and purpose: Who besides your instructor will see your portfolio? How can you most appropriately appeal to these readers?

- Choose pieces that show your strengths as a writer, and decide how many to include.

- Consider organization: what arrangement will make most sense to readers?

- Think about what layout and design will present your work most effectively.

- Be sure to get responses to your portfolio from classmates, friends, and your instructor. Ask if they find the portfolio easy to read and easy to follow.

- Edit and proofread very carefully, remembering that typos are often particularly hard to catch in digital texts.

9c A student's portfolio cover letter

The digital resources for this book include a reflective statement written by student James Kung to accompany his portfolio for his first-year college composition course. (See the inside back cover for more details.)

10 Writing in Academic Genres

Writing is important in every discipline or field, but putting your writing to work for you means different things in different fields. One of your jobs as a student is to learn to enter the conversations going on in different academic disciplines—learning to "talk the talk" and "walk the walk" in each one. You will begin to get a sense of such differences as you prepare assignments for courses in the humanities, social sciences, and natural sciences.

10a Recognizing expectations of disciplines and genres

It's frustrating to know that there is no one single "correct" style of communication in any country, including the United States. In addition, effective written styles differ from effective oral styles (Chapter 11), and what is considered good writing in one field of study may not be viewed as appropriate in another. Even the variety of English often referred to as "standard" covers a wide range of styles (19a). In each discipline you study, you will learn how to use different sets of conventions, strategies, and resources.

Early in your writing in any field, consider the **genre** or kind of text the instructor expects you to write: a lab report for biology, for example, or a review of the literature for psychology. If you are not sure what kind of text you are supposed to write, ask your instructor for clarification. (Examples may also be available at your school's writing center.) You may want to find multiple examples so that you can develop a sense of how different writers approach the same writing task.

Academic, Professional, and Public Writing: Academic Work in Any Discipline > Video Prompt
Academic, Professional, and Public Writing: Writing for the Humanities > Student Writing (2)

10b Understanding vocabularies, styles, and evidence in academic genres

As you become familiar with the vocabularies, styles, and methods of proof used in the fields you study, you will slowly come to use them with ease—that is, to be an "insider" in a particular discipline.

Vocabulary. A good way to enter into the conversation of a field or discipline is to study its vocabulary. Highlight key terms in your reading or notes to help you distinguish any specialized terms. If you find only a little specialized vocabulary, try to master the new terms quickly by reading your textbook carefully, asking your instructor questions, and looking up key words or phrases.

Style. Study writing in the field to identify its stylistic features.

- How would you describe the overall tone of the writing? Do writers in the field usually strive for an objective stance? (See 1g.)
- Do they use the first person (*I*) or prefer such terms as *one* or *the investigator*? What is the effect of this choice?
- In general, how long are the sentences and paragraphs?
- Are verbs generally active or passive—and why? (See 21e.)
- How does the writing integrate visual elements—graphs, tables, charts, photographs, or maps—or include video or sound?
- How is the writing organized? Does it typically include certain features, such as an abstract, a discussion of methods, headings, or other formatting elements?

Evidence. As you grow familiar with any area of study, you will develop a sense of what it takes to prove a point in that field. As you read assigned materials, consider the following questions about evidence:

- How do writers in the field use precedent and authority?
- What kinds of quantitative data (items that can be counted and measured) and qualitative data (items that can be systematically observed) are used—and why?

🎨 **Academic, Professional, and Public Writing: Writing for the Social Sciences > Student Writing**

- How is logical reasoning used? How are definition, cause and effect, analogy, and example used in this discipline?
- What are the primary materials—the firsthand sources of information—in this field? What are the secondary materials—the sources of information derived from others? (See 13b.)
- How is research used and integrated into the text?
- What documentation style is typically used in this field? (See Chapters 45–48.)

EVIDENCE IN THE HUMANITIES. Evidence for assignments in the humanities may come from a primary source you are examining, such as a poem, a philosophical treatise, an artifact, or a painting. For certain assignments, secondary sources such as journal articles or reference works will also provide useful evidence. Ground your analysis of each source in key questions about the work you are examining that will lead you to a thesis.

EVIDENCE IN THE SOCIAL SCIENCES. You will need to understand both the quantitative and qualitative evidence used in your sources as well as other evidence you may create from research you conduct on your own. Summarizing and synthesizing information drawn from sources will be key to your success.

EVIDENCE IN THE NATURAL AND APPLIED SCIENCES. You will probably draw on two major sources of evidence: research—including studies, experiments, and analyses—conducted by credible scientists, and research you conduct by yourself or with others. Each source should provide a strong piece of evidence for your project.

10c Using conventional patterns and formats

To produce effective writing in a discipline, you need to know the field's generally accepted formats for organizing and presenting evidence. A typical laboratory report, for instance, follows a fairly standard organizational framework (often the "introduction, methods, results, and discussion" format known as IMRAD) and has a certain look.

Academic, Professional, and Public Writing: Writing for the Natural and Applied Sciences > Student Writing (2)

Ask your instructor to recommend some excellent examples of the kind of writing you will do in the course, or consult major scholarly journals to consider these questions about format:

- What types of documents are common in this field? What is the purpose of each?
- Do articles or other documents typically begin with an abstract? (See Chapter 13.)
- How is each type of text organized? What are its main parts? How are they labeled?
- What assumptions does the text take for granted? What points does it emphasize?

Remember that there is a close connection between the writing patterns and formats a particular area of study uses and the work that scholars in that field undertake.

10d Adapting genre structures

Learning to borrow and adapt transitional devices and pieces of sentence structure from other writing in the genre you are working in is one way to help you learn the conventions of that discipline. Don't copy the whole structure, however, or your borrowed sentences may seem plagiarized (Chapter 15). Find sample sentence structures from similar genres but on different topics so that you borrow a typical structure (which does not belong to anyone) rather than the idea or the particular phrasing. Write your own sentences first, and look at other people's sentences just to guide your revision.

ABSTRACT FROM A SOCIAL SCIENCE PAPER

Using the interpersonal communications research of J. K. Brilhart and G. J. Galanes, along with T. Hartman's personality assessment, I observed and analyzed the group dynamics of my project collaborators in a communications course. Based on results of the Hartman personality assessment, I predicted that a single leader would emerge. However, complementary individual

---

strengths and gender differences encouraged a distributed leadership style.

EFFECTIVE BORROWING OF STRUCTURES

Drawing on the research of Deborah Tannen on conversational styles, I analyzed the conversational styles of six first-year students at DePaul University. Based on Tannen's research, I expected that the three men I observed would use features typical of male conversational style and the three women would use features typical of female conversational style. In general, these predictions were accurate; however, some exceptions were also apparent.

11 Creating Presentations

No doubt you will be assigned to create presentations throughout your college career. Yet many students say that they aren't completely comfortable with the "stand and deliver" format. This chapter will help you put your best foot forward in presentations.

11a Considering task, purpose, and audience

Think about how much time you have to prepare; where the presentation will take place; how long the presentation is to be; whether you will use written-out text or note cards; whether visual aids, handouts, or other accompanying materials are called for; and what equipment you will need. If you are making a group presentation, you will need time to divide duties and to practice with your classmates.

Consider the purpose of your presentation. Are you to lead a discussion? teach a lesson? give a report? make a proposal? present research findings? engage a group in an activity?

Consider your audience. What do they know about your topic, what opinions do they already hold about it, and what do they need to know to follow your presentation and perhaps accept your point of view?

11b Writing a memorable introduction and conclusion

Listeners tend to remember beginnings and endings most readily. Consider making yours memorable by using a startling statement, opinion, or question; a vivid anecdote; or a powerful quotation or image. Make sure at the end that the audience gets the main takeaway!

11c Using explicit structure and signpost language

Organize your presentation clearly and carefully, and give an overview of your main points at the outset. (You may wish to recall these points toward the end of the talk.) Then pause between major points, and use signpost language as you move from one idea to the next. Such signposts should be clear and concrete: *The second crisis point in the breakup of the Soviet Union occurred hard on the heels of the first* instead of *Another thing about the Soviet Union's problems. . . .* You can also offer signposts by repeating key words and ideas; avoiding long, complicated sentences; and using as many concrete verbs and nouns as possible. If you are talking about abstract ideas, try to provide concrete examples for each.

11d Preparing a text for ease of presentation

If you decide to speak from a full text of your presentation, use fairly large double- or triple-spaced print that will be easy to read. End each page with the end of a sentence so that you won't have to pause while you turn a page. Whether you speak from a full text, a detailed outline, note cards, or points on flip charts or slides, mark the places where you want to pause, and highlight the words you want to emphasize. (If you are using presentation software, print out a paper version and mark it up.)

11e Planning visuals

Visuals carry a lot of the message the speaker wants to convey, so think of your visuals not as add-ons but as a major means of getting your points across. Many speakers use presentation software (such as PowerPoint or Prezi) to help keep themselves on track and to guide the audience. In addition, posters, flip charts, chalkboards, or interactive whiteboards can also help you make strong visual statements.

When you work with visuals for your own presentation, remember that they must be large enough to be easily seen and read. Be sure the information is simple, clear, and easy to understand. And remember *not* to read from your visuals or turn your back on your audience as you refer to them. Most important, make sure your visuals engage and help your listeners rather than distract them from your message. Try out each visual on your classmates, friends, or roommates: if they do not clearly grasp the meaning and purpose of the visual, scrap it and try again.

You may also want to prepare handouts for your audience: pertinent bibliographies, for example, or text too extensive to be presented otherwise. Unless the handouts include material you want your audience to use while you speak, distribute them at the end of the presentation.

Slides. Here are some guidelines for preparing effective slides:

- Don't put too much information on one slide; one simple word or picture may make your point most effectively. Avoid using more than three to five bullet points (or more than fifty words) on any slide, and never read them to your audience. Instead, say something to enhance, explain, or emphasize what's on the slide.

- Use light backgrounds in a darkened room, dark backgrounds in a lighted one.

- Make sure that audio or video clips with sound are clearly audible.

- Use only images that are large and sharp enough to be clearly visible to your audience.

▶ Checklist

Reviewing Your Presentation

Before your instructor or another audience evaluates your presentation, do a review for yourself:

▶ Does your presentation have a clear thesis, a compelling introduction and conclusion, and a simple, clear structure?

▶ Do you use sources to support your points and demonstrate your knowledge? Do you include a works-cited slide at the end of the presentation?

▶ Is your use of media (posters, slides, video clips, and so on) appropriate for your topic and thesis? If you are using slides, will they appeal to your audience and make your points effectively?

▶ Do you use clear signpost language and effective repetition?

▶ Are you satisfied with your delivery—your tone and projection of voice, pacing, and stance?

11f Practicing

Set aside enough time to practice your presentation—including the use of all visuals—at least twice. You might also record your rehearsals, or practice in front of a mirror or with friends who can comment on content and style.

Timing your run-throughs will tell you whether you need to cut (or expand) material to make the presentation an appropriate length.

11g Delivering the presentation

To calm your nerves and get off to a good start, know your material thoroughly and use the following strategies to good advantage before, during, and after your presentation:

• Visualize your presentation with the aim of feeling comfortable during it.

- Consider doing some deep-breathing exercises before the presentation, and concentrate on relaxing; avoid too much caffeine.
- If possible, stand up. Most speakers make a stronger impression standing rather than sitting.
- Face your audience, and make eye contact as much as possible.
- Allow time for questions.
- Thank the audience at the end of your presentation.

11h A student's presentation

For her presentation "Words, Images, and the Mystical Way They Work Together in Alison Bechdel's *Fun Home*," Shuqiao Song developed a series of very simple slides aimed at underscoring her points and keeping her audience focused on them. The digital resources for this book include her full presentation. (See the inside back cover for more details.)

12 Writing to Make Something Happen in the World

A large group of college students participating in a research study were asked, "What is good writing?" The students kept coming back to one central idea: good writing "makes something happen in the world." They felt particular pride in the writing they did for family, friends, and community groups—and for many extracurricular activities that were meaningful to them. At some point during your college years or soon after, you are highly likely to create writing that is not just something that you turn in for a grade but writing that you do because you want to make a difference. The writing that matters most to many students and citizens, then, is writing that gets up off the page or screen, puts on its working boots, and marches out to get something done!

 Checklist

Characteristics of Writing That Makes Something Happen

▶ Public writing has a very clear *purpose*.

▶ It is intended for a specific *audience* and addresses those people directly.

▶ It uses the *genre* most suited to its purpose and audience (a poster, a newsletter, a brochure, a letter to the editor), and it appears in a *medium* (print, online, or both) where the intended audience will see it.

▶ It generally uses straightforward, everyday *language*.

12a Deciding what should happen

When you decide to write to make something happen, you'll generally have some idea of what effect you want that writing to have on your readers. Clarify what actions you want them to take in response to your writing, and then think about what people you most want to reach. Who will be interested in the topic you are writing about?

12b Connecting with your audience

Once you have a target audience in mind, you'll need to think carefully about where and how you are likely to find them, how you can get their attention so they will read what you write, and what you can say to get them to achieve your purpose.

If you want to convince your neighbors to pool time, effort, and resources to build a local playground, then you have a head start: you already know something about what they value and about what appeals would get their attention and convince them to join in this project. If you want to create a flash mob to publicize ineffective security at chemical plants near your city, on the other hand, you

will need to reach as many people as possible, most of whom you will not know.

Genre and media. Even if you know the members of your audience, you still need to think about the genre and medium that will be most likely to reach them. To get neighbors involved in the playground project previously mentioned, you might decide that a print flyer delivered door-to-door and posted at neighborhood gathering places would work best. For a flash mob, however, an easily forwarded message—text, tweet, or email—will probably work best.

Appropriate language. For all public writing, think carefully about the audience you want to reach—as well as *unintended* audiences your message might reach. Doing so can help you craft writing that will be persuasive without being offensive.

Timing. Making sure your text will appear in a timely manner is crucial to the success of your project. If you want people to plan to attend an event, present your text to them at least two weeks ahead of time. If you are issuing a newsletter or blog, make sure that you create posts or issues often enough to keep people interested (but not so often that readers can't or won't keep up). If you are reporting information based on something that has already happened, make it available as soon as possible so that your audience won't consider your report "old news."

12c Sample writing that makes something happen in the world

Look on the following pages for some examples of the forms public writing can take.

Fundraising web page

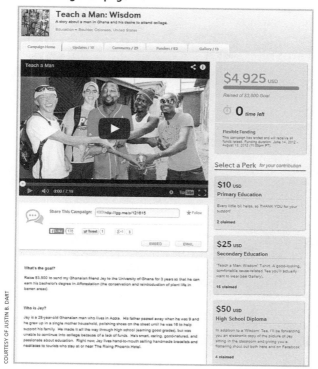

Student Justin Dart created this fundraising web page with a very clear purpose: to crowd-source the funding to help Jey, a young street vendor in Accra, Ghana, get a college education. Using the Indiegogo template, Justin posted a video spelling out the background and purpose of his fundraiser, a short written description of the project, and a list of perks for donors at various levels. Other tabs offered updates from Justin on his progress, comments from donors, photos, and more. To reach as many people as possible, Justin shared this page with his friends and acquaintances and urged them to share it on social media outlets. Justin ended up raising enough to pay for Jey's university tuition for his college career, as well as housing and incidentals.

Web comic

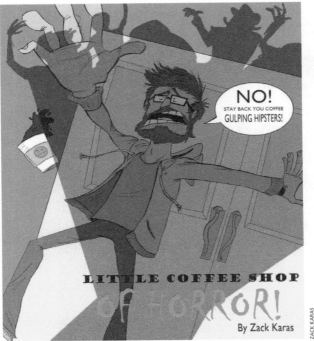

Student Zack Karas worked with a team of classmates on an assign-
ment to do field research in a public space. His group chose a local
coffee shop, and after conducting observations of the environment
and the interactions among people there, they presented a critical
analysis of the coffee-drinking scene to the rest of the class.

Zack then used his team's coffee shop experience as the basis for
a comic, which he posted on a blog created to host his artwork. The
final panels include a twist: Zack's comic avatar fails to recognize
that he, like many of the customers, is also a "post-ironic hipster . . .
with facial hair, a hoodie, and an iPhone." Turning the report into
a comic allowed Zack to reach an audience beyond his classmates—
readers who share his interest in humor, online comics, and the
critique of the coffee-culture demographic.

Newsletter

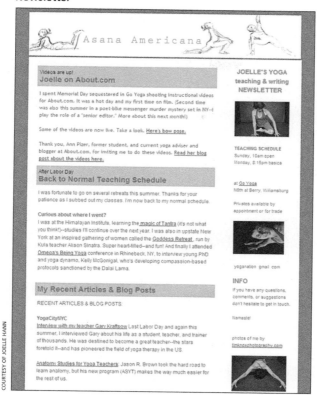

As with the creators of the fundraising web page and web comic, yoga teacher Joelle Hann has a clear purpose in mind for her e-newsletter: to provide information to her audience—students and others interested in her yoga classes and developments in the yoga community. Emailing the newsletter to her subscribers allows Joelle to reach an interested audience quickly and to provide links to more of the content she's discussing, and it also means that she can include photos, illustrations, and color to enhance her document's design impact.

Research

Writing
Processes

Writing That
Works

Research

Language

Grammar

Style

Punctuation/
Mechanics

Documentation

13   Conducting Research

Your employer asks you to recommend the best software for a project. You need to plan a week's stay in Toronto. Your instructor assigns a term project about a groundbreaking musician. Each of these situations calls for research, for examining various kinds of sources—and each calls for you to assess the data you collect, synthesize your findings, and come up with an original recommendation or conclusion. Many tasks that call for research require that your work culminate in a written document—whether print or digital—that refers to and lists the sources you used.

13a   Beginning the research process

For academic research assignments, once you have a topic you need to move as efficiently as possible to analyze the research assignment, articulate a research question to answer, and form a hypothesis. Then, after your preliminary research is complete, you can refine your hypothesis into a working thesis and begin your research in earnest.

Considering the context for a research project. Ask yourself what the *purpose* of the project is—perhaps to describe, survey, analyze, persuade, explain, classify, compare, or contrast. Then consider your *audience*. Who will be most interested, and what will they need to know? What assumptions might they hold? What response do you want from them?

You should also examine your own *stance* or *attitude* toward your topic. Do you feel curious, critical, confused, or some other way about it? What influences have shaped your stance?

For a research project, consider how many and what *kinds of sources* you need to find. What kinds of evidence will convince your audience? What visuals—charts, photographs, and so on—might you need? Would it help to do field research, such as interviews, surveys, or observations?

Finally, consider practical matters, such as how long your project will be, how much time it will take, and when it is due.

Formulating a research question and hypothesis. After ana-
lyzing your project's context, work from your general topic to a
research question and a hypothesis.

TOPIC	Farming
NARROWED TOPIC	Small family farms in the United States
ISSUE	Making a living from a small family farm
RESEARCH QUESTION	How can small family farms in the United States successfully compete with big agriculture?
HYPOTHESIS	Small family farmers can succeed by growing specialty products that consumers want and by participating in farmers' markets and community-supported agriculture programs that forge relationships with customers.

After you have explored sources to test your hypothesis and sharp-
ened it by reading, writing, and talking with others, you can refine
it into a working thesis (2b).

WORKING THESIS	Although recent data show that small family farms are more endangered than ever, some enterprising farmers have reversed the trend by growing specialized products and connecting with consumers through farmers' markets and community-supported agriculture programs.

Planning research. Once you have formulated your hypoth-
esis, determine what you already know about your topic and try
to remember where you got your information. Think hard about
the kinds of sources you expect to consult—articles, print or digital
books, specialized reference works, experts on your own campus,
and so on—and the number you think you will need, how current
they should be, and where you might find them.

13b Choosing among types of sources

Keep in mind some important differences among types of sources.

Primary and secondary sources. Primary sources provide you with firsthand knowledge, while secondary sources report on or analyze the research of others. Primary sources are basic sources of raw information, including your own field research; films, works of art, or other objects you examine; literary works you read; and eyewitness accounts, photographs, news reports, and historical documents. Secondary sources are descriptions or interpretations of primary sources, such as researchers' reports, reviews, biographies, and encyclopedia articles. What constitutes a primary or secondary source depends on the purpose of your research. A film review, for instance, serves as a secondary source if you are writing about the film but as a primary source if you are studying the critic's writing.

Scholarly and popular sources. Nonacademic sources like magazines can help you get started on a research project, but you will usually want to depend more on authorities in a field, whose work generally appears in scholarly journals in print or online. The following list will help you to distinguish between scholarly and popular sources:

SCHOLARLY	POPULAR
Title often contains the word *Journal*	*Journal* usually does not appear in title
Source is available mainly through libraries and library databases	Source is generally available outside of libraries (at newsstands or from a home Internet connection)
Few or no commercial advertisements	Many advertisements
Authors are identified with academic credentials	Authors are usually journalists or reporters hired by the publication, not academics or experts
Summary or abstract appears on first page of article; articles are fairly long	No summary or abstract; articles are fairly short
Articles cite sources and provide bibliographies	Articles may include quotations but do not cite sources or provide bibliographies

SCHOLARLY

POPULAR

Older and more current sources. Most projects can benefit from both older, historical sources and more current ones. Some older sources are classics; others are simply dated.

13c Using library resources

Almost any research project should begin with resources in your school library, so you might begin by paying a visit.

Reference librarians. Your library's staff—especially reference librarians—can be a valuable resource. You can talk with a librarian about your research project and get specific recommendations about databases and other helpful places to begin your research. Many libraries also have online tours and chat rooms where students can ask questions.

Catalogs. Library catalogs can tell you whether a book is housed in the library and, if so, offer a call number that enables you to find the book on the shelf. Browsing through other books near the

 Checklist

Effective Search Techniques

You can access many online catalogs, databases, and websites without actually going to the library. You can search the Internet by using carefully chosen keywords to limit the scope of your search, and refine your search depending on what you find.

▶ Advanced search tools let you focus your search more narrowly—by combining terms with AND or eliminating them with NOT, by specifying dates and media types, and so on—so they may give you more relevant results.

▶ If you don't see an advanced search option, start with keywords. (Simply entering terms in the search box may bring up an advanced search option.) Check the first page or two of results. If you get many irrelevant options, think about how to refine your keywords to get more targeted results.

▶ Databases and search engines don't all refine searches the same way—for instance, some use AND, while others use the + symbol. Look for tips on making the most of the search tool you're using.

▶ Most libraries classify material using the *Library of Congress Subject Headings*, or LCSH. When you find a library source that seems especially relevant, be sure to use the subject headings for that source as search terms to bring up all the entries under each heading.

one you've found in the catalog can help you locate other works related to your topic. Catalogs also indicate whether you can find a particular periodical, either in print or in an online database, at the library.

Indexes and databases.   Remember that most college libraries subscribe to a large number of indexes and databases that students can access for free, and these sources contain much information that you will not have access to in a general Google search. Some databases include the full text of articles from newspapers, magazines, journals, and other works; some offer only short abstracts

(summaries), which give an overview so you can decide whether to spend time finding and reading the whole text. Indexes of reviews provide information about a potential source's critical reception.

Check with a librarian for discipline-specific indexes and databases related to your topic.

Reference works. General reference works, such as encyclopedias, biographical resources, almanacs, digests, and atlases, can help you get an overview of a topic, identify subtopics, find more specialized sources, and identify keywords for searches.

Bibliographies. Bibliographies—lists of sources—in books or articles related to your topic can lead you to other valuable resources. Ask a librarian whether your library has more extensive bibliographies related to your research topic.

Other resources. Your library can help you borrow materials from other libraries (this can take time, so plan ahead). Check with reference librarians, too, about audio, video, multimedia, and art collections; government documents; and other special collections or archives that student researchers may be able to use.

13d Finding useful Internet sources

Many college students prefer to begin their research with general Internet searches, and much information—including authoritative sources identical to those your library provides—can be found online. But remember that library databases come from identifiable and professionally edited resources—often with materials that you can't access for free. Thus, you need to take special care to find out which information online is reliable and which is not (14a).

Internet searches. Research using a search tool such as Google usually begins with a keyword search (see the Checklist on the facing page). Many keyword searches bring up thousands of hits; you may find what you need on the first page or two of results, but if not, choose new keywords that lead to more specific sources.

Bookmarking tools. Today's powerful bookmarking tools can help you browse, sort, and track resources online. Social bookmarking sites allow users to tag information and share it with others. Users' tags are visible to all other users. If you find a helpful site, you can check how others have tagged it and browse similar tags for related information. You can also sort and group information with tags. Fellow users whose tags you trust can become part of your network so you can follow their sites of interest.

Web browsers can also help you bookmark online resources. However, unlike bookmarking tools in a browser, which are tied to one machine, you can use social bookmarking tools wherever you have an Internet connection.

Authoritative sources online. Many sources online are authoritative and reliable. You can browse collections in online virtual libraries, for example, or collections housed in government sites such as the Library of Congress, the National Institutes of Health, and the U.S. Census Bureau. For current national news, consult online versions of reputable newspapers such as the *Washington Post*, or electronic sites for news services such as C-SPAN. Google Scholar can help you limit searches to scholarly works.

Some journals (such as those from Berkeley Electronic Press) and general-interest magazines (such as *Salon*) are published only online; many other print publications make at least some of their content available free on the web.

13e　Doing field research

For many research projects, you will need to collect field data. Consider *where* you can find relevant information, *how* to gather it, and *who* might be your best providers of information. You may also want to talk with your instructor about any field research you plan to do, to make sure your research will not violate your college's guidelines for doing research that involves people.

Interviews. Some information is best obtained by asking direct questions of other people. If you can talk with an expert—in person, on the telephone, or online—you may get information you cannot obtain through any other kind of research.

- Determine your exact purpose, and be sure it relates to your research question and your hypothesis.
- Set up the interview well in advance. Specify how long it will take, and if you wish to record the session, ask permission to do so.
- Prepare a written list of factual and open-ended questions. If the interview proceeds in a direction that seems fruitful, do not feel that you have to ask all of your prepared questions.
- Record the subject, date, time, and place of the interview.
- Thank those you interview, either in person or in a letter or email.

Observation.   Trained observers report that making a faithful record of an observation requires intense concentration and mental agility.

- Determine the purpose of the observation, and be sure it relates to your research question and hypothesis.
- Brainstorm about what you are looking for, but don't be rigidly bound to your expectations.
- Develop an appropriate system for recording data. Consider using a split notebook or page: on one side, record your observations directly; on the other, record your thoughts or interpretations.
- Record the date, time, and place of observation.

Opinion surveys.   Surveys usually depend on questionnaires. On any questionnaire, the questions should be clear and easy to understand and designed so that you can analyze the answers without difficulty. Questions that ask respondents to say *yes* or *no* or to rank items on a scale are easiest to tabulate.

- Write out your purpose, and determine the kinds of questions to ask.
- Figure out how to reach respondents—either online via email, apps, or social media; over the phone; or in person.
- Draft questions that call for short, specific answers.
- Test the questions on several people, and revise questions that seem unfair, ambiguous, or too hard or time-consuming.

- Draft a cover letter or invitation email. Be sure to state a deadline.
- If you are using a print questionnaire, leave adequate space for answers.
- Proofread the questionnaire carefully.

14 Evaluating Sources and Taking Notes

All research builds on the careful and sometimes inspired use of sources—that is, on research done by others. Since you want the information you glean from sources to be reliable and persuasive, evaluate each potential source carefully. Especially with online sources, practice what Howard Rheingold calls "crap detection," which means identifying information that is faulty or deceptive. Rheingold recommends finding three separate credible online sources that corroborate the point you want to make.

14a Evaluating the usefulness and credibility of potential sources

Use these guidelines to assess the value of a source, and add useful sources to your working bibliography with notes about why you need them.

- **Your purpose.** What will this source add to your research project? Does it help you support a major point, demonstrate that you have thoroughly researched your topic, or help establish your own credibility through its authority?
- **Relevance.** Is the source closely related to your research question? You may need to read beyond the title and opening paragraph to check for relevance.
- **Publisher's credentials.** What do you know about the publisher of the source you are using? For example, is it a major newspaper known for integrity in reporting, or is it a tabloid? Is the publisher

a popular source, or is it sponsored by a professional or scholarly organization?

- **Author's credentials.** Is the author an expert on the topic? An author's credentials may be presented in the article, book, or website, or you can search the Internet for information on the author.

- **Date of publication.** Recent sources are often more useful than older ones, particularly in fields that change rapidly. However, the most authoritative works may be older ones. The publication dates of Internet sites can often be difficult to pin down. And even for sites that include the dates of posting, remember that the material posted may have been composed sometime earlier.

- **Accuracy of source.** How accurate and complete is the information in the source? How thorough is the bibliography or list of works cited that accompanies the source? Can you find other sources that corroborate what your source is saying?

- **Stance of source.** Identify the source's point of view or rhetorical stance, and scrutinize it carefully. Does the source present facts, or does it interpret or evaluate them? If it presents facts, what is included and what is omitted, and why? If it interprets or evaluates information that is not disputed, the source's stance may be obvious, but at other times you will need to think carefully about the source's goals. What does the author or sponsoring group want—to convince you of an idea? sell you something? call you to action in some way?

- **Cross-referencing.** Is the source cited in other works? If you see your source cited by others, looking at how they cite it and what they say about it can provide additional clues to its credibility.

- **Level of specialization.** General sources can be helpful as you begin your research, but you may then need the authority or currency of more specialized sources. On the other hand, extremely specialized works may be very hard to understand.

- **Audience of source.** Was the source written for the general public? specialists? advocates or opponents?

For more on evaluating web sources and articles, see the source maps on pp. 82–85.

SOURCE MAP: Evaluating Web Sources

Is the sponsor credible?

1 Who is the **sponsor or publisher** of the source? See what information you can get from the URL. The domain names for government sites may end in *.gov* or *.mil* and for educational sites in *.edu*. The ending *.org* may—but does not always—indicate a nonprofit organization. If you see a tilde (~) or percent sign (%) followed by a name, or if you see a word such as *users* or *members*, the page's creator may be an individual, not an institution. In addition, check the header and footer, where the sponsor may be identified. The web page shown on p. 83 comes from a site sponsored by the nonprofit Nieman Foundation for Journalism at Harvard University.

2 Look for an *About* page or a link to a home page for background information on the sponsor. Is a mission statement included? What are the sponsoring organization's purpose and point of view? Does the mission statement seem balanced? What is the purpose of the site (to inform, to persuade, to advocate for a cause, to advertise, or something else)? Does the information on the site come directly from the sponsor, or is the material reprinted from another source? If it is reprinted, check the original.

Is the author credible?

3 What are the **author's credentials**? Look for information accompanying the material on the page. You can also run a search on the author to find out more. Does the author seem qualified to write about this topic?

Is the information credible and current?

4 When was the information **posted or last updated**? Is it recent enough to be useful?

5 Does the page document sources with **footnotes or links**? If so, do the sources seem credible and current? Does the author include any additional resources for further information? Look for ways to corroborate the information the author provides.

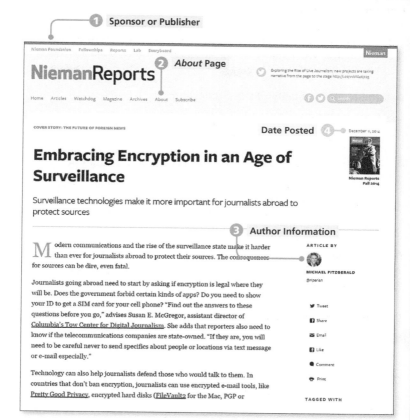

1 Sponsor or Publisher

Nieman Foundation   Fellowships   Reports   Lab   Storyboard

Nieman

NiemanReports

2 About Page

Exploring the Rise of Live Journalism: new projects are taking narrative from the page to the stage http://t.co/vvbMa6jb25

Home   Articles   Watchdog   Magazine   Archives   About   Subscribe

COVER STORY: THE FUTURE OF FOREIGN NEWS

Date Posted **4**   December 11, 2014

Embracing Encryption in an Age of Surveillance

Nieman Reports
Fall 2014

Surveillance technologies make it more important for journalists abroad to protect sources

3 Author Information

M odern communications and the rise of the surveillance state make it harder than ever for journalists abroad to protect their sources. The consequences for sources can be dire, even fatal.

Journalists going abroad need to start by asking if encryption is legal where they will be. Does the government forbid certain kinds of apps? Do you need to show your ID to get a SIM card for your cell phone? "Find out the answers to these questions before you go," advises Susan E. McGregor, assistant director of Columbia's Tow Center for Digital Journalism. She adds that reporters also need to know if the telecommunications companies are state-owned. "If they are, you will need to be careful never to send specifics about people or locations via text message or e-mail especially."

Technology can also help journalists defend those who would talk to them. In countries that don't ban encryption, journalists can use encrypted e-mail tools, like Pretty Good Privacy, encrypted hard disks (FileVault2 for the Mac, PGP or

ARTICLE BY

MICHAEL FITZGERALD
@riparian

🐦 Tweet
📘 Share
✉ Email
👍 Like
💬 Comment
🖨 Print

TAGGED WITH

83

SOURCE MAP: Evaluating Articles

Determine the relevance of the source.

1 Look for an **abstract**, which provides a summary of the entire article. Is this source directly related to your research? Does it provide useful information and insights? Will your readers consider it persuasive support for your thesis?

Determine the credibility of the publication.

2 Consider the publication's **title**. Words in the title such as *Journal, Review,* and *Quarterly* may indicate that the periodical is a scholarly source. Most research projects rely on authorities in a particular field, whose work usually appears in scholarly journals. For more on distinguishing between scholarly and popular sources, see 13b.

3 Try to determine the **publisher or sponsor**. The journal on p. 85 is published by the University of Illinois. Academic presses such as this one generally review articles carefully before publishing them and bear the authority of their academic sponsors.

Determine the credibility of the author.

4 Evaluate the **author's credentials**. In this case, they are given in a note, which indicates that the author is a college professor.

Determine the currency of the article.

5 Look at the **publication date**, and think about whether your topic and your credibility depend on your use of very current sources.

Determine the accuracy of the article.

6 Look at the **sources cited** by the author of the article. Here, they are listed in a bibliography. Ask yourself whether the works the author has cited seem credible and current. Are any of these works cited in other articles you've considered?

In addition, consider the following questions:

- What is the article's stance or point of view? What are the author's goals? What does the author want you to know or believe?

- How does this source fit in with your other sources? Does any of the information it provides contradict or challenge other sources?

ELIZABETH TUCKER

Changing Concepts of Childhood: Children's Folklore Scholarship since the Late Nineteenth Century

1 Abstract

This essay examines children's folklore scholarship from the late nineteenth century to the present, tracing key concepts from the Gilded Age to the contemporary era. These concepts reflect significant social, cultural, political, and scientific changes. From the "savage child" to the "secret-keeping child," the "magic-making child," the "cerebral child," the "taboo-breaking child," the "monstrous child," and others, scholarly representations of young people have close connections to the eras in which they developed. Nineteenth-century children's folklore scholarship relied on evolutionism; now evolutionary biology provides a basis for children's folklore research, so we have re-entered familiar territory.

SINCE 1977, WHEN THE American Folklore Society decided to form a new section for scholars interested in young people's traditions, I have belonged to the Children's Folklore Section. It has been a joy to contribute to this dynamic organization, which has significantly influenced children's folklore scholarship and children's book authors' focus on folk tradition. This essay examines children's folklore scholarship from the late nineteenth century to the present, tracing key concepts from the Gilded Age to the contemporary era in the English language. These concepts reflect significant social, cultural, political, and scientific changes that have occurred since William Wells Newell, the first secretary of the American Folklore Society and the first editor of the *Journal of American Folklore*, published *Games and Songs of American Children* in 1883. They also reveal some very interesting commonalities. Those of us who pursue children's folklore scholarship today may consider ourselves to be light years away from nineteenth-century scholars' research but may find, when reading nineteenth-century works, that we have stayed fairly close to our scholarly "home base."

Before examining concepts of childhood that folklorists have developed, I will offer a working definition [...] the beginning of childhood studies. I will also sum [...] work during the past thirty-four years. Acco [...] childhood con [...] "the state or stage of lif [...] a child; the tim [...] birth to puberty" (201 [...] [...] e between childhood and adolescence, which begins at puberty and follows pre-adolescence. The fol [...] re

2 Title of Publication
Journal of American Folklore

4 Author's Credentials

ELIZABETH TUCKER is Professor of English at Binghamton University

Journal of American Folklore 125(498):389–410

3 Publisher
Board of Trustees of the University of Illinois

5 Publication Date
2012

6 Sources Cited

and Humanities 3:145–60.
[...] [...] 2014. Why Children's Studies? Centre for [...]
[...] ca/pdf/papers/Carole.Carpenter.pdf.
[...] rancis. 1896. *The Child and Childhood* [...]
[...] Fay. 1990. *Parenting with Love and* [...] Pinon Press.
Conrad, JoAnn. 2002. The War on Youth: A Modern Oedipal Tragedy. *Children's Folklore Review* 24(1–2):33–42.
Crandall, Bryan Ripley. 2009. Cow Project. bryanripleycrandall.files.wordpress.com/2009/05/slbscow-project.pdf.
Darwin, Charles. 1859. *On the Origin of Species by Means of Natural Selection, or the Preservation of Favoured Races in the Struggle for Life* (1st edition). London: John Murray.
Dégh, Linda. 2001. *Legend and Belief.* Bloomington: Indiana University Press.
Dorson, Richard M. 1968. *The British Folklorists: A History.* Chicago: University of Chicago Press.
Douglas, Norman. [1916] 1968. *London Street Games.* Detroit: Singing Tree Press.

14b Reading and interpreting sources

After you have determined that a source is potentially useful, read it carefully and critically, asking yourself the following questions about how this research fits your writing project:

- How relevant is this material to your research question and hypothesis?
- Does the source include counterarguments that you should address?
- How persuasive is the evidence? Does it represent opposing viewpoints fairly? Will the source be convincing to your audience?
- Will you need to change your thesis to account for this information?
- What quotations or paraphrases from this source might you want to use?

As you read and take notes on your sources, keep in mind that you will need to present data and sources to other readers so that they can understand your point.

14c Synthesizing sources

Analysis requires you to take apart something complex (such as an article in a scholarly journal) and look closely at each part to understand how the parts fit together into an effective (or ineffective) whole. Academic writing also calls for *synthesis*—grouping similar pieces of information together and looking for patterns—so you can put your sources and your own knowledge together in an original argument. Synthesis is the flip side of analysis: you assemble the parts into a new whole.

To synthesize sources for a research project, try the following tips:

- **Don't just grab a quotation and move on.** Rather, read the material carefully. (See Chapter 7.)
- **Understand the purpose of each source.** Make sure the source is relevant and necessary to your argument.
- **Determine the important ideas in each source.** Take notes on each source (14d). Identify and summarize the key ideas.

Research: Evaluating Sources > LearningCurve (2)
Research: Integrating Sources > Storyboards

- **Formulate a position.** Figure out how the pieces fit together. Look for patterns. After considering multiple perspectives, decide what you have to say.

- **Summon evidence to support your position.** You might use paraphrases, summaries, or direct quotations from your sources as evidence (15a), or your personal experience or prior knowledge. Keep your ideas central.

- **Consider counterarguments.** Acknowledge the existence of valid opinions that differ from yours, and try to understand them before explaining why they are incorrect or incomplete.

- **Combine your source materials effectively.** Be careful to avoid simply summarizing all of your research. Try to weave the various sources together rather than discussing each of your sources one by one.

Using sources effectively can pose challenges. A national study of first-year college writing found that student writers trying to incorporate research sometimes used sources that were not directly relevant to their point, too specific to support the larger claim being made, or otherwise ineffective. Another study showed that students tend to use sources *only* from the first one or two pages of a source, suggesting that they may not really know how relevant it is. Even after you have evaluated a source, take time to look at how well the source works in your specific situation. (If you change the focus of your work after you have begun doing research, be especially careful to check whether your sources still fit.)

14d Taking notes

While note-taking methods vary from one researcher to another, for each note you should (1) record enough information to help you recall the major points of the source; (2) put the information in the form in which you are most likely to incorporate it into your research project, whether a quotation, summary, or paraphrase; and (3) note all the information you will need to cite the source accurately. Keep a running list that includes citation information for each source in an electronic file or on note cards that you can

rearrange and alter as your project takes shape. This working bibliography will simplify the process of documenting sources for your final project.

Quoting. Quoting involves bringing a source's exact words into your text. Use an author's exact words when the wording is so memorable or expresses a point so well that you cannot improve or shorten it without weakening it, when the author is a respected authority whose opinion supports your ideas, or when an author challenges or disagrees profoundly with others in the field.

- Copy quotations carefully, with punctuation, capitalization, and spelling exactly as in the original.
- Enclose the quotation in quotation marks (39a).
- Use brackets if you introduce words of your own into the quotation or make changes in it (40b). Use ellipses if you omit words from the quotation (40f). If you later incorporate the quotation into

Quotation-Style Note

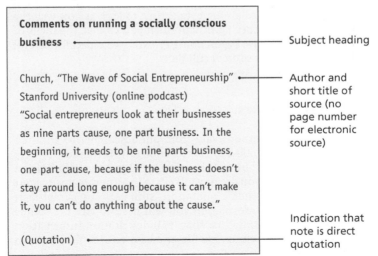

Comments on running a socially conscious business ——— Subject heading

Church, "The Wave of Social Entrepreneurship" ——— Author and short title of source (no page number for electronic source)

Stanford University (online podcast)

"Social entrepreneurs look at their businesses as nine parts cause, one part business. In the beginning, it needs to be nine parts business, one part cause, because if the business doesn't stay around long enough because it can't make it, you can't do anything about the cause."

(Quotation) ——— Indication that note is direct quotation

your research project, copy it from the note precisely, including brackets and ellipses.

- Record the author's name, shortened title of the source, and page number(s) on which the quotation appeared. Make sure you have a corresponding working-bibliography entry with complete source information.

- Label the note with a subject heading, and then identify it as a quotation.

Paraphrasing. When you paraphrase, you're putting brief material from an author (including major and minor points, usually in the order they are presented) into *your own words and sentence structures.* If you wish to cite some of the author's words within the paraphrase, enclose them in quotation marks.

- Include all main points and any important details from the original source in the same order in which the author presents them, but in your own words. Put the original source aside to avoid following the wording too closely.

- If you want to include any language from the original, enclose it in quotation marks.

- Save your comments, elaborations, or reactions for another note.

- Record the author, shortened title, and page number(s), if the source has them, on which the original material appeared.

- Make sure you have a corresponding working-bibliography entry.

- Label the note with a subject heading, and identify it as a paraphrase to avoid confusion with a summary.

- Recheck to be sure that the words and sentence structures are your own and that they express the author's meaning accurately.

The following examples of paraphrases resemble the original material either too little or too much.

ORIGINAL

Language play, the arguments suggest, will help the development of pronunciation ability through its focus on the properties of sounds and sound contrasts, such as rhyming. Playing with

word endings and decoding the syntax of riddles will help the acquisition of grammar. Readiness to play with words and names, to exchange puns and to engage in nonsense talk, promotes links with semantic development. The kinds of dialogue interaction illustrated above are likely to have consequences for the development of conversational skills. And language play, by its nature, also contributes greatly to what in recent years has been called *metalinguistic awareness*, which is turning out to be of critical importance in the development of language skills in general and of literacy skills in particular.

—David Crystal, *Language Play* (180)

UNACCEPTABLE PARAPHRASE: STRAYING FROM THE AUTHOR'S IDEAS

Crystal argues that playing with language—creating rhymes, figuring out how riddles work, making puns, playing with names, using invented words, and so on—helps children figure out a great deal about language, from the basics of pronunciation and grammar to how to carry on a conversation. Increasing their understanding of how language works in turn helps them become more interested in learning new languages and in pursuing education (180).

This paraphrase starts off well enough, but it moves away from paraphrasing the original to inserting the writer's ideas; Crystal says nothing about learning new languages or pursuing education.

UNACCEPTABLE PARAPHRASE: USING THE AUTHOR'S WORDS

Crystal suggests that language play, including rhyme, helps children improve pronunciation ability, that looking at word endings and decoding the syntax of riddles allows them to understand grammar, and that other kinds of dialogue interaction teach conversation. Overall, language play may be of critical importance in the development of language and literacy skills (180).

Because the highlighted phrases are either borrowed from the original without quotation marks or changed only superficially, this paraphrase plagiarizes.

UNACCEPTABLE PARAPHRASE: USING THE AUTHOR'S SENTENCE STRUCTURES

Language play, Crystal suggests, will improve pronunciation by zeroing in on sounds such as rhymes. Having fun with word endings and analyzing riddle structure will help a person acquire grammar. Being prepared to play with language, to use puns and talk nonsense, improves the ability to use semantics. These playful methods of communication are likely to influence a person's ability to talk to others. And language play inherently adds enormously to what has recently been known as *metalinguistic awareness*, a concept of great magnitude in developing speech abilities generally and literacy abilities particularly (180).

Here is a paraphrase of the same passage that expresses the author's ideas accurately and acceptably:

ACCEPTABLE PARAPHRASE: IN THE STUDENT WRITER'S OWN WORDS

Crystal argues that playing with language—creating rhymes, figuring out riddles, making puns, playing with names, using invented words, and so on—helps children figure out a great deal, from the basics of pronunciation and grammar to how to carry on a conversation. This kind of play allows children to understand the overall concept of how language works, a concept that is key to learning to use—and read—language effectively (180).

Summarizing. A summary is a significantly shortened version of a passage or even a whole chapter, article, film, or other work that captures main ideas *in your own words*. Unlike a paraphrase, a summary uses just enough information to record the points you wish to emphasize.

- Put the original aside to write your summary. If you later decide to include language from the original, enclose it in quotation marks.

- Record the author, shortened title, and page number(s) on which the original material appeared. For online or multimedia sources without page numbers, record any information that will help readers find the material.

- Make sure you have a corresponding working-bibliography entry.
- Label the note with a subject heading, and identify it as a summary to avoid confusion with a paraphrase.
- Recheck to be sure you have captured the author's meaning and that the words are entirely your own.

Annotating sources. You can annotate copies or printouts of sources you intend to use with your thoughts and questions as well as highlighting interesting quotations and key terms.

Try not to rely too heavily on copying or printing out whole pieces, however; you still need to read the material very carefully. And resist the temptation to treat copied material as notes, an action that could lead to inadvertent plagiarizing. Using a different color for text pasted from a source will help prevent this problem.

Summary Note

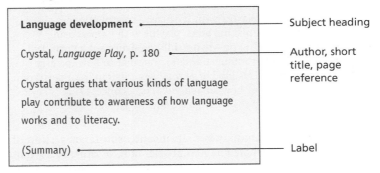

Language development — Subject heading

Crystal, *Language Play*, p. 180 — Author, short title, page reference

Crystal argues that various kinds of language play contribute to awareness of how language works and to literacy.

(Summary) — Label

⊕ *For Multilingual Writers*

Identifying Sources

While some language communities and cultures expect audiences to recognize the sources of important documents and texts, thereby eliminating the need to cite them directly, conventions for writing in North America call for careful attribution of any quoted, paraphrased, or summarized material. When in doubt, explicitly identify your sources.

15 Integrating Sources and Avoiding Plagiarism

In some ways, there is really nothing new under the sun, in writing and research as well as in life. Whatever writing you do has been influenced by what you have already read and experienced. As you work on your research project, you will need to know how to integrate and acknowledge the work of others. And all writers need to understand current definitions of plagiarism (which have changed over time and differ from culture to culture) as well as the concept of intellectual property—those works protected by copyright and other laws—so that they can give credit where credit is due.

15a Integrating quotations, paraphrases, and summaries

Integrate source materials into your writing with care to ensure that the integrated materials make grammatical and logical sense.

Quotations. Because your research project is primarily your own work, limit your use of quotations to those necessary to your thesis or memorable for your readers.

Short quotations should run in with your text, enclosed by quotation marks. Longer quotations should be set off from the text (39a). Integrate all quotations into your text so that they flow smoothly and clearly into the surrounding sentences. Be sure that the sentence containing the quotation is grammatically complete, especially if you incorporate a quotation into your own words.

SIGNAL PHRASES. Introduce the quotation with a signal phrase or signal **verb**, such as those highlighted in these examples.

► As Eudora Welty notes, "Learning stamps you with its moments. Childhood's learning," she continues, "is made up of moments. It isn't steady. It's a pulse" (9).

► In her essay, Haraway strongly opposes those who condemn technology outright, arguing that we must not indulge in a "demonology of technology" (181).

Choose a signal verb that is appropriate to the idea you are express-
ing and that accurately characterizes the author's viewpoint. Other
signal verbs include words such as *acknowledges, agrees, asserts,
believes, claims, concludes, describes, disagrees, lists, objects, offers,
remarks, reports, reveals, says, suggests,* and *writes.*

When you follow the Modern Language Association (MLA) style,
used in the examples in this chapter, put verbs in signal phrases in
the **present tense**. For *Chicago* style, use the present tense (or use
the **past tense** to emphasize a point made in the past).

If you are using American Psychological Association (APA) style
to describe research results, use the past tense or the **present per-
fect tense** (*the study showed, the study has shown*) in your signal
phrase. Use the present tense to explain implications of research
(*for future research, these findings suggest*).

When using the Council of Science Editors (CSE) style, in gen-
eral use the present tense for research reports and the past tense
to describe specific methods or observations, or to cite published
research.

BRACKETS AND ELLIPSES. In direct quotations, enclose in brackets any
words you change or add, and indicate any deletions with ellipsis
points.

▶ "There is something wrong in the [Three Mile Island] area," one
  farmer told the Nuclear Regulatory Commission after the plant
  accident ("Legacy" 33).

▶ Economist John Kenneth Galbraith pointed out that "large
  corporations cannot afford to compete with one another. . . . In
  a truly competitive market someone loses" (Key 17).

Be careful that any changes you make in a quotation do not alter
its meaning. Use brackets and ellipses sparingly; too many make for
difficult reading and might suggest that you have removed some of
the context for the quotation.

Paraphrases and summaries.   Introduce paraphrases and sum-
maries clearly, usually with a signal phrase that includes the author
of the source, as the highlighted words in this example indicate.

▶ Professor of linguistics Deborah Tannen illustrates how communication between women and men breaks down and then suggests that a full awareness of "genderlects" can improve relationships (297).

15b Integrating visuals and media

Choose visuals and media wisely, whether you use video, audio, photographs, illustrations, charts and graphs, or any other kinds of images. Integrate all visuals and media smoothly into your text.

- **Does each visual or media file make a strong contribution to the message?** Purely decorative visuals and media may weaken the power of your writing.
- **Is each fair to your subject?** An obviously biased perspective may seem unfair to your audience.
- **Is each appropriate for your audience?**

While it is considered "fair use" to use such materials in an essay or other project for a college class, once that project is published on the web, you might infringe on copyright protections if you do not ask the copyright holder for permission to use the visual or media file. If you have questions about whether your work might infringe on copyright, ask your instructor for help.

Like quotations, paraphrases, and summaries, visuals and media need to be introduced and commented on in some way.

- Refer to the visual or media element in the text *before* it appears: *As Fig. 3 demonstrates.*
- Explain or comment on the relevance of the visual or media file. This can appear *after* the visual.
- Check the documentation system you are using to make sure you label visual and media elements appropriately; MLA, for instance, asks that you number and title tables and figures (*Table 1: Average Amount of Rainfall by Region*).
- If you are posting your work publicly, make sure you have permission to use any copyrighted visuals.

15c Knowing which sources to acknowledge

As you carry out research, it is important to understand the distinction between materials that require acknowledgment (in in-text citations, footnotes, or endnotes; and in the list of works cited or bibliography) and those that do not.

While you need to prepare accurate and thorough citations in most formal academic assignments, it's also important to understand that much of the writing you do outside of college will not require formal citations. In writing on social media, for example, or even in highly respected newspapers and magazines like the *New York Times* or the *Atlantic*, providing a link is often the only "citation" the authors need. So learn to be flexible: use formal citations when called for in formal college work, and weave in and acknowledge your sources more informally in most out-of-college writing.

Materials that do not require acknowledgment. You do not usually need to cite a source for the following:

- Common knowledge—facts that most readers are already familiar with
- Facts available in a wide variety of sources, such as encyclopedias, almanacs, or textbooks
- Your own findings from field research. You should, however, acknowledge people you interview as individuals rather than as part of a survey.

Materials that require acknowledgment. You should cite all of your other sources to be certain to avoid plagiarism. Follow the documentation style required (see Chapters 45–48), and list the source in a bibliography or list of works cited. Be especially careful to cite the following:

- Sources for quotations, paraphrases, and summaries that you include
- Facts not widely known or arguable assertions
- All visuals from any source, including your own artwork, photographs you have taken, and graphs or tables you create from data found in a source
- Any help provided by a friend, an instructor, or another person

Research: Acknowledging Sources and Avoiding Plagiarism > LearningCurve (2)
Research: Acknowledging Sources and Avoiding Plagiarism > Tutorial

15d Avoiding plagiarism

Academic integrity enables us to trust those sources we use and to demonstrate that our own work is equally trustworthy. Plagiarism is especially damaging to one's academic integrity, whether it involves inaccurate or incomplete acknowledgment of one's sources in citations—sometimes called unintentional plagiarism—or deliberate plagiarism that is intended to pass off one writer's work as another's.

Whether it is intentional or not, plagiarism can have serious consequences. Students who plagiarize may fail the course or be expelled. Others who have plagiarized, even inadvertently, have had degrees revoked or have been stripped of positions or awards.

Unintentional plagiarism. If your paraphrase is too close to the wording or sentence structure of a source (even if you identify the source); if after a quotation you do not identify the source (even if you include the quotation marks); or if you fail to indicate clearly the source of an idea that you did not come up with on your own, you may be accused of plagiarism even if your intent was not to plagiarize. This inaccurate or incomplete acknowledgment of one's sources often results either from carelessness or from not learning how to borrow material properly.

⊕ For Multilingual Writers

Thinking about Plagiarism as a Cultural Concept

Many cultures do not recognize Western notions of plagiarism, which rest on a belief that writers can own their language and ideas. Indeed, in many cultures and communities, using the words and ideas of others without attribution is considered a sign of deep respect as well as an indication of knowledge. In academic writing in the United States, however, you should credit all materials except those that are common knowledge, that are available in a wide variety of sources, or that are your own creations or your own findings from field research.

Take responsibility for your research and for acknowledging all sources accurately. To guard against unintentional plagiarism, photocopy or print out sources and identify the needed quotations right on the copy. You can also insert footnotes or endnotes into the text as you write.

Deliberate plagiarism.   Deliberate plagiarism—such as handing in an essay written by a friend or purchased or downloaded from an essay-writing company; cutting and pasting passages directly from source materials without marking them with quotation marks and acknowledging their sources; failing to credit the source of an idea or concept in your text—is what most people think of when they hear the word *plagiarism.* This form of plagiarism is particularly troubling because it represents dishonesty and deception: those who intentionally plagiarize present someone else's hard work as their own and claim knowledge they really don't have, thus deceiving their readers.

Deliberate plagiarism is also fairly simple to spot: your instructor will be well acquainted with your writing and likely to notice any sudden shifts in the style or quality of your work. In addition, by typing a few words from a project into a search engine, your instructor can identify "matches" very easily.

16 Writing a Research Project

When you are working on a research project, there comes a time to draw the strands of your research together and articulate your conclusions in writing.

16a Drafting your text

Once you have all the information you think you'll need, try arranging your notes and visuals to identify connections, main ideas, and possible organization. You may also want to develop a working outline, a storyboard, or an idea map.

Research: Writing a Research Project > Video Prompt

For almost all research projects, drafting should begin well before the deadline in case you need to gather more information or do more drafting. Begin drafting wherever you feel most confident. If you have an idea for an introduction, begin there.

Working title and introduction. The title and introduction set the stage for what is to come. Ideally, the title announces the subject in an intriguing or memorable way. The introduction should draw readers in and provide any background they will need to understand your discussion.

Conclusion. A good conclusion helps readers know what they have learned. One effective strategy is to begin with a reference to your thesis and then expand to a more general conclusion that reminds readers why your discussion is significant. Try to conclude with something that will have an impact—but avoid sounding preachy.

16b Reviewing and revising a research project

Once you've completed your draft, reread it slowly and carefully. As you do so, reconsider the project's purpose and audience, your stance and thesis, and the evidence you have gathered. Then, ask others to read and respond to your draft. (For more on reviewing and revising, see Chapter 4.)

16c Preparing a list of sources

Once you have a final draft with your source materials in place, you are ready to prepare your list of sources. Create an entry for each source used in your final draft, consulting your notes and working

For Multilingual Writers

Asking Experienced Writers to Review a Thesis

You might find it helpful to ask one or two classmates who have more experience with the particular type of academic writing to look at your explicit thesis. Ask if the thesis is as direct and clear as it can be, and revise accordingly.

bibliography. Then double-check your draft to make sure that you have listed every source mentioned in the in-text citations or notes and that you have omitted any sources not cited in your project. (For guidelines on documentation styles, see Chapters 45–48.)

16d Editing and proofreading

When you have revised your draft, check grammar, usage, spelling, punctuation, and mechanics. Proofread the final version of your project, and carefully consider the advice of spell checkers and grammar checkers before accepting it. (For more information on editing, see 4c.)

Researching Writing
and Literacy
at UCF

Research questions in composition courses at UCF, with a few exceptions, are generally concerned with contextualized instances of writing and literacy. You learn to navigate genres used by particular communities, research how language causes members of communities to interact, and begin to understand how writing (in a broad sense that includes more than just text inscription) has shaped your own experience of the world around you. When beginning to ask research questions about writing and literacy, observations of your own writing practices and experiences can help you find your research foundation.

Once you've established a useful research question, it's time to start considering how to answer it. This section on researching writing and literacy, designed especially for First-Year Writing students at the University of Central Florida, will explore primary and secondary research methods to help you conduct successful, academic research. Note that all student work referenced throughout the pages that follow can be read in full, in a previous issue of *Stylus*, at **writingandrhetoric.cah.ucf.edu/stylus/issues.php**.

A   Choosing primary and secondary sources

To respond to any research question, a writer must collect evidence to prove or disprove a hypothesis or to support a claim. Once you have identified a solid research question, you must decide whether you need to collect *primary* and/or *secondary sources* to support your research aims.

Writers can choose from among several types of sources to support their research. When considering sources to support an argument, writers must study them for information that can serve as specific *evidence* to address aspects of their claims, all the while keeping their target audience in mind. What kind of evidence will likely be convincing to the target audience? If researchers are reviewing the existing literature on a topic or are trying to understand what has already been written about an issue before conducting a study of their own, they must search for sources that provide information about the ongoing conversation concerning that topic or issue. Then the researchers might collect data to answer a clearly defined research question that has grown out of reading those sources.

"**Choosing primary and secondary sources,**" and "**An Insider's View,**" from Susan Miller-Cochran, Roy Stamper, and Stacey Cochran's *An Insider's Guide to Academic Writing: A Brief Rhetoric*, pp. 60–62. Copyright © 2016 by Bedford/St. Martin's.

An Insider's View: Primary Research in Writing Studies

Moriah McCracken, Writing Studies

"I like to try to introduce my students to qualitative research in their first year, when our students have to interview a professor. sometimes I'll help them develop survey questions and question-naires so they can have that kind of experience, and I'll teach them about double-entry notebooks so they can do some observations in the classroom. I like to bring in qualitative methods so that students realize there are different kinds of questions to ask, and depending on my question, I'm going to have to try something a little bit different and learn how to do this kind of research in my discipline."

Primary sources include the results of data that researchers might collect on their own. If you're making a claim about how to interpret a work of art and you've studied the piece carefully for images and symbols that you discuss in your argument, then the work of art is your primary source. Or perhaps you've designed and conducted a survey of people's experiences with a particular phenomenon. In this case, the results you've gathered from your survey are a primary source from which you can provide evidence to answer a research question or support an argument. Other forms of primary sources include original historical documents and results from interviews you may have conducted.

Based on the scope of your argument and the expectations of your audience, you may also need to engage **secondary sources**, or research collected by and/or commented on by others. Let's say that your literature professor wants you to offer an interpretation of a poem. You study the poem carefully as your primary source and arrive at a conclusion or claim about the work. But imagine that the assignment also requires you to use scholarly opinions to support your own position or interpretation. As a result, you spend time in the library or searching online databases to locate articles or books by scholars who provide their own interpretations or perspectives on the poem. The articles or books you rely on to support your inter-pretation are secondary sources because the interpretations were developed by others, commenting on the poem. Likewise, if you cite

as part of your own argument the results of a survey published in an academic article, then that article serves as a secondary source of information to you. Other secondary sources include newspapers and magazines, textbooks, and encyclopedias. Many of the researched arguments you'll produce in college will require you to use both primary and secondary sources as support.

B Determining primary research methods

Your research should be inquiry-driven. Therefore, the primary research you conduct should be responsive to your questions. Making a decision about what type of primary research data to gather should not be an arbitrary choice. Think about the questions you are trying to answer, and select the research methods that are best suited to answering those questions. Do you want to see an in-depth profile of a particular type of writer's process? Case study, which will be discussed below, seems like an appropriate research method. But taking a survey of many people seems less appropriate to the task. Selecting the right research methods means having a clear understanding of what answers you seek. The following sections lay out some possible primary research methods that you might use when researching writing, literacy, or several other areas of study.

Ethnography. The root "ethno" means "people" or "culture." Combined with "graphy," which means a "description or image," ethnography can be thought of as a description of a group of people or culture in context. **Ethnography** is founded on the idea that the best way to get a full understanding of how people interact is to actually observe groups of people in their environment. This should be done without being intrusive, and often, ethnography is carried out when the researcher is a member of the group being studied. (We call this participant observation.) In writing studies, we use ethnography as a way of understanding how writing functions in a community and how communication serves to trigger interactions between people. A researcher may have some hypotheses about what they will find while observing the group, but generally, the observation will dictate the results of the study. You might not

have a clear idea of what you will find in observation. But you will leave the observation with a great deal more knowledge than you had previously. Ethnography can help writing studies scholars:

- Identify how texts and text genres operate in the environment
- Identify how individuals communicate around texts in the environment
- Identify how individuals gain, maintain, and assert authority through communication in the environment
- Identify how any other element in the situation impacts writing or literacy

In a research essay written for Composition I, "The Game within the Games: The Behaviors, Language, and Virtual Norms of *Rune-Scape*," UCF student writer Matthew Ceriale uses an ethnographic approach to interrogate how the jargon of online game players is attached to social norms and behaviors in the *Runescape* environment. By combining a thorough analysis of the genres of the *Runescape* community, observation of community members playing the game, and interviews with community members, Ceriale traces patterns in language that indicate particular types of community behaviors. Matthew's study was published in the Spring 2013 issue of *Stylus*.

Case studies.   **Case studies** are similar to ethnographic studies in that both approachs are interested in ascertaining a clear picture of peoples' writing in context. But while ethnography seeks to obtain a picture of a whole writing community or environment, case study attempts to understand a specific activity or the actions of an individual. In writing studies, we use case studies to gain thorough insight into how, why, and when an individual writes or performs some particular activity. Case studies involve observing an individual in context and describing what is observed. A key element of successful case studies is the use of extensive interviews that seek out in-depth understanding of the participants' writing history and activity. Case studies can help writing studies scholars understand:

- How an individual's environment or community leads them to write and communicate

- How an individual's writing history contributes to their writing behaviors or identity

Student writer Camilla Perez successfully uses case study with three participants in "'Spanglish' and Its Effects on L1 and L2," written for Composition II. The well-planned case study, which was published in the Spring 2013 Knights Write Showcase special issue of *Stylus*, looks closely at the participants' history of language and writing through hour-long interviews, observation, and analysis of their responses to a writing prompt. Use the resulting data, Camilla argues that "Spanglish" is a third language that develops as students attempt to assimilate English as a second language.

Surveys.   **Surveys** are used in a variety of fields in order to obtain a clear understanding of trends in large populations. Surveys are commonly used in writing studies when attempting to gain insight into the writing habits of many writers in an environment. If attempting to draw some conclusions about all First-Year Writing students at UCF, it might make sense to survey a representative sample of those students, if access to all of them is unavailable. Smaller sample surveys allow you to trace tentative trends toward useful questions that you or other researcher can answer. When composing a survey, it's important to identify the exact population you want to participate and make any assumptions of the survey clear in the written results. Writing studies scholars use surveys to:

- Understand the perspectives of multiple writers
- Explore the impact of a particular writing environment, prompt, or class on several writers
- Trace trends in writing perspectives that can lead to questions requiring more in-depth analysis

In a Compostion II essay, "Preparing to Be a Doctor in High School: A Study of Underrepresented Pre-Medical Students' Gains from Advanced Placement (AP) courses," Sara Bolivar Wagers deployed a survey to several fellow UCF students majoring in science fields.

By limiting her focus to science-related majors and identifying success rates of underrepresented student populations in AP courses, Wagers was able to conduct a follow-up focus group that

helped answer more complex questions. She concluded that success in AP chemistry and biology courses was not the only predetermining factor in students' success in science majors at UCF. Her entire study can be found in the Spring 2014 Knights Write Showcase special issue of *Stylus*.

Archival research.   **Archival research** engages scholars in the use of physical or digital library archives for the purpose of developing a historical perspective that can inform our understanding of current developments on a research subject. In writing studies, archival research is often used to understand trends in writing and course history; it is also often used as a means of tracing histories through written documents by performing textual analysis on them as "rhetorical artifacts." News clippings, photographs, pamphlets, memos, and messages are just a few of the many rhetorical artifacts that can be analyzed when performing archival research. Writing studies scholars use archival research in order to:

- Trace the historical development of writing procedures in a particular context or environment and understand the history's influence on the present
- Trace the development of a location or population, or the history of a culture, through textual analysis of historical documents referred to as rhetorical artifacts

In his Composition II study, "A Historical Approach to the Progression of LGBTQ Treatment and Acceptance at the University of Central Florida," Jacob Smith uses the John C. Hitt collection in the UCF library archives to gain a historical perspective on the University's acceptance of the lesbian, gay, bisexual, transsexual, and questioning community on campus. Through analysis of several historical documents, including a newcomer packet distributed to members of the 1994 Gay, Lesbian, and Bisexual Student Union, Smith concludes that the UCF community was, largely, ahead of national trends in acceptance of the LGBTQ community. His full study can be read in the Spring 2014 issue of *Stylus*.

Textual analysis.   **Textual analysis** is the breaking down of a particular text in order to ascertain its underlying themes,

Contributions for **"Archival research"** by Marcy Galbreath, University of Central Florida.

motivations, purposes, and rhetorical impact. Specifically, textual analysis interrogates specific passages or portions of texts in order to determine their meaning in an identified context. Textual analysis is at the heart of writing studies scholarship, and many of the other primary research methods covered here require some use of textual analysis.

Some of us first became familiar with textual analysis in high school, by performing literary analysis, where we try to draw conclusions about the themes of a novel. Textual analysis in writing studies does not necessarily require that the objects of study be literature (e.g., poems, novels, short stories, and so on)—though it certainly can interrogate such genres. Textual analysis tries to understand a subject text as it is situated in a cultural, environmental, or community context. The types of texts that can be analyzed are limitless (and can include non-print objects), but the aim is to try to understand how and why a text came to exist in the way that it did. Here are just a few of the phenomena that writing scholars use textual analysis to understand:

- The ideological motivations of a text
- The impact of a text on a given audience
- The narrative themes of a text and their impact
- The power relationships between the author of a text and its readers
- How a text is contextualized within a community or context
- How a text helps to shape community and group communication standards
- How a text initiates particular types of conversations

In her Composition I study "Exploiting the American Dream: The Political Rhetoric of Julian Castro," Katelyn Van De Water textually analyzes San Antonio Mayor Julian Castro's speech from the 2012 Democratic National Convention. Van De Water pulls particular passages from Castro's speech that illustrate him drawing on the theme of the "American Dream" (shared by the audience) in order to promote the presidential candidacy of Barack Obama and discredit that of Mitt Romney. Her full study can be found in the Fall 2013 issue of *Stylus*.

Three specific types of textual analysis—**rhetorical analysis, genre analysis**, and **multimodal textual analysis**—are often used by writing and literacy scholars, and are explored in greater detail below.

RHETORICAL ANALYSIS. Writing and literacy scholars often seek to discover why a particular argument was structured or delivered in a specific way. Rhetorical analysis allows researchers in many disciplines to find the motivations for and impact of a piece of discourse on its audience. When using the method, researchers look closely at both the text and the real-world environment (e.g., the time, place, institution) in which the text was written. These observations help the researcher understand how the purpose, writer/speaker (sometimes referred to as the *rhetor*), audience, and environment influenced the construction of the argument and its intended or unintended effects. We often call this placing a text in its *rhetorical situation*. Writing and rhetoric scholars use rhetorical analysis to:

- Discover the motivations of a writer/speaker
- Understand why a writer/speaker made particular language choices
- Determine how the environment surrounding a text assisted or inhibited the writer/speaker from achieving his/her intended goals
- Interrogate how a writer/speaker and audience negotiate what is considered effective language in the environment
- Understand how audiences are likely to react to a particular argument

In a Composition I essay titled "Intertextuality and Understanding Dave Chappelle's Comedy," David Galvez uses effective rhetorical analysis to ask why a particular skit performed by the comedian was effective as a comic text. Galvez argues that Chappelle's comedic depiction of President George W. Bush at the U.N. was effective because it took into account his audience's perspectives—their disagreement with Bush's policies and their affiliation with African American culture. David's full study was published in the Spring 2011 issue of *Stylus*.

GENRE ANALYSIS.   In the context of writing studies, genres are texts that are distinguished by their repeated and predictable characteristics and that arise in separate but similar rhetorical situations. Genre analysis tends to give additional attention to formatting and structural features that is not always present in rhetorical analysis. If you were to picture a syllabus, for example, and describe what it looks like and what kind of information it contains, what would you point out? You would probably say that syllabi tend to include the name of the course, contact information for the professor, a course calendar, a grading scale, and so on. Over and over again, instructors follow this format for the purposes of preparing students for class. "The syllabus" is a textual genre with repeated and predictable characteristics. You know what's coming even before you receive it.

Beyond structure, genre analysis leads to real-world actions and conversations that have important effects on the community's environment. You can probably list several actions you take after reading a syllabus, for example. When writing scholars perform genre analysis, they look for repeated features across a genre and attempt to determine the motivation and function of their use in similar (or varying) ways. Looking closely at genres can help us see how communities deploy discourse and communication in accordance with goals, values, and beliefs. Writing and rhetoric scholars use genre analysis to:

- Understand the complex ways in which communities use texts to communicate among members
- Understand how communities use texts to recruit new members
- Understand how communities use language to represent their values to community members and non-community members
- Understand how communities characterize the world around them and why
- Understand how communities achieve their goals

In a Composition II study titled "The Genres of Chi Omega: An Activity Analysis," Victoria Marro analyzed the genres employed by Chi Omega, including a national magazine, chapter newsletters, announcements, chapter websites, and rule books. With text-based interviews, Marro was able to place each of the genres into the

varying contexts of different chapters of Chi Omega. She found that each chapter used different genres based on their particular needs and context. No matter the genres, however, each chapter used their texts to mediate goals shared across *all* chapters of the Chi Omega community. Victoria's full study can be found in the Spring 2012 issue of *Stylus*.

MULTIMODAL TEXT ANALYSIS. As digital technologies have developed, it has become increasingly necessary for writing scholars to recognize the multimodal nature of texts when considering how they function within communities and contexts. Multimodal text analysis is the process of textual analysis that questions how textual, visual, auditory, and other text elements operate to deliver messages and meaning. In the screenshot below, you can see, for example, how one might interrogate a website. Annotations highlight questions related to the textual features of a digital publication, the Department of Writing and Rhetoric's website.

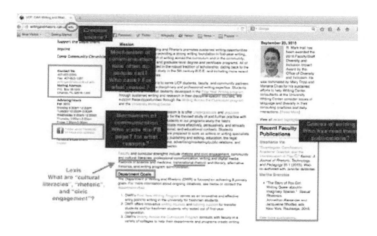

Skills in reading multimodal genres are also used in analysis. For example, the credibility of a web page may also be determined by its URL. Multimodal text analysis allows writing and rhetoric scholars to:

Contributions for **"Multimodal text analysis"** by Yumani Davis, University of Central Florida.

- Understand the relationship between visual, textual, and auditory, features of a text, and how those features mediate the author's message
- Understand how audiences of a multimodal text are likely to react to its features
- Understand how various mechanisms of communication are deployed in context
- Understand how rhetors use digital technologies to effectively or ineffectively persuade audiences

In a Composition II study, "Looking Through the Semiotic Lens: Rhetorical Sponsors of Civic Engagement in Cyberpublics," Paige Preston analyzes three blogs of varying content, *Humans of New York*, *Dress Profesh*, and *Blue Velvet: Re-dressing New Orleans in Katrina's Wake*, in order to understand their use of rhetoric to promote civic engagement by their readers. She successfully interrogates the textual and visual elements of the blogs in order to determine that they all promote civic awareness and engagement in online spaces also known as cyberpublics. According to Preston, each blog uses rhetoric to undermine "entrenched, social truths." Her full study can be found in the Fall 2015 issue of *Stylus*.

Interviews

Interviews are often conducted in conjunction with several of the other primary research methods detailed here. Writing studies scholars use interviews for a variety of purposes: to learn about participants' histories and experiences with writing, to learn from insiders how writing works in communities, to learn how writers encounter and engage in specific texts and their processes, and to learn about complex and unseen activities that writers bring to literacy and that may not be apparent without talking directly to the practitioner. Interviewing participants can be rewarding because you learn how writing works and has been experienced from an emic perspective—that is, from the perspective of an insider, or the person with the experience—rather than relying on outside observation. Choose

interviewing as your research method if you seek insider (emic) knowledge of the phenomena being studied.

There are two typical types of interviews and interview questions: structured and semi-structured. **Structured interviews** are those where the interviewers do not deviate from a pre-written set of questions. **Semi-structured interviews** are those where predetermined questions and topics serve more to guide than rule the conversation. The interviewer ask questions, listens attentively to areas of importance, and asks pertinent follow-up questions. In this scenario, the interviewer often follows the interviewee's lead in terms of content while also using any pre-written questions as a touchstone.

A researcher will choose structured or semi-structured interviews. They will also choose open- or closed-ended questions. Open-ended questions can draw out a participants' experiences or stories, as well as a personal or community schema for how writing works or has worked for them. Open-ended questions invite explanation, detail, and context and avoid *yeses*, *nos*, or clearly defined responses. The **literacy history interview** is common in writing studies research, as researchers often seek to understand a writer's past and how it has come to affect his or her present. Open-ended questions about moments of change and challenge in literacy history might look like the following:

- Can you tell me about any of writing that was a new kind of meaning for you?
- How was it different from or similar to writing you have done in the past?
- What challenges have you experienced learning to read and write here?
- Why do you think those experiences where challenging?
- How have you tried to solve or overcome those challenges?

Researchers interested in literacy history can also ask closed-ended questions that are similarly useful. These tend to seek specific answers. For instance:

- What languages did you speak at home growing up?
- What sorts of schools did you attend?

- What kinds of writing and reading do you do in your classes (both for assignments and self-initiated, like notes)?

For a useful example of how to effectively use both open- and closed-ended interview questions in order to answer complex research questions, see Yadilex Ali's "The Shift in Parental Literacy Sponsorship and Its Value According to the Children of Immigrants," which can be found in the Fall 2015 volume of *Stylus*. Ali uses interviews in her case study of three children of immigrants in order to understand how their various personal experiences led to different types of experiences with reading and writing. She interrogates her participants' responses in order to draw complex conclusions about the relationship between immigrant parents and their children as students. Take a look at Ali's interview questions and see the range of open- and closed-ended questions that all work in service of her overall goal: to learn about the impacts of migration on literacy sponsorship. As you can see, she uses a mix of questions:

- Tell me a little about where your parents are from and their journey to America. (*open*)
- Describe how your parents influenced your development and experience learning to read and write. (*open*)
- Did you teach yourself? More than your parents taught you? Why? If so, what materials did you use? (*closed*)
- What economic class do you think your parents belonged to upon arriving in America? (*closed*)
- How to do believe your parents' income affected your reading and writing skills (e.g., in terms of buying educational games, books, CDs, and so on)? (*open*)

While literacy history interviews are common in writing Studies, **text-based interviews** can also be very useful to help writess focus on an artifact at hand and interrogate specifics about the histories and current or future uses of a specific text. **Text-based interviews** are a useful subset of the interview method. As writing studies scholars, we try to discover the value, purposes, and composing history of a text situated in a context. Sometimes we are able to ascertain this through textual analysis, ethnographic observation, or other methods. But, it can also be very useful ask the author or users of a text questions about its uses, purposes, and development. You might ask

your research participant(s) some of the following questions* after reading the collected text:

- What function or purpose does this text serve? What work does it do?
- Who created this text? Who uses this text, and what do they use it for?
- What can you tell me about how this text was created?
- What kinds of talk occur when people use this text?
- How long have you been using these kinds of texts?
- How did you learn to use this text and other texts like it?
- Where is this text kept?
- How many different people have likely seen this text?
- What kinds of technologies were used in the production and use of this text?
- Does this text get used in conjunction with other kinds of texts? If so, which ones?
- Does this text lead to other kinds of texts? If so, which ones?

In her essay "Fanfiction, Poetry, Blogs, and Journals: A Case Study of the Connection between Extracurricular and Academic Writings," Marissa Penzato challenges some of the conclusions drawn by professional writing studies scholar Nancy Sommers regarding the inexperience of student writers. To support her claim that student writing processes are more complicated than Sommers outlines, Penzato performs case studies with four fanfiction writers, reading several examples of her case study participants' fanfiction, blogs, and poetry. After developing questions based on her reading, she interviewed her participants based on their texts. By asking participants how their texts developed, Penzato links their writing experiences to their writing processes and identities. Her full study can be read in the Spring 2012 issue of *Stylus*.

C Tracing patterns in primary research data

Now that you've successfully conducted your primary research with one of these methods, it's time to make sense of the resulting data. In

*Developed by Professor Kevin Roozen.

qualitative research, we call things like interview responses, texts that you analyze, and observations of communities "data," even though they are not quantifiable. At the end of your research, the amount of data you have may be somewhat daunting. So how do you make sense of all of this? The following section on looking for themes in primary data, adapted Mansfield from Gery W. Ryan and H. Russell Bernard, will help you get started.

Looking for "themes" or recurring ideas in primary, qualitative data

1. **Look for repeating words and phrases.** If a word or phrase shows up many times in your interview or observation data, take note of it. Count how many times it surfaces. The fact that the word or phrase is used frequently might suggest that it is important. The word might also summarize a key idea. Be sure to note synonyms of the word or phrase. If the repeated word is "power," for example, pay attention to words like "authority," too.

2. **Pay attention to "indigenous categories."** Indigenous words are "local terms that may sound unfamiliar or are used in unfamiliar ways." (They are similar to the specialized vocabulary of a particular group, or "lexis.") In addition to noting these unique words, pay attention to how they are used and how they are organized into the group's vocabulary. (Are there multiple versions of the same word? What versions of words are used most often?)

3. **Note Key Words in Context (KWICs).** Similar to the two steps listed above, be sure to note not only key words a group uses, but also *how* those words are used. According to Gery W. Ryan and H. Russell Bernard, "if you want to understand a concept, then look at how it is used. In this technique, researchers identify key words and then systematically search the . . . text to find all instances of the word or phrase. Each time they find a word, they make a copy of it and its immediate context. Themes get identified by physically sorting the examples into piles of similar meaning."

Contributions for **"Tracing patterns in primary research data"** by Lissa Pompos Mansfield, University of Central Florida; **"Looking for 'themes' or recurring ideas in primary, qualitative data"** adapted from Gery W. Ryan and H. Russell Bernard's "Techniques to Identify Themes in Qualitative Data," http://www.analytictech.com/mb870/readings /ryan-bernard_techniques_to_identify_themes_in.htm.

4. **Compare and contrast texts.** Try "interviewing" (or asking questions about) your text by studying each line of your transcript or notes separately. Then, compare the previous line to the next line. Some questions to keep in mind while you are studying each line/note: "What is this [line/sentence/note/statement] about?" "How does it differ from the preceding or following statements?" "What kinds of things [like ideas or key words] are mentioned in both?" and "What does [this statement] remind me of [based on other things I have read]?"

5. **Approach the data like a social scientist.** Pay attention to things like "evidence of social conflict, cultural contradictions, informal methods of social control, things that people do in managing impersonal social relationships, methods by which people acquire and maintain achieved and ascribed status, and information about how people solve problems." Also, note the setting and context of your observations, the perspectives of the people you interview and

Advice for Visualizing Your Themes

▶ **Mark up your texts.** Use highlighters, underlining, and other "marking" tools to help you note important pieces of data or passages of text .

▶ **Scan (or "eyeball") texts to see what stands out.** Oftentimes, the most prominent words or features of a document also hint at the main ideas of a text .

▶ **Cut, sort, and reassemble.** When you know that certain pieces of data (such as a quote or a note) are important, but you don't know how these pieces fit into the "big picture" of your theme, cut them into separate pieces . Then, look at all your pieces separately and try to group them together based on similar ideas or features . When you have these groups, determine what each piece in the group has in common with the other pieces and why this commonality might be important . These large groups might give you some hints at the larger "theme."

observe, and their ways of thinking about "people, objects, processes, activities, events, and relationships."

6. **Search for missing information.** What is *not* mentioned in your data? Is something absent, and why might that be the case? Sometimes, the fact that people *don't* discuss something hints at its importance. Also, absences in your data can point to assumptions the person/group makes. (For example, the president of an organization might not state the reasons for taking a specific action because he/she assumes that all other members of the group already know those reasons.)

7. **Decipher metaphors and analogies.** Look for examples of when the person/ group describes a concept in terms of a metaphor, analogy, or simile. This is a common way for people to relate their thoughts, behaviors, or feelings about an experience to some other idea. If a metaphor is used, determine the meaning of the comparison. For example, if your interviewee says "our group works like a well-oiled machine," they are comparing the group to an object that has connotations of labor/work, power, and other ideas.

8. **Look at transitions between ideas.** In both written and oral communication, writers/speakers take turns communicating and often mark their progression between ideas with words like "so," "now," "then," "next," "also," "in addition," "because," and so on. According to Ryan and Bernard, "In written texts, new paragraphs are often used by authors to indicate either subtle or abrupt shifts in topics. In oral speech, pauses, change in tone, or particular phrases may indicate thematic transitions." Paying attention to transitions might help you to see how talk is divided between participants, how ideas and topics change over time, and so on.

9. **Look at connectors.** Pay attention to words or phrases that "indicate relationships among things." If there is a causal (i.e., cause and effect) relationship between ideas, words like "because," "since," and "as a result" might be used. If there is a conditional (if/then) relationship between ideas, words like "if," "then," "rather than," and "instead of" might be used. If there is a chronological relationship between ideas, words like "before," "after," "then," and "next" might be used.

Tips for Academic Research

▶ Research typically begins with a research question, which establishes the purpose and scope of a project. As you develop research questions, keep in mind the following evaluative criteria: personal investment, debatable subject, researchable issue, feasibility, and contribution.

▶ A researcher who has established a clear focus for her research, or who has generated a claim, must decide on the kinds of sources needed to support the research focus: primary, secondary, or both.

▶ While both scholarly and popular sources may be appropriate sources of evidence in differing contexts, be sure to understand what distinguishes these types of sources so that you can choose evidence types purposefully.

▶ Primary sources are the results of data that researchers might collect on their own. These results could include data from surveys, interviews, or questionnaires. Secondary sources include research collected by and/or commented on by others. These might include information taken from newspaper articles, magazines, scholarly journal articles, and scholarly books, to name a few.

▶ Keep in mind that as you do research, you will likely have cause to refine your search terms. This process involves carefully selecting or narrowing the terms you use to locate information via search engines or databases.

▶ Be aware of the challenges of conducting basic searches for sources via internet search engines like Google. While Google Scholar may be a better means of searching for sources in the academic context, researchers often rely on more specialized research databases.

▶ Peer-reviewed academic journals are an excellent source of information for academic arguments. The publication process for journal articles is typically much shorter than for books, so using journal articles allows you access to the most current research.

(continues on next page)

Tips for Academic Research, *continued*

▶ Be aware of the strategies you can use to integrate the ideas of others into your own writing: summarizing, paraphrasing, and/ or quoting.

▶ When you integrate the words or ideas of others, take care to ensure that you are documenting their words and ideas carefully to avoid instances of plagiarism, and make sure you understand what constitutes plagiarism at your institution and/or in your individual classes. Follow appropriate rules for documenting your sources and constructing a bibliography. in academic contexts, this often means using MLA, APA, or CSE documentation systems.

D An annotated student essay

The culmination of research is the scholarly research article or essay. In UCF composition courses, students use the primary data and secondary sources they have gathered in order to make an effective argument that contributes to an academic conversation. On the following page, you will find Tiffany Gagnon's "The Disinhibition of Reddit Users." Gagnon uses both primary and secondary research to make an effective argument about the environmental and community factors that lead to Reddit user disinhibition when communicating online. The text has been annotated—pay close attention to the comments in the margins; these point out the effective use of primary and secondary research data that Gagnon uses in her essay. Note that, although Tiffany's essay was originally composed in 2013, citations have been updated to reflect the latest MLA documentation guidelines (2016).

Tiffany Gagnon

Adele Richardson

ENC 1102

Spring 2013

The Disinhibition of Reddit Users

Introduction

    There has been much research on the effects of anonymity in online communities and the disinhibition of its users. People experiencing online disinhibition act differently online than they would in offline settings (Chester and O'Hara 195, 197, 200-01; Lee 3; Suler "The Online" 321-24). Benign online disinhibition is characterized by the revealing of personal thoughts and showing unusual kindness (Suler "The Online" 321). Toxic online disinhibition describes disinhibited, harmful behavior that likely would not occur offline life (Lapidot-Lefler and Barak 434; Suler "The Online" 321). Disinhibited users are unlikely to "maintain accountability of identity"; however, it should be noted that disinhibition "does not necessarily lead to deceptive, dishonest, and fraudulent behavior" (Lee 3).

    Researchers recognize dissociative anonymity (a resistance to attach to offline identity) as the foundation of online disinhibition. It results in decreased feelings of vulnerability and increased self-disclosure and acting out (Lapidot-Lefler and Barak 435; Suler "The Online" 322). Noam Lapidot-Lefler and Azy Barak define anonymity as an "unidentifiability aspect. . . rather than namelessness," encompassing the concepts of pseudonymity and the withholding of identifying information (Lapidot-Lefler and Barak 435, 440-42). On another note, users that were surveyed in anonymous online communities feel that anonymity contributes to negativity found in the forums, but a majority of users still support anonymity because they feel that it leads to more lively discussion (Rosenberry 12-13).

Notice how Gagnon attributes this concept *to multiple authors using a string citation. Doing so shows readers that the concept is generally accepted by the field and that it can operate as a starting point for the academic conversation.*

Using secondary sources effectively can mean placing ideas from authors in relation to each other. Gagnon associates two concepts *as opposite categories of disinhibition, providing a fuller conception of the term for her readers. Throughout her introduction, Gagnon will continue to borrow ideas from various authors in a way that creatively frames her research.*

Introduction sections establish the context for an essay. Sometimes, as in the case of Gagnon's text, they also review relevant secondary sources that will be used to support the author's argument. Other times, this review of sources is deployed in another section called the "Literature Review."

Invisibility is the inability to see physical responses from others while online that would ordinarily affect what people were to express in face-to-face settings (Lapidot-Lefler and Barak 435-36; Suler "The Online" 322-23). Asynchronicity also plays a role. When conversations are easily left and returned to, people do not have to deal with other's immediate responses (Suler "The Online" 322-23).

Rhetorical awareness is comprehension of one's purpose, motivations, audience, and the constraints on presenting discourse (Gee 489-90; Grant-Davie 106-11). The motivation is known as exigence; the rhetors are responsible for the discourse; the audience is who the discourse is intended for; and constraints are factors that hinder or help the discourse (Grant Davie 106-11). People recognize places of open online communication and may reveal private information even though they are aware of its public nature (Lee 3). James Paul Gee discusses metaknowledge in a rhetorical situation, "the ability to manipulate, analyze, [and] to resist while advancing" in the community, indicating rhetorical awareness and an understanding of a community's functions in order to advance within it (Gee 489-90).

People take on an identity in an environment usually by showing favorable parts of their personality (Suler "Identity" 457-58; Wardle 524-25). They can make the choice of who they are and may use this power towards self-actualization by practicing positive personality characteristics, while others may take on a harmful identity (Suler "Identity" 457-58). There are also users who want to "receive and not show too much" by engaging in lurking behaviors by simply observing the community (Suler "Identity" 456, 459). Elizabeth Wardle argues that users construct their identities through their rhetorical choices, writing in ways that are appropriate in the community to help establish a positive social identity (Wardle 525).

Suler and Grant-Davie have done excellent jobs at explaining online disinhibition and rhetorical situation, respectively, and there

---

Many UCF composition students are required to frame their own research interests in the context of writing and rhetoric studies. The key is to make sure that this framing is a clear foundation of the research. Gagnon will draw on Gee, Grant-Davie, and Wardle, all authors usually assigned in UCF composition courses, to clearly position her argument as one that is valuable to writing and rhetoric scholars. The essay isn't just a report on disinhibition, but how anonymity online leads to rhetorical choices by disinhibited Reddit users.

This is one of Gagnon's most important paragraphs. She first establishes what work has been accomplished by previous scholars. Then, she positions her own essay as an extension of these authors' ideas by situating her research in the particular context of Reddit. Remember, academic writers need to clearly be engaged in academic conversations. Here, Gagnon shows she has listened to what others have said about disinhibition and rhetoric and will now argue for her own, new position.

Gagnon 3

have been many studies conducted to explain the disinhibition in different communities. However, I would like to build on these studies with my own on the disinhibition of users within a popular social media website: Reddit. My research focuses on the evidence of online disinhibition displayed in posted content resulting from the anonymity of Reddit users.

Methodology

As a Reddit visitor for two years, I am quite familiar with the site and believed that this environment could be valuable to the discussion on online disinhibition. To observe Reddit for the presence of this effect, I developed the following research question:

How do Reddit's users embrace and take advantage of their anonymity within the site?

From there, my research took on the role of digital discourse community ethnography, and comprehending the basic workings of Reddit is crucial to understanding how users can interact on the site.

This social media site is coined "the front page of the Internet." Current news and entertainment found on the web quickly end up on Reddit. The site functions through its registered users who submit content while others vote to rank how high it appears on the page. Registered users can also leave comments on posts. Anyone can access Reddit, but only the registered users may submit, comment, and vote. They can also create and subscribe to subreddits—sub-communities—of Reddit that discuss a specific topic. Registration does not require any information about offline identity.

I observed popular subreddits as well as the discussion surrounding controversial topics involving Reddit. I used notecards to record my observations and bookmarked links back to my observed content's original source. Data was collected over a two-week period from topics on Reddit and comment threads. Several comments from

The methodology section of a scholarly essay is where the author details his/her primary research methods so that they can be scrutinized and possibly replicated.

Gagnon's research question is contextualized, answerable, and potentially valuable to other writing and rhetoric scholars.

Which of the primary research methods described in section B involves the observation of people in a community with as little impact on the community as possible? Ethnography! Gagnon uses ethnographic research in order to collect important data for her argument.

Gagnon 4

users were recorded; however, usernames were not recorded for the sake of privacy.

I did note if a user was clearly using a "throwaway" account, an account created to dissociate a comment from one's usual Reddit username. I determined a throwaway account from a main account by these criteria:

1. The account history contains only the comment related to it.
2. The username contains the word "throwaway" or is directly related to the content of the observed comment.

Gagnon reveals her additional use of case study methods to offer readers an in-depth look at this famous Reddit user.

For a section of my study, I focus on one user in particular: Michael Brutsch, pseudonym *violentacrez*, because of his harmful behavior on Reddit that became known to the offline public. He is not currently an active member of Reddit, as he was banned last year, but he has he had a lasting impact on the community.

I examined my data for instances of online disinhibition. I considered the factors that are playing a role in the disinhibition that Reddit users can experience. I recognized the rhetorical situations of individual content by considering what subreddit the content had been posted in, its purpose, and the audience. My presence during discussion was not known; therefore, it was not possible for users to feel a need to adjust their behavior as a result of my observation.

Results and Discussion

Ask Reddit: Spill Your Life to Strangers

The subreddit *Ask Reddit* is a community where users may pose thought-provoking questions to discuss. While observing some of the top discussions, I found this very popular topic: "Throwaway time! What's your secret that could literally ruin your life if it came out?" "Throwaway" refers to the "throwaway accounts" I described. The following are responses to this thread written under throwaway accounts:

Gagnon 5

1. "I once helped out my female friend's family by taking care of their cat for a week. . . I would snoop around their house. I found my friend's diary, and read the entire thing. I used this information to get her to like me, and she is currently my wife."

2. "When I was 13, I was molested by a guy who dragged me into an alley. . . . My friend doesn't believe me. I've never told anyone because I don't want them to react the way my 'friend' did."

3. "I faked the last two years of college."

4. "Everyone thinks I have a good job and roommates but I've been homeless and a prostitute for over a year."

These Reddit users are using this confession thread as a place to share secrets that are weighing on them. Throwaway accounts are an example of a Reddit user's power over their anonymity. They can make the choice to dissociate from their Reddit identity further by simply using an alternate pseudonym and then leaving it behind. This dissociative anonymity allows them to feel more willing to self-disclose with the community (Suler "The Online" 322). They can share their secret and walk away from any further discussion, as the conversation is asynchronous. No immediate reactions from others have to be dealt with, and the conversation can be resumed whenever the user decides, if at all (Suler "The Online" 322- 23). For instance, in comment 2, the user clearly expresses that (s)he has never told anyone else about the incident, but the comment discloses it to anyone who reads it. Even though the user is discussing the secret publicly, invisibility and asynchronous conversation allow the user to leave the conversation freely. Anyone who posts a secret does not worry about eye contact with the people they are telling, and physical signs of disapproval are not there to inhibit what the user is willing to share (Suler "The Online" 322).

In these sentences, Gagnon effectively transitions from the reporting of data to making an argument based on that data. Notice how her argument "Throwaway accounts are an example of Reddit user's power over their anonymity" is supported by Suler's conclusions about how online users become disinhibited.

Looking for expert argument construction? Check this out. Earlier in the paragraph, Gagnon offered a few claims based on the data she gathered. In these lines, she defends her position by clearly analyzing one specific piece of her ethnographic data. When your instructors say "Show, don't tell," this is what they mean.

Gagnon 6

Creation of throwaway accounts demonstrates the rhetorical
awareness of the users creating them: they understand the purpose
of the thread is not to be able to identify anyone based on their
response, but to provide shocking confessions for entertainment. The
four users behind comments 1-4 recognize that their usual Reddit
pseudonym is not important or relevant. This metaknowledge gives
them an advantage with authority over their anonymity (Gee 489-90).
Understanding that it is acceptable to create an account to simply
ditch it once it serves its purpose allows users to resist single-
pseudonym conformity and advance in discussion in the community.
The user is aware that they are the rhetor behind the comment, and
therefore serve as its authorial voice (Grant-Davie 108). Audience
can influence what identity the user—the rhetor—will assume, but
when it is possible to remain anonymous, the user may consider the
audience's presence much less than in an identifying situation.

Pseudonyms allow Reddit users to be more honest about
themselves in their comments. Andrea Chester and Agi O'Hara also
found that the students in their study using pseudonyms claimed
to do so to be more honest (Chester and O'Hara 200). Even though
Reddit is public, the discussions such as the confessions listed above
still appear on the site. Disclosing private information has been found
to occur in public online settings when pseudonyms allow for a lack
of accountability (Lee 2-3). Users are unlikely to be worried that their
confession comments will affect them in their offline life.

Gone Wild: *Show Your Body to Reddit*

Gone Wild is a subreddit described as a place for adults to
post pictures of their nude bodies. By reviewing account histories,
I observed that a majority of the users post their pictures from
an account that is not associated with other parts of Reddit.
Furthermore, most photos I observed did not contain a face, or faces
were at least partially hidden. Titles for posted photos are usually
flirty and provocative.

Margin notes:

In this paragraph, Gagnon's ethnographic research methodology requires textual analysis. She draws conclusions based on what people have written on the Reddit feed.

At the end of several sections, Gagnon deploys a paragraph that ties each section's argument to her overall exploration of disinhibited Reddit users. An expert rhetorical move, these paragraphs serve to remind readers of the overall message of the cohesive essay.

Gagnon 7

Gone Wild allows its posters to create an identity driven by sexual attraction, while dissociating from their offline identity as well as their usual Reddit identity if an alternate account is being used. Creating a *Gone Wild* identity can be a person's way of attaining a "new, idealized way of being" (Suler "Identity" 457). They may be fulfilling a self-esteem or self-expression need. Those wishing to successfully create an identity on *Gone Wild* must follow a specific way of writing and presenting themselves in the community. Members of a community must be comfortable with writing and rhetorical conventions of the community (Wardle 524-25). Failing to provide the types of photos that viewers are looking for on *Gone Wild* will cause the user to fail to achieve a positive identity among the community. In addition, failing to produce flirtatious titles and descriptions can minimize the authority of the user among viewers.

Withholding offline identity on *Gone Wild* by hiding identifying features indicates that the user is aware of the context of the community, and the consequences that could be faced in offline life if identity is revealed. It is clear that they wish to remain anonymous when they have hidden their face from camera's view, and some users will black out any obvious identifying features, such as tattoos, as necessary. Attempts at separating their online actions from their offline identity leads to the dissociative anonymity that gives many users the courage to post their photos.

Random Acts of *Benign Disinhibition*

There are many subreddits that use a variation of the name *Random Acts of . . .* to identify the community as a place for requesting, exchanging, and helping out others in need of something specific. An example is *Random Acts of Christmas*. During the holiday season, users can make requests for and offer holiday gifts for children when parents are faced with difficult financial times. When searching through posts about last holiday season, I found a parent graciously thanking the community for their help:

Notice Gagnon's continued use of framing concepts offered by Suler. Gagnon is following through with the promise she made in her introduction: She's extending the academic conversation by applying Suler's concepts in a particular context.

In addition to the disinhibition frameworks provided by Suler, Gagnon effectively relies on writing and rhetoric scholars to explore the rhetorical choices of Reddit users. Here, Wardle helps her understand the genre standards of the *Gone Wild* community.

Gagnon 8

"So remember all those books y'all sent my little girls?! Well, I'd like to hug you all again and say another big THANK YOU. . . . [M]y daughter's school just called me and said. . . her reading average has improved from a 70 to a 92! I know it's because of all the extra reading she's been doing!"

The kindness and generosity seen in these *Random Act* communities can be described as benign online disinhibition (Suler "The Online" 321). This is not to say that the generous Reddit users are unkind in their offline lives, but to imply that they take advantage of these opportunities to make a difference in someone's life that they may not have been able to otherwise. Moreover, in offline life, people can be shy to offer their help to others. These subreddits allow an anonymous way to affect a stranger's life positively. Expressing generosity online can be an opportunity to practice positive character traits and help in accomplishing self-actualization (Suler "The Online" 457).

Part of ethnographic research can include historical research. In this section, Gagnon is able to draw on researched history of two particular cases in the Reddit community in order to make an argument about online disinhibition.

Misinterpreting Anonymity:
The Applebee's Waitress and the Google Employee

In February 2013, a waitress posted in the subreddit *Atheism* a picture of a check she found both insulting and amusing. For the "tip" section of the check, the customer, whom the waitress identified as a pastor, wrote, "I give God 10%, why do you get 18%?" and left the waitress without a tip. The photo and story went viral and according to news posted to Reddit, the waitress was soon identified as "Chelsea" and the pastor as "Ms. Bell." Chelsea reported that she "withheld any identifying information" in her Reddit post and that she "posted the note as a lighthearted joke," After her exposure, Applebee's reportedly fired her for exposing the customer's check and signature.

A similar story involves a Google employee hired as a "Chrome Specialist" who enthusiastically posted a photo of his new work

uniform on Reddit. In the thread, he mentioned that he had been trained to promote the Chromebook computer in stores such as Best Buy. His post and mention of his training violated the nondisclosure agreement he had with Google, and Google identified and fired him.

Chelsea did not expect to lose her job by posting the photo of the check on Reddit. She is a victim of misinterpreting her anonymity on Reddit. She failed to remain anonymous or develop the rhetorical awareness necessary to see the possible consequences of her actions. She once had the authority as the rhetor behind the posted photo and description, but her audience that was responsible for her exposure caused her to lose that authorial voice (Grant-Davie 108-10). As result, her post easily backfired on her.

The ex-Google employee also lost his authority as the rhetor. The photo he posted quickly led to an interesting discussion thread, but when it was exposed that he was being fired over the Reddit post and violation of his nondisclosure agreement, opinion of him quickly turned sour. Reddit users commented how ignorant he was to have so easily violated his agreement with Google. He went from having an identity as an interesting new Google employee to being the misinformed man who made a poor decision that cost him his job. In developing an online identity, he did not maintain offline accountability for his actions or take into account how public they were (Lee 3).

Violentacrez: An Exposed Case of Toxic Disinhibition

Violentacrez is the online pseudonym behind a now-banned Reddit account of 49 year-old Michael Brutsch. On Reddit, Brutsch had created many distasteful subreddits, some which still remain today. He was banned from Reddit in October 2012 and his identity had been revealed by Gawker.com, later followed by his interview with CNN. Brutsch's employer fired him shortly following his exposure (Roy).

Gagnon 10

An example of a subreddit created by violentacrez is *Jailbait,* a place for photos of eye-catching underage girls. The subreddit is now banned because of obvious controversy that arose, but many of violentacrez's other subreddits remain. *Pics of Dead Kids* is a subreddit that still remains, albeit it is not very active. The title is to the point: users may post pictures found on the Internet—usually very gory—of dead children. It is an unsettling community filled with appalling pictures and comments, but it represents the freedom expressed online and the types of things people may view or post when they are hidden behind a computer screen.

Brutsch admits he "didn't really think" about what he was doing on Reddit, and he referred to his username in the third-person during his CNN interview. He also expressed regret over the interview in the first place (Roy). This displays his dissociation with his online identity, violentacrez, from his offline identity, because he went as far as referring to his username as if it was not himself behind that identity. Brutsch visited dark territory of the internet—and created it—but has not been proven to explore such territory in his offline life. I knew of his existence on Reddit when his account had yet to be banned. He had achieved an identity described as "the creepy uncle of Reddit," which was almost humorous without looking into his account activity. Reddit did not take action to ban this user until the controversy led to exposure of his offline identity.

It is likely that Brutsch had been releasing a negative aspect of his psyche into a world— Reddit—in which he did not think it could be associated with his offline identity (Suler "Identity" 457). He catered to a shock-value oriented audience, with an exigence of jolting users of Reddit and creating a famous negative identity for himself.

Lurkers: You Can't See Me

Lurkers are the users of Reddit who do not participate in discussion and do not make their presence known. They want to

---

Gagnon uses historical data in this paragraph as well, this time drawing on a CNN interview. Analysis of language use in the interview leads Gagnon to draw useful conclusions about online disinhibition through disassociation with offline identity. Writing and rhetoric scholars pay close attention to language choices when analyzing primary research data (see "Looking for 'themes' or recurring ideas in primary, qualitative data" on page R-16).

"receive and not show too much" (Suler "Identity" 459). I define them as unregistered users, or registered users who participate in discussion rarely or never. Throughout this study and my usual browsing of Reddit, I've been a lurker.

I lurk on Reddit to be entertained in times of boredom. It also serves as a place to fuel my procrastination. As much as I take from Reddit and as much as it offers me, I do not give back very much; however, I do not feel much guilt about it. I am invisible on Reddit—no one is judging me personally on my lack of contribution to the community because no one can see me. In a similar situation in offline life, I would feel more compelled to contribute to a cause if I was around people who are. But in an online setting such as Reddit, I can satisfy my need to separate my personal identity from my observation of those around me (Suler "Identity" 459).

Conclusion

Reddit is a community where online disinhibition can be found throughout, but no published study on disinhibition pertaining to Reddit users exists. My findings are a work in progress—to help narrow the gap on what we understand about the disinhibition resulting from the pseudonymous nature of Reddit. They indicate the presence of this behavior in yet another popular online environment, and point to Reddit as a source for further valuable research. The results of this study contribute to the discussion on online communities where disinhibition has been observed.

This study needs to be followed by other discussion of the psychology behind Reddit. As popular a site as Reddit is, more research needs to be done to understand the interactions that occur within it. Other pseudonymous online communities should be studied for disinhibition in comparison to findings about Reddit. It is crucial to understand what factors of pseudonymous communities can affect the disinhibition and behavior of its users.

Conclusion sections of research essays often recap the argument the author made in the whole of the essay, connect the research to larger academic discussions, and/or call for further studies.

Gagnon expresses a realistic understanding of the impact of her claims, treating them as a useful starting point for a larger academic conversation and setting up a call for further research.

Gagnon specifies her call for further research, arguing for the necessity of such research while again supplementing the value of her own study.

Gagnon 12

In these concluding sentences, Gagnon successfully ties her research to larger academic conversations.

The Internet and social media play a huge role in many people's lives today. Understanding the workings behind the socialization and how its users choose to present themselves is vital in order to fully understand why these websites captivate us so much. To understand the behavior of users of these sites is to further understand human nature. Humans act variably in face-to-face situations, but online interaction pushes people into a rhetorical situation unlike any other. Understanding behavior in these contexts can lead to discussion on the "true self" of a person, and if it even exists at all. Online disinhibition is a phenomenon that represents more than a deviation from an offline identity. It illustrates the ability of the human mind to adapt and create fluctuating identities dependent on context and experience.

Works Cited

Chester, Andrea, and Agi O'Hara. "Image, Identity and Pseudonymity in Online Discussions." *International Journal of Learning*, vol. 13, no.12, 2007, pp. 193-203. *Education Source*, doi:10.18848/1447 -9494/CGP/v13i12. Accessed 3 Feb. 2013.

Gee, James Paul. "Literacy, Discourse, and Linguistics: Introduction." Wardle and Downs, pp. 482-95.

Grant-Davie, Keith. "Rhetorical Situations and Their Constituents." Wardle and Downs, pp. 104-18.

Lapidot-Lefler, Noam, and Azy Barak. "Effects Of Anonymity, Invisibility, and Lack of Eye-Contact on Toxic Online Disinhibition." *Computers in Human Behavior*, vol. 28, no.2, 2012, pp. 434-43. *Social Sciences Citation Index*, doi:10.1016 /j.chb.2011.10.014. Accessed 3 Feb. 2013.

Lee, Hangwoo. "Privacy, Publicity, and Accountability of Self-Presentation in an On-Line Discussion Group." *Sociological Inquiry*, vol. 76, no.1, 2006, pp. 1-22. *Academic Search Premier*, doi:10.1111/j.1475-682X.2006.00142.x. Accessed 3 Feb. 2013.

Rosenberry, Jack. "Users Support Online Anonymity Despite Increasing Negativity." *Newspaper Research Journal*, vol. 32, no.2, 2011, pp. 6-19. *OmniFile Full Text Mega*, doi:10.1177/073953291103200202. Accessed 27 Feb. 2013.

Roy, Jessica. "Violentacrez Admits Doing CNN Interview Was a 'Huge Mistake.'" *Observer*, 19 Oct. 2012, observer.com/2012/10 /violentacrez-admits-doing-cnn-interview-was-a-huge-mistake. Accessed 2 Mar. 2013.

Suler, John. "Identity Management in Cyberspace." *Journal of Applied Psychoanalytic Studies*, vol. 4, no. 4, 2002, pp. 455-59. *PsycINFO*, doi:10.1023/A:1020392231924. Accessed 3 Feb. 2013.

Suler, John. "The Online Disinhibition Effect." *CyberPsychology & Behavior*, vol. 7, no. 3, 2004, pp. 321-26. *Academic Search Premier*, doi: 10.1089/1094931041291295. Accessed 3 Feb. 2013.

Gagnon 14

Wardle, Elizabeth. "Identity, Authority, and Learning to Write in New
    Workplaces." Wardle and Downs, pp. 521-35.
Wardle, Elizabeth, and Doug Downs, editors. *Writing about Writing: A
    College Reader*. Bedford/St. Martin's, 2011.

Language

Writing
Processes

Writing That
Works

Research

Language

Grammar

Style

Punctuation/
Mechanics

Documentation

17 Writing across Cultures

People today often communicate instantaneously across vast distances and cultures. Businesspeople complete multinational transactions, students take online classes at distant universities, and conversations circle the globe via social media. You may also find yourself writing to (or with) people from other cultures, language groups, and countries. In this era of rapid global communication, you must know how to write effectively across cultures.

17a Thinking about what seems "normal"

More than likely, your judgments about what is "normal" are based on assumptions that you are not aware of. Most of us tend to see our own way as the "normal" or right way to do things. If your ways seem inherently right, then perhaps you assume that other ways are somehow less than right. To communicate effectively with people across cultures, recognize the norms that guide your own behavior and how those norms differ from those of other people.

- Know that most ways of communicating are influenced by cultural contexts and differ from one culture to the next.
- Notice the ways that people from cultures other than your own communicate, and be flexible.
- Respect the differences among individuals within a culture. Don't assume that all members of a community behave in the same way or value the same things.

17b Clarifying meaning

All writers face challenges in trying to communicate across space, languages, and cultures. You can address these challenges by working to be sure that you understand what others say—and that they understand you. In such situations, take care to be explicit about the meanings of the words you use. In addition, don't hesitate to ask people to explain a point if you're not absolutely sure you

understand, and invite responses by asking whether you're making yourself clear or what you could do to be *more* clear.

17c Meeting audience expectations

When you do your best to meet an audience's expectations about how a text should work, your writing is more likely to have the desired effect. In practice, figuring out what audiences want, need, or expect can be difficult—especially when you are writing in public spaces online and your audiences can be composed of anyone, anywhere. If you know little about your potential audiences, carefully examine your assumptions about your readers.

Expectations about your authority as a writer. Writers communicating across cultures often encounter audiences who have differing attitudes about authority and about the relationship between the writer and the people being addressed. In the United States, students are frequently asked to establish authority in their writing—by drawing on personal experience, by reporting on research, or by taking a position for which they can offer strong evidence and support. But some cultures position student writers as novices, whose job is to learn from others who have greater authority. When you write, think carefully about your audience's expectations and attitudes toward authority.

- What is your relationship to those you are addressing?
- What knowledge are you expected to have? Is it appropriate for you to demonstrate that knowledge—and if so, how?
- What is your goal—to answer a question? to make a point? to agree? something else?
- What tone is appropriate? If in doubt, show respect: politeness is rarely if ever inappropriate.

Expectations about persuasive evidence. You should think carefully about how to use evidence in writing, and pay attention to what counts as evidence to members of groups you are trying to persuade. Are facts, concrete examples, or firsthand experience

convincing to the intended audience? Does the testimony of experts count heavily as evidence? What people are considered trustworthy experts, and why? Will the audience value citations from religious or philosophical texts, proverbs, or everyday wisdom? Are there other sources that would be considered strong evidence? If analogies are used as support, which kinds are most powerful?

Once you determine what counts as evidence in your own thinking and writing, consider where you learned to use and value this kind of evidence. You can ask these same questions about the use of evidence by members of other cultures.

Expectations about organization. The organizational patterns that you find pleasing are likely to be deeply embedded in your own culture. Many U.S. readers expect a well-organized piece of writing to use the following structure: introduction and thesis, necessary background, overview of the parts, systematic presentation of evidence, consideration of other viewpoints, and conclusion.

However, in cultures that value indirection, subtlety, or repetition, writers tend to prefer different organizational patterns. When writing for world audiences, think about how you can organize material to get your message across effectively. Consider where to state your thesis or main point (at the beginning, at the end, somewhere else, or not at all) and whether to use a straightforward organization or to employ digressions to good effect.

Expectations about style. Effective style varies broadly across cultures and depends on the rhetorical situation—purpose, audience, and so on. Even so, there is one important style question to consider when writing across cultures: what level of formality is most appropriate? In most writing to a general audience in the United States, a fairly informal style is often acceptable, even appreciated. Many cultures, however, tend to value a more formal approach. When in doubt, err on the side of formality in writing to people from other cultures, especially to your elders or to those in authority. Use appropriate titles (*Dr. Moss, Professor Mejía*); avoid slang and informal structures, such as **sentence fragments**; use complete words and sentences (even in email); and use first names only if invited to do so.

18 Language That Builds Common Ground

The supervisor who refers to her staff as "team members" (rather than as "my staff" or as "subordinates") has chosen language intended to establish common ground with people who are important to her. Your own language can work to build common ground if you carefully consider the sensitivities and preferences of others and if you watch for words that betray your assumptions, even though you have not directly stated them.

18a Examining assumptions and avoiding stereotypes

Unstated assumptions that enter into thinking and writing can destroy common ground by ignoring important differences. For example, a student in a religion seminar who uses *we* to refer to Christians and *they* to refer to members of other religions had better be sure that everyone in the class identifies as Christian, or some may feel left out of the discussion.

At the same time, don't overgeneralize about or stereotype a group of people. Because stereotypes are often based on half-truths, misunderstandings, and hand-me-down prejudices, they can lead to intolerance, bias, and bigotry.

Sometimes stereotypes and assumptions lead writers to call special attention to a group affiliation when it is not relevant to the point, as in *a woman plumber* or *a white basketball player*. Careful writers make sure that their language doesn't stereotype any group or individual.

18b Examining assumptions about gender

Powerful gender-related words can subtly affect our thinking and our behavior. For instance, at one time speakers commonly referred to hypothetical doctors or engineers as *he* (and then labeled a woman who worked as a doctor *a woman doctor*, as if to say, "She's an exception; doctors are normally men"). Similarly, a label like

male nurse reflects stereotyped assumptions about proper roles for men. Equally problematic is the traditional use of *man* and *mankind* to refer to people of both sexes and the use of *he* and *him* to refer generally to any human being. Because such usage ignores half of the people on earth, it hardly helps a writer build common ground.

Sexist language, those words and phrases that stereotype or ignore members of either sex or that unnecessarily call attention to gender, can usually be revised fairly easily. There are several alternatives to using masculine **pronouns** to refer to persons whose gender is unknown:

▶ <u>Lawyers</u> A lawyer must pass the bar exam before <u>he</u> can practice. <u>they</u>

▶ A lawyer must pass the bar exam before he can practice. <u>or she</u>

▶ A lawyer must pass the bar exam before <s>he can practice.</s> <u>practicing.</u>

Try to eliminate common sexist **nouns** from your writing.

INSTEAD OF	TRY USING
anchorman, anchorwoman	anchor
businessman	businessperson, business executive
congressman	member of Congress, representative
fireman	firefighter
male nurse	nurse
man, mankind	humans, human beings, humanity, the human race, humankind
policeman, policewoman	police officer
woman engineer	engineer

18c Examining assumptions about race and ethnicity

In building common ground, watch for any words that ignore differences not only among individual members of a race or ethnic group but also among subgroups. Be aware, for instance, of the many nations to which American Indians belong and of the diverse places from which Americans of Spanish-speaking ancestry come.

Preferred terms. Identifying preferred terms is sometimes not an easy task, for they can change often and vary widely.

- The word *colored* was once widely used in the United States to refer to Americans of African ancestry. By the 1950s, the preferred term had become *Negro*; in the 1960s, *black* came to be preferred by most, though certainly not all, members of that community. Then, in the late 1980s, some leaders of the community urged that *black* be replaced by *African American*. Today, *African American* and *black* (or *Black*) are both widely used.

- The word *Oriental*, once used to refer to people of East Asian descent, is now considered offensive.

- Once widely preferred, the term *Native American* is challenged by those who argue that the most appropriate way to refer to indigenous peoples is by the specific name such as *Chippewa*, *Tlingit*, or *Hopi*. It has also become common for tribal groups to refer to themselves as *Indians* or *Indian tribes*.

- Among Americans of Spanish-speaking descent, the preferred terms of reference are many: *Chicano/Chicana*, *Hispanic*, *Latin American*, *Latino/Latina*, *Mexican American*, *Dominican*, and *Puerto Rican*, to name but a few.

Clearly, then, ethnic terminology changes often enough to challenge even the most careful writers—including writers who belong to the groups they are writing about. The best advice may be to consider your words carefully, to listen for the way members of a group refer to themselves (or ask about preferences), and to check in a current dictionary for any term you're unsure of.

18d Considering other kinds of difference

Remember that your audiences may include people from many areas of the United States as well as from other countries, of many different ages and socioeconomic backgrounds, of many different abilities, of differing religious views, and of different sexual orientations. In the latter case, it's important to recognize that people inhabit a very wide range of sexualities, including gay, lesbian, bisexual, transgender, intersexual, and asexual as well as heterosexual orientations. In short, you can almost never assume that audiences are just like you or that they share your background and experiences. Keeping this range of differences in mind can help you avoid overgeneralizing or stereotyping audiences—and thus help you build common ground.

19 Varieties of Language

Comedian Dave Chappelle has said, "Every black American is bilingual. We speak street vernacular, and we speak job interview." As Chappelle understands, English comes in many varieties that differ from one another in pronunciation, vocabulary, usage, and grammar. You probably already adjust the variety of language you use depending on how well—and how formally—you know the audience you are addressing. Language variety can improve your communication with your audience if you think carefully about the effect you want to achieve.

19a Using "standard" varieties of English appropriately

The key to shifting among varieties of English and among languages is appropriateness: you need to consider when such shifts will help your audience appreciate your message and when shifts may do just the opposite. Used appropriately and wisely, *any* variety of English can serve a good purpose.

One variety of English, usually referred to as the "standard" or "standard academic," is that taught prescriptively in schools, represented

 ### For Multilingual Writers

Recognizing Global Varieties of English

Like other world languages, English is used in many countries, so it has many global varieties. For example, British English differs somewhat from U.S. English in certain vocabulary (*bonnet* for *hood* of a car), syntax (*to hospital* rather than *to the hospital*), spelling (*centre* rather than *center*), and pronunciation. If you have learned a non-American variety of English, you will want to recognize, and to appreciate, the ways in which it differs from the variety widely used in U.S. academic settings.

in this and most other textbooks, used in the national media, and written and spoken widely by those wielding social and economic power. As the language used in business and most public institutions, "standard" English is a variety you will want to be completely familiar with. "Standard" English, however, is only one of many effective varieties of English and itself varies according to purpose and audience, from the more formal style used in academic writing to the informal style characteristic of casual conversation.

19b Using varieties of English to evoke a place or community

Weaving together regionalisms and standard English can be effective in creating a sense of place. Here, an anthropologist writing about one Carolina community takes care to let the residents speak their minds—and in their own words:

> For Roadville, schooling is something most folks have not gotten enough of, but everybody believes will do something toward helping an individual "get on." In the words of one oldtime resident, "Folks that ain't got no schooling don't get to be nobody nowadays."
> —Shirley Brice Heath, *Ways with Words*

Varieties of language, including slang and colloquial expressions, can also help writers evoke other kinds of communities. (See also 20a.)

19c   Using varieties of English to build credibility with a community

Whether you are American Indian or trace your ancestry to Europe, Asia, Latin America, Africa, or elsewhere, your heritage lives on in the diversity of the English language. See how one Hawaiian writer uses a local variety of English to paint a picture of young teens hearing a "chicken skin" story from their grandmother.

> "—So, rather dan being rid of da shark, da people were stuck with many little ones, for dere mistake."
> Then Grandma Wong wen' pause, for dramatic effect, I guess, and she wen' add, "Dis is one of dose times. . . . Da time of da sharks."
> Those words ended another of Grandma's chicken skin stories. The stories she told us had been passed on to her by her grandmother, who had heard them from her grandmother. Always skipping a generation.
> —Rodney Morales, "When the Shark Bites"

Notice how the narrator of the story uses different varieties of English—presenting information necessary to the story line mostly in standard English and using a local, ethnic variety to represent spoken language. One important reason for the shift from standard English is to demonstrate that the writer is a member of the community whose language he is representing and thus to build credibility with others in the community. Take care, however, in using the language of communities other than your own. When used inappropriately, such language can have an opposite effect, perhaps destroying credibility and alienating your audience.

20   Word Choice

Deciding which word is the right word can be a challenge. It's not unusual to find many words that have similar but subtly different meanings, and each makes a different impression on your audience. For instance, the "pasta with marinara sauce" presented in a restaurant may look and taste much like the "macaroni and gravy" served

at an Italian family dinner, but the choice of one label rather than the other tells us not only about the food but also about the people serving it and the people they expect to serve it to.

20a Using appropriate formality

In an email or letter to a friend or close associate, informal language is often appropriate. For most academic and professional writing, however, more formal language is appropriate, since you are addressing people you do not know well.

EMAIL TO SOMEONE YOU KNOW WELL

▶ Myisha is great—hire her if you can!

LETTER OF RECOMMENDATION TO SOMEONE YOU DO NOT KNOW

▶ I am pleased to recommend Myisha Fisher. She will bring good ideas and extraordinary energy to your organization.

Slang and colloquial language. Slang, or extremely informal language, is often confined to a relatively small group and changes very quickly, though some slang gains wide use (*ripoff, zine*). Colloquial language, such as *a lot, in a bind*, or *snooze*, is less informal, more widely used, and longer lasting than most slang.

Writers who use slang and colloquial language run the risk of not being understood or of not being taken seriously. If you are writing for a general audience about gun-control legislation and you use the term *gat*, some readers may not know what you mean, and others may be irritated by what they see as a frivolous reference to a deadly serious subject.

Jargon. Jargon is the special vocabulary of a trade or profession, enabling members to speak and write concisely to one another. Reserve jargon for an audience that will understand your terms. The example that follows, from a blog about fonts and typefaces, uses jargon appropriately for an interested and knowledgeable audience.

FONTSHOP.COM

The Modern typeface classification is usually associated with Didones and display faces that often have too much contrast for text use. The Ingeborg family was designed with the intent of producing a Modern face that was readable at any size. Its roots might well be historic, but its approach is very contemporary. The three text weights (Regular, Bold, and Heavy) are functional and discreet while the Display weights (Fat and Block) catch the reader's eye with a dynamic form and a whole lot of ink on the paper. The family includes a boatload of extras like unicase alternates, swash caps, and a lined fill. —fontshop.com blog

Jargon can be irritating and incomprehensible—or extremely helpful. Before you use technical jargon, remember your readers: if they will not understand the terms, or if you don't know them well enough to judge, then say whatever you need to say in everyday language.

Pompous language, euphemisms, and doublespeak. Stuffy or pompous language is unnecessarily formal for the purpose, audience, or topic. It often gives writing an insincere or unintentionally humorous tone, making a writer's ideas seem insignificant or even unbelievable.

POMPOUS

▶ Pursuant to the August 9 memorandum regarding the company carbon-footprint-reduction initiative, it is incumbent upon us to endeavor to make maximal utilization of telephonic and digital communication in lieu of personal visitation.

REVISED

▶ According to the August 9 memo, the company wants us to reduce our use of oil and gas, so we should telephone or email whenever possible rather than make personal visits.

⊕ For Multilingual Writers

Avoiding Fancy Language

In writing standard academic English, which is fairly formal, students are often tempted to use many "big words" instead of simple language. Although learning impressive words can be a good way to expand your vocabulary, it is usually best to avoid flowery or fancy language in college writing. Academic writing at U.S. universities tends to value clear, concise prose.

Euphemisms are words and **phrases** that make unpleasant ideas seem less harsh. *Your position is being eliminated* seeks to soften the blow of being fired or laid off. Although euphemisms can sometimes appeal to an audience by showing that you are considerate of people's feelings, they can also sound insincere or evasive.

Doublespeak is language used to hide or distort the truth. During massive layoffs in the business world, companies may describe a job-cutting policy as *employee repositioning, deverticalization,* or *rightsizing.* The public—and particularly those who lose their jobs—recognize such terms as doublespeak.

20b Considering denotation and connotation

The words *enthusiasm, passion,* and *obsession* all carry roughly the same denotation, or dictionary meaning. But the connotations, or associations, are quite different: an *enthusiasm* is a pleasurable and absorbing interest; a *passion* has a strong emotional component and may affect someone positively or negatively; an *obsession* is an unhealthy attachment that excludes other interests.

Note the differences in connotation among the following three statements:

▸ Students Against Racism (SAR) erected a temporary barrier on the campus oval, saying the structure symbolized "the many barriers to those discriminated against by university policies."

▸ Left-wing agitators threw up an eyesore right on the oval to try to stampede the university into giving in to their demands.

► Supporters of human rights for all students challenged the
  university's investment in racism by erecting a protest barrier
  on campus.

The first statement is the most neutral, merely stating facts (and
quoting the assertion about university policy to represent it as some-
one's opinion); the second, by using words with negative connota-
tions (*agitators, eyesore, stampede*), is strongly critical; the third, by
using words with positive connotations (*supporters of human rights*)
and presenting assertions as facts (*the university's investment in rac-
ism*), gives a favorable slant to the protest.

20c Using general and specific language effectively

Effective writers balance general words (those that name groups or
classes) with specific words (those that identify individual and par-
ticular things). Abstractions, which are types of general words, refer
to things we cannot perceive through our five senses. Specific words
are often concrete, naming things we can see, hear, touch, taste, or
smell.

GENERAL	LESS GENERAL	SPECIFIC	MORE SPECIFIC
book	dictionary	abridged dictionary	the fourth edition of the *American Heritage College Dictionary*

ABSTRACT	LESS ABSTRACT	CONCRETE	MORE CONCRETE
culture	visual art	painting	van Gogh's *Starry Night*

20d Using figurative language effectively

Figurative language, or figures of speech, paints pictures in read-
ers' minds, allowing readers to "see" a point readily and clearly. Far
from being a frill, such language is crucial to understanding.

Similes, metaphors, and analogies. Similes use *like, as, as if,* or *as though* to make explicit the comparison between two seemingly different things.

▸ The comb felt as if it was raking my skin off.
—Malcolm X, "My First Conk"

Metaphors are implicit comparisons, omitting the *like, as, as if,* or *as though* of similes.

▸ The Internet is the new town square. —Jeb Hensarling

Analogies compare similar features of two dissimilar things; they explain something unfamiliar by relating it to something more familiar.

▸ The mouse genome . . . [is] the Rosetta Stone for understanding the language of life. —Tom Friend

Clichés and mixed metaphors. A cliché is an overused figure of speech, such as *busy as a bee.* By definition, we use clichés all the time, especially in speech, and many serve usefully as shorthand for familiar ideas. But if you use clichés to excess in your writing, readers may conclude that what you are saying is not very new or is even insincere.

Mixed metaphors make comparisons that are inconsistent.

▸ The lectures were like brilliant comets streaking through the
  dazzling   flashes
night sky, ~~showering~~ listeners with ~~a torrential rain~~ of insight.
           ^   ^

The images of streaking light and heavy precipitation are inconsistent; in the revised sentence, all of the images relate to light.

20e Making spell checkers work for you

Research conducted for this book shows that spelling errors have changed dramatically in the past twenty years, thanks to spell checkers. Although these programs have weeded out many once-common misspellings, they are not foolproof. Look out for these typical errors allowed by spell checkers:

- **Homonyms.** Spell checkers cannot distinguish between words such as *affect* and *effect* that sound alike but are spelled differently.
- **Proper nouns.** A spell checker cannot tell you when you misspell a name.
- **Compound words written as two words.** Spell checkers will not see a problem if you write *nowhere* incorrectly as *no where*.
- **Typos.** The spell checker will not flag *heat* even if you meant to write *heart*.

Spell checkers and wrong words.   Wrong-word errors are the most common surface error in college writing today (see pp. 2–3), and spell checkers are partly to blame. Spell checkers may suggest bizarre substitutions for proper names and specialized terms, and if you accept the suggestions automatically, you may introduce wrong-word errors. A student who typed *fantic* instead of *frantic* found that the spell checker had substituted *fanatic*, a replacement that made no sense. Be careful not to take a spell checker's recommendation without paying careful attention to the replacement word.

Adapting spell checkers to your needs.   Always proofread carefully, even after running the spell checker. The following tips can help:

- Check a dictionary if a spell checker highlights or suggests a word you are not sure of.
- If you can enter new words in your spell checker's dictionary, include names, non-English terms, or other specialized words that you use regularly. Be careful to enter the correct spelling!
- After you run the spell checker, look again for homonyms that you mix up regularly.
- Remember that spell checkers are not sensitive to capitalization.

Grammar

Writing
Processes

Writing
That Works

Research

Language

Grammar

Style

Punctuation/
Mechanics

Documentation

21 Verbs and Verb Phrases

One famous restaurant in New Orleans offers to bake, broil, pan-fry, deep-fry, poach, sauté, fricassee, blacken, or scallop any of the fish entrées on its menu. To someone ordering—or cooking—at this restaurant, the important distinctions lie entirely in the **verbs**.

21a Using regular and irregular verb forms

The past **tense** and past **participle** of a **regular verb** are formed by adding *-ed* or *-d* to the **base form**.

BASE FORM	PAST TENSE	PAST PARTICIPLE
love	loved	loved
honor	honored	honored
obey	obeyed	obeyed

An **irregular verb** does not follow the *-ed* or *-d* pattern. If you are unsure about whether a verb is regular or irregular, or what the correct form is, consult the following list or a dictionary. Dictionaries list any irregular forms under the entry for the base form.

Some common irregular verbs

BASE FORM	PAST TENSE	PAST PARTICIPLE
arise	arose	arisen
be	was/were	been
beat	beat	beaten
become	became	become
begin	began	begun
bite	bit	bitten, bit
blow	blew	blown
break	broke	broken

BASE FORM	PAST TENSE	PAST PARTICIPLE
bring	brought	brought
build	built	built
burn	burned, burnt	burned, burnt
burst	burst	burst
buy	bought	bought
catch	caught	caught
choose	chose	chosen
come	came	come
cost	cost	cost
cut	cut	cut
dig	dug	dug
dive	dived, dove	dived
do	did	done
draw	drew	drawn
dream	dreamed, dreamt	dreamed, dreamt
drink	drank	drunk
drive	drove	driven
eat	ate	eaten
fall	fell	fallen
feel	felt	felt
fight	fought	fought
find	found	found
fly	flew	flown
forget	forgot	forgotten, forgot
freeze	froze	frozen
get	got	gotten, got
give	gave	given
go	went	gone

BASE FORM	PAST TENSE	PAST PARTICIPLE
grow	grew	grown
hang (suspend)[1]	hung	hung
have	had	had
hear	heard	heard
hide	hid	hidden
hit	hit	hit
keep	kept	kept
know	knew	known
lay	laid	laid
lead	led	led
leave	left	left
lend	lent	lent
let	let	let
lie (recline)[2]	lay	lain
lose	lost	lost
make	made	made
mean	meant	meant
meet	met	met
pay	paid	paid
prove	proved	proved, proven
put	put	put
read	read	read
ride	rode	ridden
ring	rang	rung
rise	rose	risen
run	ran	run

[1]*Hang* meaning "execute by hanging" is regular: *hang, hanged, hanged.*
[2]*Lie* meaning "tell a falsehood" is regular: *lie, lied, lied.*

BASE FORM	PAST TENSE	PAST PARTICIPLE
say	said	said
see	saw	seen
send	sent	sent
set	set	set
shake	shook	shaken
shoot	shot	shot
show	showed	showed, shown
shrink	shrank	shrunk
sing	sang	sung
sink	sank	sunk
sit	sat	sat
sleep	slept	slept
speak	spoke	spoken
spend	spent	spent
spread	spread	spread
spring	sprang, sprung	sprung
stand	stood	stood
steal	stole	stolen
strike	struck	struck, stricken
swim	swam	swum
swing	swung	swung
take	took	taken
teach	taught	taught
tear	tore	torn
tell	told	told
think	thought	thought
throw	threw	thrown
wake	woke, waked	waked, woken

BASE FORM	PAST TENSE	PAST PARTICIPLE
wear	wore	worn
win	won	won
write	wrote	written

21b Building verb phrases

Verb phrases can be built up out of a main **verb** and one or more **helping** (auxiliary) **verbs**.

▶ Immigration figures are rising every year.
▶ Immigration figures have risen every year.

Verb phrases have strict rules of order. If you try to rearrange the words in either of these sentences, you will find that most alternatives are impossible. You cannot say *Immigration figures rising are every year*.

Putting auxiliary verbs in order. In the sentence *Immigration figures may have been rising*, the main verb *rising* follows three auxiliaries: *may*, *have*, and *been*. Together these auxiliaries and the main verb make up a verb phrase.

 Checklist

Editing the Verbs in Your Writing

▶ Check verb endings that cause you trouble. (21a)
▶ Double-check forms of *lie* and *lay*, *sit* and *set*, *rise* and *raise*. (21d)
▶ Refer to action in a literary work in the present tense. (21e)
▶ Check that verb tenses in your writing express meaning accurately. (21e and 21f)
▶ Use passive voice appropriately. (21g)

- *May* is a modal that indicates possibility; it is followed by the base form of a verb.
- *Have* is an auxiliary verb that in this case indicates the perfect tense; it must be followed by a past participle (*been*).
- Any form of *be*, when it is followed by a present participle ending in *-ing* (such as *rising*), indicates the progressive tense.
- *Be* followed by a past participle, as in *New immigration policies have* <u>*been passed*</u> *in recent years*, indicates the passive voice (21g).

As shown in the following chart, when two or more auxiliaries appear in a verb phrase, they must follow a particular order based on the type of auxiliary: (1) modal, (2) a form of *have* used to indicate a perfect tense, (3) a form of *be* used to indicate a progressive tense, and (4) a form of *be* used to indicate the passive voice. (Very few sentences include all four kinds of auxiliaries.)

	Modal	Perfect *Have*	Progressive *Be*	Passive *Be*	Main Verb	
Sonia	—	has	—	been	invited	to visit a family in Prague.
She	should	—	—	be	finished	with school soon.
The invitation	must	have	—	been	sent	in the spring.
She	—	has	been	—	studying	Czech.
She	may	—	be	—	feeling	nervous.
She	might	have	been	—	expecting	to travel elsewhere.
The trip	will	have	been	being	planned	for a month by the time she leaves.

Only one modal is permitted in a verb phrase.

> _be able to_
> She will ~~can~~ speak Czech much better soon.
>   ^

Forming auxiliary verbs. Whenever you use an auxiliary, check the form of the word that follows.

MODAL + BASE FORM. Use the base form of a verb after _can, could, will, would, shall, should, may, might,_ and _must: Alice <u>can read</u> Latin._ In many other languages, modals like _can_ or _must_ are followed by the **infinitive** (_to_ + base form). Do not substitute an infinitive for the base form in English.

> Alice can ~~to~~ read Latin.

PERFECT _HAVE, HAS,_ OR _HAD_ + PAST PARTICIPLE. To form the perfect tenses, use _have, has,_ or _had_ with a past participle: _Everyone <u>has gone</u> home. They <u>have been</u> working all day._

PROGRESSIVE _BE_ + PRESENT PARTICIPLE. A progressive form of the verb is signaled by two elements, a form of the auxiliary _be_ (_am, is, are, was, were, be,_ or _been_) and the _-ing_ form of the next word: _The children <u>are studying</u>._ Be sure to include both elements.

> _are_
> The children studying science.
>   ^
> _studying_
> The children are ~~study~~ science.
>   ^

Some verbs are rarely used in progressive forms. These are verbs that express unchanging conditions or mental states rather than deliberate actions: _believe, belong, hate, know, like, love, need, own, resemble, understand._

PASSIVE _BE_ + PAST PARTICIPLE. Use _am, is, are, was, were, being, be,_ or _been_ with a past participle to form the passive voice.

> Tagalog is spoken in the Philippines.

Notice that the word following the progressive _be_ (the present participle) ends in _-ing,_ but the word following the passive _be_ (the past participle) never ends in _-ing._

| PROGRESSIVE | Meredith is studying music. |
| PASSIVE | Natasha was taught by a famous violinist. |

If the first auxiliary in a verb phrase is a form of *be* or *have*, it must show either present or past tense and must agree with the subject: *Meredith has played in an orchestra.*

21c Using infinitives and gerunds

Knowing whether to use an **infinitive** (*to read*) or a **gerund** (*reading*) in a sentence may be a challenge.

INFINITIVE

▶ My adviser urged me to apply to several colleges.

GERUND

▶ Applying took a great deal of time.

In general, infinitives tend to represent intentions, desires, or expectations, while gerunds tend to represent facts. The infinitive in the first sentence conveys the message that the act of applying was desired but not yet accomplished, while the gerund in the second sentence calls attention to the fact that the application process was actually carried out.

The association of intention with infinitives and facts with gerunds can often help you decide whether to use an infinitive or a gerund when another verb immediately precedes it.

INFINITIVES

▶ Kumar expected to get a good job after graduation.
▶ Last year, Jorge decided to become a math major.
▶ The strikers have agreed to go back to work.

GERUNDS

▶ Jerzy enjoys going to the theater.
▶ We resumed working after our coffee break.
▶ Alycia appreciated getting candy from Sean.

A few verbs can be followed by either an infinitive or a gerund. With some, such as *begin* and *continue*, the choice makes little difference in meaning. With others, however, the difference in meaning is striking.

▶ **Carlos was working as a medical technician, but he stopped to study English.**

The infinitive indicates that Carlos left his job because he intended to study English.

▶ **Carlos stopped studying English when he left the United States.**

The gerund indicates that Carlos actually studied English but then stopped.

The distinction between fact and intention is a tendency, not a rule, and other rules may override it. Always use a gerund—not an infinitive—directly following a **preposition**.

▶ This fruit is safe for ~~to eat.~~ *eating.*

You can also remove the preposition and keep the infinitive.

▶ This fruit is safe ~~for~~ to eat.

 ## For Multilingual Writers

Checking Usage with Search Engines

Search engines such as Google can provide a useful way of checking sentence structure and word usage. For example, if you are not sure whether you should use an **infinitive** form (*to* verb) or a **gerund** (*-ing*) for the verb *confirm* after the main verb *expect*, you can search for both *"expected confirming"* and *"expected to confirm"* to see which search term yields more results. A search for *"expected to confirm"* yields many more hits than a search for *"expected confirming."* These results indicate that *expected to confirm* is the more commonly used expression. Be sure to click through a few pages of the search engine's results to make sure that most results come from ordinary sentences rather than from headlines or phrases that may be constructed differently from standard English.

21d Using *lie* and *lay, sit* and *set, rise* and *raise*

These pairs of verbs cause confusion because both verbs in each pair have similar-sounding forms and somewhat related meanings. In each pair, one verb is transitive, meaning that it is followed by a direct **object** (*I lay the package on the counter*). The other is intransitive, meaning that it does not have an object (*He lies on the floor, unable to move*). The best way to avoid confusing these verbs is to memorize their forms and meanings.

BASE FORM	PAST TENSE	PAST PARTICIPLE	PRESENT PARTICIPLE	-S FORM
lie (recline)	lay	lain	lying	lies
lay (put)	laid	laid	laying	lays
sit (be seated)	sat	sat	sitting	sits
set (put)	set	set	setting	sets
rise (get up)	rose	risen	rising	rises
raise (lift)	raised	raised	raising	raises

> The doctor asked the patient to ~~lay~~ on his side.
    lie

> Tamika ~~sat~~ the vase on the table.
    set

> Jaime ~~rose~~ himself to a sitting position.
    raised

21e Using verb tenses

Tenses show when the verb's action takes place. The three **simple tenses** are the **present tense**, the **past tense**, and the **future tense**.

PRESENT TENSE	I ask, write
PAST TENSE	I asked, wrote
FUTURE TENSE	I will ask, will write

More complex aspects of time are expressed through **progressive**, **perfect**, and **perfect progressive** forms of the simple tenses.

PRESENT PROGRESSIVE	she is asking, is writing
PAST PROGRESSIVE	she was asking, was writing
FUTURE PROGRESSIVE	she will be asking, will be writing
PRESENT PERFECT	she has asked, has written
PAST PERFECT	she had asked, had written
FUTURE PERFECT	she will have asked, will have written
PRESENT PERFECT PROGRESSIVE	she has been asking, has been writing
PAST PERFECT PROGRESSIVE	she had been asking, had been writing
FUTURE PERFECT PROGRESSIVE	she will have been asking, will have been writing

The simple tenses locate an action only within the three basic time frames of present, past, and future. Progressive forms express continuing actions; perfect forms express completed actions; perfect progressive forms express actions that continue up to some point in the present, past, or future.

Special purposes of the present tense.   When writing about action in literary works, use the present tense.

▶ Ishmael slowly ~~realized~~ all that ~~was~~ at stake in the search for the
    white whale.

(above "realized": realizes; above "was": is)

General truths or scientific facts should be in the present tense, even when the **predicate** in the main **clause** is in the past tense.

▶ Pasteur demonstrated that his boiling process ~~made~~ milk safe to
    drink.

(above "made": makes)

In general, when you are quoting, summarizing, or paraphrasing a work, use the present tense.

▶ Adam Banks ~~wrote~~ that we should "fly on, reaching for the stars
    we cannot yet map, see, or scan."

(above "wrote": writes)

But when using APA (American Psychological Association) style, report the results of your experiments or another researcher's work in the past tense (*wrote, noted*) or the present perfect (*has discovered*). (For more on APA style, see Chapter 46.)

▸ Comer (1995) ~~notes~~ ^noted^ that protesters who deprive themselves of food are seen not as dysfunctional but rather as "caring, sacrificing, even heroic" (p. 5).

21f Sequencing verb tenses

Careful and accurate use of tenses is important for clear writing. When you use the appropriate tense for each action, readers can follow time changes easily.

▸ By the time he lent her the money, she ^had^ declared bankruptcy.

The revision makes clear that the bankruptcy occurred before the loan.

21g Using active and passive voice

Voice tells whether a **subject** is acting (*He questions us*) or being acted upon (*He is questioned*). When the subject is acting, the verb is in the **active voice**; when the subject is being acted upon, however, the verb is in the **passive voice**. Most contemporary writers use the active voice as much as possible because it makes their prose stronger and livelier. To shift a sentence from passive to active voice, make the performer of the action the subject of the sentence.

▸ ^My sister took the^ ~~The~~ prizewinning photograph. ~~was taken by my sister.~~

Use the passive voice when you want to emphasize the recipient of an action rather than the performer of the action.

▸ Colonel Muammar el-Qaddafi was killed during an uprising in his hometown of Surt.

In scientific and technical writing, use the passive voice to focus attention on what is being studied.

▶ The volunteers' food intake **was** closely **monitored**.

21h Using mood appropriately

The **mood** of a verb indicates the writer's attitude toward what he or she is saying. The indicative mood states facts or opinions and asks questions: *I did the right thing.* The imperative mood gives commands and instructions: *Do the right thing.* The subjunctive mood (used primarily in **dependent clauses** beginning with *that* or *if*) expresses wishes and conditions that are contrary to fact: *If I were doing the right thing, I'd know it.*

The present subjunctive uses the base form of the verb with all subjects.

▶ It is important that children **be** ready for a new sibling.

The past subjunctive is the same as the simple past except for the verb *be*, which uses *were* for all subjects.

▶ He spent money as if he **had** infinite credit.
▶ If the store **were** better located, it would attract more customers.

Because the subjunctive creates a rather formal tone, many people today substitute the indicative mood in informal conversation.

INFORMAL

▶ If the store **was** better located, it would attract more customers.

For academic or professional writing, use the subjunctive in the following contexts:

CLAUSES EXPRESSING A WISH

                          were
▶ He wished that his brother **was** still living nearby.
                         ^

THAT CLAUSES EXPRESSING A REQUEST OR DEMAND

▶ The plant inspector insists that a supervisor ~~is~~ on site at all times.
      be

IF CLAUSES EXPRESSING A CONDITION THAT DOES NOT EXIST

▶ If public transportation ~~was~~ widely available, fewer Americans
      were
would commute by car.

One common error is to use *would* in both clauses. Use the subjunctive in the *if* clause and *would* in the other clause.

▶ If I ~~would have~~ played harder, I would have won.
    had

21i Using conditional sentences appropriately

English distinguishes among many different types of conditional sentences: sentences that focus on questions and that are introduced by *if* or its equivalent. Each of the following examples makes different assumptions about the likelihood that what is stated in the *if* **clause** is true.

▶ If you *practice* (or *have practiced*) writing often, you *learn* (or *have learned*) what your main problems are.

This sentence assumes that what is stated in the *if* clause may be true; any verb tense that is appropriate in a simple sentence may be used in both the *if* clause and the main clause.

▶ If you *practice* writing for the rest of this term, you *will* (or *may*) *understand* the process better.

This sentence makes a prediction and again assumes that what is stated may turn out to be true. Only the main clause uses the future tense (*will understand*) or a modal that can indicate future time (*may understand*). The *if* clause must use the present tense.

▶ If you *practiced* (or *were to practice*) writing every day, it *would* eventually *seem* easier.

This sentence indicates doubt that what is stated will happen. In the *if* clause, the verb is either past—actually, past subjunctive (21h)—or

were to + the base form, though it refers to future time. The main clause contains *would* + the base form of the main verb.

▶ If you *practiced* writing on Mars, *you would find* no one to read your work.

This sentence imagines an impossible situation. Again, the past subjunctive is used in the *if* clause, although here past time is not being referred to, and *would* + the base form is used in the main clause.

▶ If you *had practiced* writing in ancient Egypt, you *would have used* hieroglyphics.

This sentence shifts the impossibility back to the past; obviously you won't find yourself in ancient Egypt. But a past impossibility demands a form that is "more past": the past perfect in the *if* clause and *would* + the present perfect form of the main verb in the main clause.

22 Nouns and Noun Phrases

Everyday life is filled with **nouns**: orange *juice, hip-hop,* the morning *news,* a *bus* to *work, meetings, pizza, email, Diet Coke, errands, dinner* with *friends,* a *chapter* in a good *book.* Every language includes nouns. In English, articles (*a* book, *an* email, *the* news) often accompany nouns.

22a Understanding count and noncount nouns

Nouns in English can be either **count nouns** or **noncount nouns**. Count nouns refer to distinct individuals or things that can be directly counted: *a doctor, an egg, a child; doctors, eggs, children.* Noncount nouns refer to masses, collections, or ideas without distinct parts: *milk, rice, courage.* You cannot count noncount nouns except with a preceding **phrase**: <u>*a glass of*</u> milk, <u>*three grains of*</u> rice, <u>*a little*</u> courage.

⁂ Grammar: Parts of Speech > LearningCurve (4)
   Grammar: Parts of Sentences > LearningCurve (2)

Count nouns usually have singular and plural forms: *tree, trees.*
Noncount nouns usually have only a singular form: *grass.*

COUNT	NONCOUNT
people (plural of *person*)	humanity
tables, chairs, beds	furniture
letters	mail
pebbles	gravel
suggestions	advice

Some nouns can be either count or noncount, depending on their
meaning.

COUNT	Before video games, children played with marbles.
NONCOUNT	The palace floor was made of marble.

When you learn a noun in English, you will therefore need to learn
whether it is count, noncount, or both. Many dictionaries provide
this information.

22b Using determiners

Determiners are words that identify or quantify a noun, such as *this*
study, all people, his suggestions.

COMMON DETERMINERS

- the articles *a, an, the*
- *this, these, that, those*
- *my, our, your, his, her, its, their*
- possessive nouns and noun phrases (*Sheila's paper, my friend's book*)
- *whose, which, what*
- *all, both, each, every, some, any, either, no, neither, many, much,*
  (a) few, (a) little, several, enough
- the numerals *one, two,* etc.

These determiners . . .	. . . can precede these noun types	Examples
a, an, each, every	singular count nouns	a book an American each word every Buddhist
this, that	singular count nouns noncount nouns	this book that milk
(a) *little, much*	noncount nouns	a little milk much affection
some, enough	noncount nouns plural count nouns	some milk enough trouble some books enough problems
the	singular count nouns plural count nouns noncount nouns	the doctor the doctors the information
these, those, (a) *few, many,* *both, several*	plural count nouns	these books those plans a few ideas many students both hands several trees

Determiners with singular count nouns.   Every singular count noun must be preceded by a determiner. Place any adjectives between the determiner and the noun.

►   my
  sister
  ∧

►   the
  growing population
  ∧

►   that
  old neighborhood
  ∧

Determiners with plural nouns or noncount nouns. Non-count and plural nouns sometimes have determiners and sometimes do not. For example, *This research is important* and *Research is important* are both acceptable but have different meanings.

22c Using articles

Articles (*a*, *an*, and *the*) are a type of determiner. In English, choosing which article to use—or whether to use an article at all—can be challenging. Although there are exceptions, the following general guidelines can help.

Using *a* or *an*. Use indefinite articles *a* and *an* with singular count nouns. Use *a* before a consonant sound (*a car*) and *an* before a vowel sound (*an uncle*). Consider sound rather than spelling: *a house, an hour.*

A or *an* tells readers they do not have enough information to identify specifically what the noun refers to. Compare the following sentences:

▶ I need a new coat for the winter.

▶ I saw a coat that I liked at Dayton's, but it wasn't heavy enough.

The coat in the first sentence is hypothetical rather than actual. Since it is indefinite to the writer and the reader, it is used with *a*, not *the*. The second sentence refers to an actual coat, but since the writer cannot expect the reader to know which one, it is used with *a* rather than *the*.

If you want to speak of an indefinite quantity rather than just one indefinite thing, use *some* or *any* with a noncount noun or a plural count noun. Use *any* in either negative sentences or questions.

▶ This stew needs some more salt.

▶ I saw some plates that I liked at Gump's.

▶ This stew doesn't need any more salt.

Using *the*.   Use the definite article *the* with both count and non-count nouns whose identity is known or is about to be made known to readers. The necessary information for identification can come from the noun phrase itself, from elsewhere in the text, from context, from general knowledge, or from a **superlative**.

► Let's meet at ^the^ fountain in front of Dwinelle Hall.

The phrase *in front of Dwinelle Hall* identifies the specific fountain.

► Last Saturday, a fire that started in a restaurant spread to a nearby clothing store. ~~Store~~ ^The store^ was saved, although it suffered water

damage.

The word *store* is preceded by *the*, which directs our attention to the information in the previous sentence, where the store is first identified.

► She asked him to shut ^the^ door when he left her office.

The context shows that she is referring to her office door.

► ^The pope^ ~~Pope~~ is expected to visit Mexico City in February.

There is only one living pope.

► She is now one of ^the^ best hip-hop artists in the neighborhood.

The superlative *best* identifies the noun *hip-hop artists*.

No article.   Noncount and plural count nouns can be used without an article to make generalizations:

► In this world nothing is certain but death and taxes.
                                                    —Benjamin Franklin

Franklin refers not to a particular death or specific taxes but to death and taxes in general, so no article is used with *death* or with *taxes*.

English differs from many other languages that use the definite article to make generalizations. In English, a sentence like *The ants live in colonies* can refer only to particular, identifiable ants, not to ants in general.

23 Subject-Verb Agreement

In everyday terms, the word *agreement* refers to an accord of some sort: you reach an agreement with your boss about salary; friends agree to go to a movie; the members of a family agree to share household chores. This meaning covers grammatical **agreement** as well. Verbs must agree with their subjects in number (singular or plural) and in **person** (first, second, or third).

To make a verb in the **present tense** agree with a third-person singular subject, add -*s* or -*es* to the **base form**.

▶ A vegetarian diet lowers the risk of heart disease.

To make a verb in the present tense agree with any other subject, use the base form of the verb.

▶ I miss my family.

▶ They live in another state.

Have and *be* do not follow the -*s* or -*es* pattern with third-person singular subjects. *Have* changes to *has*; *be* has irregular forms in both the present tense and the **past tense**.

▶ War is hell.

▶ The soldier was brave beyond the call of duty.

23a Checking for words between subject and verb

Make sure the verb agrees with the simple **subject** and not with another **noun** that falls in between.

                    have
▶ Many books on the best-seller list has little literary value.

The simple subject is *books*, not *list*.

Be careful when you use *as well as, along with, in addition to, together with,* and similar phrases. They do not make a singular subject plural.

▷ A passenger, as well as the driver, ~~were~~ injured in the accident.
(was)

Though this sentence has a grammatically singular subject, it would be clearer with a compound subject: *The driver and a passenger were injured in the accident.*

23b Checking agreement with compound subjects

Compound subjects joined by *and* are generally plural.

▷ A backpack, a canteen, and a rifle ~~was~~ issued to each recruit.
(were)

When subjects joined by *and* are considered a single unit or refer to the same person or thing, they take a singular verb form.

▷ The lead singer and chief songwriter *wants* to make the new songs available online.

The singer and songwriter are the same person.

▷ Drinking and driving ~~remain~~ a major cause of highway accidents and fatalities.
(remains)

In this sentence, *drinking and driving* is considered a single activity, and a singular verb is used.

With subjects joined by *or* or *nor*, the verb agrees with the part closer to the verb.

▷ Neither my roommate nor my neighbors *like* my loud music.

▷ Either the witnesses or the defendant *is* lying.

If you find this sentence awkward, put the plural noun closer to the verb: *Either the defendant or the witnesses <u>are</u> lying.*

> ## Checklist

Editing for Subject-Verb Agreement

- ▶ Identify the subject that goes with each verb to check for agreement problems. (23a)
- ▶ Check compound subjects joined by *and, or,* and *nor.* (23b)
- ▶ Check any collective-noun subjects to determine whether they refer to a group as a single unit or as multiple members. (23c)
- ▶ Check indefinite-pronoun subjects. Most take a plural verb. (23d)

23c   Making verbs agree with collective nouns

Collective nouns—such as *family, team, audience, group, jury, crowd, band, class,* and *committee*—and fractions can take either singular or plural verbs, depending on whether they refer to the group as a single unit or to the multiple members of the group. The meaning of a sentence as a whole is your guide.

- ▶ After deliberating, the jury *reports* its verdict.

  The jury acts as a single unit.

- ▶ The jury still *disagree* on a number of counts.

  The members of the jury act as multiple individuals.

- ▶ Two-thirds of the park ~~have~~ has burned.

  Two-thirds refers to the single portion of the park that burned.

- ▶ One-third of the student body ~~was~~ were commuters.

  One-third here refers to the students who commuted as individuals.

Treat phrases starting with *the number of* as singular and with *a number of* as plural.

SINGULAR   The number of applicants for the internship *was* unbelievable.

PLURAL   A number of applicants *were* put on the waiting list.

23d Making verbs agree with indefinite pronouns

Indefinite pronouns do not refer to specific persons or things. Most take singular verb forms.

SOME COMMON INDEFINITE PRONOUNS

another	each	much	one
any	either	neither	other
anybody	everybody	nobody	somebody
anyone	everyone	no one	someone
anything	everything	nothing	something

▸ Of the two jobs, neither holds much appeal.

▸ Each of the plays ~~depict~~ *depicts* a hero undone by a tragic flaw.

Both, few, many, others, and *several* are plural.

▸ Though many apply, few are chosen.

All, any, enough, more, most, none, and *some* can be singular or plural, depending on the noun they refer to.

▸ All of the cake *was* eaten.

▸ All of the candidates *promise* to improve the schools.

23e Making verbs agree with *who, which,* and *that*

When the relative **pronouns** *who, which,* and *that* are used as subjects, the verb agrees with the **antecedent** of the pronoun (26b).

▶ Fear is an ingredient that goes into creating stereotypes.

▶ Guilt and fear are ingredients that go into creating stereotypes.

Problems often occur with the words *one of the*. In general, *one of the* takes a plural verb, while *the only one of the* takes a singular verb.

▶ Carla is one of the employees who always ~~works~~ *work* overtime.

> Some employees always work overtime. Carla is among them. Thus *who* refers to *employees*, and the verb is plural.

▶ Ming is the only one of the employees who always ~~work~~ *works* overtime.

> Only one employee, Ming, always works overtime. Thus *one* is the antecedent of *who*, and the verb form must be singular.

23f Making linking verbs agree with subjects

A **linking verb** should agree with its subject, which usually precedes the verb, not with the subject complement, which follows it.

▶ These three key treaties ~~is~~ *are* the topic of my talk.

> The subject is *treaties*, not *topic*.

▶ Nero Wolfe's passion ~~were~~ *was* orchids.

> The subject is *passion*, not *orchids*.

23g Making verbs agree with subjects that end in *-s*

Some words that end in *-s* seem to be plural but are singular in meaning and thus take singular verb forms.

▶ Measles still ~~strike~~ ^{strikes} many Americans.

Some nouns of this kind (such as *statistics* and *politics*) may be either singular or plural, depending on context.

| SINGULAR | Statistics *is* a course I really dread. |
| PLURAL | The statistics in that study *are* questionable. |

23h Checking for subjects that follow the verb

In English, verbs usually follow subjects. When this order is reversed, make the verb agree with the subject, not with a noun that happens to precede it.

▶ Beside the barn ~~stands~~ ^{stand} silos filled with grain.

The subject, *silos*, is plural, so the verb must be *stand*.

In sentences beginning with *there is* or *there are* (or *there was* or *there were*), *there* is just an introductory word; the subject follows the verb.

▶ There are five basic positions in classical ballet.

23i Making verbs agree with titles and words used as words

Titles and words used as words always take singular verb forms, even if their own forms are plural.

▶ *One Writer's Beginnings* ~~describe~~ ^{describes} Eudora Welty's childhood.

▶ *Steroids* ~~are~~ ^{is} a little word that packs a big punch in the world of sports.

23j Considering spoken forms of *be*

Conventions for subject-verb agreement with *be* in spoken or vernacular varieties of English may differ from those of academic English. For instance, an Appalachian speaker might say "I been down" rather than "I have been down"; a speaker of African American vernacular might say "He be at work" rather than "He is at work," indicating that the person in question is habitually at work. You may want to quote such spoken phrases in your writing or to use them for special effect, but for much academic and professional writing, it's safest to follow the conventions of academic English. (For information on using varieties of English appropriately, see Chapter 19.)

24 Adjectives and Adverbs

Adjectives and **adverbs** can add indispensable differences in meaning to the words they describe or modify. In basketball, for example, there is an important difference between a *flagrant* foul and a *technical* foul, a layup and a *reverse* layup, and an *angry* coach and an *abusively angry* coach. In each instance, the **modifiers** are crucial to accurate communication.

Adjectives modify **nouns** and **pronouns**; they answer the questions *which? how many?* and *what kind?* Adverbs modify **verbs**, adjectives, and other adverbs; they answer the questions *how? when? where?* and *to what extent?* Many adverbs are formed by adding *-ly* to adjectives (*slight, slightly*), but some are formed in other ways (*outdoors*) or have forms of their own (*very*).

24a Using adjectives after linking verbs

When adjectives come after **linking verbs** (such as *is*), they usually describe the **subject**: *I am patient*. Note that in specific sentences, certain verbs may or may not be linking verbs—*appear, become, feel, grow, look, make, prove, seem, smell, sound,* and *taste,* for instance.

Grammar: Parts of Speech > LearningCurve (4)
Grammar: Parts of Sentences > LearningCurve (2)

 For Multilingual Writers

Using Adjectives with Plural Nouns

In Spanish, Russian, and many other languages, adjectives agree in number with the nouns they modify. In English, adjectives do not change number in this way: *the kittens are cute* (not *cutes*).

When a word following one of these verbs modifies the subject, use an adjective; when it modifies the verb, use an adverb.

ADJECTIVE   Fluffy looked angry.

ADVERB   Fluffy looked angrily at the poodle.

Linking verbs suggest a state of being, not an action. In the preceding examples, *looked angry* suggests the state of being angry; *looked angrily* suggests an angry action.

In everyday conversation, you will often hear (and perhaps use) adjectives in place of adverbs. For example, people often say *go quick* instead of *go quickly*. When you write in academic and professional English, however, use adverbs to modify verbs, adjectives, and other adverbs.

▶ You can feel the song's meter if you listen ~~careful.~~ *carefully.*

▶ The audience was ~~real~~ *really* disappointed by the show.

Good, well, bad, and *badly.*   The modifiers *good, well, bad,* and *badly* cause problems for many writers because the distinctions between *good* and *well* and between *bad* and *badly* are often not observed in conversation. Problems also arise because *well* can function as either an adjective or an adverb.

▶ I look ~~well~~ *good* in blue.

▶ Now that the fever has broken, I feel ~~good~~ *well* again.

>   *well.*
> He plays the trumpet ~~good.~~
>   ^
>   *bad*
> I feel ~~badly~~ for the Toronto fans.
>   ^
>   *badly.*
> Their team played ~~bad.~~
>   ^

24b Using comparatives and superlatives

Most adjectives and adverbs have three forms: positive, **comparative**, and **superlative**. You usually form the comparative and superlative of one- or two-syllable adjectives by adding *-er* and *-est*: *short, shorter, shortest*. With some two-syllable adjectives, longer adjectives, and most adverbs, use *more* and *most* (or *less* and *least*): *scientific, more scientific, most scientific; elegantly, more elegantly, most elegantly*. Some short adjectives and adverbs have irregular comparative and superlative forms: *good, better, best; badly, worse, worst*.

Comparatives versus superlatives. In academic writing, use the comparative to compare two things; use the superlative to compare three or more things.

> Rome is a much *older* city than New York.

>   *oldest*
> Damascus is one of the ~~older~~ cities in the world.
>   ^

Double comparatives and superlatives. Double comparatives and superlatives are those that unnecessarily use both the *-er* or *-est* ending and *more* or *most*. Occasionally, these forms can add a special emphasis, as in the title of Spike Lee's movie *Mo' Better Blues*. In academic and professional writing, however, it's safest not to use *more* or *most* before adjectives or adverbs ending in *-er* or *-est*.

> Paris is the ~~most~~ loveliest city in the world.

Absolute concepts. Some readers consider modifiers such as *perfect* and *unique* to be absolute concepts; according to this view, a thing is either unique or it isn't, so modified forms of the concept

don't make sense. However, many seemingly absolute words have multiple meanings, all of which are widely accepted as correct. For example, *unique* may mean *one of a kind* or *unequaled*, but it can also simply mean *distinctive* or *unusual*.

If you think your readers will object to a construction such as *more perfect* (which appears in the U.S. Constitution), then avoid such uses.

25 Modifier Placement

To be effective, **modifiers** should clearly refer to the words they modify and should be positioned close to those words. Consider this command:

> DO NOT USE THE ELEVATORS IN CASE OF FIRE.

Should we avoid the elevators altogether, or only in case there is a fire? Repositioning the modifier *in case of fire* eliminates such confusion—and makes clear that we are to avoid the elevators only if there is a fire: IN CASE OF FIRE, DO NOT USE THE ELEVATORS.

25a Revising misplaced modifiers

Modifiers can cause confusion or ambiguity if they are not close enough to the words they modify or if they seem to modify more than one word in the sentence.

▶ She teaches a seminar this term <del>on voodoo</del> at Skyline College. *on voodoo*

The voodoo is not at the college; the seminar is.

▶ <del>Billowing from the window, he</del> saw clouds of smoke. *He* ... *billowing from the window.*

People cannot billow from windows.

▶ Nixon told reporters that he planned to get out of politics. <del>after he lost the 1962 race.</del> *After he lost the 1962 race,*

Nixon did not predict that he would lose the race.

Limiting modifiers. Be especially careful with the placement of limiting modifiers such as *almost, even, just, merely,* and *only.* In general, these modifiers should be placed right before or after the words they modify. Putting them in other positions may produce not just ambiguity but a completely different meaning.

AMBIGUOUS	The court *only* hears civil cases on Tuesdays.
CLEAR	The court hears only civil cases on Tuesdays.
CLEAR	The court hears civil cases on Tuesdays only.

Squinting modifiers. If a modifier can refer either to the word before it or to the word after it, it is a squinting modifier. Put the modifier where it clearly relates to only a single word.

SQUINTING	Students who practice writing *often* will benefit.
REVISED	Students who often practice writing will benefit.
REVISED	Students who practice writing will often benefit.

25b Revising disruptive modifiers

Disruptive modifiers interrupt the connections between parts of a sentence, making it hard for readers to follow the progress of the thought.

▶ ~~Vegetables will, if they are cooked too long,~~ lose most of their nutritional value.

If they are cooked too long, vegetables will

Split infinitives. In general, do not place a modifier between the *to* and the **verb** of an **infinitive** (*to often complain*). Doing so makes it hard for readers to recognize that the two go together.

▶ Hitler expected the British to fairly quickly ~~surrender.~~ surrender

In certain sentences, however, a modifier sounds awkward if it does not split the infinitive. Most language experts consider split

infinitives acceptable in such cases. Another option is to reword the sentence to eliminate the infinitive altogether.

SPLIT   I hope *to* almost *equal* my last year's income.

REVISED   I hope that I will earn almost as much as I did last year.

25c Revising dangling modifiers

Dangling modifiers are words or **phrases** that modify nothing in the rest of a sentence. They often *seem* to modify something that is implied but not actually present in the sentence. Dangling modifiers frequently appear at the beginnings or ends of sentences, as in the following example.

DANGLING   Exploding in rapid bursts of red, white, and blue, the picnickers cheered for the Fourth of July celebration.

REVISED   With fireworks exploding in rapid bursts of red, white, and blue, the picnickers cheered for the Fourth of July celebration.

To revise a dangling modifier, often you need to add a **subject** that the modifier clearly refers to; sometimes you have to turn the modifier into a phrase or a **clause**.

▶ Reluctantly, the hound was given to a neighbor.
our family gave

In the original sentence, was the dog reluctant, or was someone else who is not mentioned reluctant?

▶ As a young boy, his grandmother told stories of her years as a migrant worker.
When he was

His grandmother was never a young boy.

▶ Thumbing through the magazine, my eyes automatically noticed the perfume ads.
My *as I was thumbing through the magazine.*

Eyes cannot thumb through a magazine.

26 Pronouns

As words that stand in for **nouns, pronouns** carry a lot of weight in our everyday discourse. The following directions show why it's important for a pronoun to refer clearly to a specific noun or pronoun **antecedent**:

▶ When you see a dirt road on the left side of Winston Lane, follow it for two more miles.

The word *it* could mean either the dirt road or Winston Lane.

26a Considering a pronoun's role in the sentence

Most speakers of English usually know intuitively when to use *I, me,* and *my.* The choices reflect differences in **case,** the form a pronoun takes to indicate its function in a sentence. Pronouns functioning as **subjects** or subject complements are in the subjective case (*I*); those functioning as **objects** are in the objective case (*me*); those functioning as possessives are in the possessive case (*my*).

SUBJECTIVE	OBJECTIVE	POSSESSIVE
I	me	my/mine
we	us	our/ours
you	you	your/yours
he/she/it	him/her/it	his/her/hers/its
they	them	their/theirs
who/whoever	whom/whomever	whose

Problems tend to occur in the following situations.

In subject complements.   Americans routinely use the objective case for subject complements in conversation: *Who's there? It's me.* If the subjective case for a subject complement sounds stilted or

▶ Checklist

Editing Pronouns

▶ Make sure all pronouns in subject complements are in the subjective case. (26a)

▶ Check for correct use of *who, whom, whoever,* and *whomever.* (26a)

▶ In compound structures, check that pronouns are in the same case they would be in if used alone. (26a)

▶ When a pronoun follows *than* or *as,* complete the sentence mentally to determine whether the pronoun should be in the subjective or objective case. (26a)

▶ Check that pronouns agree with indefinite-pronoun antecedents, and revise sexist pronouns. (26b)

▶ Identify the antecedent that a pronoun refers to. Supply one if none appears in the sentence. If more than one possible antecedent is present, revise the sentence. (26c)

awkward (*It's I*), try rewriting the sentence using the pronoun as the subject (*I'm here*).

> She was the
> ▶ ~~The~~ first person to see Kishore after the awards. ~~was she.~~

Before gerunds. Pronouns before a **gerund** should be in the possessive case.

> his
> ▶ The doctor argued for ~~him~~ writing a living will.

With *who, whoever, whom,* and *whomever.* Today's speakers tend not to use *whom* and *whomever,* which can create a very formal tone. But for academic and professional writing in which formality is appropriate, remember that problems distinguishing between *who* and *whom* occur most often in two situations: when they begin a question, and when they introduce a **dependent clause** (29c). You can determine whether to use *who* or *whom* at the beginning of a question by answering the question using a personal pronoun. If

the answer is in the subjective case, use *who*; if it is in the objective case, use *whom*.

> Whom
> ► ~~Who~~ did you visit?
> I visited *them*. *Them* is objective, so *whom* is correct.

> Who
> ► ~~Whom~~ do you think wrote the story?
> I think *she* wrote the story. *She* is subjective, so *who* is correct.

If the pronoun acts as a subject or subject complement in the clause, use *who* or *whoever*. If the pronoun acts as an object in the clause, use *whom* or *whomever*.

> who
> ► Anyone can hypnotize a person ~~whom~~ wants to be hypnotized.
> The verb of the clause is *wants*, and its subject is *who*.

> Whomever
> ► ~~Whoever~~ the party suspected of disloyalty was executed.
> *Whomever* is the object of *suspected* in the clause *whomever the party suspected of disloyalty*.

In compound structures. When a pronoun is part of a compound subject, complement, or object, put it in the same case you would use if the pronoun were alone.

> he
> ► When ~~him~~ and Zelda were first married, they lived in New York.

> her
> ► The boss invited ~~she~~ and her family to dinner.

> me.
> ► This morning saw yet another conflict between my sister and ~~I~~.

In elliptical constructions. Elliptical constructions are sentences in which some words are understood but left out. When an elliptical construction ends in a pronoun, put the pronoun in the case it would be in if the construction were complete.

> ► His sister has always been more athletic than *he* [is].

In some elliptical constructions, the case of the pronoun depends on the meaning intended.

▶ Willie likes Lily more than *she* [likes Lily].

She is the subject of the omitted verb *likes.*

▶ Willie likes Lily more than [he likes] *her*.

Her is the object of the omitted verb *likes.*

With *we* and *us* before a noun. If you are unsure about whether to use *we* or *us* before a noun, use whichever pronoun would be correct if the noun were omitted.

We
▶ ~~Us~~ fans never give up hope.

Without *fans,* *we* would be the subject.

us
▶ The Broncos depend on ~~we~~ fans.

Without *fans,* *us* would be the object of the preposition *on.*

26b Making pronouns agree with antecedents

The **antecedent** of a pronoun is the word the pronoun refers to. Pronouns and antecedents are said to agree when they match up in **person**, number, and gender.

SINGULAR   The choirmaster raised his baton.

PLURAL   The boys picked up their music.

Compound antecedents. Whenever a compound antecedent is joined by *or* or *nor,* the pronoun agrees with the nearer or nearest antecedent. If the parts of the antecedent are of different genders, however, this kind of sentence can be awkward and may need to be revised.

AWKWARD   Neither Annie nor Lu Ming got *his* work done.

REVISED   Annie didn't get *her* work done, and neither
             did Lu Ming.

When a compound antecedent contains both singular and plural parts, the sentence may sound awkward unless the plural part comes last.

▶ Neither the blog nor the newspapers would reveal their sources.

Collective-noun antecedents. A collective noun such as *herd*, *team*, or *audience* may refer to a group as a single unit. If so, use a singular pronoun.

▶ The *committee* presented *its* findings to the board.

When a collective noun refers to the members of the group as individuals, however, use a plural pronoun.

▶ The *herd* stamped *their* hooves and snorted nervously.

Indefinite-pronoun antecedents. **Indefinite pronouns** do not refer to specific persons or things. Most indefinite pronouns are always singular; a few are always plural. Some can be singular or plural depending on the context.

▶ One of the ballerinas lost her balance.

▶ Many in the audience jumped to their feet.

SINGULAR   *Some* of the furniture was showing *its* age.

PLURAL   *Some* of the farmers abandoned *their* land.

Sexist pronouns. Pronouns often refer to antecedents that may be either male or female. Writers used to use a masculine pronoun, known as the "generic *he*," to refer to such antecedents: *Everyone should know his legal rights.* However, such wording ignores or even excludes females—and thus should be revised: *Everyone should know his or her legal rights,* for example, or *People should know their legal rights.*

26c Making pronouns refer to clear antecedents

If a pronoun does not refer clearly to a specific antecedent, readers will have trouble making the connection between the two.

Ambiguous antecedents. In cases where a pronoun could refer to more than one antecedent, revise the sentence to make the meaning clear.

> The car went over the bridge just before ~~it~~ *the bridge* fell into the water.

What fell into the water—the car or the bridge? The revision makes the meaning clear.

> Kerry told Ellen, *"I* ~~that she~~ should be ready soon."

Reporting Kerry's words directly, in quotation marks, eliminates the ambiguity.

Vague use of *it, this, that,* and *which*. The words *it, this, that,* and *which* often function as a shortcut for referring to something mentioned earlier. Like other pronouns, each must refer to a specific antecedent.

> When the senators realized the bill would be defeated, they tried
> to postpone the vote but failed. *The entire effort* ~~It~~ was a fiasco.

> Jasmine just found out that she won the lottery, ~~which~~ *and her sudden wealth* explains
> her resignation.

Indefinite use of *you, it,* and *they*. In conversation, we often use *you, it,* and *they* in an indefinite sense in such expressions as *you never know* and *on television, they said.* In academic and professional writing, however, use *you* only to mean "you, the reader," and *they* or *it* only to refer to a clear antecedent.

> Commercials try to make ~~you~~ *people* buy without thinking.

> ~~On the~~ *The* Weather Channel, ~~it~~ reported a powerful earthquake in
> China.

> ~~In France, they~~ *Many restaurants in France* allow dogs ~~in many restaurants.~~

Implied antecedents. A pronoun may suggest a noun antecedent that is implied but not present in the sentence.

> Detention centers routinely blocked efforts by ~~detainees'~~ families
> and lawyers to locate ~~them.~~ *detainees.*

 Prepositions and Prepositional Phrases

Words such as *to* and *from*, which show the relations between other words, are **prepositions**. They are one of the more challenging elements of English writing.

27a Choosing the right preposition

Even if you usually know where to use prepositions, you may have difficulty knowing which preposition to use. Each of the most common prepositions has a wide range of different applications, and this range never coincides exactly from one language to another. See, for example, how *in* and *on* are used in English.

▶ The peaches are in the refrigerator.

▶ The peaches are on the table.

▶ Is that a diamond ring on your finger?

The Spanish translations of these sentences all use the same preposition (*en*), a fact that might lead you astray in English.

There is no easy solution to the challenge of using English prepositions idiomatically, but a few strategies can make it less troublesome.

Know typical examples. The **object** of the preposition *in* is often a container that encloses something; the object of the preposition *on* is often a horizontal surface that supports something touching it.

IN   The peaches are *in* the refrigerator.

There are still some pickles *in* the jar.

ON   The peaches are *on* the table.

Learn related examples. Prepositions that are not used in typical ways may still show some similarities to typical examples.

IN   You shouldn't drive *in* a snowstorm.

Like a container, the falling snow surrounds the driver. The preposition *in* is used for many weather-related expressions.

ON   Is that a diamond ring *on* your finger?

The preposition *on* is used to describe things you wear.

Use your imagination. Mental images can help you remember figurative uses of prepositions.

IN   Michael is *in* love.

Imagine a warm bath—or a raging torrent—in which Michael is immersed.

ON   I've just read a book *on* social media.

Imagine the book sitting on a shelf labeled "Social Media."

Learn prepositions as part of a system. In identifying the location of a place or an event, the three prepositions *in*, *on*, and *at* can be used. *At* specifies the exact point in space or time; *in* is required for expanses of space or time within which a place is located or an event takes place; and *on* must be used with the names of streets (but not exact addresses) and with days of the week or month.

AT   There will be a meeting tomorrow *at* 9:30 AM *at* 160
          Main Street.

IN   I arrived *in* the United States *in* January.

ON   The airline's office is *on* Fifth Avenue.

          I'll be moving to my new apartment *on* September 30.

27b Using two-word verbs idiomatically

Some words that look like prepositions do not always function as prepositions. Consider the following sentences:

▶ The balloon rose *off* the ground.

▶ The plane took *off* without difficulty.

In the first sentence, *off* is a preposition that introduces the prepositional phrase *off the ground*. In the second sentence, *off* neither functions as a preposition nor introduces a prepositional phrase. Instead, it combines with *took* to form a two-word **verb** with its own meaning. Such a verb is called a phrasal verb, and the word *off*, when used in this way, is called an adverbial particle. Many prepositions can function as particles to form phrasal verbs.

The verb + particle combination that makes up a phrasal verb is a single entity that cannot usually be torn apart.

▶ The plane took *off* without difficulty. ~~off~~.

Exceptions include some phrasal verbs that are transitive, meaning that they take a direct **object**. Some of these verbs have particles that may be separated from the verb by the object.

▶ I *picked up my baggage* at the terminal.

▶ I *picked my baggage up* at the terminal.

If a personal **pronoun** is used as the direct object, it *must* separate the verb from its particle.

▶ I picked up *it* ~~it~~ at the terminal.

In idiomatic two-word verbs where the second word is a preposition, the preposition can never be separated from the verb.

▶ We *ran into* our neighbor on the train. [not *ran our neighbor into*]

The combination *run* + *into* has a special meaning (find by chance). Therefore, *run into* is a two-word verb.

28 Comma Splices and Fused Sentences

A **comma splice** results from placing only a comma between **independent clauses**—groups of words that can stand alone as a sentence. We often see comma splices used effectively to give slogans a catchy rhythm.

▶ Dogs have owners, cats have staff.   —Bumper Sticker

A related construction is a **fused sentence**, or run-on, which results from joining two independent clauses with no punctuation or connecting word between them. The bumper sticker as a fused sentence would be "Dogs have owners cats have staff."

In academic and professional English, using comma splices or fused sentences will almost always be identified as an error, so be careful if you are using them for special effect.

28a Separating the clauses into two sentences

The simplest way to revise comma splices or fused sentences is to separate them into two sentences.

> COMMA SPLICE   My mother spends long hours every spring
>
> tilling the soil and moving manure/.
>
> ᴛhis part of gardening is nauseating.

If the two clauses are very short, making them two sentences may sound abrupt and terse, so some other method of revision is probably preferable.

28b Linking the clauses with a comma and a coordinating conjunction

If the two clauses are closely related and equally important, join them with a comma and a **coordinating conjunction** (*and*, *but*, *or*, *nor*, *for*, *so*, or *yet*).

> FUSED SENTENCE   Interest rates fell, so people began borrowing
>
> more money.

28c Linking the clauses with a semicolon

If the ideas in the two clauses are closely related and you want to give them equal emphasis, link them with a semicolon.

COMMA SPLICE   This photograph is not at all realistic/; it uses
                     dreamlike images to convey its message.

Be careful when you link clauses with a **conjunctive adverb** like *however* or *therefore* or with a **transition** like *in fact*. In such sentences, the two clauses must be separated by a semicolon or by a comma and a coordinating conjunction.

COMMA SPLICE   Many developing countries have high

                     birthrates/; therefore, most of their citizens

                     are young.

28d   Rewriting the two clauses as one independent clause

Sometimes you can reduce two spliced or fused independent clauses to a single independent clause.

                   Most
FUSED SENTENCE   A large part of my mail is advertisements

                   and
                   most of the rest is bills.

⊕ For Multilingual Writers

Judging Sentence Length

In U.S. academic contexts, readers sometimes find a series of short sentences "choppy" and undesirable. If you want to connect two independent clauses into one sentence, join them using one of the methods discussed in this chapter to avoid creating a comma splice or fused sentence. Another useful tip for writing in American English is to avoid writing several very long sentences in a row. If you find this pattern in your writing, try breaking it up by including a shorter sentence occasionally.

28e Rewriting one independent clause as a dependent clause

When one independent clause is more important than the other, try converting the less important one to a **dependent clause** by adding an appropriate **subordinating conjunction**.

COMMA SPLICE
Although
Zora Neale Hurston is now regarded as one of America's major novelists, she died in obscurity.

In the revision, the writer emphasizes the second clause and makes the first one into a dependent clause by adding the subordinating conjunction *although*.

FUSED SENTENCE The arts and crafts movement called for
, which reacted against mass production,
handmade objects. ~~it reacted against mass production.~~

In the revision, the writer chooses to emphasize the first clause (the one describing what the movement advocated) and make the second clause into a dependent clause.

28f Linking the two clauses with a dash

In informal writing, you can use a dash to join the two clauses, especially when the second clause elaborates on the first clause.

COMMA SPLICE Exercise trends come and go; this year yoga
—
is hot.

29 Sentence Fragments

Sentence fragments are often used to make writing sound conversational, as in this Facebook status update:

Realizing that there are no edible bagels in this part of Oregon. Sigh.

Fragments—groups of words that are punctuated as sentences but are not sentences—are often seen in intentionally informal writing and in public writing, such as advertising, that aims to attract attention or give a phrase special emphasis. But think carefully before using fragments for special effect in academic or professional writing, where readers might regard them as errors.

29a Revising phrase fragments

A **phrase** is a group of words that lacks a **subject**, a **verb**, or both. When a phrase is punctuated like a sentence, it becomes a fragment. To revise a phrase fragment, attach it to an independent clause, or make it a separate sentence.

▶ CNN is broadcasting the debates. ~~With~~ *with* discussions afterward.

With discussions afterward is a prepositional phrase, not a sentence. The editing combines the phrase with an independent clause.

▶ The town's growth is controlled by zoning laws. *a* A strict set of regulations for builders and corporations.

A strict set of regulations for builders and corporations is a phrase renaming *zoning laws*. The editing attaches the fragment to the sentence containing that noun.

▶ Kamika stayed out of school for three months after Linda was born. *She did so to* ~~To~~ recuperate and to take care of her baby.

The revision—adding a subject (*she*) and a verb (*did*)—turns the fragment into a separate sentence.

Fragments beginning with transitions. If you introduce an example or explanation with a transitional word or phrase like *also*, *for example*, *such as*, or *that*, be certain you write a sentence, not a fragment.

▶ Joan Didion has written on many subjects. *such* ~~Such~~ as the Hoover Dam and migraine headaches.

The second word group is a phrase, not a sentence. The editing combines it with an independent clause.

29b Revising compound-predicate fragments

A fragment occurs when one part of a compound **predicate** lacks a subject but is punctuated as a separate sentence. Such a fragment usually begins with *and*, *but*, or *or*. You can revise it by attaching it to the independent clause that contains the rest of the predicate.

▶ They sold their house/ ~~And~~ ^{and} moved into an apartment.

29c Revising clause fragments

A **dependent clause** contains both a subject and a verb, but it cannot stand alone as a sentence; it depends on an independent clause to complete its meaning. A dependent clause usually begins with a **subordinating conjunction**, such as *after, because, before, if, since, that, though, unless, until, when, where, while, who,* or *which*. You can usually combine dependent-clause fragments with a nearby independent clause.

▶ When I decided to switch to part-time work/, I gave up a lot of my earning potential.

If you cannot smoothly attach a clause to a nearby independent clause, try deleting the opening subordinating word and turning the dependent clause into a sentence.

▶ Most injuries in automobile accidents occur in two ways. ~~When~~ ^{An} ~~an~~ occupant either is hurt by something inside the car or is thrown from the car.

Style

Writing
Processes

Writing
That Works

Research

Language

Grammar

Style

Punctuation/
Mechanics

Documentation

30 Consistency and Completeness

If you listen carefully to the conversations around you, you will hear speakers use different styles to get their points across. The words, tone, and structure they choose have a big impact on your impression of them—their personality and credibility, for example—and their ideas. Often, you will hear inconsistent and incomplete structures. For instance, during an NPR interview with journalist Shankar Vedantam, comedian Aziz Ansari discussed recent changes in modern romance:

> One of the big changes for people that are, like, dating now is you have more options than any generation of people ever. You know, when we talked to people that were living in retirement homes and stuff, it was really interesting. They talked about how, like—especially with the women it was really interesting. You know, they were saying, like, well, you know, I was 20 years old. I was living with my parents. I didn't have the opportunity to pursue education or my own career. . . . And there was some guy that lived in the neighborhood. He was pretty nice. And I wanted to get out of the house, and I was like, all right, I'll get married.

Because Ansari is talking casually, some of his sentences begin one way but then move in another direction. The mixed structures pose no problem for listeners, but sentences such as these can be confusing in writing.

30a Revising faulty sentence structure

Beginning a sentence with one grammatical pattern and then switching to another one confuses readers.

MIXED   The fact that I get up at 5:00 AM, a wake-up time
         that explains why I'm always tired in the evening.

This sentence starts out with a **subject** (*The fact*) followed by a **dependent clause** (*that I get up at 5:00 AM*). The sentence needs a

predicate to complete the **independent clause**, but instead it moves to another **phrase** followed by a dependent clause (*a wake-up time that explains why I'm always tired in the evening*), and a **fragment** results.

> REVISED   The fact that I get up at 5:00 AM explains why I'm
>   always tired in the evening.

Deleting *a wake-up time that* changes the rest of the sentence into a predicate.

> REVISED   I get up at 5:00 AM, a wake-up time that explains
>   why I'm always tired in the evening.

Deleting *The fact that* turns the beginning of the sentence into an independent clause.

30b   Matching subjects and predicates

Another kind of mixed structure, called faulty predication, occurs when a subject and predicate do not fit together grammatically or simply do not make sense together.

▶ A characteristic that I admire is ~~a person who is generous.~~ *generosity.*
  A person is not a characteristic.

▶ The rules of the corporation ~~expect~~ *require that* employees ~~to~~ be on time.
  Rules cannot expect anything.

Is when, is where, the reason . . . is because.   Although you will often hear these expressions in everyday use, such constructions are inappropriate in academic or professional writing.

▶ A stereotype is ~~when someone characterizes~~ *an unfair characterization of* a group ~~unfairly.~~

▶ Spamming is ~~where companies send~~ *the practice of sending* electronic junk mail.

▶ ~~The reason~~ I like to play soccer ~~is~~ because it provides aerobic exercise.

30c Using consistent compound structures

Sometimes writers omit certain words in compound structures. If the omitted word does not fit grammatically with other parts of the compound, the omission can be inappropriate.

► His skills are weak, and his performance only ^{is} average.

The omitted verb *is* does not match the verb in the other part of the compound (*are*), so the writer needs to include it.

30d Making complete comparisons

When you compare two or more things, the comparison must be complete and clear.

► I was often embarrassed because my parents were so different. *from my friends' parents.*

Adding *from my friends' parents* completes the comparison.

UNCLEAR	Aneil always felt more affection for his brother than his sister.
CLEAR	Aneil always felt more affection for his brother than his sister did.
CLEAR	Aneil always felt more affection for his brother than he did for his sister.

31 Coordination and Subordination

You may notice a difference between your spoken and your written language. In speech, people tend to use *and* and *so* as all-purpose connectors.

He enjoys psychology, and he has to study hard.

The meaning of this sentence may be perfectly clear in speech, which provides clues with voice, facial expressions, and gestures.

In writing, however, the same sentence could have more than one meaning.

Although he enjoys psychology, he has to study hard.

He enjoys psychology although he has to study hard.

The first sentence links two ideas with a **coordinating conjunction**, *and*; the other two sentences link ideas with a **subordinating conjunction**, *although*. A coordinating conjunction gives the ideas equal emphasis, and a subordinating conjunction emphasizes one idea more than another.

31a Relating equal ideas

When you want to give equal emphasis to different ideas in a sentence, link them with a coordinating conjunction (*and, but, for, nor, or, so, yet*) or a semicolon.

▶ They acquired horses, **and** their ancient nomadic spirit was suddenly free of the ground.

▶ There is perfect freedom in the mountains, **but** it belongs to the eagle and the elk, the badger and the bear.

—N. Scott Momaday, *The Way to Rainy Mountain*

Coordination can help make explicit the relationship between two separate ideas.

▶ My son watches *The Simpsons* religiously/; ~~Forced~~ to choose, he
would probably take Homer Simpson over his sister.

> *forced*

Connecting these two sentences with a semicolon strengthens the connection between two closely related ideas.

When you connect ideas in a sentence, make sure that the relationship between the ideas is clear.

▶ **Surfing the Internet is a common way to spend leisure time,**
~~and~~ **it should not replace human contact.**

> *but*

What does being a common form of leisure have to do with replacing human contact? Changing *and* to *but* better relates the two ideas.

31b Distinguishing main ideas

Subordination allows you to distinguish major points from minor points or to bring supporting details into a sentence. If, for instance, you put your main idea in an **independent clause**, you might then put any less significant ideas in **dependent clauses**, **phrases**, or even single words. The following sentence highlights the subordinated point:

▶ Mrs. Viola Cullinan was a plump woman who lived in a three-bedroom house somewhere behind the post office.
> —Maya Angelou, "My Name Is Margaret"

The dependent clause adds some important information about Mrs. Cullinan, but it is subordinate to the independent clause.

Notice that the choice of what to subordinate rests with the writer and depends on the intended meaning. Angelou might have given the same basic information differently:

▶ Mrs. Viola Cullinan, a plump woman, lived in a three-bedroom house somewhere behind the post office.

Subordinating the information about Mrs. Cullinan's size to that about her house would suggest a slightly different meaning. As a writer, you must think carefully about what you want to emphasize and subordinate information accordingly.

Subordination also establishes logical relationships among different ideas. These relationships are often specified by subordinating conjunctions.

SOME COMMON SUBORDINATING CONJUNCTIONS

after	if	though
although	in order that	unless
as	once	until
as if	since	when
because	so that	where
before	than	while
even though	that	

The following sentence highlights the subordinate clause and italicizes the subordinating word:

▶ She usually rested her smile until late afternoon *when* her women friends dropped in and Miss Glory, the cook, served them cold drinks on the closed-in porch.
　　　　　　　　　　　—Maya Angelou, "My Name Is Margaret"

Using too many coordinate structures can be monotonous and can make it hard for readers to recognize the most important ideas. Subordinating lesser ideas can help highlight the main ideas.

▶ Many people check email in the evening, and so they turn on the
　　　　　　　　　Though they
computer. ~~They~~ may intend to respond only to urgent messages,
　　　　　^　　　　　　　　　　　　　　　　which
a friend sends a link to a blog post, ~~and~~ they decide to read ~~it~~ for
　　　　　　　　　　　　　Eventually,　　　^
just a short while~~,~~. ~~and~~ they get engrossed in Facebook, and they
　　　　　　　　　^
end up spending the whole evening in front of the screen.

Determining what to subordinate

　　　　Although our
▶ ~~Our~~ new boss can be difficult, ~~although~~ she has revived and
　^
maybe even saved the division.

The editing puts the more important information—that the new boss has saved part of the company—in an independent clause and subordinates the rest.

Avoiding excessive subordination. When too many subordinate clauses are strung together, readers may have trouble keeping track of the main idea expressed in the independent clause.

TOO MUCH SUBORDINATION

▶ Philip II sent the Spanish Armada to conquer England, which was ruled by Elizabeth, who had executed Mary because she was plotting to overthrow Elizabeth, who was a Protestant, whereas Mary and Philip were Roman Catholics.

REVISED

▶ Philip II sent the Spanish Armada to conquer England, which was ruled by Elizabeth, a Protestant. She had executed Mary, a Roman Catholic like Philip, because Mary was plotting to overthrow her.

Putting the facts about Elizabeth executing Mary into an independent clause makes key information easier to recognize.

32 Conciseness

If you have a Twitter account, you probably know a lot about being concise—that is, about getting messages across in no more than 140 characters. In 2011, *New York Times* editor Bill Keller tweeted, "Twitter makes you stupid. Discuss." That little comment drew a large number of responses, including one from his wife that read, "I don't know if Twitter makes you stupid, but it's making you late for dinner. Come home."

No matter how you feel about the effects of Twitter on the brain (or stomach!), you can make any writing more effective by choosing words that convey exactly what you mean to say.

32a Eliminating redundant words

Sometimes writers add words for emphasis, saying that something is large *in size* or red *in color* or that two ingredients should be combined *together*. The italicized words are redundant (unnecessary for meaning), as are the deleted words in the following examples.

▶ ~~Compulsory~~ A attendance at assemblies is required.

▶ The auction featured ~~contemporary~~ "antiques" made recently.

▶ Many different forms of hazing occur, such as physical ~~abuse~~ and mental abuse.

32b Eliminating empty words

Words that contribute little or no meaning to a sentence include vague **nouns** like *area*, *kind*, *situation*, and *thing* as well as vague **modifiers** like *definitely*, *major*, *really*, and *very*. Delete such words, or find a more specific way to say what you mean.

> The ~~h~~ousing ~~situation~~ can ~~have a really significant impact~~ strongly influence
>
> ~~on the social aspect of~~ a student's life. social

32c Replacing wordy phrases

Many common **phrases** can be reduced to a word or two with no loss in meaning.

WORDY	CONCISE
at all times	always
at that point in time	then
at the present time	now/today
due to the fact that	because
for the purpose of	for
in order to	to
in spite of the fact that	although
in the event that	if

32d Simplifying sentence structure

Using the simplest grammatical structures can tighten and strengthen your sentences considerably.

> Hurricane Katrina, ~~which was certainly~~ one of the most
>
> powerful storms ever to hit the Gulf Coast, caused damage. widespread
>
> ~~to a very wide area.~~

Strong verbs. *Be* **verbs** (*is, are, was, were, been*) often result in wordiness.

> ~~harms~~
> A high-fat, high-cholesterol diet ~~is bad for~~ your heart.
>   ^

Expletives. Sometimes expletive constructions such as *there is, there are,* and *it is* introduce a topic effectively; often, however, your writing will be better without them.

>   M
> ~~There are m~~any people ~~who~~ fear success because they believe
>   ^
> they do no~~t~~ deserve it.

>   P   need
> ~~It is necessary for p~~residential candidates to perform well on
>   ^   ^
> television.

Active voice. Some writing situations call for the passive **voice,** but it is always wordier than the active—and often makes for dull or even difficult reading (see 21g).

> *Gower*
> ~~In Gower's research, it was~~ found that pythons often dwell
> ^
> in trees.

33 Parallelism

If you look and listen, you will see parallel grammatical structures in everyday use. Bumper stickers often use parallelism to make their messages memorable (*Minds are like parachutes; both work best when open*), as do song lyrics and jump-rope rhymes. In addition to creating pleasing rhythmic effects, parallelism can help clarify meaning.

33a Making items in a series or list parallel

All items in a series should be in parallel form—all **nouns,** all **verbs,** all prepositional **phrases,** and so on. Parallelism makes a series both graceful and easy to follow.

▶ In the eighteenth century, armed forces could fight in open fields and on the high seas. Today, they can clash on the ground anywhere, on the sea, under the sea, and in the air.

—Donald Snow and Eugene Brown, *The Contours of Power*

The parallel structure of the phrases (highlighted here), and of the sentences themselves, highlights the contrast between the eighteenth century and today.

▶ The quarter horse skipped, pranced, and ~~was sashaying~~ onto the track.
sashayed

▶ The children ran down the hill, skipped over the lawn, and into the swimming pool.
jumped

▶ The duties of the job include baby-sitting, housecleaning, and ~~preparation of~~ meals.
preparing

Items that are in a list, in a formal outline, and in headings should be parallel.

▶ Kitchen rules: (1) Coffee to be made only by library staff.

(2) Coffee service to be closed at 4:00 AM. (3) Doughnuts to be kept in cabinet. (4) ~~No faculty members should handle~~ ~~coffee materials.~~
Coffee materials not to be handled by faculty.

33b Making paired ideas parallel

Parallel structures can help you pair two ideas effectively. The more nearly parallel the two structures are, the stronger the connection between the ideas will be.

▶ I type in one place, but I write all over the house.
—Toni Morrison

▶ Writers are often more interesting on the page than they are in ~~person.~~
the flesh.

In these examples, the parallel structures help readers see an important contrast between two ideas or acts.

With conjunctions. When you link ideas with *and, but, or, nor, for, so,* or *yet,* try to make the ideas parallel in structure. Always use the same structure after both parts of a **correlative conjunction**: *either . . . or, both . . . and, neither . . . nor, not . . . but, not only . . . but also, just as . . . so,* and *whether . . . or.*

▶ Consult a friend in your class ~~or~~ who is good at math.

who is

▶ The wise politician promises the possible and ~~should accept~~ the inevitable.

accepts

▶ I wanted not only to go away to school but also to New England.

live in

33c Using words necessary for clarity

In addition to making parallel elements grammatically similar, be sure to include any words—**prepositions**, articles, verb forms, and so on—that are necessary for clarity.

▶ We'll move to a city in the Southwest or Mexico.

in

To a city in Mexico or to Mexico in general? The editing clarifies this.

34 Shifts

A shift in writing is an abrupt change that results in inconsistency. Sometimes a writer or speaker will shift deliberately, as Geneva Smitherman does in this passage from *Word from the Mother*:

> There are days when I optimistically predict that Hip Hop will survive—and thrive. . . . In the larger realm of Hip Hop culture, there is cause for optimism as we witness Hip Hop younguns tryna git they political activist game togetha.

Smitherman's shift from formal academic language to vernacular speech calls out for and holds our attention. Although writers make shifts for good rhetorical reasons, unintentional shifts can be confusing to readers.

34a Revising shifts in tense

If **verbs** in a passage refer to actions occurring at different times, they may require different **tenses**. Be careful, however, not to change tenses without a good reason.

▶ A few countries produce almost all of the world's illegal drugs,
   affects
   but addiction ~~affected~~ many countries.

34b Revising shifts in voice

Do not shift between the **active voice** (she *sold* it) and the **passive voice** (it *was sold*) without a reason. Sometimes a shift in voice is justified, but often it only confuses readers.

▶ Two youths approached ~~me,~~ and ~~I was~~ asked for my wallet.
   me

   The original sentence shifts from active to passive voice, so it is unclear who asked for the wallet.

34c Revising shifts in point of view

Unnecessary shifts in point of view between first person (*I* or *we*), second person (*you*), and third person (*he, she, it, one,* or *they*), or between singular and plural subjects, can be very confusing to readers.

   You
▶ ~~One~~ can do well on this job if you budget your time.

   Is the writer making a general statement or giving advice to someone? Revising the shift eliminates this confusion.

34d Revising shifts between direct and indirect discourse

When you quote someone's exact words, you are using direct discourse: *She said, "I'm an editor."* When you report what someone says without repeating the exact words, you are using indirect

discourse: *She said she was an editor.* Shifting between direct and indirect discourse in the same sentence can cause problems, especially with questions.

▸ Bob asked what could ~~he~~ ^he^ do to help~~?~~ ^.^

The editing eliminates an awkward shift by reporting Bob's question indirectly. It could also be edited to quote Bob directly: *Bob asked, "What can I do to help?"*

34e Revising shifts in tone and diction

Watch out for shifts in your tone (overall attitude toward a topic or audience) and word choice. These shifts can confuse readers and leave them wondering what your real attitude is.

INCONSISTENT TONE

The question of child care forces a society to make profound decisions about its values. If some conservatives had their way, June Cleaver would still be in the kitchen baking cookies for Wally and the Beaver and waiting for Ward to bring home the bacon, but with only one income, the Cleavers would be lucky to afford hot dogs.

REVISED

The question of child care forces a society to make profound decisions about its values. Some conservatives believe that women with young children should not work outside the home, but many mothers are forced to do so for financial reasons.

The shift in diction from formal to informal makes readers wonder whether the writer is presenting a serious analysis or a humorous satire. As revised, the passage makes more sense because the words are consistently formal.

Punctuation/
Mechanics

Writing
Processes

Writing
That Works

Research

Language

Grammar

Style

**Punctuation/
Mechanics**

Documentation

35 Commas

It's hard to go through a day without encountering directions of some kind, and commas often play a crucial role in how you interpret instructions. See how important the comma is in the following directions for making hot cereal:

> Add Cream of Wheat slowly, stirring constantly.

That sentence tells the cook to *add the cereal slowly*. If the comma came before the word *slowly*, however, the cook might add all of the cereal at once and *stir slowly*.

35a Setting off introductory elements

In general, use a comma after any word, **phrase**, or **clause** that precedes the **subject** of the sentence.

▶ However, health care costs keep rising.

▶ Wearing new tap shoes, Audrey prepared for the recital.

▶ To win the game, players need both skill and luck.

▶ Fingers on the keyboard, Maya waited for the test to begin.

▶ While her friends watched, Lila practiced her gymnastics routine.

Some writers omit the comma after a short introductory element that does not seem to require a pause after it. However, you will never be wrong if you use a comma.

35b Separating clauses in compound sentences

A comma usually precedes a **coordinating conjunction** (*and, but, or, nor, for, so,* or *yet*) that joins two **independent clauses** in a compound sentence.

▶ The climbers must reach the summit today, or they will have to turn back.

With very short clauses, you can sometimes omit the comma (*She saw her chance and she took it*). But always use the comma if there is a chance the sentence will be misread without it.

▶ I opened the heavy junk drawer, and the cabinet door jammed.

▶ Checklist

Editing for Commas

Research for this book shows that five of the most common errors in college writing involve commas.

▶ Check that a comma separates an introductory word, phrase, or clause from the main part of the sentence. (35a)

▶ Look at every sentence that contains a coordinating conjunction (*and, but, for, nor, or, so,* or *yet*). If the groups of words before and after this conjunction both function as complete sentences, use a comma before the conjunction. (35b)

▶ Look at each adjective clause beginning with *which, who, whom, whose, when,* or *where* and at each phrase and appositive. If the rest of the sentence would have a different meaning without the clause, phrase, or appositive, do not set off the element with commas. (35c)

▶ Make sure that adjective clauses beginning with *that* are not set off with commas. Do not use commas between subjects and verbs, verbs and objects or complements, or prepositions and objects; to separate parts of compound constructions other than compound sentences; to set off restrictive clauses; or before the first or after the last item in a series. (35i)

▶ Do not use a comma alone to separate your sentences. (See Chapter 28.)

Use a semicolon rather than a comma when the clauses are long and complex or contain their own commas.

▶ When these early migrations took place, the ice was still confined to the lands in the far north; but eight hundred thousand years ago, when man was already established in the temperate latitudes, the ice moved southward until it covered large parts of Europe and Asia.

—Robert Jastrow, *Until the Sun Dies*

35c Setting off nonrestrictive elements

Nonrestrictive elements are word groups that do not limit, or restrict, the meaning of the noun or pronoun they modify. Setting nonrestrictive elements off with commas shows your readers that the information is not essential to the meaning of the sentence. **Restrictive elements**, on the other hand, *are* essential to meaning and should *not* be set off with commas. The same sentence may mean different things with and without the commas:

▶ The bus drivers rejecting the management offer remained on strike.

▶ The bus drivers, rejecting the management offer, remained on strike.

The first sentence says that only *some* bus drivers, the ones rejecting the offer, remained on strike. The second says that *all* the drivers did.

Since the decision to include or omit commas influences how readers will interpret your sentence, you should think especially carefully about what you mean and use commas (or omit them) accordingly.

RESTRICTIVE   Drivers *who have been convicted of drunken driving* should lose their licenses.

In the preceding sentence, the clause *who have been convicted of drunken driving* is essential because it explains that only drivers who have been convicted of drunken driving should lose their licenses. Therefore, it is *not* set off with commas.

NONRESTRICTIVE   The two drivers involved in the accident, *who have been convicted of drunken driving*, should lose their licenses.

In this sentence, however, the clause *who have been convicted of drunken driving* is not essential to the meaning because it does not limit what it modifies, *The two drivers involved in the accident,* but merely provides additional information about these drivers. Therefore, the clause *is* set off with commas.

To decide whether an element is restrictive or nonrestrictive, mentally delete the element, and see if the deletion changes the meaning of the rest of the sentence. If the deletion *does* change the meaning, you should probably not set the element off with commas. If it *does not* change the meaning, the element probably requires commas.

Adjective and adverb clauses.

An adjective clause that begins with *that* is always restrictive; do not set it off with commas. An adjective clause beginning with *which* may be either restrictive or nonrestrictive; however, some writers prefer to use *which* only for nonrestrictive clauses, which they set off with commas.

RESTRICTIVE CLAUSES

▶ The claim *that men like seriously to battle one another to some sort of finish* is a myth.

—John McMurtry, "Kill 'Em! Crush 'Em! Eat 'Em Raw!"

The adjective clause is necessary to the meaning because it explains which claim is a myth; therefore, the clause is not set off with commas.

▶ The man,/ who rescued Jana's puppy,/ won her eternal gratitude.

The adjective clause is necessary to the meaning because it identifies the man, so it takes no commas.

NONRESTRICTIVE CLAUSES

▶ I borrowed books from the rental library of Shakespeare and Company, which was the library and bookstore of Sylvia Beach at 12 rue de l'Odeon. —Ernest Hemingway, *A Moveable Feast*

The adjective clause is not necessary to the meaning of the independent clause and therefore is set off with a comma.

An adverb clause that follows a main clause does *not* usually require a comma to set it off unless the adverb clause expresses contrast.

► The park became a popular gathering place, although nearby residents complained about the noise.

The adverb clause expresses contrast; therefore, it is set off with a comma.

Phrases. Participial **phrases** may be restrictive or nonrestrictive. Prepositional phrases are usually restrictive, but sometimes they are not essential to the meaning of a sentence and thus are set off with commas.

NONRESTRICTIVE PHRASES

► The NBA star's little daughter, refusing to be ignored, interrupted the interview.

Using commas around the participial phrase makes it nonrestrictive.

Appositives. An **appositive** is a **noun** or noun phrase that renames a nearby noun. When an appositive is not essential to identify what it renames, it is set off with commas.

NONRESTRICTIVE APPOSITIVES

► Savion Glover, the award-winning dancer, taps like poetry in motion.

Savion Glover's name identifies him; the appositive *the award-winning dancer* provides extra information.

RESTRICTIVE APPOSITIVES

► Mozart's opera/ *The Marriage of Figaro*/ was considered revolutionary.

The phrase is restrictive because Mozart wrote more than one opera. Therefore, it is *not* set off with commas.

35d Separating items in a series

▷ He has plundered our seas, ravaged our coasts, burnt our towns, and destroyed the lives of our people.

— Declaration of Independence

You may see a series with no comma after the next-to-last item, particularly in newspaper writing. Occasionally, however, omitting the comma can cause confusion.

▷ All the cafeteria's vegetables—broccoli, green beans, peas, and carrots—were cooked to a gray mush.

Without the comma after *peas*, you wouldn't know if there were three choices (the third being a *mixture* of peas and carrots) or four.

Coordinate adjectives—two or more adjectives that relate equally to the noun they modify—should be separated by commas.

▷ The long, twisting, muddy road led to a shack in the woods.

In a sentence like *The cracked bathroom mirror reflected his face*, however, *cracked* and *bathroom* are not coordinate because *bathroom mirror* is the equivalent of a single word, which is modified by *cracked*. Hence they are *not* separated by commas.

You can usually determine whether adjectives are coordinate by inserting *and* between them. If the sentence makes sense with the *and* added, the adjectives are coordinate and should be separated by commas.

▷ They are sincere *and* talented *and* inquisitive researchers.

The sentence makes sense with the *and*s, so the adjectives should be separated by commas: *They are sincere, talented, inquisitive researchers.*

▷ Byron carried an elegant ~~and~~ pocket watch.

The sentence does not make sense with *and*, so the adjectives *elegant* and *pocket* should not be separated by commas: *Byron carried an elegant pocket watch.*

35e Setting off parenthetical and transitional expressions

Parenthetical expressions add comments or information. Because they often interrupt the flow of a sentence, they are usually set off with commas.

▶ Some studies have shown that chocolate, of all things, helps prevent tooth decay.

Transitions (such as *as a result*), **conjunctive adverbs** (such as *however*), and other expressions used to connect parts of sentences are usually set off with commas.

▶ Ozone is a by-product of dry cleaning, for example.

35f Setting off contrasting elements, interjections, direct address, and tag questions

▶ I asked you, *not your brother*, to sweep the porch.
▶ *Holy cow*, did you see that?
▶ Remember, *sir*, that you are under oath.
▶ The governor did not veto the bill, *did she?*

35g Setting off parts of dates and addresses

Dates. Use a comma between the day of the week and the month, between the day of the month and the year, and between the year and the rest of the sentence, if any.

▶ On Wednesday, November 26, 2008, gunmen arrived in Mumbai by boat.

Do not use commas with dates in inverted order or with dates consisting of only the month and the year.

▶ She dated the letter 5 August 2016.
▶ Thousands of Germans swarmed over the wall in November 1989.

Addresses and place names. Use a comma after each part of an address or a place name, including the state if there is no ZIP code. Do not precede a ZIP code with a comma.

▶ Forward my mail to the Department of English, The Ohio State University, Columbus, Ohio 43210.

▶ Portland, Oregon, is much larger than Portland, Maine.

35h Setting off quotations

Commas set off a quotation from words used to introduce or identify the source of the quotation. A comma following a quotation goes *inside* the closing quotation mark.

▶ A German proverb warns, "Go to law for a sheep, and lose your cow."

▶ "All I know about grammar," said Joan Didion, "is its infinite power."

Do not use a comma following a question mark or an exclamation point.

▶ "Out, damned spot!/" cries Lady Macbeth.

Do not use a comma to introduce a quotation with *that* or when you do not quote a speaker's exact words.

▶ The writer of Ecclesiastes concludes that/ "all is vanity."

▶ Patrick Henry declared/ that he wanted either liberty or death.

35i Avoiding unnecessary commas

Excessive use of commas can spoil an otherwise fine sentence.

Around restrictive elements. Do not use commas to set off restrictive elements—elements that limit, or define, the meaning of the words they modify or refer to (35c).

▶ I don't let my children watch movies/ that are violent.

▶ The actor/ Benicio Del Toro/ might win the award.

Between subjects and verbs, verbs and objects or comple-ments, and prepositions and objects. Do not use a comma between a subject and its **verb**, a verb and its **object** or complement, or a **preposition** and its object.

▶ Watching movies late at night/ allows me to relax.

▶ Parents must decide/ what time their children should go to bed.

▶ The winner of/ the prize for community service stepped forward.

In compound constructions. In compound constructions other than compound sentences, do not use a comma before or after a coordinating conjunction that joins the two parts (35b).

▶ Improved health care/ and more free trade were two of the administration's goals.

The *and* joins parts of a compound subject, which should not be separated by a comma.

▶ Mark Twain trained as a printer/ and worked as a steamboat pilot.

The *and* joins parts of a compound predicate, which should not be separated by a comma.

In a series. Do not use a comma before the first or after the last item in a series.

▶ The auction included/ furniture, paintings, and china.

▶ The swimmer took slow, elegant, powerful/ strokes.

36 Semicolons

The following public-service announcement, posted in New York City subway cars, reminded commuters what to do with a used newspaper at the end of the ride:

Please put it in a trash can; that's good news for everyone.

The semicolon in the subway announcement separates two clauses that could have been written as separate sentences. Semicolons, which create a pause stronger than that of a comma but not as strong as the full pause of a period, show close connections between related ideas.

36a Linking independent clauses

Although a comma and a **coordinating conjunction** often join **independent clauses** (35b), semicolons provide writers with subtler ways of signaling closely related clauses. The clause following a semicolon often restates an idea expressed in the first clause; it sometimes expands on or presents a contrast to the first.

▶ **Immigration acts were passed; newcomers had to prove, besides moral correctness and financial solvency, their ability to read.** —Mary Gordon, "More Than Just a Shrine"

The semicolon gives the sentence an abrupt rhythm that suits the topic: laws that imposed strict requirements.

If two independent clauses joined by a coordinating conjunction contain commas, you may use a semicolon instead of a comma before the conjunction to make the sentence easier to read.

▶ **Every year, whether the Republican or the Democratic party is in office, more and more power drains away from the individual to feed vast reservoirs in far-off places; and we have less and less say about the shape of events which shape our future.** —William F. Buckley Jr., "Why Don't We Complain?"

A semicolon should link independent clauses joined by a **conjunctive adverb** such as *however* or *therefore* or a **transition** such as *as a result* or *for example*.

▶ **The circus comes as close to being the world in microcosm as anything I know; in a way, it puts all the rest of show business in the shade.** —E. B. White, "The Ring of Time"

36b Separating items in a series containing other punctuation

Ordinarily, commas separate items in a series (35d). But when the items themselves contain commas or other punctuation, semicolons make the sentence clearer.

▶ Anthropology encompasses archaeology, the study of ancient civilizations through artifacts/; linguistics, the study of the structure and development of language/; and cultural anthropology, the study of language, customs, and behavior.

36c Avoiding misused semicolons

Use a comma, not a semicolon, to separate an independent clause from a **dependent clause** or **phrase**.

▶ The police found fingerprints;/, which they used to identify the thief.

▶ The new system would encourage students to register for courses online;/, thus streamlining registration.

Use a colon, not a semicolon, to introduce a series or list.

▶ The reunion tour includes the following bands;/: Urban Waste, Murphy's Law, Rapid Deployment, and Ism.

37 End Punctuation

Periods, question marks, and exclamation points often appear in advertising to create special effects:

You have a choice to make.

Where can you turn for advice?

Ask our experts today!

End punctuation tells us how to read each sentence—as a matter-of-fact statement, a question for the reader, or an enthusiastic exclamation.

37a Using periods

Use a period to close sentences that make statements or give mild commands.

▶ **All books are either dreams or swords.** —Amy Lowell

▶ **Don't use a fancy word if a simpler word will do.**
—George Orwell, "Politics and the English Language"

A period also closes indirect questions, which report rather than ask questions.

▶ **I asked how old the child was.**

In American English, periods are used with most abbreviations. However, more and more abbreviations are currently appearing without periods.

Mr.	MD	BCE or B.C.E.
Ms.	PhD	AD or A.D.
Sen.	Jr.	PM or p.m.

Some abbreviations rarely if ever appear with periods. These include the postal abbreviations of state names, such as *FL* and *TN*, and most groups of initials (*GE, CIA, AIDS, YMCA, UNICEF*). If you are not sure whether a particular abbreviation should include periods, check a dictionary or follow the particular style guidelines you are using for a research paper. (For more about abbreviations, see Chapter 42.)

Do not use an additional period when a sentence ends with an abbreviation that has its own period.

▶ **The social worker referred me to John Pintz Jr./**

37b Using question marks

Use question marks to close sentences that ask direct questions.

▶ **How is the human mind like a computer, and how is it different?**
—Kathleen Stassen Berger and Ross A. Thompson,
The Developing Person through Childhood and Adolescence

Question marks do not close indirect questions, which report rather than ask questions.

▶ She asked whether I opposed his nomination?

37c Using exclamation points

Use an exclamation point to show surprise or strong emotion. Use these marks sparingly because they can distract your readers or suggest that you are exaggerating.

▶ **In those few moments of geologic time will be the story of all that has happened since we became a nation. And what a story it will be!**
— James Rettie, "But a Watch in the Night"

37d Using end punctuation in informal writing

In informal writing, especially on social media, writers today are more likely to omit end punctuation entirely. Research also shows that ellipses (. . .), or "dots," are on the rise; they can be used to signal a trailing off of a thought, to raise questions about what is being left out, to leave open the possibility of further communication, or simply to indicate that the writer doesn't want or need to finish the sentence. Exclamation marks can convey an excited or a chatty tone, so they are used more frequently in informal writing. And some writers have argued that using a period at the end of a text or tweet rather than no punctuation at all can suggest that the writer is irritated or angry. The meaning of end punctuation is changing in informal contexts, so pay attention to how others communicate, and use what you learn in your own social writing.

38 Apostrophes

The little apostrophe can make a big difference in meaning. The following sign at a neighborhood swimming pool, for instance, says something different from what the writer probably intended:

Please deposit your garbage (and your guests) in the trash receptacles before leaving the pool area.

The sign indicates that the guests, not their garbage, should be deposited in trash receptacles. Adding a single apostrophe would offer a more neighborly statement: *Please deposit your garbage (and your guests') in the trash receptacles before leaving the pool area.*

38a   Signaling possessive case

The possessive case denotes ownership or possession. Add an apostrophe and -*s* to form the possessive of most singular **nouns**, including those that end in -*s*, and of **indefinite pronouns** (23d). The possessive forms of personal **pronouns** do not take apostrophes: *yours, his, hers, its, ours, theirs.*

▶ The bus's fumes overpowered her.

▶ George Lucas's movies have been wildly popular.

▶ Anyone's guess is as good as mine.

Plural nouns.   To form the possessive case of plural nouns not ending in -*s*, add an apostrophe and -*s*. For plural nouns ending in -*s*, add only the apostrophe.

▶ The men's department sells business attire.

▶ The clowns' costumes were bright green and orange.

Compound nouns.   For compound nouns, make the last word in the group possessive.

▶ Both her daughters-in-law's birthdays fall in July.

Two or more nouns.   To signal individual possession by two or more owners, make each noun possessive.

▶ Great differences exist between Jerry Bruckheimer's and Ridley Scott's films.

   Bruckheimer and Scott produce different films.

To signal joint possession, make only the last noun possessive.

▶ **Wallace and Gromit's creator is Nick Park.**
  Wallace and Gromit have the same creator.

38b Signaling contractions

Contractions are two-word combinations formed by leaving out certain letters, which are replaced by an apostrophe (*it is, it has/ it's; will not/won't*).

Contractions are common in conversation and informal writing. Academic and professional work, however, often calls for greater formality.

Distinguishing *its* and *it's*. *Its* is a possessive **pronoun**—the possessive form of *it*. *It's* is a contraction for *it is* or *it has*.

▶ This disease is unusual; its symptoms vary from person to person.

▶ It's a difficult disease to diagnose.

38c Understanding apostrophes and plural forms

Many style guides now advise against using apostrophes for plurals.

▶ The gymnasts need marks of 8s and 9s in order to qualify for the finals.

Other guidelines call for an apostrophe and -*s* to form the plural of numbers, letters, and words referred to as terms.

▶ The five Shakespeare's in the essay were spelled five different ways.

Check your instructor's preference.

39 Quotation Marks

"Hilarious!" "A great family movie!" "A must see!" The quotation marks are a key component of statements like these from movie ads; they make the praise more believable by indicating that it comes

from people other than the movie promoter. Quotation marks identify a speaker's exact words or the titles of short works.

39a Signaling direct quotation

▷ The crowd chanted "Yes, we can" as they waited for the speech to begin.

▷ She smiled and said, "Son, this is one incident that I will never forget."

Use quotation marks to enclose the words of each speaker within running dialogue. Mark each shift in speaker with a new paragraph.

> "I want no proof of their affection," said Elinor; "but of their engagement I do."
> "I am perfectly satisfied of both."
> "Yet not a syllable has been said to you on the subject, by either of them." —Jane Austen, *Sense and Sensibility*

Single quotation marks. Single quotation marks enclose a quotation within a quotation. Open and close the quoted passage with double quotation marks, and change any quotation marks that appear *within* the quotation to single quotation marks.

▷ Baldwin says, "The title 'The Uses of the Blues' does not refer to music; I don't know anything about music."

Long quotations. To quote a passage that is more than four typed lines, set the quotation off by starting it on a new line and indenting it one-half inch from the left margin. This format, known as block quotation, does not require quotation marks.

> In "Suspended," Joy Harjo tells of her first awareness of jazz as a child:
>> My rite of passage into the world of humanity occurred then, via jazz. The music made a startling bridge between the familiar and strange lands, an appropriate vehicle for . . . we were there when jazz was born. I recognized it, that humid afternoon in my formative years, as a way to speak beyond the confines of ordinary language. I still hear it. (84)

This block quotation, including the ellipsis dots and the page number in parentheses at the end, follows the style of the Modern Language Association, or MLA (see Chapter 45). The American Psychological Association, or APA, has different guidelines for setting off block quotations (see Chapter 46).

Poetry. When quoting poetry, if the quotation is brief (fewer than four lines), include it within your text. Separate the lines of the poem with slashes, each preceded and followed by a space, in order to tell the reader where one line of the poem ends and the next begins.

> In one of his best-known poems, Robert Frost remarks, "Two roads diverged in a yellow wood, and I—/ I took the one less traveled by / And that has made all the difference."

To quote more than three lines of poetry, indent the block one-half inch from the left margin. Do not use quotation marks. Take care to follow the spacing, capitalization, punctuation, and other features of the original poem.

> The duke in Robert Browning's poem "My Last Duchess" is clearly a jealous, vain person, whose arrogance is illustrated through this statement:
>
>> She thanked men—good! but thanked
>> Somehow—I know not how—as if she ranked
>> My gift of a nine-hundred-years-old name
>> With anybody's gift. (lines 31–34)

39b Identifying titles of short works and definitions

Use quotation marks to enclose the titles of short poems, short stories, articles, essays, songs, sections of books, and episodes of television and radio programs. Quotation marks also enclose definitions.

▸ **The essay "The Art of Stephen Curry" analyzes some reasons for the success of the Warriors' star.**

▶ In social science, the term *sample size* means "the number of individuals being studied in a research project."
> —Kathleen Stassen Berger and Ross A. Thompson,
> *The Developing Person through Childhood and Adolescence*

39c Using quotation marks with other punctuation

Periods and commas go *inside* closing quotation marks.

▶ "Don't compromise yourself," said Janis Joplin. "You are all you've got."

Colons, semicolons, and footnote numbers go *outside* closing quotation marks.

▶ I felt one emotion after finishing "Eveline": sorrow.

▶ Tragedy is defined by Aristotle as "an imitation of an action that is serious and of a certain magnitude."[1]

Question marks, exclamation points, and dashes go *inside* if they are part of the quoted material, *outside* if they are not.

PART OF THE QUOTATION

▶ The cashier asked, "Would you like to super-size that?"

NOT PART OF THE QUOTATION

▶ What is the theme of "The Birth-Mark"?

39d Avoiding misused quotation marks

Do not use quotation marks for indirect quotations—those that do not use someone's exact words.

▶ Mother smiled and said that /"she was sure she would never forget the incident./"

Do not use quotation marks merely to add emphasis to particular
words or phrases.

▷ The hikers were startled by the appearance of a "gigantic" grizzly bear.

Do not use quotation marks around slang or colloquial language;
they create the impression that you are apologizing for using those
words. If you have a good reason to use slang or a colloquial term,
use it without quotation marks.

▷ After our twenty-mile hike, we were completely exhausted and
ready to "turn in."

40 Other Punctuation

Parentheses, brackets, dashes, colons, slashes, and ellipses are every-
where. Every URL includes colons and slashes, many sites use brackets
or parentheses to identify updates and embedded media, and dashes
and ellipses are increasingly common in writing that expresses con-
versational informality.

You can also use these punctuation marks for more formal pur-
poses: to signal relationships among parts of sentences, to create
particular rhythms, and to help readers follow your thoughts.

40a Using parentheses

Use parentheses to enclose material that is of minor or secondary
importance in a sentence—material that supplements, clarifies, com-
ments on, or illustrates what precedes or follows it.

> Inventors and men of genius have almost always been regarded as fools at the beginning **(and very often at the end)** of their careers.
> —Fyodor Dostoyevsky

> During my research, I found problems with the flat-rate income tax **(a single-rate tax with no deductions)**.

Parentheses are also used to enclose textual citations and numbers or letters in a list.

> Freud and his followers have had a most significant impact on the ways abnormal functioning is understood and treated **(Joseph, 1991)**. —Ronald J. Comer, *Abnormal Psychology*

The in-text citation in this sentence shows the style of the American Psychological Association (APA).

> Five distinct styles can be distinguished: **(1)** Old New England, **(2)** Deep South, **(3)** Middle American, **(4)** Wild West, and **(5)** Far West or Californian. —Alison Lurie, *The Language of Clothes*

With other punctuation. A period may be placed either inside or outside a closing parenthesis, depending on whether the parenthetical text is part of a larger sentence. A comma, if needed, is always placed *outside* a closing parenthesis (and never before an opening one).

> Gene Tunney's single defeat in an eleven-year career was to a flamboyant and dangerous fighter named Harry Greb **("The Human Windmill")**, who seems to have been, judging from boxing literature, the dirtiest fighter in history.
> —Joyce Carol Oates, "On Boxing"

40b Using brackets

Use brackets to enclose any parenthetical elements in material that is itself within parentheses. Brackets should also be used to enclose any explanatory words or comments that you are inserting into a quotation.

> Eventually, the investigation had to examine the major agencies (including the National Security Agency **[NSA]**) that were conducting covert operations.

▶ Massing notes that "on average, it [Fox News] attracts more than eight million people daily—more than double the number who watch CNN."

The bracketed words *Fox News* clarify the meaning of *it* in the original quotation.

In the quotation in the following sentence, the artist Gauguin's name is misspelled. The bracketed word *sic*, which means "so," tells readers that the person being quoted—not the writer who has picked up the quotation—made the mistake.

▶ One admirer wrote, "She was the most striking woman I'd ever seen—a sort of wonderful combination of Mia Farrow and one of Gaugin's [*sic*] Polynesian nymphs."

40c Using dashes

Use dashes to insert a comment or to highlight material in a sentence.

▶ The pleasures of reading itself—who doesn't remember?—were like those of Christmas cake, a sweet devouring.
                              —Eudora Welty, "A Sweet Devouring"

A single dash can be used to emphasize material at the end of a sentence, to mark a sudden change in tone, to indicate hesitation in speech, or to introduce a summary or an explanation.

▶ In the twentieth century it has become almost impossible to moralize about epidemics—except those which are transmitted sexually.
                              —Susan Sontag, *AIDS and Its Metaphors*

▶ In walking, the average adult person employs a motor mechanism that weighs about eighty pounds—sixty pounds of muscle and twenty pounds of bone.   —Edwin Way Teale

Dashes give more emphasis than parentheses to the material they enclose or set off. Many word-processing programs automatically convert two typed hyphens with no spaces before or after into a solid dash.

40d Using colors

Use a colon to introduce an explanation, an example, an appositive, a series, a list, or a quotation.

▶ At the baby's one-month birthday party, Ah Po gave him the Four Valuable Things: ink, inkslab, paper, and brush.
　　　　　　　　　　　　　　　　　—Maxine Hong Kingston, *China Men*

Use a colon rather than a comma to introduce a quotation when the lead-in is a complete sentence on its own.

▶ The 2013 State of the Union address ended with a bold challenge: "Well into our third century as a nation, it remains the task of us all . . . to be the authors of the next great chapter in our American story."

Colons are also used after salutations in letters; with numbers indicating hours, minutes, and seconds; with ratios; with biblical chapters and verses; with titles and subtitles; and in bibliographic entries.

▶ Dear Dr. Chapman:
▶ 4:59 PM
▶ a ratio of 5:1
▶ Ecclesiastes 3:1
▶ *The Joy of Insight: Passions of a Physicist*
▶ Boston: Bedford/St. Martin's, 2016

Misused colons. Do not put a colon between a **verb** and its **object** or complement (unless the object is a quotation), between a **preposition** and its object, or after such expressions as *such as*, *especially*, and *including*.

▶ Some natural fibers are: cotton, wool, silk, and linen.
▶ In poetry, additional power may come from devices such as: simile, metaphor, and alliteration.

40e Using slashes

Use a slash to separate alternatives.

▶ Then there was Daryl, the cabdriver/bartender.
—John L'Heureux, *The Handmaid of Desire*

Use a slash, preceded and followed by a space, to divide lines of poetry quoted within running text.

▶ The speaker of Sonnet 130 says of his mistress, "I love to hear her speak, yet well I know / That music hath a far more pleasing sound."

Slashes also separate parts of fractions and Internet addresses.

40f Using ellipses

An ellipsis is three equally spaced dots that indicate that something has been omitted from a quoted passage. Just as you should carefully use quotation marks around any material that you are quoting directly from a source, so you should carefully use an ellipsis to indicate that you have left out part of a quotation that otherwise appears to be a complete sentence. Ellipses have been used in the following example to indicate two omissions—one in the middle of the first sentence and one at the end of the second sentence.

ORIGINAL TEXT

▶ The quasi-official division of the population into three economic classes called high-, middle-, and low-income groups rather misses the point, because as a class indicator the amount of money is not as important as the source.
—Paul Fussell, "Notes on Class"

WITH ELLIPSES

▶ As Paul Fussell argues, "The quasi-official division of the population into three economic classes . . . rather misses the point. . . ."

When you omit the last part of a quoted sentence, add a period before the ellipsis—for a total of four dots. Be sure a complete sentence comes before the four dots. If your shortened quotation ends with a source citation (such as a page number, a name, or a title), place the documentation source in parentheses after the three ellipsis points and the closing quotation mark but before the period.

▶ Packer argues, "The Administration is right to reconsider its strategy . . ." (34).

You can also use an ellipsis to indicate a pause or a hesitation in speech in the same way that you can use a dash for that purpose. (For more uses of ellipses in informal writing, see 37d.)

▶ Then the voice, husky and familiar, came to wash over us—"The winnah, and still heavyweight champeen of the world . . . Joe Louis."
—Maya Angelou, *I Know Why the Caged Bird Sings*

41 Capital Letters

Capital letters are a key signal in everyday life. Look around any store to see their importance: you can shop for Levi's or *any* blue jeans, for Pepsi or *any* cola, for Kleenex or *any* tissue. In each of these instances, the capital letter indicates the name of a particular brand.

41a Capitalizing the first word of a sentence

With very few exceptions, capitalize the first word of a sentence. If you are quoting a full sentence, capitalize its first word.

▶ Kennedy said, "Let us never negotiate out of fear."

Capitalization of a nonquoted sentence following a colon is optional.

▶ Gould cites the work of Darwin: The [*or* the] theory of natural selection incorporates the principle of evolutionary ties among all animals.

Capitalize a sentence within parentheses unless the parenthetical sentence is inserted into another sentence.

▶ Gould cites the work of Darwin. (Other researchers cite more recent evolutionary theorists.)

▶ Gould cites the work of Darwin (see p. 150).

When citing poetry, follow the capitalization of the original poem. Though most poets capitalize the first word of each line in a poem, some do not.

▶ Morning sun heats up the young beech tree
leaves and almost lights them into fireflies
—June Jordan, "Aftermath"

41b Capitalizing proper nouns and proper adjectives

Capitalize proper **nouns** (those naming specific persons, places, and things) and most **adjectives** formed from proper nouns. All other nouns are common nouns and are not capitalized unless they are used as part of a proper noun: *a street*, but *Elm Street*.

Capitalized nouns and adjectives include personal names; nations, nationalities, and languages; months, days of the week, and holidays (but not seasons of the year); geographical names; structures and monuments; ships, trains, aircraft, and spacecraft; organizations, businesses, and government institutions; academic institutions and courses; historical events and eras; and religions, with their deities, followers, and sacred writings. For trade names, follow the capitalization you see in company advertising or on the product itself.

PROPER	COMMON
Alfred Hitchcock, Hitchcockian	a director
Brazil, Brazilian	a nation, a language
Pacific Ocean	an ocean
Challenger	a spaceship
Library of Congress	a federal agency

Political Science 102	a political science course
the Qur'an	a holy book
Catholicism	a religion
Cheerios, iPhone	cereal, a smartphone
Halloween	a holiday in the fall

41c Capitalizing titles before proper names

When used alone or following a proper name, most titles are not capitalized. One common exception is the word *president*, which many writers capitalize whenever it refers to the President of the United States.

Professor Gordon Chang	my history professor
Dr. Teresa Ramirez	Teresa Ramirez, our doctor

41d Capitalizing titles of works

Capitalize most words in titles of books, articles, speeches, stories, essays, plays, poems, documents, films, paintings, and musical compositions. Do not capitalize articles (*a, an, the*), **prepositions**, **conjunctions**, and the *to* in an **infinitive** unless they are the first or last words in a title or subtitle.

Walt Whitman: A Life	Declaration of Independence
"As Time Goes By"	*Hamilton*
"Crazy in Love"	*The Living Dead*

41e Revising unnecessary capitalization

Capitalize compass directions only if the word designates a specific geographical region.

▷ John Muir headed west, motivated by the desire to explore.

▷ Water rights are an increasingly contentious issue in the West.

 For Multilingual Writers

Learning English Capitalization

Capitalization systems vary considerably. Arabic, Chinese, Hebrew, and Hindi, for example, do not use capital letters at all. English may be the only language to capitalize the first-person singular pronoun (*I*), but Dutch and German capitalize some forms of the second-person pronoun (*you*)—and German also capitalizes all nouns.

Capitalize family relationships only if the word is used as part of a name or as a substitute for the name.

▶ When she was a child, my mother shared a room with my aunt.

▶ I could always tell when Mother was annoyed with Aunt Rose.

42 Abbreviations and Numbers

Anytime you look up an address, you see an abundance of abbreviations and numbers, as in the following listing from a Google map:

Tarrytown Music Hall   13 Main St   Tarrytown, NY

Abbreviations and numbers allow writers to present detailed information in a small amount of space.

42a Using abbreviations

Certain titles are normally abbreviated.

Ms. Susanna Moller   Henry Louis Gates Jr.

Mr. Mark Otuteye   Karen Lancry, MD

Religious, academic, and government titles should be spelled out in academic writing but can be abbreviated in other writing when they appear before a full name.

Rev. Fleming Rutledge   Reverend Rutledge

Prof. Jaime Mejía   Professor Mejía

Sen. Christopher Dodd   Senator Dodd

Business, government, and science terms. As long as you can be sure your readers will understand them, use common abbreviations such as *PBS*, *NASA*, and *DNA*. If an abbreviation may be unfamiliar, spell out the full term the first time you use it, and give the abbreviation in parentheses; after that, you can use the abbreviation by itself. Use abbreviations such as *Co.*, *Inc.*, *Corp.*, and *&* only if they are part of a company's official name.

▶ The Comprehensive Test Ban (CTB) Treaty was first proposed in the 1950s. For those nations signing it, the CTB would bring to a halt all nuclear weapons testing.

▶ Sears, Roebuck & Co. was the only large ~~corp.~~ in town.
                                         corporation
                                              ^

With numbers. The following abbreviations are acceptable with specific years and times.

399 BCE ("before the common era") *or* 399 BC ("before Christ")

49 CE ("common era") *or* AD 49 (*anno Domini*, Latin for "year of our Lord")

11:15 AM (*or* a.m.)

9:00 PM (*or* p.m.)

Symbols such as % and $ are acceptable with figures (*$11*) but not with words (*eleven dollars*). Units of measurement can be abbreviated in charts and graphs (*4 in.*) but not in the body of a paper (*four inches*).

In notes and source citations. Some Latin abbreviations required in notes and in source citations are not appropriate in the body of a paper.

cf.   compare (*confer*)

e.g.   for example (*exempli gratia*)

et al.   and others (*et alii* or *et aliae*)

etc.	and so forth (*et cetera*)
i.e.	that is (*id est*)
N.B.	note well (*nota bene*)

In addition, except in notes and source citations, do not abbreviate such terms as *chapter*, *page*, and *volume* or the names of months, states, cities, or countries. Two exceptions are *Washington, D.C.*, and *U.S.* The latter abbreviation is acceptable as an **adjective** but not as a **noun**: *U.S. borders* but *in the United States.*

42b   Using numbers

If you can write out a number in one or two words, do so. Use figures for longer numbers.

▸ Her screams were ignored by ~~38~~ people.
  thirty-eight

▸ A baseball is held together by ~~two hundred sixteen~~ red stitches.
  216

If one of several numbers *of the same kind* in the same sentence requires a figure, you should use figures for all the numbers in that sentence.

▸ An audio system can range in cost from ~~one hundred dollars~~ to $2,599.
  $100

When a sentence begins with a number, either spell out the number or rewrite the sentence.

▸ *Taxpayers spent sixteen million dollars for*
  119 years of CIA labor. ~~cost taxpayers sixteen million dollars.~~

In general, use figures for the following:

ADDRESSES	23 Main Street; 175 Fifth Avenue
DATES	September 17, 1951; 6 June 1983; 4 BCE; the 1860s
DECIMALS AND FRACTIONS	65.34; 8½
EXACT AMOUNTS OF MONEY	$7,348; $1.46 trillion; $2.50; thirty-five (*or* 35) cents

PERCENTAGES	*77* percent (*or* 77%)
SCORES AND STATISTICS	an 8–3 Red Sox victory; an average age of 22
TIME OF DAY	6:00 AM (*or* a.m.)

 Italics

The slanted type known as *italics* is more than just a pretty typeface. Indeed, italics give words special meaning or emphasis. In the sentence "Many people read *People* on the subway every day," the italics (and the capital letter) tell us that *People* is a publication. You may use your computer to produce italic type; if not, underline words that you would otherwise italicize.

43a Italicizing titles

In general, use italics for titles and subtitles of long works; use quotation marks for shorter works (39b).

BOOKS	*Fun Home: A Family Tragicomic*
CHOREOGRAPHIC WORKS	Agnes de Mille's *Rodeo*
FILMS AND VIDEOS	*Star Wars*
LONG MUSICAL WORKS	*The Magic Flute*
LONG POEMS	*Bhagavad Gita*
MAGAZINES AND JOURNALS	*Ebony;* the *New England Journal of Medicine*
NEWSPAPERS	the Cleveland *Plain Dealer*
PAINTINGS AND SCULPTURE	Georgia O'Keeffe's *Black Iris*
PAMPHLETS	Thomas Paine's *Common Sense*
PLAYS	*Les Misérables*
RADIO SERIES	*All Things Considered*

ALBUM-LENGTH RECORDINGS	*The Ramones Leave Home*
SOFTWARE	*Quicken*
TELEVISION SERIES	*Breaking Bad*

Do not italicize titles of sacred books, such as the Bible and the Qur'an; public documents, such as the Constitution and the Magna Carta; or your own papers.

43b Italicizing words, letters, and numbers used as terms

▶ On the back of his jersey was the famous *24*.

▶ One characteristic of some New York speech is the absence of postvocalic *r*—for example, pronouncing the word *four* as "fouh."

43c Italicizing non-English words

Italicize words from other languages unless they have become part of English—like the French "bourgeois" or the Italian "pasta," for example. If a word is in an English dictionary, it does not need italics.

▶ At last one of the phantom sleighs gliding along the street would come to a stop, and with gawky haste Mr. Burness in his fox-furred *shapka* would make for our door.

—Vladimir Nabokov, *Speak, Memory*

43d Italicizing names of aircraft, ships, and trains

| *Spirit of St. Louis* | Amtrak's *Silver Star* | U.S.S. *Iowa* |

43e Using italics for emphasis

Italics can help create emphasis in writing, but use them sparingly for this purpose. It is usually better to create emphasis with sentence structure and word choice.

▶ Great literature and a class of literate readers are nothing new in India. What is new is the emergence of a gifted generation of Indian writers *working in English.* —Salman Rushdie

44 Hyphens

Hyphens are undoubtedly confusing to many people—hyphen problems are now one of the twenty most common surface errors in student writing (see p. 10). The confusion is understandable. Over time, the conventions for hyphen use in a given word can change (*tomorrow* was once spelled *to-morrow*). New words, even compounds such as *firewall*, generally don't use hyphens, but controversy continues to rage over whether to hyphenate *email* (or is it *e-mail?*). And some words are hyphenated when they serve one kind of purpose in a sentence and not when they serve another.

44a Using hyphens with compound words

Compound nouns. Some are one word (*rowboat*), some are separate words (*hard drive*), and some require hyphens (*sister-in-law*). You should consult a dictionary to be sure.

Compound adjectives. Hyphenate most compound **adjectives** that precede a noun, but not those that follow a noun.

| a *well-liked* boss | My boss is *well liked.* |
| a *six-foot* plank | The plank is *six feet long.* |

In general, the reason for hyphenating compound adjectives is to make meaning clear.

▶ **Designers often use potted plants as living‑room dividers.**

Without the hyphen, *living* may seem to modify *room dividers.*

Never hyphenate an *-ly* adverb and an adjective.

▶ **They used a widely⁄distributed mailing list.**

Fractions and compound numbers. Use a hyphen to write out fractions and to spell out compound numbers from twenty-one to ninety-nine.

one‑seventh   fifty‑four thousand

44b Using hyphens with prefixes and suffixes

The majority of words containing prefixes or suffixes are written without hyphens, such as *antiwar* or *Romanesque*. Following are some exceptions:

BEFORE CAPITALIZED BASE WORDS	un-American, non-Catholic
WITH FIGURES	pre-1960, post-1945
WITH CERTAIN PREFIXES AND SUFFIXES	all-state, ex-partner, self-possessed, quasi-legislative, mayor-elect, fifty-odd
WITH COMPOUND BASE WORDS	pre-high school, post-cold war
FOR CLARITY OR EASE OF READING	re-cover, anti-inflation, troll-like

Re-cover means "cover again"; the hyphen distinguishes it from *recover*, meaning "get well." In *anti-inflation* and *troll-like*, the hyphens separate confusing clusters of vowels and consonants.

> ## Checklist

Editing for Hyphens

▶ Double-check compound words to be sure they are properly closed up, separated, or hyphenated. If in doubt, consult a dictionary. (44a)

▶ Check all terms that have prefixes or suffixes to see whether you need hyphens. (44b)

▶ Do not hyphenate two-word verbs or word groups that serve as subject complements. (44c)

44c Avoiding unnecessary hyphens

Unnecessary hyphens are at least as common a problem as omitted ones. Do not hyphenate the parts of a two-word verb such as *depend on, turn off,* or *tune out* (27b).

▶ Each player must pick⁄up a medical form before football tryouts.

The words *pick up* act as a verb and should not be hyphenated.

However, be careful to check that two words do indeed function as a verb in the sentence; if they function as an adjective, a hyphen may be needed.

▶ Let's sign up for the early class.

The verb *sign up* should not have a hyphen.

▶ Where is the sign-up sheet?

The adjective *sign-up,* which modifies the noun *sheet,* needs a hyphen.

Do not hyphenate a subject complement—a word group that follows a linking verb (such as a form of *be* or *seem*) and describes the subject.

▶ Audrey is almost three⁄years⁄old.

Documentation

Writing
Processes

Writing That
Works

Research

Language

Grammar

Style

Punctuation/
Mechanics

Documentation

45 MLA Style

Many fields in the humanities ask students to follow Modern Language Association (MLA) style to format manuscripts and to document various kinds of sources. This chapter introduces MLA guidelines. For further reference, consult the *MLA Handbook*, Eighth Edition (2016).

45a Understanding MLA citation style

Why does academic work call for very careful citation practices when writing for the general public may not? The answer is that readers of your academic work expect source citations for several reasons:

- Source citations demonstrate that you've done your homework on your topic and that you are a part of the conversation surrounding it. Careful citation shows your readers what you know, where you stand, and what you think is important.
- Source citations show your readers that you understand the need to give credit when you make use of someone else's intellectual property. Especially in academic writing, when it's better to be safe than sorry, include a citation for any source you think you might need to cite. (See 15c.)
- Source citations give explicit directions to guide readers who want to look for themselves at the works you're using.

The guidelines for MLA style help you with this last purpose, giving you instructions on exactly what information to include in your citation and how to format that information.

45b Considering the context of your sources

New kinds of sources crop up regularly. As the *MLA Handbook* confirms, there are often several "correct" ways to cite a source, so you will need to think carefully about *your own context* for using the source so you can identify the pieces of information that you

should emphasize or include and any other information that might be helpful to your readers.

Elements of MLA citations. The first step is to identify elements that are commonly found in most works writers cite.

AUTHOR AND TITLE. The first two elements, both of which are needed for many sources, are the author's name and the title of the work. Each of these elements is followed by a period.

Author. Title.

Even in these elements, your context is important. The author of a novel may be obvious, but who is the "author" of a television episode? The director? The writer? The show's creator? The star? The answer may depend on the focus of your own work. If an actor's performance is central to your discussion, then MLA guidelines ask you to identify the actor as the author. If the plot is your focus, you might name the writer of the episode as the author.

CONTAINER. The next step is to identify elements of what the MLA calls the "container" for the work. The context in which you are discussing the source and the context in which you find the source will help you determine what counts as a container in each case. If you watch a movie in a theater, you won't identify a separate container after the film title. But if you watch the same movie as part of a DVD box set of the director's work, the container title is the name of the box set. If you read an article in a print journal, the first container will be the journal that the article appears in. If you read it online, the journal may also be part of a second, larger container, such as a database. Thinking about a source as nested in larger containers may help you to visualize how a citation works.

The elements you may include in the "container" part of your citation include the following, in this order: the title of the larger container, if it's different from the title of the work; the names of any contributors such as editors or translators; the version or edition; the volume and issue numbers; the publisher or sponsor; the date of publication; and a location such as the page numbers,

DOI, permalink, or URL. These elements are separated by commas, and the end of the container is marked with a period.

Author. Title. Container title, contributor names, version or edition, volume and issue numbers, publisher, date, location.

Most sources won't include all these pieces of information, so include only the elements that are available and relevant to create an acceptable citation. If you need a second container—for instance, if you are citing an article from a journal you found in a database—you simply add it after the first one, beginning with the container title and including as many of the same container elements as you can find. The rest of this chapter offers many examples of how elements and containers are combined to create citations.

Examples from student work

ARTICLE IN A DATABASE. David Craig, whose research writing appears in 45f, found a potentially useful article in Academic Search Premier, a database he accessed through his library website. Many databases are digital collections of articles that originally appeared in print periodicals, and the articles usually have the same written-word content as they did in print form, without changes or updates.

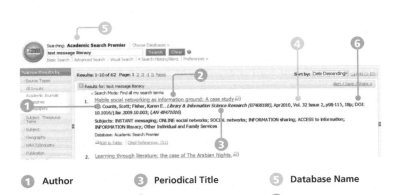

① **Author**   ③ **Periodical Title**   ⑤ **Database Name**

② **Article Title**   ④ **Print Publication**   ⑥ **DOI**
                              Data

From the page shown on p. 216, David Craig was able to click through to read the full text of the article. He printed this computer screen in case he needed to cite the article: the image has all the information that he would need to create a complete MLA citation, including the original print publication information for the article, the name of the database, and the location (here, a "digital object identifier" or DOI, which provides the source's permanent location). A complete citation for this article would look like this:

Counts, Scott, and Karen E. Fisher. "Mobile Social Networking as
 Information Ground: A Case Study." *Library and Information Science
 Research*, vol. 32, no. 2, Apr. 2010, pp. 98-115. *Academic Search
 Premier*, doi:10.1016/j.lisr.2009.10.003.

Note that the periodical, *Library and Information Science Research*, is the first container of the article, and the database, *Academic Search Premier*, is the second container. Notice, too, that the first container includes just four relevant elements—the journal title, number (here, that means the volume and issue numbers), date, and page numbers; and the second container includes just two—the database title and location. Publisher information is not readily available for journals and databases, so it is not required.

Types of sources.   Look at the Directory to MLA Style on pp. 227–28 for guidelines on citing various types of sources, including print books, print periodicals (journals, magazines, and newspapers), digital written-word sources, and other sources (films, artwork) that consist mainly of material other than written words. A digital version of a source may include updates or corrections that the print version of the same work lacks, so MLA guidelines ask you to indicate where you found the source. If you can't find a model exactly like the source you've selected, see "Citing sources that don't match any model exactly" on p. 229.

Parts of citations.   MLA citations appear in two parts—a brief in-text citation in parentheses in the body of your written text, and a full citation in the list of works cited, to which the in-text citation directs readers. A basic in-text citation includes the author's name and the page number (for a print source), but many variations on this format are discussed in 45d.

In the text of his research project (see 45f), David Craig quotes material from a print book and from an online report. He cites both parenthetically, pointing readers to entries on his list of works cited, as shown on p. 268. These examples show just two of the many ways to cite sources using in-text citations and a list of works cited. You'll need to make case-by-case decisions based on the types of sources you include.

> for good reason. According to David Crystal, an internationally recognized scholar of linguistics at the University of Wales, as young children develop and learn how words string together to express ideas, they go through many phases of language play. The singsong rhymes and nonsensical chants of preschoolers are vital to learning language, and a healthy appetite for wordplay leads to a better command of language later in life (182).

Craig 10

...nd in SAT
...n Is Yielding
...Concern. College
Board, 2002.

Crystal, David. *Language Play.* U of Chicago P, 1998.

Ferguson, Niall. "Texting Makes U Stupid." *Newsweek,* vol. 158, no. 12, 19 Sept. 2011, p. 11. *EBSCOHost,* connection.ebscohost.com/c/articles/65454341/texting-makes-u-stupid.

Leibowitz, Wendy R. "Technology Transforms Writing and the Teaching of Writing." *Chronicle of Higher Education,* 26 Nov. 1999, pp. A67-A68.

Lenhart, Amanda. *Teens, Smartphones, & Texting.* Pew Research Center, 19 Mar. 2012, www.pewinternet.org/files/old-media//Files/Reports/2012/PIP_Teens_Smartphones_and_Texting.pdf.

Lenhart, Amanda, et al. *Writing, Technology & Teens.* Pew Research Center, 24 Apr. 2008, www.pewinternet.org/2008/04/24/writing-technology-and-teens/.

Lenhart, Amanda, and Oliver Lewis. *Teenage Life Online: The Rise of the Instant-Message Generation and the Internet's Impact on Friendships and Family Relationships.* Pew Research Center, 21 June 2001, www.pewinternet.org/2001/06/20/the-rise-of-the-instant-message-generation/.

> is rising among the young. According to the Pew Internet & American Life Project, 85 percent of those aged twelve to seventeen at least occasionally write text messages, instant messages, or comments on social networking sites (Lenhart et al.) In 2001, the most conservative estimate based on

...'?" *Bedford Bits,* 9 Apr. 2015, ...'the-english-community/bedford ...ma-queen.

...ext-Messaging Skills Can Score ...11 Mar. 2005, www ...sc.html.

"SAT Trends 2011." *Collegeboard.org,* 14 Sept. 2011, research.collegeboard.org/programs/sat/data/archived/cb-seniors-2011/tables.

Explanatory notes.   MLA citation style asks you to include explanatory notes for information that doesn't readily fit into your text but is needed for clarification or further explanation. In addition, MLA permits bibliographic notes for information about or evaluation of a source, or to list multiple sources that relate to a single point. Use superscript numbers in the text to refer readers to the notes, which may appear as endnotes (under the heading *Notes* on a separate page immediately before the list of works cited) or as footnotes at the bottom of each page where a superscript number appears.

EXAMPLE OF SUPERSCRIPT NUMBER IN TEXT

Although messaging relies on the written word, many messagers disregard standard writing conventions. For example, here is a snippet from an IM conversation between two teenage girls:[1]

EXAMPLE OF EXPLANATORY NOTE

1. This transcript of an IM conversation was collected on 20 Nov. 2016. The teenagers' names are concealed to protect their privacy.

45c Following MLA manuscript format

The MLA recommends the following format for the manuscript of a research paper. However, check with your instructor before preparing the final draft of a print work.

First page and title.   The MLA does not require a title page. Type each of the following items on a separate line on the first page, beginning one inch from the top and flush with the left margin: your name, the instructor's name, the course name and number, and the date. Double-space between each item; then double-space again and center the title. Double-space between the title and the beginning of the text.

Margins and spacing.   Leave one-inch margins at the top and bottom and on both sides of each page. Double-space the entire text, including set-off quotations, notes, and the list of works cited. Indent the first line of a paragraph one-half inch. Indent set-off quotations one-half inch.

Page numbers. Include your last name and the page number on each page, one-half inch below the top and flush with the right margin.

Long quotations. When quoting a long passage (more than four typed lines), set the quotation off by starting it on a new line and indenting each line one-half inch from the left margin. Do not enclose the passage in quotation marks (39a).

Headings. MLA style allows, but does not require, headings. However, many students and instructors find them helpful. (See 3b for guidelines on using headings and subheadings.)

Visuals. Visuals (such as photographs, drawings, charts, graphs, and tables) should be placed as near as possible to the relevant text. (See 15b for guidelines on incorporating visuals into your text.) Tables should have a label and number (*Table 1*) and a clear caption. The label and caption should be aligned on the left, on separate lines. Give the source information below the table. All other visuals should be labeled *Figure* (abbreviated *Fig.*), numbered, and captioned. The label and caption should appear on the same line, followed by source information. Remember to refer to each visual before it appears in your text, indicating how it contributes to the point(s) that you are making.

45d Creating MLA in-text citations

MLA style requires a citation in the text of a writing project for every quotation, paraphrase, summary, or other material requiring documentation (see 15c). In-text citations document material from other sources with both signal phrases and parenthetical references. Parenthetical references should include the information your readers need to locate the full reference in the list of works cited at the end of the text. An in-text citation in MLA style gives the reader two kinds of information: (1) it indicates which source on the works-cited page the writer is referring to, and (2) it explains where in the source the material quoted, paraphrased, or summarized can be found, if the source has page numbers or other numbered sections.

The basic MLA in-text citation includes the author's last name either in a signal phrase introducing the source material (see 15a) or in parentheses at the end of the sentence. For sources with stable page numbers, it also includes the page number in parentheses at the end of the sentence.

SAMPLE CITATION USING A SIGNAL PHRASE

In his discussion of Monty Python routines, Crystal notes that the group relished "breaking the normal rules" of language (107).

SAMPLE PARENTHETICAL CITATION

A noted linguist explains that Monty Python humor often relied on "bizarre linguistic interactions" (Crystal 108).

(For digital sources without stable page numbers, see model 3.)

Note in the examples on the following pages where punctuation is placed in relation to the parentheses.

DIRECTORY TO MLA STYLE

MLA style for in-text citations

1. AUTHOR NAMED IN A SIGNAL PHRASE. The MLA recommends using the author's name in a signal phrase to introduce the material and citing the page number(s) in parentheses.

> Lee claims that his comic-book creation, Thor, was "the first regularly published superhero to speak in a consistently archaic manner" (199).

2. AUTHOR NAMED IN A PARENTHETICAL REFERENCE. When you do not mention the author in a signal phrase, include the author's last name before the page number(s), if any, in the parentheses. Use no punctuation between the author's name and the page number(s).

> The word *Bollywood* is sometimes considered an insult because it implies that Indian movies are merely "a derivative of the American film industry" (Chopra 9).

3. DIGITAL OR NONPRINT SOURCE. Give enough information in a signal phrase or in parentheses for readers to locate the source in your list of works cited. Many works found online or in electronic databases lack stable page numbers; you can omit the page number in such cases. However, if you are citing a work with stable pagination, such as an article in PDF format, include the page number in parentheses.

DIGITAL SOURCE WITHOUT STABLE PAGE NUMBERS

> As a *Slate* analysis explains, "Prominent sports psychologists get praised for their successes and don't get grief for their failures" (Engber).

DIGITAL SOURCE WITH STABLE PAGE NUMBERS

> According to Whitmarsh, the British military had experimented with using balloons for observation as far back as 1879 (328).

If the source includes numbered sections, paragraphs, or screens, include the abbreviation (*sec.*), paragraph (*par.*), or screen (*scr.*) number in parentheses.

4. TWO AUTHORS. Use both authors' last names in a signal phrase or in parentheses.

> Gilbert and Gubar point out that in the Grimm version of "Snow White," the king "never actually appears in this story at all" (37).

5. THREE OR MORE AUTHORS. Use the first author's name and *et al.* ("and others"), unless your instructor asks you to list every name.

> Similarly, as Belenky et al. assert, examining the lives of women expands our understanding of human development (7).

6. ORGANIZATION AS AUTHOR. Give the group's full name in a signal phrase; in parentheses, abbreviate any common words in the name.

> Any study of social welfare involves a close analysis of "the impacts, the benefits, and the costs" of its policies (Social Research Corp. iii).

7. UNKNOWN AUTHOR. Use the full title, if it is brief, in your text — or the first word of the title in parentheses.

> One analysis defines *hype* as "an artificially engendered atmosphere of hysteria" (*Today's* 51).

8. AUTHOR OF TWO OR MORE WORKS CITED IN THE SAME PROJECT. If your list of works cited has more than one work by the same author, include the title of the work you are citing in a signal phrase or the first word of the title in parentheses to prevent reader confusion.

> Gardner shows readers their own silliness in his description of a "pointless, ridiculous monster, crouched in the shadows, stinking of dead men, murdered children, and martyred cows" (*Grendel* 2).

9. TWO OR MORE AUTHORS WITH THE SAME LAST NAME. Include the author's first *and* last names in a signal phrase or first initial and last name in a parenthetical reference.

> Children will learn to write if they are allowed to choose their own subjects, James Britton asserts, citing the Schools Council study of the 1960s (37-42).

10. MULTIVOLUME WORK. In a parenthetical reference, note the volume number first and then the page number(s), with a colon and one space between them.

> Modernist writers prized experimentation and gradually even sought to blur the line between poetry and prose, according to Forster (3: 150).

If you name only one volume of the work in your list of works cited, include only the page number in the parentheses.

11. LITERARY WORK. Because literary works are usually available in many different editions, cite the page number(s) from the edition you used followed by a semicolon, and then give other identifying information that will lead readers to the passage in any edition. Indicate the act and/or scene in a play (*37; sc. 1*). For a novel, indicate the part or chapter (*175; ch. 4*).

> In utter despair, Dostoyevsky's character Mitya wonders aloud about the "terrible tragedies realism inflicts on people" (376; bk. 8, ch. 2).

For a poem, cite the part (if there is one) and line(s), separated by a period. If you are citing only line numbers, use the word *line(s)* in the first reference (*lines 33-34*).

> Whitman speculates, "All goes onward and outward, nothing collapses, / And to die is different from what anyone supposed, and luckier" (6.129-30).

For a verse play, give only the act, scene, and line numbers, separated by periods.

> The witches greet Banquo as "lesser than Macbeth, and greater" (1.3.65).

12. WORK IN AN ANTHOLOGY OR COLLECTION. For an essay, short story, or other piece of prose reprinted in an anthology, use the name of the author of the work, not the editor of the anthology, but use the page number(s) from the anthology.

> Narratives of captivity play a major role in early writing by women in the United States, as demonstrated by Silko (219).

13. SACRED TEXT. To cite a sacred text such as the Qur'an or the Bible, give the title of the edition you used, the book, and the chapter and verse (or their equivalent) separated by a period. In your text, spell out the names of books. In parenthetical references, use

abbreviations for books with names of five or more letters (*Gen.* for *Genesis*).

> He ignored the admonition "Pride goes before destruction, and a haughty spirit before a fall" (*New Oxford Annotated Bible,* Prov. 16.18).

14. ENCYCLOPEDIA OR DICTIONARY ENTRY. An entry from a reference work—such as an encyclopedia or a dictionary—without an author will appear on the works-cited list under the entry's title. Enclose the entry title in quotation marks, and place it in parentheses. Omit the page number for print reference works that arrange entries alphabetically.

> The term *prion* was coined by Stanley B. Prusiner from the words *proteinaceous* and *infectious* and a suffix meaning *particle* ("Prion").

15. GOVERNMENT SOURCE WITH NO AUTHOR NAMED. Because entries for sources authored by government agencies will appear on your list of works cited under the name of the country (see 45e, item 69), your in-text citation for such a source should include the name of the country as well as the name of the agency responsible for the source.

> To reduce the agricultural runoff into the Chesapeake Bay, the United States Environmental Protection Agency has argued that "[h]igh nutrient loading crops, such as corn and soybean, should be replaced with alternatives in environmentally sensitive areas" (2-26).

16. ENTIRE WORK. Include the reference in the text, without any page numbers.

> Krakauer's *Into the Wild* both criticizes and admires the solitary impulses of its young hero, which end up killing him.

17. INDIRECT SOURCE (AUTHOR QUOTING SOMEONE ELSE). Use the abbreviation *qtd. in* to indicate that you are quoting from someone else's report of a source.

> As Arthur Miller says, "When somebody is destroyed everybody finally contributes to it, but in Willy's case, the end product would be virtually the same" (qtd. in Martin and Meyer 375).

18. TWO OR MORE SOURCES IN ONE CITATION. Separate the information with semicolons.

Economists recommend that *employment* be redefined to include unpaid domestic labor (Clark 148; Nevins 39).

19. VISUAL. When you include an image in your text, number it and include a parenthetical reference (*see Fig. 2*). Number figures (photos, drawings, cartoons, maps, graphs, and charts) and tables separately. Each visual should include a caption with the figure or table number and information about the source—either a complete citation or enough information to direct readers to the works-cited entry.

This trend is illustrated in a chart distributed by the College Board as part of its 2011 analysis of aggregate SAT data (see Fig. 1).

Soon after the preceding sentence, readers find the following figure and a caption referring them to the entry in the list of works cited (see 45f):

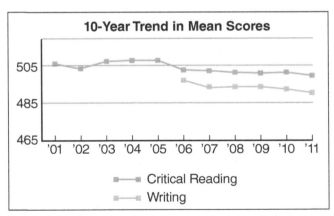

Fig. 1. Ten-year trend in mean SAT reading and writing scores (2001-2011). Data source: "SAT Trends 2011."

An image that you create might appear with a caption like this:

Fig. 4. Young women reading magazines. Personal photograph by author.

45e Creating an MLA list of works cited

A list of works cited is an alphabetical list of the sources you have referred to in your essay. (If your instructor asks you to list everything you have read as background, call the list *Works Consulted*.)

 Checklist

Citing Sources That Don't Match Any Model Exactly

What should you do if your source doesn't match any of the models exactly? Suppose, for instance, that your source is a translated essay that appears in the fifth edition of an anthology.

▶ Identify a basic model to follow. For example, if you decide that your source looks most like an essay in an anthology, you would start with a citation that looks like model 10.

▶ After listing author and title information (if given), enter as many of the elements of the container as you can find (see 45b): title of the larger container, if any; other contributors, such as editor or translator; version or edition; volume; publisher; date; and page numbers or other location information such as a URL or DOI. End the container with a period. If the container is nested in a larger container, collect the information from the second container as well.

▶ If you aren't sure which model to follow or how to create a combination model with multiple containers, ask your instructor.

Formatting a list of works cited

- Start your list on a separate page after the text of your document and any notes.
- Center the heading *Works Cited* (not italicized or in quotation marks) one inch from the top of the page.
- Begin each entry flush with the left margin, but indent subsequent lines one-half inch. Double-space the entire list.
- List sources alphabetically by the first word. Start with the author's name, if available, or the editor's name. If no author or editor is given, start with the title.
- List the author's last name first, followed by a comma and the first name. If a source has two authors, the second author's name appears first name first (see model 2).
- Capitalize every important word in titles and subtitles. Italicize titles of books and long works, but put titles of shorter works in quotation marks.

Guidelines for author listings

The list of works cited is always arranged alphabetically. The in-text citations in your writing point readers toward particular sources on the list.

NAME CITED IN SIGNAL PHRASE IN TEXT

Crystal explains . . .

NAME IN PARENTHETICAL CITATION IN TEXT

. . . (Crystal 107).

BEGINNING OF ENTRY ON LIST OF WORKS CITED

Crystal, David.

Models 1–5 explain how to arrange author names. The information that follows the name depends on the type of work you are citing — a book (models 6–27); a print periodical (models 28–34); a written text from a digital source, such as an article from a website or database (models 35–51); sources from art, film, comics, or other media, including live performances (models 52–67); and academic, government, and legal sources (models 68–75). Consult the model that most closely resembles the source you are using.

1. ONE AUTHOR. Put the last name first, followed by a comma, the first name (and initial, if any), and a period.

Crystal, David.

2. MULTIPLE AUTHORS. For two authors, list the first author with the last name first (see model 1). Follow this with a comma, the word *and*, and the name of the second author with the first name first.

Gilbert, Sandra M., and Susan Gubar.

For three or more authors, list the first author followed by a comma and *et al.* ("and others").

> Lupton, Ellen, et al.

3. ORGANIZATION OR GROUP AUTHOR. Give the name of the group, government agency, corporation, or other organization listed as the author.

> Getty Trust.

> United States. Government Accountability Office.

4. UNKNOWN AUTHOR. When the author is not identified, begin the entry with the title, and alphabetize by the first important word. Italicize titles of books and long works, but put titles of articles and other short works in quotation marks.

> "California Sues EPA over Emissions."

> *New Concise World Atlas.*

5. TWO OR MORE WORKS BY THE SAME AUTHOR. Arrange the entries alphabetically by title. Include the author's name in the first entry, but in subsequent entries, use three hyphens followed by a period. (For the basic format for citing a book, see model 6. For the basic format for citing an article from an online newspaper, see model 38.)

> Chopra, Anupama. "Bollywood Princess, Hollywood Hopeful." *The New York Times*, 10 Feb. 2008, nyti.ms/1QEtNpF.

> ---. *King of Bollywood: Shah Rukh Khan and the Seductive World of Indian Cinema.* Warner Books, 2007.

Note: Use three hyphens only when the work is by *exactly* the same author(s) as the previous entry.

Print books

6. BASIC FORMAT FOR A BOOK. Begin with the author name(s). (See models 1–5.) Then include the title and subtitle, the publisher, and

the publication year. The source map on pp. 234–35 shows where to find this information in a typical book.

> Crystal, David. *Language Play*. U of Chicago P, 1998.

Note: Place a period and a space after the name and title, and end with a period. Place a comma after the publisher, and in the publisher's name, omit *Co.* or *Inc.*, and abbreviate *University Press* to *UP*.

7. AUTHOR AND EDITOR BOTH NAMED

> Bangs, Lester. *Psychotic Reactions and Carburetor Dung*. Edited by Greil
> Marcus, Alfred A. Knopf, 1988.

Note: To cite the editor's contribution instead, begin the entry with the editor's name.

> Marcus, Greil, editor. *Psychotic Reactions and Carburetor Dung*. By Lester
> Bangs, Alfred A. Knopf, 1988.

8. EDITOR, NO AUTHOR NAMED

> Wall, Cheryl A., editor. *Changing Our Own Words*: *Essays on Criticism,*
> *Theory, and Writing by Black Women*. Rutgers UP, 1989.

9. ANTHOLOGY. Cite an entire anthology the same way you would cite a book with an editor and no named author (see model 8).

> Walker, Dale L., editor. *Westward*: *A Fictional History of the American West*.
> Forge Books, 2003.

10. WORK IN AN ANTHOLOGY OR CHAPTER IN A BOOK WITH AN EDITOR. List the author(s) of the selection; the selection title, in quotation marks; the title of the book, italicized; the words *edited by* and the name(s) of the editor(s); the publisher; the year; and the abbreviation *pp.* with the selection's page numbers.

> Komunyakaa, Yusef. "Facing It." *The Seagull Reader,* edited by Joseph
> Kelly, W. W. Norton, 2000, pp. 126-27.

Note: To provide original publication information for a reprinted selection, use the original publication information as a second container (see 45b):

> Byatt, A. S. "The Thing in the Forest." *The O. Henry Prize Stories 2003*,
>> edited by Laura Furman, Anchor Books, 2003, pp. 3-22. Originally
>> published in *The New Yorker*, 3 June 2002, pp. 80-89.

11. TWO OR MORE ITEMS FROM THE SAME ANTHOLOGY. List the anthology as one entry (see model 9). Also list each selection separately with a cross-reference to the anthology.

> Estleman, Loren D. "Big Tim Magoon and the Wild West." Walker, pp. 391-404.

> Salzer, Susan K. "Miss Libbie Tells All." Walker, pp. 199-212.

12. TRANSLATION

> Bolaño, Roberto. *2666*. Translated by Natasha Wimmer, Farrar, Straus and
>> Giroux, 2008.

13. BOOK WITH BOTH TRANSLATOR AND EDITOR. List the editor's and translator's names after the title, in the order they appear on the title page.

> Kant, Immanuel. *"Toward Perpetual Peace" and Other Writings on Politics,*
>> *Peace, and History*. Edited by Pauline Kleingeld, translated by David L.
>> Colclasure, Yale UP, 2006.

14. TRANSLATION OF A SECTION OF A BOOK. If different translators have worked on various parts of the book, identify the translator of the part you are citing.

> García Lorca, Federico. *"The Little Mad Boy."* Translated by W. S. Merwin.
>> *The Selected Poems of Federico García Lorca*, edited by Francisco
>> García Lorca and Donald M. Allen, Penguin, 1969, pp. 51-53.

15. TRANSLATION OF A BOOK BY AN UNKNOWN AUTHOR

> *Grettir's Saga*. Translated by Denton Fox and Hermann Palsson, U of
>> Toronto P, 1974.

Take information from the book's title page and copyright page (on the reverse side of the title page), not from the book's cover or a library catalog.

1 **Author.** List the last name first. End with a period. For variations, see models 2–5.

2 **Title.** Italicize the title and any subtitle; capitalize all major words. End with a period.

3 **Publisher.** Identify the publisher's name as given on the book's title page. If more than one publisher appears on the title page, separate the names with a slash, leaving a space before and after the slash. If no publisher is listed on the title page, check the copyright page. Abbreviate *University* and *Press* as *U* and *P* (*Oxford UP*). Omit terms such as *Company* and *Incorporated*. Follow the publisher's name with a comma.

4 **Year of publication.** If more than one copyright date is given, use the most recent one. End with a period.

A citation for the book on p. 235 would look like this:

Patel, Raj. *The Value of Nothing: How to Reshape Market Society and Redefine Democracy.* Picador, 2009.

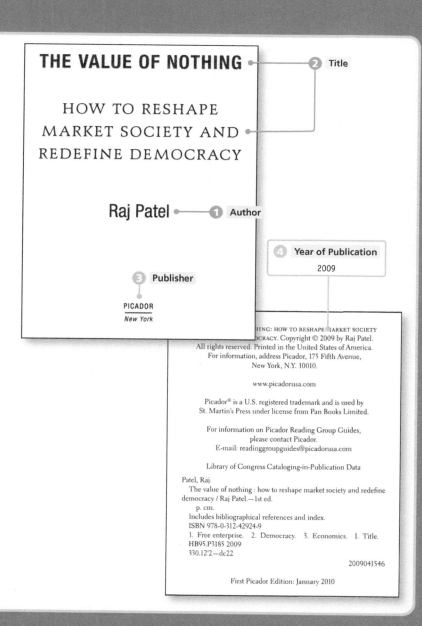

THE VALUE OF NOTHING

2 Title

HOW TO RESHAPE MARKET SOCIETY AND REDEFINE DEMOCRACY

Raj Patel

1 Author

4 Year of Publication
2009

3 Publisher

PICADOR
New York

HING: HOW TO RESHAPE MARKET SOCIETY
OCRACY. Copyright © 2009 by Raj Patel.
All rights reserved. Printed in the United States of America.
For information, address Picador, 175 Fifth Avenue,
New York, N.Y. 10010.

www.picadorusa.com

Picador® is a U.S. registered trademark and is used by
St. Martin's Press under license from Pan Books Limited.

For information on Picador Reading Group Guides,
please contact Picador.
E-mail: readinggroupguides@picadorusa.com

Library of Congress Cataloging-in-Publication Data

Patel, Raj.
   The value of nothing : how to reshape market society and redefine
democracy / Raj Patel.—1st ed.
      p. cm.
   Includes bibliographical references and index.
   ISBN 978-0-312-42924-9
   1. Free enterprise.   2. Democracy.   3. Economics.   I. Title.
   HB95.P3185 2009
   330.12'2—dc22

                                                       2009041546

First Picador Edition: January 2010

16. BOOK IN A LANGUAGE OTHER THAN ENGLISH. Include a translation of the title in brackets, if necessary.

> Benedetti, Mario. *La borra del café* [*The Coffee Grind*]. Editorial
>
> Sudamericana, 2000.

17. GRAPHIC NARRATIVE OR COMIC. If the words and images are created by the same person, cite a graphic narrative just as you would with a book (model 6).

> Bechdel, Alison. *Are You My Mother? A Comic Drama*. Houghton Mifflin
>
> Harcourt, 2012.

If the work is a collaboration, indicate the author or illustrator who is most important to your research before the title of the work. List other contributors after the title, in the order of their appearance on the title page. Label each person's contribution to the work.

> Stavans, Ilan, writer. *Latino USA: A Cartoon History*. Illustrated by Lalo
>
> Arcaraz, Basic Books, 2000.

18. EDITION OTHER THAN THE FIRST

> Walker, John A. *Art in the Age of Mass Media*. 3rd ed., Pluto Press, 2001.

19. ONE VOLUME OF A MULTIVOLUME WORK. Give the number of the volume cited after the title. Including the total number of volumes after the publication date is optional.

> Ch'oe, Yong-Ho, et al., editors. *Sources of Korean Tradition*. Vol. 2,
>
> Columbia UP, 2000. 2 vols.

20. TWO OR MORE VOLUMES OF A MULTIVOLUME WORK

> Ch'oe, Yong-Ho, et al., editors. *Sources of Korean Tradition*. Columbia UP,
>
> 2000. 2 vols.

21. PREFACE, FOREWORD, INTRODUCTION, OR AFTERWORD. After the writer's name, describe the contribution. After the title, indicate the book's author (with *by*) or editor (with *edited by*).

> Atwan, Robert. Foreword. *The Best American Essays 2002*, edited by
>
> Stephen Jay Gould, Houghton Mifflin, 2002, pp. viii-xii.

Moore, Thurston. Introduction. *Confusion Is Next: The Sonic Youth Story*, by
Alec Foege, St. Martin's Press, 1994, p. xi.

22. ENTRY IN A REFERENCE BOOK. For a well-known encyclopedia, note the edition (if identified) and year of publication. If the entries are alphabetized, omit the page number.

Kettering, Alison McNeil. "Art Nouveau." *World Book Encyclopedia*, 2002 ed.

23. BOOK THAT IS PART OF A SERIES. Cite the series name (and number, if any) from the title page.

Nichanian, Marc, and Vartan Matiossian, editors. *Yeghishe Charents: Poet of
the Revolution*. Mazda, 2003. Armenian Studies Ser. 5.

24. REPUBLICATION (MODERN EDITION OF AN OLDER BOOK). Indicate the original publication date after the title.

Austen, Jane. *Sense and Sensibility*. 1813. Dover Publications, 1996.

25. MORE THAN ONE PUBLISHER'S NAME. If the title page gives two publishers' names, separate them with a slash. Include spaces on both sides of the slash.

Hornby, Nick. *About a Boy*. Riverhead / Penguin Putnam, 1998.

26. BOOK WITH A TITLE WITHIN THE TITLE. Do not italicize the title of a book or other long work within a book title. For an article title within a title, italicize as usual and place the article title in quotation marks.

Mullaney, Julie. *Arundhati Roy's* The God of Small Things: *A Reader's Guide*.
Continuum, 2002.

Rhynes, Martha. *"I, Too, Sing America": The Story of Langston Hughes*.
Morgan Reynolds Publishing, 2002.

27. SACRED TEXT. To cite any individual published editions of sacred books, begin the entry with the title.

Qur'an: The Final Testament (Authorized English Version) with Arabic Text.
Translated by Rashad Khalifa, Universal Unity, 2000.

Print periodicals

Begin with the author name(s). (See models 1–5.) Then include the article title, the title of the periodical, the date and volume information, and the page numbers. The source map on pp. 240–41 shows where to find this information in a sample periodical.

28. ARTICLE IN A PRINT JOURNAL. Follow the journal title with a comma; the abbreviation *vol.* and volume number; a comma; the abbreviation *no.* and issue number; a comma; the month (abbreviated except for May, June, and July), day (if given), and the year or the season and year of publication; a comma; and the abbreviation *p.* or *pp.* and page numbers.

> Gigante, Denise. "The Monster in the Rainbow: Keats and the Science of
>
> Life." *PMLA*, vol. 117, no. 3, May 2002, pp. 433-48.

29. ARTICLE IN A PRINT MAGAZINE. Provide the date from the magazine cover instead of volume or issue numbers.

> Surowiecki, James. "The Stimulus Strategy." *The New Yorker*, 25 Feb. 2008,
>
> p. 29.

> Taubin, Amy. "All Talk?" *Film Comment*, Nov.-Dec. 2007, pp. 45-47.

30. ARTICLE IN A PRINT NEWSPAPER. Include the edition (if listed) and the section number or letter (if listed).

> Fackler, Martin. "Japan's Foreign Minister Says Apologies to Wartime Victims
>
> Will Be Upheld." *The New York Times*, 9 Apr. 2014, late ed., p. A6.

Note: For locally published newspapers, add the city in brackets after the name if it is not part of the name: *Globe and Mail [Toronto]*.

31. ARTICLE THAT SKIPS PAGES. When an article skips pages, give only the first page number and a plus sign.

> Tyrnauer, Matthew. "Empire by Martha." *Vanity Fair*, Sept. 2002, pp. 364+.

32. EDITORIAL OR LETTER TO THE EDITOR. Include the writer's name, if given, and the title, if any. Then end with the label *Editorial* or *Letter*.

"California Dreaming." *The Nation*, 25 Feb. 2008, p. 4. Editorial.

MacEwan, Valerie. *The Believer*, vol. 12, no. 1, Jan. 2014, p. 4. Letter.

33. REVIEW

Nussbaum, Emily. "Change Agents: Review of *The Americans* and *Silicon Valley*." *The New Yorker*, 31 Mar. 2014, p. 68.

Schwarz, Benjamin. Review of *The Second World War: A Short History*, by R. A. C. Parker, *The Atlantic Monthly*, May 2002, pp. 110-11.

34. UNSIGNED ARTICLE

"Performance of the Week." *Time*, 6 Oct. 2003, p. 18.

Digital written-word sources

Digital sources such as websites differ from print sources in the ease with which they can be changed, updated, or eliminated. The most commonly cited electronic sources are documents from websites and databases.

35. WORK FROM A DATABASE. The basic format for citing a work from a database appears in the source map on pp. 244–45.

For a periodical article that you access in an online database through a library subscription service such as Academic Search Premier, begin with the author's name (if given); the title of the work, in quotation marks; the title of the periodical, italicized; and the volume/issue and date of the print version of the work (see models 28–34). Include the page numbers from the print version. Then give the name of the online database, italicized, and the DOI or permalink for the article; if neither is available, give the URL of the database home page, omitting the protocol (*http://*).

Collins, Ross F. "Cattle Barons and Ink Slingers: How Cow Country Journalists Created a Great American Myth." *American Journalism*, vol. 24, no. 3, Summer 2007, pp. 7-29. *Communication and Mass Media Complete*, www.ebscohost.com/academic/communication-mass -media-complete.

① **Author.** List the last name first. End with a period. For variations, see models 2–5.

② **Article title.** Put the title and any subtitle in quotation marks; capitalize all major words. Place a period inside the closing quotation mark.

③ **Periodical title.** Italicize the title; capitalize all major words. End with a comma.

④ **Volume and issue / Date of publication.** Give the abbreviation *vol.* and the volume number, and the abbreviation *no.* and the issue number, if the periodical provides them. List day (if given), month (abbreviated except for May, June, and July), and year, or season and year, of publication. Put commas after the volume, issue, and date.

⑤ **Page numbers.** Give the abbreviation *p.* (for "page") or *pp.* (for "pages") and the inclusive page numbers. If the article skips pages, put the first page number and a plus sign. End with a period.

A citation for the article on p. 241 would look like this:

Quart, Alissa. "Lost Media, Found Media: Snapshots from the Future of Writing." *Columbia Journalism Review*, May/June 2008, pp. 30-34.

③ Periodical Title

COLUMBIA
JOURNALISM
REVIEW
May/June 2008 · cjr.org

④ Date of Publication
May/June 2008

The Fu
Wri

Nonfiction's
ALISSA QUA

Kindle isn't
EZRA KLEIN

UNDER TH
A reporter
that got hi
CAMERON M

LOVE THY
The religio
TIM TOWNS

Lost Media,
Found Media

Snapshots from the future of writing

BY ALISSA QUART

② Article Title

① Author
ALISSA QUART

If there were an ashram for people who worship contemplative long-form journalism, it would be the Nieman Conference on Narrative Journalism. This March, at the Sheraton Boston Hotel, hundreds of journalists, authors, students, and aspirants came for the weekend event. Seated on metal chairs in large conference rooms, we learned about muscular storytelling (the Q-shaped narrative structure—who knew?). We sipped cups of coffee and ate bagels and heard about reporting history through letters and public documents and how to evoke empathy for our subjects, particularly our most marginal ones. As we listened to reporters discussing great feats—exposing Walter Reed's fetid living quarters for wounded soldiers, for instance—we also renewed our pride in our profession. In short, the conference exemplified the best of the older media models, the ones that have so recently fallen into economic turmoil.

Yet even at the weekend's strongest lectures on interview
... we couldn't ignore the
... knew as writers that
... ssing require months
..., and that we were all
... oney to do that. It was
always hard for nonfiction writers, but something seems to have changed. For those of us who believed in the value of the journalism and literary nonfiction of the past, we had

become like the people at the ashram after the guru has died.

Right now, journalism is more or less divided into two camps, which I will call Lost Media and Found Media. I went to the Nieman conference partially because I wanted to see how the forces creating this new division are affecting and afflicting the Lost Media world that I love best, not on the institutional level, but for reporters and writ-
ers them... ... ... des
pe... ... ... pa-
pers and magazines that are currently struggling with layoffs, speedups, hiring freezes, buyouts, the death or shrinkage of ... ... ns, lim-
it... ... ... rk, the
er... ... ... he gen-
er... ... ... bition.
It... ... ... peting
with hordes of ever-younger competi-
tors willing to write and publish online for free, the fade-out of established journalistic career paths, and, perhaps most crucially, a muddled sense of the meritorious, as blogs level and scramble the value and status of print publications, and of professional writers. The glamour and influence once associated with a magazine elite seem to have faded, becoming a sort of pastiche of winsome articles about yearning and boxers and dinners at Elaine's.

Found Media-ites, meanwhile, are the bloggers, the contributors to Huffington Post-type sites that aggregate blogs, as well as other work that somebody else paid for, and the new nonprofits and pay-per-article schemes that aim to save journalism from 20 percent profit-margin demands. Although these elements are often disparate, together they compose the new media landscape. In economic terms, I mean all the outlets for nonfiction writing that seem to be thriving in the new era or striving to fill niches that Lost Media is giving up in a new order. Stylistically, Found Media tends to feel spontaneous, almost accidental. It's a domain dominated by the young, where writers get points not for following traditions or burnishing them but for amateur and hybrid vigor, for creating their own venues and their own genres. It is about public expression and community—not quite John Dewey's Great Community, which the critic Eric Alterman alluded to in a recent *New Yorker* article on newspapers, but rather a fractured form of Dewey's ideal: call it Great Communities.

To be a Found Media journalist or pundit, one need not be elite, expert, or trained; one must simply produce punchy intellectual property that is in conversation with groups of

⑤ Page Numbers
30–34

Illustration by Tomer Hanuka

 Checklist

Citing Works from Websites

When citing online sources, give as many of the following elements as you can find:

1. **Author.** Provide the author of the work, if you can find one. End with a period.

2. **Title.** Give the title of the work you are citing, ending with a period. If the work is part of a larger container (such as a video on YouTube), put the title in quotation marks.

3. **Website title.** If the title you identified is not the name of the website itself, list the website title, in italics, followed by a comma.

4. **Publisher or sponsor.** If the site's publisher or sponsor is different from the title of the site, identify the publisher or sponsor, followed by a comma. If the name is very similar to the site title, omit the publisher.

5. **Date of publication.** Give the date of publication or latest update, followed by a comma.

6. **Permalink or URL.** Give a permalink (if you can find one) or URL. End with a period.

7. **Date of access.** If the work does not include any date, add "Accessed" and the day, month (abbreviated, except for May, June, and July), and year you accessed the source. End with a period. If you provided a date before the URL, omit the access date.

36. ARTICLE FROM A JOURNAL ON THE WEB. Begin an entry for an online journal article as you would one for a print journal article (see model 28). End with the online location (permalink, DOI, or URL) and a period.

> Clark, Msia Kibona. "Hip Hop as Social Commentary in Accra and Dar es Salaam." *African Studies Quarterly*, vol. 13, no. 3, Summer 2012, asq.africa.ufl.edu/files/Clark-V131s3.pdf.

37. ARTICLE IN A MAGAZINE ON THE WEB. List the author, article title, and name of the magazine. Then identify the date of publication, and provide a permalink or DOI, if one is available, or a URL.

> Landhuis, Esther. "Is Dementia Risk Falling?" *Scientific American,*
>
> 25 Jan. 2016, www.scientificamerican.com/article/is-dementia
>
> -risk-falling/.

38. ARTICLE IN A NEWSPAPER ON THE WEB. After the name of the newspaper, give the publication date and the permalink (if you can find one) or URL.

> Shyong, Frank. "Sriracha Showdown Intensifies as Irwindale Declares
>
> Public Nuisance." *Los Angeles Times,* 10 Apr. 2014, articles.latimes
>
> .com/2014/apr/10/local/la-me-in-sriracha-irwindale-public-nuisance
>
> -20140410.

39. DIGITAL BOOK. Provide information as for a print book (see models 6–27); then give the digital container title and any other relevant information, including the location.

> Euripides. *The Trojan Women.* Translated by Gilbert Murray, Oxford UP,
>
> 1915. *Internet Sacred Text Archive,* 2011, www.sacred-texts.com/cla/
>
> eurip/trok_w.htm.

If you read the book on an e-reader such as a Kindle or Nook, specify the type of reader file you used.

> Schaap, Rosie. *Drinking with Men: A Memoir.* Riverhead / Penguin,
>
> 2013. Kindle.

40. ONLINE POEM. Include the poet's name, the title of the poem, and the print publication information (if any) for the first container. For the second container, give the title, the date, and the DOI, permalink, or URL.

> Geisel, Theodor. "Too Many Daves." *The Sneetches and Other*
>
> *Stories,* Random House, 1961. *Poetry Foundation,* 2015, www
>
> .poetryfoundation.org/poem/171612.

Library subscriptions—such as EBSCOhost and Academic Search Premier—provide access to huge databases of articles.

1 **Author.** List the last name first. End with a period. For variations, see models 2–5.

2 **Article title.** Enclose the title and any subtitle in quotation marks. End with a period.

3 **Periodical title.** Italicize it. Follow it with a comma.

4 **Volume and issue/Date of publication.** List the volume and issue number, if any, separated by commas. Use the abbreviations *vol.* and *no.* Then, add the date of publication, including the day (if given), month, and year, in that order. Last, add a comma.

5 **Page numbers.** Give the inclusive page numbers, using the abbreviations *p.* or *pp.* End with a period.

6 **Database name.** Italicize the name of the database. End with a period.

7 **Location.** Give the DOI or other permalink, if available. If not, give the URL for the home page of the database.

A citation for the article on p. 245 would look like this:

Arnett, Robert P. "*Casino Royale* and Franchise Remix: James Bond as Superhero." *Film Criticism*, vol. 33, no. 3, Spring 2009, pp. 1-16. *Academic Search Premier*, www.ebscohost.com/academic/academic-search-premier.

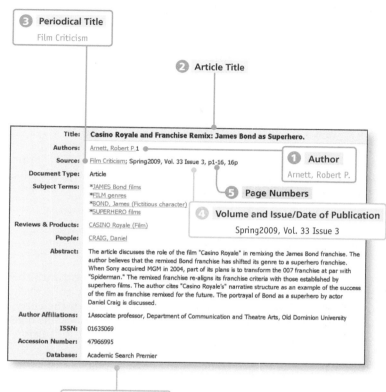

③ Periodical Title
Film Criticism

② Article Title

Title:	**Casino Royale and Franchise Remix: James Bond as Superhero.**
Authors:	Arnett, Robert P.1
Source:	Film Criticism; Spring2009, Vol. 33 Issue 3, p1-16, 16p
Document Type:	Article
Subject Terms:	*JAMES Bond films *FILM genres *BOND, James (Fictitious character) *SUPERHERO films
Reviews & Products:	CASINO Royale (Film)
People:	CRAIG, Daniel
Abstract:	The article discusses the role of the film "Casino Royale" in remixing the James Bond franchise. The author believes that the remixed Bond franchise has shifted its genre to a superhero franchise. When Sony acquired MGM in 2004, part of its plans is to transform the 007 franchise at par with "Spiderman." The remixed franchise re-aligns its franchise criteria with those established by superhero films. The author cites "Casino Royale's" narrative structure as an example of the success of the film as franchise remixed for the future. The portrayal of Bond as a superhero by actor Daniel Craig is discussed.
Author Affiliations:	1Associate professor, Department of Communication and Theatre Arts, Old Dominion University
ISSN:	01635069
Accession Number:	47966995
Database:	Academic Search Premier

① Author
Arnett, Robert P.

⑤ Page Numbers

④ Volume and Issue/Date of Publication
Spring2009, Vol. 33 Issue 3

⑥ Database Name
Academic Search Premier

41. ONLINE EDITORIAL OR LETTER TO THE EDITOR. Include the author's name (if given) and the title (if any). Follow the appropriate model for the type of source you are using. (Check the directory on pp. 227–28.) End with the label *Editorial* or *Letter*.

> "Migrant Children Deserve a Voice in Court." *The New York Times*, 8 Mar.
>
> 2016, nyti.ms/1LO8bKK. Editorial.

> Starr, Evva. "Local Reporting Thrives in High Schools." *The Washington*
>
> *Post*, 4 Apr. 2014, wpo.st/7hmJ1. Letter.

42. ONLINE REVIEW. Cite an online review as you would a print review (see model 33). End with the name of the website, the date of publication, and the URL or permalink.

> O'Hehir, Andrew. "Aronofsky's Deranged Biblical Action Flick." *Salon*,
>
> 27 May 2014, www.salon.com/2014/03/27/noah_aronofskys
>
> _deranged_biblical_action_flick/.

43. ENTRY IN AN ONLINE REFERENCE WORK OR WIKI. Begin with the title unless the author is named. (A wiki, which is collectively edited, will not include an author.) Include the title of the entry; the name of the work, italicized; the sponsor or publisher; the date of the latest update; and the location (permalink or URL). Before using a wiki as a source, check with your instructor.

> Cartwright, Mark. "Apollo." *Ancient History Encyclopedia*, 18 May 2012,
>
> www.ancient.eu/apollo/.

> "Gunpowder Plot." *Wikipedia*, 4 Mar. 2016, en.wikipedia.org/wiki/
>
> Gunpowder_Plot.

44. SHORT WORK FROM A WEBSITE. For basic information for citing a work on a website that is not part of a regularly published journal, magazine, or newspaper, see the source map on pp. 248–49. Treat a short work from a website as you would an online reference entry (see model 43). Include all of the following elements that are available: the author; the title of the document, in quotation marks; the name of the website, italicized; the name of the publisher or

sponsor (if the name is different from the name of the site); the date of the publication; and the location. If the site gives no date, end with *Accessed* and your date of access.

> Bali, Karan. "Kishore Kumar." *Upperstall.com,* upperstall.com/profile/
> kishore-kumar/. Accessed 2 Mar. 2016.

> "Our Mission." *Trees for Life International,* 2011, www.treesforlife.org/
> our-work/our-mission.

45. ENTIRE WEBSITE. Follow the guidelines for a work from the web, beginning with the name of the author or editor (if any), followed by the title of the website, italicized; the name of the sponsor or publisher (if different from the name of the site); the date of publication or last update; and the location.

> Glazier, Loss Pequeño, director. *Electronic Poetry Center.* State U of New
> York Buffalo, 1994-2016, epc.buffalo.edu/.

> *Weather.com.* Weather Channel Interactive, 1995-2016, weather.com/.

For a personal website, include the name of the person who created the site as you would with a site's author or editor. If the site is undated, end with your date of access.

> Enright, Mike. *Menright.com.* www.menright.com. Accessed 30 Mar. 2016.

46. BLOG. For an entire blog, give the author's name; the title of the blog, italicized; the date; and the URL. If the site is undated, end with your access date.

> Levy, Carla Miriam. *Filmi Geek.* 2006-2015, www.filmigeek.com.

> *Little Green Footballs.* littlegreenfootballs.com. Accessed 4 Mar. 2016.

Note: To cite a blogger who writes under a pseudonym, begin with the pseudonym and then put the writer's real name (if you know it) in parentheses.

> Atrios (Duncan Black). *Eschaton.* www.eschatonblog.com. Accessed
> 8 Mar. 2016.

MLA SOURCE MAP: Works from Websites

You may need to browse other parts of a site to find some of the following elements, and some sites may omit elements. Uncover as much information as you can.

1 **Author.** List the last name first. End with a period. If no author is given, begin with the title. For variations, see models 2–5.

2 **Title of work.** Enclose the title and any subtitle of the work in quotation marks.

3 **Title of website.** Give the title of the entire website, italicized. Follow it with a comma.

4 **Publisher or sponsor.** Look for the sponsor's name at the bottom of the home page. If the sponsor's name is roughly the same as the site title, omit the sponsor. Follow it with a comma.

5 **Date of publication or latest update.** Give the most recent date, followed by a period.

6 **Location.** Give the permalink, if you can find one, or the site's URL, followed by a period.

7 **Date of access.** If the site is undated, end with *Accessed* and the date.

A citation for the work on p. 249 would look like this:

Tønnesson, Øyvind. "Mahatma Gandhi, the Missing Laureate."
Nobelprize.org, 2015, www.nobelprize.org/nobel_prizes/themes/
peace/gandhi/.

6 Location · · · · · **3** Title of Website · · · · · **2** Title of Work

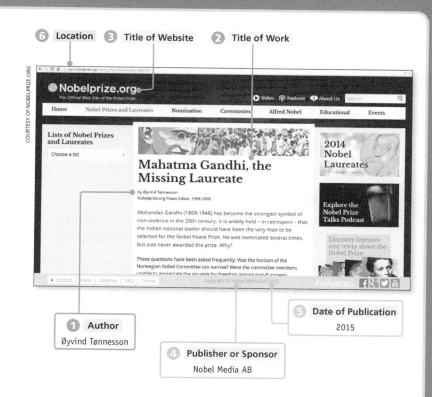

1 Author
Øyvind Tønnesson

4 Publisher or Sponsor
Nobel Media AB

5 Date of Publication
2015

47. ONLINE INTERVIEW. Start with the name of the person interviewed. Give the title, if there is one. If not, give a descriptive label such as *Interview*, neither italicized nor in quotation marks, and the interviewer, if relevant; the title of the site; the sponsor or publisher (if there is one); the date of publication; and the URL.

> Ladd, Andrew. "What Ends: An Interview with Andrew Ladd." Interview
>
> by Jill. *Looks & Books*, 25 Feb. 2014, www.looksandbooks
>
> .com/2014/02/25/what-ends-an-interview-with-andrew-ladd/.

48. POST OR COMMENT ON A BLOG OR DISCUSSION GROUP. Give the author's name; the title of the post, in quotation marks; the title of the site, italicized; the date of the post; and the URL.

> Edroso, Roy. "Going Down with the Flagship." *Alicublog*, 24 Feb. 2016,
>
> alicublog.blogspot.com/2016/02/going-down-with-flagship.html.

For a comment on an online post, give the writer's name or screen name; a label such as *Comment on*, not italicized; the title of the article commented on; and the label *by* and the article author's name. End with the citation information for the type of article.

> JennOfArk. Comment on "Going Down with the Flagship," by Roy Edroso.
>
> *Alicublog*, 24 Feb. 2016, alicublog.blogspot.com/2016/02/going
>
> -down-with-flagship.html#disqus_thread.

49. POSTING ON A SOCIAL NETWORKING SITE. To cite a posting on Facebook, Instagram, or another social networking site, include the writer's name; up to 140 characters of the posting, in quotation marks (or a description such as *Photograph*, not italicized and not in quotation marks, if there's no text); the name of the site, italicized; the date of the post; and the location of the post (URL).

> Cannon, Kevin. "Portrait of Norris Hall in #Savannah, GA — home (for
>
> a few months, anyway) of #SCAD's sequential art department."
>
> *Instagram*, Mar. 2014, www.instagram.com/p/lgmqk4i6DC/.

50. EMAIL OR MESSAGE. Include the writer's name; the subject line, in quotation marks, if one is provided, or a descriptive message such as *Text message*; *Received by* (not italicized or in quotation

marks) followed by the recipient's name; and then the date of the message.

> Carbone, Nick. "Screen vs. Print Reading." Received by Karita dos Santos,
> 17 Apr. 2016.

51. TWEET. Begin with the writer's Twitter handle, and put the real name, if known, in parentheses. Include the entire tweet, in quotation marks. Give the site name in italics (*Twitter*), the date and time of the message, and the tweet's URL.

> @Lunsfordhandbks (Andrea A. Lunsford). "Technology & social media
> have changed the way we write. That doesn't mean literacy has
> declined https://community.macmillan.com/groups/macmillan-news/
> blog/2016/02/24/the-literacy-revolution... @MacmillanLearn."
> *Twitter*, 24 Feb. 2016, 10:17 a.m., twitter.com/LunsfordHandbks/
> status/702512638937460736.

Visual, audio, multimedia, and live sources

52. FILM (THEATRICAL, DVD, OR OTHER FORMAT). If you cite a particular person's work, start with that name. If not, start with the title of the film; then name the director, distributor, and year of release. Other contributors, such as writers or performers, may follow the director. If you cite a feature from a disc, treat the film as the first container and the disc as the second container.

> Bale, Christian, performer. *The Big Short*. Directed by Adam McKay,
> Paramount Pictures, 2015.

> Lasseter, John. Introduction. *Spirited Away*, directed by Hayao Miyazaki,
> 2001. Walt Disney Video, 2003, disc 1.

53. ONLINE VIDEO. Cite an online video as you would a short work from a website (see model 44).

> Weber, Jan. "As We Sow, Part 1: Where Are the Farmers?" *YouTube*, 15 Mar.
> 2008, www.youtube.com/watch?v=_cdcDpMf6qE.

54. TELEVISION (BROADCAST OR ON THE WEB). For a show broadcast on television, begin with the title of the program, italicized (for an

entire series), or the title of the episode, in quotation marks. Then list important contributors (writer, director, actor); season and episode number (for a specific episode); the network; the local station and city, if the show appeared on a local channel; and the broadcast date(s).

> *Breaking Bad.* Created by Vince Gilligan, performances by Bryan Cranston, Aaron Paul, and Anna Gunn, AMC, 2008-2013.

> "Time Zones." *Mad Men*, written by Matthew Weiner, directed by Scott Hornbacher, season 7, episode 1, AMC, 13 Apr. 2014.

For a show accessed on a network website, include the URL after the date of posting.

> "Time Zones." *Mad Men*, written by Matthew Weiner, directed by Scott Hornbacher, season 7, episode 1, AMC, 13 Apr. 2014, www.amc.com/ shows/mad-men/season-7/episode-01-time-zones.

55. RADIO (BROADCAST OR ON THE WEB). If you are citing a particular episode or segment, cite a radio broadcast as you would a television episode (see model 54).

> "Tarred and Feathered." *This American Life*, narrated by Ira Glass, WNYC, 11 Apr. 2013.

For a show or segment accessed on the web, include the website title and URL after the date of posting.

> "Obama's Failures Have Made Millennials Give Up Hope." *The Rush Limbaugh Show*, narrated by Rush Limbaugh, Premiere Radio Networks, 14 Apr. 2014, RushLimbaugh.com, www.rushlimbaugh.com/daily/2014/04/14/ obama_s_failures_have_made_millennials_give_up_hope.

56. TELEVISION OR RADIO INTERVIEW. List the person interviewed and then the title, if any. If the interview has no title, use the label *Interview* and the name of the interviewer, if relevant. Then identify the source. End with information about the program and the interview date(s). (For an online interview, see model 47.)

> Russell, David O. Interview by Terry Gross. *Fresh Air*, WNYC, 20 Feb. 2014.

57. PERSONAL INTERVIEW. List the person who was interviewed; the label *Telephone interview, Personal interview,* or *E-mail interview;* and the date the interview took place.

> Freedman, Sasha. Personal interview. 10 Nov. 2015.

58. SOUND RECORDING. List the name of the person or group you wish to emphasize (such as the composer, conductor, or band); the title of the recording or composition; the artist, if appropriate; the manufacturer; and the year of issue. If you are citing a particular song or selection, include its title, in quotation marks.

> Bach, Johann Sebastian. *Bach: Violin Concertos.* Performances by Itzhak
>
> Perlman and Pinchas Zukerman, English Chamber Orchestra, EMI, 2002.

> Sonic Youth. "Incinerate." *Rather Ripped,* Geffen, 2006.

Note: If you are citing instrumental music that is identified only by form, number, and key, do not underline, italicize, or enclose it in quotation marks.

> Grieg, Edvard. Concerto in A minor, op. 16. Conducted by Eugene Ormandy,
>
> Philadelphia Orchestra, RCA, 1989.

59. MUSICAL COMPOSITION. When you are not citing a specific published version, first give the composer's name, followed by the title.

> Mozart, Wolfgang Amadeus. *Don Giovanni,* K527.

> Mozart, Wolfgang Amadeus. Symphony no. 41 in C major, K551.

Note: Cite a published score as you would a book. If you include the date that the composition was written, do so immediately after the title.

> Schoenberg, Arnold. *Chamber Symphony No. 1 for 15 Solo Instruments,*
>
> *Op. 9.* 1906. Dover, 2002.

60. VIDEO GAME. Start with the developer or author (if any). After the title, give the distributor and the date of publication.

> Harmonix. *Rock Band Blitz.* MTV Games, 2012.

61. LECTURE OR SPEECH. For a live lecture or speech, list the speaker; the title (if any), in quotation marks; the sponsoring institution or group; the place; and the date. Add the label *Lecture* or *Speech* after the date if readers will not otherwise be able to identify the work.

> Eugenides, Jeffrey. Portland Arts and Lectures. Arlene Schnitzer Concert
>
> Hall, Portland, OR, 30 Sept. 2003.

For a lecture or speech on the web, cite as you would a short work from a website (see model 44).

> Burden, Amanda. "How Public Spaces Make Cities Work." *TED.com*, Mar.
>
> 2014, www.ted.com/talks/amanda_burden_how_public_spaces
>
> _make_cities_work.

62. LIVE PERFORMANCE. List the title, the appropriate names (such as the writer or performer), the place, and the date.

> *The Sea Ranch Songs.* By Aleksandra Vrebalov, performed by the Kronos
>
> Quartet, White Barn, The Sea Ranch, CA, 23 May 2015.

63. DIGITAL FILE OR PODCAST. A citation for a downloadable digital file — one that exists independently, not only on a website — begins with citation information required for the type of source (a photograph or sound recording, for example).

> "Return to the Giant Pool of Money." *This American Life,* narrated by Ira
>
> Glass, NPR, 25 Sept. 2009, www.thisamericanlife.org/radio-archives/
>
> episode/390/Return-To-The-Giant-Pool-of-Money.

Cite a podcast that you view or listen to online as you would a short work from a website (see model 44).

> Fogarty, Mignon. "Begs the Question: Update." *QuickandDirtyTips.com,*
>
> Macmillan, 6 Mar. 2014, www.quickanddirtytips.com/education/
>
> grammar/begs-the-question-update.

64. WORK OF ART OR PHOTOGRAPH. List the artist's or photographer's name; the work's title, italicized; and the date of composition. Then

cite the name of the museum or other location and the city. To cite a reproduction in a book, add the publication information. To cite online artwork, add the title of the database or website, italicized, and the URL or permalink.

> Bronzino, Agnolo. *Lodovico Capponi.* 1550-55, Frick Collection, New York.
>
> *General William Palmer in Old Age.* 1810, National Army Museum, London. *White Mughals: Love and Betrayal in Eighteenth-Century India,* by William Dalrymple, Penguin Books, 2002, p. 270.
>
> Hassam, Childe. *Isles of Shoals,* 1899, Minneapolis Institute of Arts, collections.artsmia.org/art/45/isles-of-shoals-childe-hassam.

65. MAP OR CHART. Cite a map or chart as you would a book or a short work within a longer work. For an online source, include the location. End with the label *Map* or *Chart* if needed for clarity.

> "Australia." *Perry-Castaneda Library Map Collection,* U of Texas, 1999, www .lib.utexas.edu.maps.australia_pol99.jpg.
>
> *California.* Rand McNally, 2002. Map.

66. CARTOON OR COMIC STRIP. List the artist's name; the title of the cartoon or comic strip, in quotation marks; and the usual publication information for a print periodical (see models 28–34) or a short work from a website (model 44). You may end with a label (*Cartoon* or *Comic strip*) for clarity.

> Flake, Emily. *The New Yorker,* 13 Apr. 2015, p. 66. Cartoon.
>
> Munroe, Randall. "Heartbleed Explanation." *xkcd.com,* xkcd.com/1354/. Comic strip.

67. ADVERTISEMENT. Include the label *Advertisement* at the end of the entry.

> Ameritrade. *Wired,* Jan. 2014, p. 47. Advertisement.
>
> Lufthansa. *The New York Times,* 16 Apr. 2014, www.nytimes.com. Advertisement.

Other sources (including digital versions)

If an online version is not shown in this section, use the appropriate model for the source and then end with a DOI, permalink, or URL.

68. REPORT OR PAMPHLET. Follow the guidelines for a print book (models 6–27) or a digital book (model 39).

> Rainie, Lee, and Maeve Duggan. *Privacy and Information Sharing.* Pew
>
> Research Center, 14 Jan. 2016, www.pewinternet.org/files/2016/01/
>
> PI_2016.01.14_Privacy-and-Info-Sharing_FINAL.pdf.

69. GOVERNMENT PUBLICATION. Begin with the author, if identified. Otherwise, start with the name of the government, followed by the agency. For congressional documents, cite the number, session, and house of Congress; the type (*Report, Resolution, Document*); and the number. End with the publication information. For online versions, follow the models for a short work from a website (model 44), an entire website (model 45), or a digital file (model 63).

> Gregg, Judd. *Report to Accompany the Genetic Information Act of 2003.*
>
> US 108th Congress, 1st session, Senate Report 108-22, Government
>
> Printing Office, 2003.

> United States, Department of Health and Human Services, National
>
> Institutes of Health. *Keep the Beat Recipes: Deliciously Healthy*
>
> *Dinners.* Oct. 2009, healthyeating.nhlbi.nih.gov/pdfs/Dinners
>
> _Cookbook_508-compliant.pdf.

70. PUBLISHED PROCEEDINGS OF A CONFERENCE. Cite the proceedings as you would a book.

> Cleary, John, and Gary Gurtler, editors. *Proceedings of the Boston Area*
>
> *Colloquium in Ancient Philosophy 2002.* Brill Academic Publishers, 2003.

71. DISSERTATION. Enclose the title in quotation marks. Add the label *Dissertation*, the school, and the year the work was accepted.

> Thompson, Brian. "I'm Better Than You and I Can Prove It: Games, Expertise,
>
> and the Culture of Competition." Dissertation, Stanford U, 2015.

Note: Cite a published dissertation as a book, adding the identification *Dissertation* and the university after the title.

72. DISSERTATION ABSTRACT. Cite the abstract as you would an unpublished dissertation (model 71). For an abstract that uses *Dissertation Abstracts International*, include the volume, year, and page number.

> Huang-Tiller, Gillian C. "The Power of the Meta-Genre: Cultural, Sexual, and
> Racial Politics of the American Modernist Sonnet." Dissertation, U of
> Notre Dame, 2000. Abstract. *Dissertation Abstracts International*, vol. 61,
> 2000, p. 1401.

> Moore, Courtney L. "Stress and Oppression: Identifying Possible Protective
> Factors for African American Men." Dissertation, Chicago School of
> Professional Psychology, 2016. Abstract. *ProQuest Dissertations and
> Theses*, search.proquest.com/docview/1707351557.

73. UNPUBLISHED LETTER. Cite a published letter as a work in an anthology (see model 10). If the letter is unpublished, follow this form:

> Anzaldúa, Gloria. Letter to the author. 10 Sept. 2002.

74. MANUSCRIPT OR OTHER UNPUBLISHED WORK. List the author's name; the title (if any) or a description of the material; any identifying numbers; and the name of the library or research institution housing the material, if applicable.

> Woolf, Virginia. "The Searchlight." Papers of Virginia Woolf, 1902-1956,
> Series III, Box 4, Item 184, Smith College, Northampton.

75. LEGAL SOURCE. To cite a court case, give the names of the first plaintiff and defendant, the case number, the name of the court, and the date of the decision. To cite an act, give the name of the act followed by its Public Law (*Pub. L.*) number, its Statutes at Large (*Stat.*) cataloging number, and the date the act was enacted.

> Citizens United vs. FEC. 558 US 310. Supreme Court of the US. 2010.
> Legal Information Institute, Cornell U Law School, www.law.cornell
> .edu/supct/pdf/08-205P.ZS.

Museum and Library Services Act of 2003. Pub. L. 108-81. Stat. 117.991.
25 Sept. 2003.

Note: You do not need an entry on the list of works cited when you cite articles of the U.S. Constitution and laws in the U.S. Code.

45f A sample student research project, MLA style

A brief research essay by David Craig appears on the following pages. David followed the MLA guidelines described in this chapter.

½"

Craig 1

1"

David Craig

Professor Turkman

English 219

18 December 2014

Messaging: The Language of Youth Literacy

The English language is under attack. At least, that is what
many people seem to believe. From concerned parents to local
librarians, everyone seems to have a negative comment on the state
of youth literacy today. They fear that the current generation of
grade school students will graduate with an extremely low level of
literacy, and they point out that although language education hasn't
changed, kids are having more trouble reading and writing than in
the past. When asked about the cause of this situation, many adults
pin the blame on technologies such as texting and instant messaging,
arguing that electronic shortcuts create and compound undesirable
reading and writing habits and discourage students from learning
conventionally correct ways to use language. But although the
arguments against messaging are passionate, evidence suggests that
they may not hold up.

The disagreements about messaging shortcuts are profound,
even among academics. John Briggs, an English professor at the
University of California, Riverside, says, "Americans have always
been informal, but now the informality of precollege culture is so
ubiquitous that many students have no practice in using language
in any formal setting at all" (qtd. in McCarroll). Such objections are
not new; Sven Birkerts of Mount Holyoke College argued in 1999
that "[students] read more casually. They strip-mine what they
read" online and consequently produce "quickly generated, casual
prose" (qtd. in Leibowitz A67). However, academics are also among
the defenders of texting and instant messaging (IM), with

Name, instruc-
tor, course, and
date aligned
at left

Title centered

Opens with
attention-
getting
statement

Background on
the problem of
youth literacy

Explicit thesis
statement
concludes
introductory
paragraph

Indirect
quotation uses
"qtd. in" and
name of web
source on list
of works cited

Marginal annotations indicate effective choices or MLA-style formatting.

Craig 2

Writer's last
name and
page number
at upper right
corner of every
page

Definition and
example of
messaging

some suggesting that messaging may be a beneficial force in the
development of youth literacy because it promotes regular contact
with words and the use of a written medium for communication.

Texting and instant messaging allow two individuals who
are separated by any distance to engage in real-time, written
communication. Although such communication relies on the written
word, many messengers disregard standard writing conventions. For
example, here is a snippet from an IM conversation between two
teenage girls:[1]

> Teen One: sorry im talkinto like 10 ppl at a time
> Teen Two: u izzyful person
> Teen Two: kwel
> Teen One: hey i g2g

As this brief conversation shows, participants must use words to
communicate via texting and messaging, but their words do not have

Writer consid-
ers argument
that youth
literacy is in
decline

Figure
explained in
text and cited
in parentheti-
cal reference

Discussion of
Figure 1

Explanatory
note adds
information
not found in
list of works
cited

to be in standard English.

The issue of youth literacy does demand attention because
standardized test scores for language assessments, such as the verbal
and writing sections of the College Board's SAT, have declined in
recent years. This trend is illustrated in a chart distributed by the
College Board as part of its 2011 analysis of aggregate SAT data (see
Fig. 1).

The trend lines illustrate a significant pattern that may lead
to the conclusion that youth literacy is on the decline. These lines
display the ten-year paths (from 2001 to 2011) of reading and writing
scores, respectively. Within this period, the average verbal score
dropped a few points — and appears to be headed toward a further
decline in the future.

1. This transcript of an IM conversation was collected on 20
Nov. 2014. The teenagers' names are concealed to protect privacy.

Craig 3

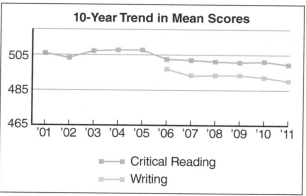

10-Year Trend in Mean Scores

505

485

465

'01 '02 '03 '04 '05 '06 '07 '08 '09 '10 '11

■———■ Critical Reading
■———■ Writing

Fig. 1. Ten-year trend in mean SAT reading and writing scores
(2001-2011). Data source: "2011 SAT Trends."

> Figure labeled, titled, and credited to source; inserted at appropriate point in text

Based on the preceding statistics, parents and educators
appear to be right about the decline in youth literacy. And this
trend coincides with another phenomenon: digital communication is
rising among the young. According to the Pew Internet & American
Life Project, 85 percent of those aged twelve to seventeen at least
occasionally write text messages, instant messages, or comments
on social networking sites (Lenhart et al.). In 2001, the most
conservative estimate based on Pew numbers showed that American
youths spent, at a minimum, nearly three million hours per day on
instant messaging services (Lenhart and Lewis 20). These numbers
are now exploding thanks to texting, which was "the dominant daily
mode of communication" for teens in 2012 (Lenhart), and messaging
on popular social networking sites such as Facebook and Tumblr.

In the interest of establishing the existence of a messaging
language, I analyzed 11,341 lines of text from IM conversations

> Writer accepts part of critics' argument; transition to next point

> For a web source with no page numbers, only author names appear in parentheses

> Writer's field research described

Craig 4

between youths in my target demographic: U.S. residents aged twelve to seventeen. Young messagers voluntarily sent me chat logs, but they were unaware of the exact nature of my research. Once all of the logs had been gathered, I went through them, recording the number of times messaging language was used in place of conventional words and phrases. Then I generated graphs to display how often these replacements were used.

During the course of my study, I identified four types of messaging language: phonetic replacements, acronyms, abbreviations, and inanities. An example of phonetic replacement is using *ur* for *you are*. Another popular type of messaging language is the acronym; for a majority of the people in my study, the most common acronym was *lol*,

Findings of
field research
presented

a construction that means *laughing out loud*. Abbreviations are also common in messaging, but I discovered that typical IM abbreviations, such as *etc.*, are not new to the English language. Finally, I found a class of words that I call "inanities." These words include completely new words or expressions, combinations of several slang categories, or simply nonsensical variations of other words. My favorite from this category is *lolz*, an inanity that translates directly to *lol* yet includes a terminating *z* for no obvious reason.

In the chat transcripts that I analyzed, the best display of typical messaging lingo came from the conversations between two thirteen-year-old Texan girls, who are avid IM users. Figure 2 is a

Figure
introduced and
explained

graph showing how often they used certain phonetic replacements and abbreviations. On the *y*-axis, frequency of replacement is plotted, a calculation that compares the number of times a word or phrase is used in messaging language with the total number of times that it is communicated in any form. On the *x*-axis, specific messaging words and phrases are listed.

Craig 5

My research shows that the Texan girls use the first ten phonetic replacements or abbreviations at least 50 percent of the time in their normal messaging writing. For example, every time one of them writes *see*, there is a parallel time when *c* is used in its place. In light of this finding, it appears that the popular messaging culture contains at least some elements of its own language. It also seems that much of this language is new: no formal dictionary yet identifies the most common messaging words and phrases. Only in the heyday of the telegraph or on the rolls of a stenographer would you find a similar situation, but these "languages" were never a popular medium of youth communication. Texting and instant messaging, however, are very popular among young people and continue to generate attention and debate in academic circles.

> Discussion of findings presented in Figure 2

My research shows that messaging is certainly widespread, and it does seem to have its own particular vocabulary, yet these two factors alone do not mean it has a damaging influence on youth literacy. As noted earlier, however, some people claim that

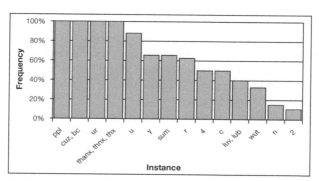

Fig. 2. Usage of phonetic replacements and abbreviations in messaging.

> Figure labeled and titled

Craig 6

Writer returns
to opposition
argument

For author of
web source
named in
signal phrase,
no parentheti-
cal citation
needed

Transition
to support
of thesis
and refutation
of critics

Linguistic
authority cited
in support
of thesis

Author of print
source named
in signal
phrase, so
parenthetical
citation
includes only
page number

the new technology is a threat to the English language. In an article provocatively titled "Texting Makes U Stupid," historian Niall Ferguson argues, "The good news is that today's teenagers are avid readers and prolific writers. The bad news is that what they are reading and writing are text messages." He goes on to accuse texting of causing the United States to "[fall] behind more literate societies."

The critics of messaging are numerous. But if we look to the field of linguistics, a central concept — metalinguistics — challenges these criticisms and leads to a more reasonable conclusion — that messaging has no negative impact on a student's development of or proficiency with traditional literacy.

Scholars of metalinguistics offer support for the claim that messaging is not damaging to those who use it. As noted earlier, one of the most prominent components of messaging language is phonetic replacement, in which a word such as *everyone* becomes *every1*. This type of wordplay has a special importance in the development of an advanced literacy, and for good reason. According to David Crystal, an internationally recognized scholar of linguistics at the University of Wales, as young children develop and learn how words string together to express ideas, they go through many phases of language play. The singsong rhymes and nonsensical chants of preschoolers are vital to learning language, and a healthy appetite for wordplay leads to a better command of language later in life (182).

As justification for his view of the connection between language play and advanced literacy, Crystal presents an argument for metalinguistic awareness. According to Crystal, *metalinguistics* refers to the ability to "step back" and use words to analyze how language works:

Craig 7

If we are good at stepping back, at thinking in a more abstract way about what we hear and what we say, then we are more likely to be good at acquiring those skills which depend on just such a stepping back in order to be successful—and this means, chiefly, reading and writing. . . . [T]he greater our ability to play with language, . . . the more advanced will be our command of language as a whole. (Crystal 181)

If we accept the findings of linguists such as Crystal that metalinguistic awareness leads to increased literacy, then it seems reasonable to argue that the phonetic language of messaging can also lead to increased metalinguistic awareness and, therefore, increases in overall literacy. As messagers develop proficiency with a variety of phonetic replacements and other types of texting and messaging words, they should increase their subconscious knowledge of metalinguistics.

Metalinguistics also involves our ability to write in a variety of distinct styles and tones. Yet in the debate over messaging and literacy, many critics assume that either messaging or academic literacy will eventually win out in a person and that the two modes cannot exist side by side. This assumption is, however, false. Human beings ordinarily develop a large range of language abilities, from the formal to the relaxed and from the mainstream to the subcultural. Mark Twain, for example, had an understanding of local speech that he employed when writing dialogue for *Huckleberry Finn*. Yet few people would argue that Twain's knowledge of this form of English had a negative impact on his ability to write in standard English.

However, just as Mark Twain used dialects carefully in dialogue, writers must pay careful attention to the kind of language

Block format for a quotation of more than four lines

Ellipses and brackets indicate omissions and changes in quotation

Writer links Crystal's views to thesis

Another refutation of critics' assumptions

Example from well-known work of literature used as support

Craig 8

they use in any setting. Composition specialist Andrea A. Lunsford
backs up this idea in a blog post:

Email correspondence cited in support of claim

> [W]here English is concerned, there is never one solitary right
> way to proceed: everything depends on the rhetorical situation
> and the intended purpose.

The analytical ability that is necessary for writers to choose
an appropriate tone and style in their writing is, of course,
metalinguistic in nature because it involves the comparison of two or

Writer synthesizes evidence for claim

more language systems. Thus, youths who grasp multiple languages
will have a greater natural understanding of metalinguistics.
More specifically, young people who possess both messaging and
traditional skills stand to be better off than their peers who have
been trained only in traditional or conventional systems. Far from
being hurt by their online pastime, instant messagers can be aided in
standard writing by their experience with messaging language.

Transition to final point

Alternative explanation for decline in literacy

The fact remains, however, that youth literacy seems to
be declining. What, if not messaging, is the main cause of this
phenomenon? According to the College Board, which collects data
on several questions from its test takers, course work in English
composition classes has decreased by 14 percent between 1992
and 2002 (Carnahan and Coletti 11). The possibility of messaging
causing a decline in literacy seems inadequate when statistics
on English education for US youths provide other evidence of the
possible causes. Simply put, students in the United States are
not getting as much practice in academic writing as they used to.
Rather than blaming texting and messaging language alone for the
decline in literacy and test scores, we must also look toward our
schools' lack of focus on the teaching of standard English skills.

Craig 9

My findings indicate that the use of messaging poses virtually
no threat to the development or maintenance of formal language
skills among American youths aged twelve to seventeen. Diverse
language skills tend to increase a person's metalinguistic awareness
and, thereby, his or her ability to use language effectively to achieve
a desired purpose in a particular situation. The current decline in
youth literacy is not due to the rise of texting and messaging. Rather,
fewer young students seem to be receiving an adequate education
in the use of conventional English. Unfortunately, it may always be
fashionable to blame new tools for old problems, but in the case of
messaging, that blame is not warranted. Although messaging may
expose literacy problems, it does not create them.

Transition to
conclusion

Concluding
paragraph
sums up
argument
and reiterates
thesis

Craig 10

Works Cited

Carnahan, Kristin, and Chiara Coletti. *Ten-Year Trend in SAT Scores Indicates Increased Emphasis on Math Is Yielding Results: Reading and Writing Are Causes for Concern.* College Board, 2002.

Crystal, David. *Language Play.* U of Chicago P, 1998.

Ferguson, Niall. "Texting Makes U Stupid." *Newsweek,* vol. 158, no. 12, 19 Sept. 2011, p. 11. *EBSCOHost,* connection .ebscohost.com/c/articles/65454341/texting-makes-u-stupid.

Leibowitz, Wendy R. "Technology Transforms Writing and the Teaching of Writing." *Chronicle of Higher Education,* 26 Nov. 1999, pp. A67-A68.

Lenhart, Amanda. *Teens, Smartphones, & Texting.* Pew Research Center, 19 Mar. 2012, www.pewinternet.org/files/old-media// Files/Reports/2012/PIP_Teens_Smartphones_and_Texting.pdf.

Lenhart, Amanda, et al. *Writing, Technology & Teens.* Pew Research Center, 24 Apr. 2008, www.pewinternet.org/2008/04/24/ writing-technology-and-teens/.

Lenhart, Amanda, and Oliver Lewis. *Teenage Life Online: The Rise of the Instant-Message Generation and the Internet's Impact on Friendships and Family Relationships.* Pew Research Center, 21 June 2001, www.pewinternet.org/2001/06/20/the-rise-of-the -instant-message-generation/.

Lunsford, Andrea A. "Are You a 'Comma Queen'?" *Bedford Bits,* 9 Apr. 2015, community.macmillan.com/community/the-english -community/bedford-bits/blog/2015/04/09/are-you-a-comma -queen.

McCarroll, Christina. "Teens Ready to Prove Text-Messaging Skills Can Score SAT Points." *Christian Science Monitor,* 11 Mar. 2005, www.csmonitor.com/2005/0311/p01s02-ussc.html.

"SAT Trends 2011." *Collegeboard.org,* 14 Sept. 2011, research .collegeboard.org/programs/sat/data/archived/cb-seniors -2011/tables.

Heading centered

Report

Print book

Article from database

Print news-paper article

Downloaded file

Online report

Subsequent lines of each entry indented

Blog post

Online news-paper article

Graph source

46 APA Style

Chapter 46 discusses the basic formats prescribed by the American Psychological Association (APA), guidelines that are widely used for research in the social sciences. For further reference, consult the *Publication Manual of the American Psychological Association*, Sixth Edition (2010).

46a Understanding APA citation style

Why does academic work call for very careful citation practices when writing for the general public may not? The answer is that readers of academic work expect source citations for several reasons:

- Source citations demonstrate that you've done your homework on your topic and that you are a part of the conversation surrounding it.

- Source citations show that you understand the need to give credit when you make use of someone else's intellectual property. (See Chapter 15.)

- Source citations give explicit directions to guide readers who want to look for themselves at the works you're using.

The guidelines for APA style tell you exactly what information to include in your citation and how to format that information.

Types of sources. Look at the Directory to APA Style on pp. 278–79 for guidelines on citing various types of sources—print books (or parts of print books), print periodicals (journals, magazines, and newspapers), and digital written-word sources (an online article or a book on an e-reader). A digital version of a source may include updates or corrections that the print version lacks, so it's important to provide the correct information for readers. For sources that consist mainly of material other than written words—such as a film, song, or artwork—consult the "other sources" section of the directory. And if you can't find a model exactly like the source you've selected, see the box on p. 281.

ARTICLES FROM WEB AND DATABASE SOURCES. You need a subscription to look through most databases, so individual researchers almost always gain access to articles in databases through the computer system of a school or public library that pays to subscribe. The easiest way to tell whether a source comes from a database, then, is that its information is *not* generally available for free. Many databases are digital collections of articles that originally appeared in edited print periodicals, ensuring that an authority has vouched for the accuracy of the information. Such sources often have more credibility than free material available on the web.

Parts of citations. APA citations appear in two parts of your text—a brief in-text citation in the body of your written text and a full citation in the list of references, to which the in-text citation directs readers. The most straightforward in-text citations include the author's name, the publication year, and the page number, but many variations on this basic format are discussed in 46c.

In the text of her research essay (see 46e), Tawnya Redding includes a paraphrase of material from an online journal that she accessed through the publisher's website. She cites the authors' names and the year of publication in a parenthetical reference, pointing readers to the entry for "Baker, F., & Bor, W. (2008)" in her references list, shown on p. 309.

Content notes. APA style allows you to use content notes, either at the bottom of the page or on a separate page at the end of the text, to expand or supplement your text. Indicate such notes in the text by superscript numerals (^{1}). Double-space all entries. Indent the first line of each note five spaces, but begin subsequent lines at the left margin.

SUPERSCRIPT NUMBER IN TEXT

The age of the children involved in the study was an important factor in the selection of items for the questionnaire.[1]

FOOTNOTE

[1]Marjorie Youngston Forman and William Cole of the Child Study Team provided great assistance in identifying appropriate items for the questionnaire.

MOOD MUSIC 9

References

Baker, F., & Bor, W. (2008). Can music preference indicate mental
 health status in young people? *Australasian Psychiatry, 16*(4),
 284–288. Retrieved from http://www3.interscience.wiley.com
 /journal/118565538/home

George, D., Stickle, K., Rachid, F., & Wopnford, A. (2007). The

alter the mood of at-risk youth in a negative way. This view of the

correlation between music and suicide risk is supported by a meta-

analysis done by Baker and Bor (2008), in which the authors assert
 al music

that most studies reject the notion that music is a causal factor
 lescence,

and suggest that music preference is more indicative of emotional

vulnerability. However, it is still unknown whether these genres can

Taiwan. *Issues in Mental Health Nursing, 20,* 229–246. doi:
 10.1080/016128499248637

46b Following APA manuscript format

The following formatting guidelines are adapted from the APA rec-
ommendations for preparing manuscripts for publication in jour-
nals. However, check with your instructor before preparing the final
draft of a print text.

Title page.   APA does not provide specific title-page guidelines.
Center the title and include your name, the course name and num-
ber, the instructor's name, and the date. If your instructor wants you
to include a running head, place it flush left on the first line. Write
the words *Running head*, a colon, and a short version of the title (fifty
characters or fewer, including spaces) using all capital letters. On the
same line, flush with the right margin, type the number 1.

Margins and spacing.   Leave margins of at least one inch at
the top and bottom and on both sides of the page. Do not jus-
tify the right margin. Double-space the entire text, including any

headings, set-off quotations (39a), content notes, and the list of references. Indent one-half inch from the left margin for the first line of a paragraph and all lines of a quotation over forty words long.

Short title and page numbers. Place the running head and the short title in the upper left corner of each page. Place the page number in the upper right corner of each page, in the same position as on the title page.

Long quotations. For a long, set-off quotation (one having more than forty words), indent it one-half inch from the left margin, and do not use quotation marks. Place the page reference in parentheses one space after the final punctuation.

Abstract. If your instructor asks for an abstract, the abstract should go immediately after the title page, with the word *Abstract* centered about an inch from the top of the page. Double-space the text of the abstract. In most cases, a one-paragraph abstract of about one hundred words will be sufficient to introduce readers to your topic and provide a brief summary of your major thesis and supporting points.

Headings. Headings are frequently used within the text of APA-style projects. In a text with only one or two levels of headings, center the main headings; italicize the subheadings and position them flush with the left margin. Capitalize all major words; however, do not capitalize any **articles**, short **prepositions**, or **coordinating conjunctions** unless they are the first word or follow a colon.

Visuals. Tables should be labeled *Table*, numbered, and captioned. All other visuals (such as charts, graphs, photographs, and drawings) should be labeled *Figure*, numbered, and captioned with a description and the source information. Remember to refer to each visual in your text, stating how it contributes to the point(s) you are making. Tables and figures should generally appear near the relevant text; check with your instructor for guidelines on the placement of visuals.

46c Creating APA in-text citations

An in-text citation in APA style always indicates which source on the references page the writer is referring to, and it explains in what year the material was published; for quoted material, the in-text citation also indicates where in the source the quotation can be found.

Note that APA style generally calls for using the past tense or present perfect tense for signal verbs: *Baker (2003) showed* or *Baker (2003) has shown*. Use the present tense only to discuss results (*the experiment demonstrates*) or widely accepted information (*researchers agree*).

1. BASIC FORMAT FOR A QUOTATION. Generally, use the author's name in a signal phrase to introduce the cited material, and place the date, in parentheses, immediately after the author's name. The page number, preceded by *p.*, appears in parentheses after the quotation.

> Gitlin (2001) pointed out that "political critics, convinced that the media are rigged against them, are often blind to other substantial reasons why their causes are unpersuasive" (p. 141).

If the author is not named in a signal phrase, place the author's name, the year, and the page number in parentheses after the quotation: (Gitlin, 2001, p. 141). For a long, set-off quotation (more than forty words), place the page reference in parentheses one space after the final quotation.

For quotations from works without page numbers, you may use paragraph numbers, if the source includes them, preceded by the abbreviation *para.*

> Driver (2007) has noticed "an increasing focus on the role of land" in
>
> policy debates over the past decade (para. 1).

2. BASIC FORMAT FOR A PARAPHRASE OR SUMMARY. Include the author's last name and the year as in model 1, but omit the page or paragraph number unless the reader will need it to find the material in a long work.

> Gitlin (2001) has argued that critics sometimes overestimate the influence
>
> of the media on modern life.

3. TWO AUTHORS. Use both names in all citations. Use *and* in a signal phrase, but use an ampersand (&) in parentheses.

> Babcock and Laschever (2003) have suggested that many women do
>
> not negotiate their salaries and pay raises as vigorously as their male
>
> counterparts do.

> A recent study has suggested that many women do not negotiate their
>
> salaries and pay raises as vigorously as their male counterparts do (Babcock
>
> & Laschever, 2003).

4. THREE TO FIVE AUTHORS. List all the authors' names for the first reference.

> Safer, Voccola, Hurd, and Goodwin (2003) reached somewhat different
>
> conclusions by designing a study that was less dependent on subjective
>
> judgment than were previous studies.

In subsequent references, use just the first author's name followed by *et al.*

Based on the results, Safer et al. (2003) determined that the apes took significant steps toward self-expression.

5. SIX OR MORE AUTHORS. Use only the first author's name and *et al.* in every citation.

As Soleim et al. (2002) demonstrated, advertising holds the potential for manipulating "free-willed" consumers.

6. CORPORATE OR GROUP AUTHOR. If the name of the organization or corporation is long, spell it out the first time you use it, followed by an abbreviation in brackets. In later references, use the abbreviation only.

FIRST CITATION	(Centers for Disease Control and Prevention [CDC], 2006)
LATER CITATIONS	(CDC, 2006)

7. UNKNOWN AUTHOR. Use the title or its first few words in a signal phrase or in parentheses. A book's title is italicized, as in the following example; an article's title is placed in quotation marks.

The employment profiles for this time period substantiated this trend (*Federal Employment,* 2001).

8. TWO OR MORE AUTHORS WITH THE SAME LAST NAME. Include the authors' initials in each citation.

S. Bartolomeo (2000) conducted the groundbreaking study on teenage childbearing.

9. TWO OR MORE WORKS BY AN AUTHOR IN A SINGLE YEAR. Assign lowercase letters (*a, b,* and so on) alphabetically by title, and include the letters after the year.

Gordon (2004b) examined this trend in more detail.

10. TWO OR MORE SOURCES IN ONE PARENTHETICAL REFERENCE. List any sources by different authors in alphabetical order by the authors' last names, separated by semicolons: (Cardone, 1998; Lai, 2002).

List works by the same author in chronological order, separated by commas: (Lai, 2000, 2002).

11. SOURCE REPORTED IN ANOTHER SOURCE. Use the phrase *as cited in* to indicate that you are reporting information from a secondary source. Name the original source in a signal phrase, but list the secondary source in your list of references.

> Amartya Sen developed the influential concept that land reform was necessary for "promoting opportunity" among the poor (as cited in Driver, 2007, para. 2).

12. PERSONAL COMMUNICATION. Cite any personal letters, email messages, electronic postings, telephone conversations, or interviews as shown. Do not include personal communications in the reference list.

> R. Tobin (personal communication, November 4, 2006) supported his claims about music therapy with new evidence.

13. ELECTRONIC DOCUMENT. Cite a web or electronic document as you would a print source, using the author's name and date.

> Link and Phelan (2005) argued for broader interventions in public health that would be accessible to anyone, regardless of individual wealth.

The APA recommends the following for electronic sources without names, dates, or page numbers:

AUTHOR UNKNOWN
Use a shortened form of the title in a signal phrase or in parentheses (see model 7). If an organization is the author, see model 6.

DATE UNKNOWN
Use the abbreviation *n.d.* (for "no date") in place of the year: (*Hopkins, n.d.*).

NO PAGE NUMBERS
Many works found online or in electronic databases lack stable page numbers. (Use the page numbers for an electronic work in a format, such as PDF, that has stable pagination.) If paragraph numbers are

included in such a source, use the abbreviation *para.*: (*Giambetti, 2006, para. 7*). If no paragraph numbers are included but the source includes headings, give the heading and identify the paragraph in the section:

> Jacobs and Johnson (2007) have argued that "the South African media is still highly concentrated and not very diverse in terms of race and class" (South African Media after Apartheid, para. 3).

14. TABLE OR FIGURE REPRODUCED IN THE TEXT. Number figures (graphs, charts, illustrations, and photographs) and tables separately.

For a table, place the label (*Table 1*) and an informative heading (*Hartman's Key Personality Traits*) above the table; below, provide information about its source.

Table 1

Hartman's Key Personality Traits

Trait category	Color			
	Red	Blue	White	Yellow
Motive	Power	Intimacy	Peace	Fun
Strengths	Loyal to tasks	Loyal to people	Tolerant	Positive
Limitations	Arrogant	Self-righteous	Timid	Uncommitted

Note: Adapted from *The Hartman Personality Profile*, by N. Hayden. Retrieved February 24, 2016, from http://students.cs.byu.edu/~nhayden/Code/index.php

For a figure, place the label (*Figure 3*) and a caption indicating the source below the image. If you do not cite the source of the table or figure elsewhere in your text, you do not need to include the source on your list of references.

46d Creating an APA list of references

The alphabetical list of the sources cited in your document is called *References*. If your instructor asks that you list everything you have read—not just the sources you cite—call the list *Bibliography*.

DIRECTORY TO APA STYLE

APA style for references

DIRECTORY TO APA STYLE

APA style for references, *continued*

All the entries in this section of the book use hanging indent format, in which the first line aligns on the left and the subsequent lines indent one-half inch or five spaces. This is the customary APA format.

Guidelines for author listings

List authors' last names first, and use only initials for first and middle names. The in-text citations in your text point readers toward particular sources in your list of references (see 46c).

NAME CITED IN SIGNAL PHRASE IN TEXT

Driver (2007) has noted . . .

NAME IN PARENTHETICAL CITATION IN TEXT

. . . (Driver, 2007).

BEGINNING OF ENTRY IN LIST OF REFERENCES

Driver, T. (2007).

Models 1–5 below explain how to arrange author names. The information that follows the name of the author depends on the type of work you are citing—a book (models 6–15), a print periodical (models 16–23), a digital written-word source (models 24–34), or another kind of source (models 35–48).

> ## ▶ Checklist

> **Formatting a List of References**
>
> ▶ Start your list on a new page after the text of your document but before appendices or notes. Continue consecutive page numbers.
>
> ▶ Center the heading *References* one inch from the top of the page.
>
> ▶ Begin each entry flush with the left margin, but indent subsequent lines one-half inch or five spaces. Double-space the entire list.
>
> ▶ List sources alphabetically by author's last name. If no author is given, alphabetize the source by the first word of the title other than *A, An,* or *The*. If the list includes two or more works by the same author, list them in chronological order.
>
> ▶ Italicize titles and subtitles of books and periodicals. Do not italicize titles of articles, and do not enclose them in quotation marks.
>
> ▶ For titles of books and articles, capitalize only the first word of the title and the subtitle and any proper nouns or proper adjectives.
>
> ▶ For titles of periodicals, capitalize all major words.

1. ONE AUTHOR. Give the last name, a comma, the initial(s), and the date in parentheses.

Zimbardo, P. G. (2009).

2. MULTIPLE AUTHORS. List up to seven authors, last name first, with commas separating authors' names and an ampersand (&) before the last author's name.

Walsh, M. E., & Murphy, J. A. (2003).

Note: For a work with more than seven authors, list the first six, then an ellipsis (. . .), and then the final author's name.

3. CORPORATE OR GROUP AUTHOR

Resources for Rehabilitation. (2003).

 Checklist

Combining Parts of Models

What should you do if your source doesn't match the model exactly? Suppose, for instance, that your source is a translation of a republished book with an editor.

▶ Identify a basic model to follow. If you decide that your source looks most like a republished book, for example, start with a citation that looks like model 13.

▶ Look for models that show additional elements in your source. For this example, you would need elements of model 9 (for the translation) and model 7 (for the editor).

▶ Add new elements from other models to your basic model in the order that makes the most sense to you.

▶ If you still aren't sure how to arrange the pieces to create a combination model, ask your instructor.

4. UNKNOWN AUTHOR. Begin with the work's title. Italicize book titles, but do not italicize article titles or enclose them in quotation marks. Capitalize only the first word of the title and subtitle (if any) and proper nouns and proper adjectives.

Safe youth, safe schools. (2009).

5. TWO OR MORE WORKS BY THE SAME AUTHOR. List works by the same author in chronological order. Repeat the author's name in each entry.

Goodall, J. (1999).

Goodall, J. (2002).

If the works appeared in the same year, list them alphabetically by title, and assign lowercase letters (*a*, *b*, etc.) after the dates.

Shermer, M. (2002a). On estimating the lifetime of civilizations. *Scientific American, 287*(2), 33.

Shermer, M. (2002b). Readers who question evolution. *Scientific American, 287*(1), 37.

Print books

6. BASIC FORMAT FOR A BOOK. Begin with the author name(s). (See models 1–5.) Then include the publication year, title and subtitle, city of publication, country or state abbreviation, and publisher. The source map on pp. 284–85 shows where to find this information in a typical book.

> Levick, S. E. (2003). *Clone being: Exploring the psychological and social dimensions.* Lanham, MD: Rowman & Littlefield.

7. EDITOR. For a book with an editor but no author, list the source under the editor's name.

> Dickens, J. (Ed.). (1995). *Family outing: A guide for parents of gays, lesbians and bisexuals.* London, England: Peter Owen.

To cite a book with an author and an editor, place the editor's name, with a comma and the abbreviation *Ed.*, in parentheses after the title.

> Austin, J. (1995). *The province of jurisprudence determined.* (W. E. Rumble, Ed.). Cambridge, England: Cambridge University Press.

8. SELECTION IN A BOOK WITH AN EDITOR

> Burke, W. W., & Nourmair, D. A. (2001). The role of personality assessment in organization development. In J. Waclawski & A. H. Church (Eds.), *Organization development: A data-driven approach to organizational change* (pp. 55–77). San Francisco, CA: Jossey-Bass.

9. TRANSLATION

> Al-Farabi, A. N. (1998). *On the perfect state* (R. Walzer, Trans.). Chicago, IL: Kazi.

10. EDITION OTHER THAN THE FIRST

> Moore, G. S. (2002). *Living with the earth: Concepts in environmental health science* (2nd ed.). New York, NY: Lewis.

11. MULTIVOLUME WORK WITH AN EDITOR

Barnes, J. (Ed.). (1995). *Complete works of Aristotle* (Vols. 1–2). Princeton, NJ: Princeton University Press.

Note: If you are citing just one volume of a multivolume work, list that volume, not the complete span of volumes, in parentheses after the title.

12. ARTICLE IN A REFERENCE WORK

Dean, C. (1994). Jaws and teeth. In *The Cambridge encyclopedia of human evolution* (pp. 56–59). Cambridge, England: Cambridge University Press.

If no author is listed, begin with the title.

13. REPUBLISHED BOOK

Piaget, J. (1952). *The language and thought of the child*. London, England: Routledge & Kegan Paul. (Original work published 1932)

14. INTRODUCTION, PREFACE, FOREWORD, OR AFTERWORD

Klosterman, C. (2007). Introduction. In P. Shirley, *Can I keep my jersey?: 11 teams, 5 countries, and 4 years in my life as a basketball vagabond* (pp. v–vii). New York, NY: Villard-Random House.

15. BOOK WITH A TITLE WITHIN THE TITLE. Do not italicize or enclose in quotation marks a title within a book title.

Klarman, M. J. (2007). Brown v. Board of Education *and the civil rights movement*. New York, NY: Oxford University Press.

Print periodicals

Begin with the author name(s). (See models 1–5.) Then include the publication date (year only for journals, and year, month, and day for all other periodicals); the article title; the periodical title; the volume number and issue number, if any; and the page numbers. The source map on pp. 288–89 shows where to find this information in a sample periodical.

APA SOURCE MAP: Books

Take information from the book's title page and copyright page (on the reverse side of the title page), not from the book's cover or a library catalog.

1 **Author.** List all authors' last names first, and use only initials for first and middle names. For more about citing authors, see models 1–5.

2 **Publication year.** Enclose the year of publication in parentheses.

3 **Title.** Italicize the title and any subtitle. Capitalize only the first word of the title and the subtitle and any proper nouns or proper adjectives.

4 **City and state of publication, and publisher.** List the city of publication and the country or state abbreviation, a colon, and the publisher's name, dropping any *Inc.*, *Co.*, or *Publishers*.

A citation for the book on p. 285 would look like this:

Tsutsui, W. (2004). *Godzilla on my mind: Fifty years of the king of monsters*. New York, NY: Palgrave Macmillan.

First published 2004 by
PALGRAVE MACMILLAN™
175 Fifth Avenue, New York, N.Y. 10010 and
Houndmills, Basingstoke, Hampshire, England RG21 6XS.
Companies and representatives throughout the world.

PALGRAVE MACMILLAN is the global academic imprint of
the Palgrave Macmillan division of St. Martin's Press, LLC and of
Palgrave Macmillan Ltd. Macmillan® is a registered trademark in
the United States, United Kingdom and other countries. Palgrave
is a registered trademark in the European Union and other
countries.

ISBN 1–4039–6474–2

Library of Con...
Tsutsui, Willian...
Godzilla on my...
Tsutsui.
    p. cm.
  Includes bibl...
  ISBN 1–4039...
  1. Godzilla f...

PN1995.9.G63...
791.43'651—dc...

A catalogue re...
Library.

Design by Letr...

10 9 8 7 ...

Printed in the ...

Publication Year
2004

City and State of Publication
New York, N.Y.

GODZILLA® ON MY MIND

Title

Subtitle

*

Fifty Years of the King of Monsters

WILLIAM TSUTSUI — **Author**

palgrave
macmillan

Publisher

285

16. ARTICLE IN A JOURNAL PAGINATED BY VOLUME

Banks, A. (2015). Ain't no walls behind the sky, baby! Funk, flight,
　　freedom. *College Composition and Communication, 67,* 267–279.

17. ARTICLE IN A JOURNAL PAGINATED BY ISSUE. If each issue begins with page 1, include the issue number (in parentheses and not italicized) after the volume number (italicized).

Hall, R. E. (2000). Marriage as vehicle of racism among women of color.
　　Psychology: A Journal of Human Behavior, 37(2), 29–40.

18. ARTICLE IN A MAGAZINE. Include the month (and day, if given).

Solomon, A. (2014, March 17). The reckoning. *The New Yorker,*
　　(*90*)4, 36-45.

19. ARTICLE IN A NEWSPAPER. Use *p.* or *pp.* for the page number(s) of a newspaper article.

Reynolds Lewis, K. (2011, December 22). Why some business owners think
　　now is the time to sell. *The New York Times,* p. B5.

20. EDITORIAL OR LETTER TO THE EDITOR. Add an identifying label.

Zelneck, B. (2003, July 18). Serving the public at public universities
　　[Letter to the editor]. *The Chronicle Review,* p. B18.

21. UNSIGNED ARTICLE

Annual meeting announcement. (2003, March). *Cognitive Psychology, 46,*
　　227.

22. REVIEW. Identify the work reviewed.

Ringel, S. (2003). [Review of the book *Multiculturalism and the therapeutic
　　process*]. *Clinical Social Work Journal, 31,* 212–213.

23. PUBLISHED INTERVIEW. Identify the person interviewed.

Smith, H. (2002, October). [Interview with A. Thompson]. *The Sun,* pp. 4–7.

Digital written-word sources

Updated guidelines for citing digital resources are maintained at the APA's website (www.apa.org).

24. ARTICLE FROM AN ONLINE PERIODICAL. Give the author, date, title, and publication information as you would for a print document. Include both the volume and issue numbers for all journal articles. If the article has a digital object identifier (DOI), include it. If there is no DOI, write *Retrieved from* and the URL for the periodical's home page or for the article (if the article is difficult to find from the home page). For newspaper articles accessible from a searchable website, give the site URL only.

> Barringer, F. (2008, February 7). In many communities, it's not easy going
>   green. *The New York Times*. Retrieved from http://www.nytimes.com

> Cleary, J. M., & Crafti, N. (2007). Basic need satisfaction, emotional
>   eating, and dietary restraint as risk factors for recurrent overeating
>   in a community sample. *E-Journal of Applied Psychology, 2*(3), 27–39.
>   Retrieved from http://ojs.lib.swin.edu.au/index.php/ejap/article
>   /view/90/116

25. ARTICLE FROM A DATABASE. Give the author, date, title, and publication information as you would for a print document. Include both the volume and issue numbers for all journal articles. If the article has a DOI, include it. If there is no DOI, write *Retrieved from* and the URL of the journal's home page (not the URL of the database). The source map on pp. 292–93 shows where to find this information for a typical article from a database.

> Hazleden, R. (2003, December). Love yourself: The relationship of the self
>   with itself in popular self-help texts. *Journal of Sociology, 39*(4),
>   413–428. Retrieved from http://jos.sagepub.com

> Morley, N. J., Ball, L. J., & Ormerod, T. C. (2006). How the detection of
>   insurance fraud succeeds and fails. *Psychology, Crime, & Law, 12*(2),
>   163–180. doi:10.1080/10683160512331316325

APA SOURCE MAP: Articles from Print Periodicals

(1) Author. List all authors' last names first, and use only initials for first and middle names. For more about citing authors, see models 1–5.

(2) Publication date. Enclose the date in parentheses. For journals, use only the year. For magazines and newspapers, use the year, a comma, the month (spelled out), and the day, if given.

(3) Article title. Do not italicize or enclose article titles in quotation marks. Capitalize only the first word of the article title and subtitle and any proper nouns or proper adjectives.

(4) Periodical title. Italicize the periodical title (and subtitle, if any), and capitalize all major words. Follow the periodical title with a comma.

(5) Volume and issue numbers. Give the volume number (italicized) and, without a space in between, the issue number (if given) in parentheses. Follow with a comma.

(6) Page numbers. Give the inclusive page numbers of the article. For newspapers only, include the abbreviation *p.* ("page") or *pp.* ("pages") before the page numbers. End the citation with a period.

A citation for the periodical article on p. 289 would look like this:

Etzioni, A. (2006). Leaving race behind: Our growing Hispanic population creates a golden opportunity. *The American Scholar, 75*(2), 20–30.

The AMERICAN
SCHOLAR

4 Periodical Title

Spring 2006 | Vol. 75, No. 2

5 Volume and Issue Numbers

2 Publication Date

The AMERICAN
SCHOLAR

3 Article Title

Leaving Race Behind

Our growing Hispanic population creates a golden opportunity

AMITAI ETZIONI

1 Author

Some years ago the United States government asked me what my race was. I was reluctant to respond because my 50 years of practicing sociology—and some powerful personal experiences—have underscored for me what we all know to one degree or another, that racial divisions bedevil America, just as they do many other societies across the world. Not wanting to encourage these divisions, I refused to check off one of the specific racial options on the U.S. Census form and instead marked a box labeled "Other." I later found out that the federal government did not accept such an attempt to de-emphasize race, by me or by some 6.75 million other Americans who tried it. Instead the government assigned me to a racial category, one it chose for me. Learning this made me conjure up what I admit is a far-fetched association. I was in this place once before. When I was a Jewish child in Nazi Germany in the early 1930s, many Jews who saw themselves as good Germans wanted to "pass" as Aryans. But the Nazi regime would have none of it. Never mind, they told these Jews, *we determine* who is Jewish and who is not. A similar practice prevailed in the Old South, where if you had one drop of African blood you were a Negro, disregarding all other facts and considerations, including how you saw yourself.

You might suppose that in the years since my little Census-form protest

⌐ Amitai Etzioni is University Professor at George Washington University and the author of *The Monochrome Society*.

6 Page Numbers

▶ Checklist

Citing Digital Sources

When citing sources accessed online or from an electronic database, include as many of the following elements as you can find:

▶ **Author.** Give the author's name, if available.

▶ **Publication date.** Include the date of electronic publication or of the latest update, if available. When no publication date is available, use *n.d.* ("no date").

▶ **Title.** If the source is not from a larger work, italicize the title.

▶ **Print publication information.** For articles from online journals, magazines, or reference databases, give the publication title and other publishing information as you would for a print periodical (see models 16–23).

▶ **Retrieval information.** For a work from a database, do the following: if the article has a DOI (digital object identifier), include that number after the publication information; do not include the name of the database. If there is no DOI, write *Retrieved from* followed by the URL for the journal's home page (not the database URL). For a work found on a website, write *Retrieved from* and include the URL. If the work seems likely to be updated, include the retrieval date. If the URL is longer than one line, break it only before a punctuation mark; do not break *http://*.

26. ABSTRACT FOR AN ONLINE ARTICLE. Include a label.

> Gudjonsson, G. H., & Young, S. (2010). Does confabulation in memory predict suggestibility beyond IQ and memory? [Abstract]. *Personality & Individual Differences, 49*(1), 65–67. doi: 10.1016 /j.paid.2010.03.014

27. COMMENT ON AN ONLINE ARTICLE. Give the writer's real name (if known) or screen name. Use *Re:* before the title of the article, and add the label *[Comment]*.

 Checklist

Citing Sources without Models in APA Style

You may need to cite a source for which you cannot find a model in APA style. If so, collect as much information as you can find about the creator, title, sponsor, date, and so on, with the goal of helping readers find the source for themselves. Then look at the models in this section to see which one most closely matches the type of source you are using.

In an academic writing project, before citing an electronic source for which you have no model, also be sure to ask your instructor's advice.

The Lone Ranger. (2014, April 22). Re: The American middle class is no

longer the world's richest [Comment]. *The New York Times*. Retrieved

from http://www.nytimes.com/

28. REPORT OR LONG DOCUMENT FROM A WEBSITE. Include all of the following information that you can find: the author's name; the publication date (or *n.d.* if no date is available); the title of the document, italicized; and *Retrieved from* and the URL. Provide your date of access only if an update seems likely. The source map on pp. 296–97 shows where to find this information for a report from a website.

Nice, M. L., & Katzev, R. (n.d.). *Internet romances: The frequency and*

nature of romantic on-line relationships. Retrieved from http://www

.publicpolicyresearch.net/papers.html

29. SHORT WORK FROM A WEBSITE. Include the name of the work (with no italics) and the name of the site, italicized.

Zimbardo, P. G. (2013). Constructing the experiment. *Stanford*

Prison Experiment. Retrieved from http://www.prisonexp.org

/psychology/5

1 **Author.** Include the author's name as you would for a print source. List all authors' last names first, and use initials for first and middle names. For more about citing authors, see models 1–5.

2 **Publication date.** Enclose the date in parentheses. For journals, use only the year. For magazines and newspapers, use the year, a comma, the month, and the day if given.

3 **Article title.** Capitalize only the first word of the article title and the subtitle and any proper nouns or proper adjectives.

4 **Periodical title.** Italicize the periodical title.

5 **Volume and issue number.** For journals and magazines, give the volume number (italicized) and the issue number (in parentheses).

6 **Page numbers.** For journals only, give inclusive page numbers.

7 **Retrieval information.** If the article has a DOI (digital object identifier), include that number after the publication information; do not include the name of the database. If there is no DOI, write *Retrieved from* followed by the URL of the journal's home page (not the database URL).

A citation for the article on p. 293 would look like this:

Knobloch-Westerwick, S., & Crane, J. (2012). A losing battle: Effects of prolonged exposure to thin-ideal images on dieting and body satisfaction. *Communication Research, 39*(1), 79–102. doi:10.1177/0093650211400596

Article Title Periodical Title Page Numbers

Communication Research
39(1) 79–102
© The Author(s) 2012
Reprints and permission:
sagepub.com/journalsPermissions.nav
DOI: 10.1177/0093650211400596
http://crx.sagepub.com
$SAGE

A Losing Battle: Effects of Prolonged Exposure to Thin-Ideal Images on Dieting and Body Satisfaction

Volume and Issue Number

Retrieval Information

Silvia Knobloch-Westerwick[1] and Josselyn Crane[1]

Authors Publication Date

Abstract

The present study examined prolonged exposure effects of thin-ideal media messages. College-aged females participated in seven online sessions over 10 days including a baseline measures session, five daily measures, and a posttest. Two experimental groups viewed magazine pages with thin-ideal imagery. One of those groups was induced to engage in social comparisons with the thin-ideal models. The control group viewed messages with body-neutral images of women. Prolonged exposure to thin-ideal messages led to greater body satisfaction. This finding was attributed to the fact that the experimental groups reported more dieting behaviors. A mediation analysis showed that the impact of thin-ideal message exposure on body satisfaction was mediated by dieting.

Keywords

body dissatisfaction, body image, dieting, prolonged exposure, social comparison

Idealized body images in the media have been linked to unrealistic body shape aspirations and body dissatisfaction (see meta-analysis by Grabe, Ward, & Hyde, 2008), which, in turn, have been linked to numerous pathological problems, including depression, obesity, dieting, and eating disorders (e.g., Johnson & Wardle, 2005; Neumark-Sztainer, Paxton, Hannan, Haines, & Story, 2006; Ricciardelli & McCabe, 2001). However, another meta-analysis by Holmstrom (2004) found that the longer the media exposure, the *better* the individuals felt about their body. This inconsistency indicates that the factors and processes at work have not yet been fully understood and captured by the research at hand and deserve further investigation. Social comparison theory is the theoretical framework that has guided much

[1]The Ohio State University

Corresponding Author:
Silvia Knobloch-Westerwick, The Ohio State University, 154 N Oval Mall, Columbus, OH 43210
Email: knobloch-westerwick.1@osu.edu

293

30. ONLINE BOOK. Give the original print publication date, if different, in parentheses at the end of the entry.

> Russell, B. (2008). *The analysis of mind.* Retrieved from http://onlinebooks
> .library.upenn.edu/webbin/gutbook/lookup?num=2529 (Original work
> published 1921)

31. EMAIL OR PRIVATE MESSAGE. The APA stresses that any sources cited in your list of references be retrievable by your readers, so do not include entries for email messages or any postings that are not archived. Instead, cite these sources in your text as forms of personal communication (see p. 276).

32. POSTING ON PUBLIC SOCIAL MEDIA. List an online posting in the references list only if you are able to retrieve the message from an archive. Provide the author's name, the date of posting, and a few words from the post. (If you are citing Twitter, include the entire tweet.) Include other identifying information, such as *[Tweet]* or *[Facebook post]*. Then end with the date you retrieved the post and the URL of the public page.

> HeForShe. (2016, May 17). "Dads are stepping up in the fight for caregiver
> rights" #HeForShe @TIMEIdeas [Tweet]. Retrieved May 17, 2016,
> from https://twitter.com/HeforShe/status/732629285756932096

33. BLOG POST OR COMMENT. For a blog post, give the author's real name (if known) or screen name; the date (or *n.d.* if no date is given); the title, followed by the label *[Blog post]*; and the URL.

> Black, D. (2016, May 14). How to succeed [Blog post]. Retrieved from
> http://www.eschatonblog.com/2016/05/how-to-succeed.html

For a comment, put *Re:* before the title of the post commented on, and use the label *[Blog comment]*.

34. WIKI ENTRY. Use the date of posting, if there is one, or *n.d.* for "no date" if there is none. Include the retrieval date because wiki content can change frequently.

> Happiness. (2007, June 14). Retrieved March 24, 2016, from PsychWiki:
> http://www.psychwiki.com/wiki/Happiness

Other sources (including online versions)

35. GOVERNMENT PUBLICATION

> Office of the Federal Register. (2003). *The United States government manual 2003/2004.* Washington, DC: U.S. Government Printing Office.

Cite an online government document as you would a printed government work, adding the URL. If there is no date, use *n.d.*

> U.S. Public Health Service. (1999). *The surgeon general's call to action to prevent suicide.* Retrieved from http://www.mentalhealth.org /suicideprevention/calltoaction.asp

36. DATA SET

> U.S. Department of Education, Institute of Education Sciences. (2009). *NAEP state comparisons* [Data set]. Retrieved from http://nces.ed.gov /nationsreportcard/statecomparisons/

37. DISSERTATION. If you retrieved the dissertation from a database, give the database name and the accession number, if one is assigned.

> Lengel, L. L. (1968). *The righteous cause: Some religious aspects of Kansas populism.* Retrieved from ProQuest Digital Dissertations (6900033)

If you retrieve a dissertation from a website, give the type of dissertation and the institution after the title, and provide a retrieval statement.

> Meeks, M. G. (2006). *Between abolition and reform: First-year writing programs, e-literacies, and institutional change* (Doctoral dissertation, University of North Carolina). Retrieved from http://dc.lib.unc.edu/etd/

38. TECHNICAL OR RESEARCH REPORT. Give the report number, if available, in parentheses after the title.

> McCool, R., Fikes, R., & McGuinness, D. (2003). *Semantic web tools for enhanced authoring* (Report No. KSL-03-07). Retrieved from www.ksl .stanford.edu/KSL_Abstracts/KSL-03-07.html

1 Author. If one is given, include the author's name (see models 1–5). List last names first, and use only initials for first names. The site's sponsor may be the author. If no author is identified, begin the citation with the title of the document.

2 Publication date. Enclose the date of publication or latest update in parentheses. Use *n.d.* ("no date") when no publication date is available.

3 Title of work. Italicize the title. Capitalize only the first word of the title and subtitle and any proper nouns or proper adjectives.

4 Retrieval information. Write *Retrieved from* and include the URL. For a report from an organization's website, identify the organization in the retrieval statement. If the work seems likely to be updated, include the retrieval date.

A citation for the web document on p. 297 would look like this:

Parker, K., & Wang, W. (2013, March 14). *Modern parenthood: Roles of moms and dads converge as they balance work and family.* Retrieved from the Pew Research Center website: http://www.pewsocialtrends .org/2013/03/14/modern-parenthood-roles-of-moms-and-dads -converge-as-they-balance-work-and-family/

② **Publication Date**

March 14, 2013

④ **Retrieval Information**

④ **Retrieval Information**

Released: March 14, 2013

Modern Parenthood
Roles of Moms and Dads Converge as They Balance Work and Family

by *Kim Parker* and *Wendy Wang*

OVERVIEW

The way mothers and fathers spend their time has changed dramatically in the past half century. Dads are doing more housework and child care; moms more paid work outside the home. Neither has overtaken the other in their "traditional" realms, but their roles are converging, according to a new Pew Research Center analysis of long-term data on time use.

At the same time, roughly equal shares of working mothers and fathers report in a new Pew Research Center survey feeling stressed about juggling work and family life: 56% of working moms and 50% of working dads say they find it very or somewhat difficult to balance these responsibilities.

Still, there are important gender role differences. While a nearly equal share of mothers and fathers say they wish they could be at home raising their children rather than working, dads are much more likely than moms to say they want to work full time. And when it comes to what they value most in a job, working fathers place more importance on having a high-paying job, while working mothers are more concerned with having a flexible schedule.[1]

Moms and Dads, 1965-2011: Roles Converge, but Gaps Remain
Average number of hours per week spent on ...

REPORT MATERIALS
- Complete Report
- Topline Questionnaire

Quiz: Which Parent Does More in Your Home?

Slideshow: Key Findings from the Survey

Data Trends: Parental Time Use Since 1965

① **Author**

Kim Parker and *Wendy Wang*

③ **Title of Work**

39. CONFERENCE PROCEEDINGS

> Robertson, S. P., Vatrapu, R. K., & Medina, R. (2009). YouTube and Facebook: Online video "friends" social networking. In *Conference proceedings: YouTube and the 2008 election cycle* (pp. 159–176). Amherst, MA: University of Massachusetts. Retrieved from http://scholarworks.umass.edu/jitpc2009

40. PAPER PRESENTED AT A MEETING OR SYMPOSIUM, UNPUBLISHED. Cite the month of the meeting if it is available.

> Jones, J. G. (1999, February). *Mental health intervention in mass casualty disasters*. Paper presented at the Rocky Mountain Region Disaster Mental Health Conference, Laramie, WY.

41. POSTER SESSION

> Barnes Young, L. L. (2003, August). *Cognition, aging, and dementia*. Poster session presented at the 2003 Division 40 APA Convention, Toronto, Ontario, Canada.

42. PRESENTATION SLIDES

> Mader, S. (2007, March 27). *The Zen aesthetic* [Presentation slides]. Retrieved from http://www.slideshare.net/slmader/the-zen-aesthetic

43. FILM, VIDEO, DVD, OR BLU-RAY. Begin with the director, the producer, and other relevant contributors.

> Bigelow, K. (Director, Producer), Boal, M. (Producer), & Ellison, M. (Producer). (2012). *Zero dark thirty* [Motion picture]. United States: Annapurna.

If you watched the film in another medium, such as on a DVD or Blu-ray disc, indicate the medium in brackets. If the DVD or Blu-ray and the film were not released in the same year, put *Original release* and the year in parentheses at the end of the entry.

Hitchcock, A. (Director, Producer). (2010). *Psycho* [Blu-ray]. United States: Universal. (Original release 1960.)

44. ONLINE (STREAMING) AUDIO OR VIDEO FILE

Klusman, P. (2008, February 13). An engineer's guide to cats [Video file]. Retrieved from http://www.youtube.com/watch?v=mHXBL6bzAR4

Koenig, S. (2013, January 25). Petticoats in a twist [Audio file]. Retrieved from http://www.thisamericanlife.org/radio-archives/episode/485 /surrogates

45. TELEVISION PROGRAM, SINGLE EPISODE

Imperioli, M. (Writer), & Buscemi, S. (Director). (2002). Everybody hurts [Television series episode]. In D. Chase (Executive Producer), *The Sopranos*. New York, NY: Home Box Office.

46. TELEVISION SERIES

Gilligan, V. (2008-2013). *Breaking Bad* [Television series]. New York, NY: AMC.

47. PODCAST (DOWNLOADED AUDIO FILE)

Noguchi, Yugi. (2010, 24 May). BP hard to pin down on oil spill claims [Audio podcast]. *NPR Morning Edition*. Retrieved from http://www .npr.org

48. RECORDING

The Avalanches. (2001). Frontier psychiatrist. On *Since I left you* [CD]. Los Angeles, CA: Elektra/Asylum Records.

46e A sample student writing project, APA style

On the following pages is a paper by Tawnya Redding that conforms to the APA guidelines described in this chapter.

Running head: MOOD MUSIC   1

Running
head (fifty
characters
or fewer, all
capital letters)
appears flush
left on first
line of every
page, preceded
on title page
only by
Running head
and colon

Page number
appears flush
right on first
line of every
page

Title, name,
and affiliation
centered and
double-spaced

Mood Music: Music Preference and the Risk for Depression
and Suicide in Adolescents
Tawnya Redding
University of Oregon

Annotations indicate effective choices or APA-style formatting.

MOOD MUSIC   2

Abstract

There has long been concern for the effects that certain genres
of music (such as heavy metal and country) have on youth. While
a correlational link between these genres and increased risk
for depression and suicide in adolescents has been established,
researchers have been unable to pinpoint what is responsible for
this link, and a causal relationship has not been determined. This
paper will begin by discussing correlational literature concerning
music preference and increased risk for depression and suicide, as
well as the possible reasons for this link. Finally, studies concerning
the effects of music on mood will be discussed. This examination of
the literature on music and increased risk for depression and suicide
points out the limitations of previous research and suggests the need
for new research establishing a causal relationship for this link as
well as research into the specific factors that may contribute to an
increased risk for depression and suicide in adolescents.

Heading
centered and
not boldface

No indentation

Use of passive
voice appropri-
ate for social
sciences

Double-spaced
text

Clear, straight-
forward
description
of literature
under review

Conclusions
indicated

Full title,
centered and
not boldface

Paragraphs
indented

Background
information
about review
supplied

Questions
focus reader's
attention

Boldface
headings
help organize
review

Multiple
sources in one
parenthetical
citation
separated by
semicolons

Mood Music: Music Preference and the Risk for Depression and Suicide in Adolescents

Music is a significant part of American culture. Since the explosion of rock and roll in the 1950s there has been a concern for the effects that music may have on listeners, and especially on young people. The genres most likely to come under suspicion in recent decades have included heavy metal, country, and blues. These genres have been suspected of having adverse effects on the mood and behavior of young listeners. But can music really alter the disposition and create self-destructive behaviors in listeners? And if so, which genres and aspects of those genres are responsible? The following review of the literature will establish the correlation between potentially problematic genres of music such as heavy metal and country and depression and suicide risk. First, correlational studies concerning music preference and suicide risk will be discussed, followed by a discussion of the literature concerning the possible reasons for this link. Finally, studies concerning the effects of music on mood will be discussed. Despite the link between genres such as heavy metal and country and suicide risk, previous research has been unable to establish the causal nature of this link.

The Correlation Between Music and Depression and Suicide Risk

Studies over the past two decades have set out to answer this question by examining the correlation between youth music preference and risk for depression and suicide. A large portion of these studies have focused on heavy metal and country music as the main genre culprits associated with youth suicidality and depression (Lacourse, Claes, & Villeneuve, 2001; Scheel &

MOOD MUSIC   4

Westefeld, 1999; Stack & Gundlach, 1992). Stack and Gundlach
(1992) examined the radio airtime devoted to country music
in 49 metropolitan areas and found that the higher the
percentages of country music airtime, the higher the incidence
of suicides among whites. The researchers hypothesized that
themes in country music (such as alcohol abuse) promoted
audience identification and reinforced a preexisting suicidal
mood, and that the themes associated with country music
were responsible for elevated suicide rates. Similarly, Scheel
and Westefeld (1999) found a correlation between heavy metal
music listeners and an increased risk for suicide, as did Lacourse
et al. (2001).

> In parentheses, two author names joined with &; in text, names joined with *and*

Reasons for the Link: Characteristics of Those Who Listen to Problematic Music

Unfortunately, previous studies concerning music preference
and suicide risk have been unable to determine a causal relationship
and have focused mainly on establishing a correlation between
suicide risk and music preference. This leaves the question open
as to whether an individual at risk for depression and suicide is
attracted to certain genres of music or whether the music helps
induce the mood — or both. Some studies have suggested that
music preference may simply be a reflection of other underlying
problems associated with increased risk for suicide (Lacourse
et al., 2001; Scheel & Westefeld, 1999). For example, in research
done by Scheel and Westefeld (1999), adolescents who listened
to heavy metal were found to have lower scores on the Reason
for Living Inventory and several of its subscales, a self-report
measure designed to assess potential reasons for not committing
suicide. These adolescents were also found to have lower scores
on several subscales of the Reason for Living Inventory, including

> Discussion of correlation vs. causation points out limitations of previous studies

MOOD MUSIC   5

responsibility to family along with survival and coping beliefs. Other risk factors associated with suicide and suicidal behaviors include poor family relationships, depression, alienation, anomie, and drug and alcohol abuse (Lacourse et al., 2001). Lacourse et al. (2001) examined 275 adolescents in the Montreal region with a preference for heavy metal and found that this preference was not significantly related to suicide risk when other risk factors were controlled for. This was also the conclusion of Scheel and Westefeld (1999), in which music preference for heavy metal was thought to be a red flag for suicide vulnerability, suggesting that the source of the problem may lie more in personal and familial characteristics.

George, Stickle, Rachid, and Wopnford (2007) further explored the correlation between suicide risk and music preference by attempting to identify the personality characteristics of those with a preference for different genres of music. A sample of 358 individuals was assessed for preference of thirty different styles of music along with a number of personality characteristics, including self-esteem, intelligence, spirituality, social skills, locus of control, openness, conscientiousness, extraversion, agreeableness, emotional stability, hostility, and depression (George et al., 2007). The thirty styles of music were then categorized into eight factors: rebellious (for example, punk and heavy metal), classical, rhythmic and intense (including hip-hop, rap, and pop), easy listening, fringe (for example, techno), contemporary Christian, jazz and blues, and traditional Christian. The results revealed an almost comprehensively negative personality profile for those who preferred to listen to the rebellious and rhythmic and intense categories, while those who preferred classical music tended to have a comprehensively positive profile. Like Scheel and Westefeld (1999) and

MOOD MUSIC   6

Lacourse et al. (2001), this study also supports the theory that youth are drawn to certain genres of music based on already existing factors, whether they be related to personality or situational variables.

Reasons for the Link: Characteristics of Problematic Music

Another possible explanation is that the lyrics and themes of the music have an effect on listeners. In this scenario, music is thought to exacerbate an already depressed mood and hence contribute to an increased risk for suicide. This was the proposed reasoning behind higher suicide rates in whites in Stack and Gundlach's (1992) study linking country music to suicide risk. In this case, the themes associated with country music were thought to promote audience identification and reinforce preexisting self-destructive behaviors (such as excessive alcohol consumption). Stack (2000) also studied individuals with a musical preference for blues to determine whether the genre's themes could increase the level of suicide acceptability. The results demonstrated that blues fans were no more accepting of suicide than nonfans, but that blues listeners were found to have low religiosity levels, an important factor for suicide acceptability (Stack, 2000). Despite this link between possible suicidal behavior and a preference for blues music, the actual suicide behavior of blues fans has not been explored, and thus no concrete associations can be made.

The Effect of Music on Mood

While studies examining the relationship between music genres such as heavy metal, country, and blues have been able to establish a correlation between music preference and suicide risk, it is still unclear from these studies what effect music has

Transition links paragraphs

Need for more research indicated

Discussion of previous research

MOOD MUSIC   7

on the mood of the listener. Previous research has suggested
that some forms of music can both improve and depress mood
(Lai, 1999; Siedliecki & Good, 2006; Smith & Noon, 1998). Lai
(1999) found that changes in mood were more likely to be found
in an experimental group of depressed women versus a control
group. It was also found that both the experimental and control
groups showed significant increases in the tranquil mood state,
but the amount of change was not significant between the
groups (Lai, 1999). This study suggests that music can have a
positive effect on depressed individuals when they are allowed
to choose the music they are listening to. In a similar study,
Siedliecki and Good (2006) found that music can increase a
listener's sense of power and decrease depression, pain, and
disability. Researchers randomly assigned sixty African American
and Caucasian participants with chronic nonmalignant pain to
a standard music group (offering them a choice of instrumental
music types — piano, jazz, orchestra, harp, and synthesizer), a
patterning music group (asking them to choose music to ease
muscle tension, to facilitate sleep, or to decrease anxiety), or a
control group. There were no statistically significant differences
between the two music groups. However, the music groups had
significantly less pain, depression, and disability than the control
group (Siedliecki & Good, 2006). On the other hand, Martin, Clark,
and Pearce (1993) identified a subgroup of heavy metal fans who
reported feeling worse after listening to their music of choice.
Although this subgroup did exist, there was also evidence that
listening to heavy metal results in more positive affect, and it
was hypothesized that those who experience negative effects after
listening to their preferred genre of heavy metal may be most at risk
for suicidal behaviors (Martin et al., 1993).

MOOD MUSIC   8

Smith and Noon (1998) also determined that music can have a negative effect on mood. Six songs were selected for the particular theme they embodied: (1) vigorous, (2) fatigued, (3) angry, (4) depressed, (5) tense, and (6) all moods. The results indicated that selections 3–6 had significant effects on the mood of participants, with selection 6 (all moods) resulting in the greatest positive change in the mood and selection 5 (tense) resulting in the greatest negative change in mood. Selection 4 (depressed) was found to sap the vigor and increase anger/hostility in participants, while selection 5 (tense) significantly depressed participants and made them more anxious. Although this study did not specifically comment on the effects of different genres on mood, the results do indicate that certain themes can indeed depress mood. The participants for this study were undergraduate students who were not depressed, and thus it seems that certain types of music can have a negative effect on the mood of healthy individuals.

Is There Evidence for a Causal Relationship?

Despite the correlation between certain music genres (especially heavy metal) and increased risk for depression and suicidal behaviors in adolescents, it remains unclear whether these types of music can alter the mood of at-risk youth in a negative way. This view of the correlation between music and suicide risk is supported by a meta-analysis done by Baker and Bor (2008), in which the authors assert that most studies reject the notion that music is a causal factor and suggest that music preference is more indicative of emotional vulnerability. However, it is still unknown whether these genres can negatively alter mood at all, and if they can, whether the themes and lyrics associated with the music are responsible. Clearly, more research is needed to further examine

Conclusion
indicates need
for further
research

MOOD MUSIC   9

this correlation, as a causal link between these genres of music and adolescent suicide risk has yet to be shown. However, even if the theory put forth by Baker and Bon and other researchers is true, it is still important to investigate the effects that music can have on those who may be at risk for suicide and depression. Even if music genres are not the ultimate cause of suicidal behavior, they may act as a catalyst that further pushes adolescents into a state of depression and increased risk for suicidal behavior.

References

Baker, F., & Bor, W. (2008). Can music preference indicate mental health status in young people? *Australasian Psychiatry, 16*(4), 284–288. Retrieved from http://www3.interscience.wiley.com /journal/118565538/home

George, D., Stickle, K., Rachid, F., & Wopnford, A. (2007). The association between types of music enjoyed and cognitive, behavioral, and personality factors of those who listen. *Psychomusicology, 19*(2), 32–56.

Lacourse, E., Claes, M., & Villeneuve, M. (2001). Heavy metal music and adolescent suicidal risk. *Journal of Youth and Adolescence, 30*(3), 321–332.

Lai, Y. (1999). Effects of music listening on depressed women in Taiwan. *Issues in Mental Health Nursing, 20*, 229–246. doi: 10.1080/016128499248637

Martin, G., Clark, M., & Pearce, C. (1993). Adolescent suicide: Music preference as an indicator of vulnerability. *Journal of the American Academy of Child and Adolescent Psychiatry, 32*, 530–535.

Scheel, K., & Westefeld, J. (1999). Heavy metal music and adolescent suicidality: An empirical investigation. *Adolescence, 34*(134), 253–273.

Siedliecki, S., & Good, M. (2006). Effect of music on power, pain, depression and disability. *Journal of Advanced Nursing, 54*(5), 553–562. doi: 10.1111/j.1365-2648.2006.03860.x

Smith, J. L., & Noon, J. (1998). Objective measurement of mood change induced by contemporary music. *Journal of Psychiatric & Mental Health Nursing, 5*, 403–408.

Stack, S. (2000). Blues fans and suicide acceptability. *Death Studies, 24*, 223–231.

Stack, S., & Gundlach, J. (1992). The effect of country music on suicide. *Social Forces, 71*(1), 211–218. Retrieved from http:// socialforces.unc.edu/

47 *Chicago* Style

The style guide of the University of Chicago Press has long been used in history as well as in other areas of the arts and humanities. The Seventeenth Edition of *The Chicago Manual of Style* (2017) provides a complete guide to *Chicago* style, including two systems for citing sources. This chapter presents the notes and bibliography system.

47a Understanding *Chicago* citation style

Why does academic work call for very careful citation practices when writing for the general public may not? The answer is that readers of academic work expect source citations for several reasons:

- Source citations demonstrate that you've done your homework on your topic and that you are a part of the conversation surrounding it.
- Source citations show that you understand the need to give credit when you make use of someone else's intellectual property. (See Chapter 15.)
- Source citations give explicit directions to guide readers who want to look for themselves at the works you're using.

Guidelines from *The Chicago Manual of Style* will tell you exactly what information to include in your citation and how to format that information.

Types of sources. Look at the Directory to *Chicago* Style on p. 314. You will need to be careful to tell your readers whether you read a print version or a digital version of a source that consists mainly of written words. Digital magazine and newspaper articles may include updates or corrections that the print version lacks; digital books may not number pages or screens the same way the print book does. If you are citing a source with media elements—such as a film, song, or artwork—consult the "other sources" section of the directory. And if you can't find a model exactly like the source you've selected, see the box on p. 319.

ARTICLES FROM WEB AND DATABASE SOURCES. You need a subscription to look through most databases, so individual researchers almost always gain access to articles in databases through the computer system of a school or public library that pays to subscribe. The easiest way to tell whether a source comes from a database, then, is that its information is *not* generally available free to anyone with an Internet connection. Many databases are digital collections of articles that originally appeared in edited print periodicals, ensuring that an authority has vouched for the accuracy of the information. Such sources may have more credibility than free material available on the web.

Parts of citations. Citations in *Chicago* style will appear in three places in your text—a note number in the text marks the material from the source, a footnote or an endnote includes information to identify the source (or information about supplemental material), and the bibliography provides the full citation.

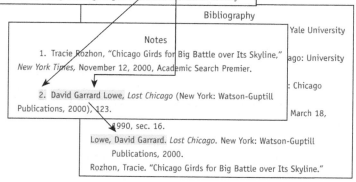

Chicago is a city for the working man. Nowhere is this more evident than in its architecture. David Garrard Lowe, author of *Lost Chicago*, notes that early Chicagoans "sought reality, not fantasy, and the reality of America as seen from the heartland did not include the pavilions of princes or the castles of kings,"² The inclination toward unadorned, sturdy buildings began in the late nineteenth century

Bibliography

Yale University

Notes

1. Tracie Rozhon, "Chicago Girds for Big Battle over Its Skyline," *New York Times*, November 12, 2000, Academic Search Premier.

2. David Garrard Lowe, *Lost Chicago* (New York: Watson-Guptill Publications, 2000), 123.

1990, sec. 16.

Lowe, David Garrard. *Lost Chicago*. New York: Watson-Guptill Publications, 2000.

Rozhon, Tracie. "Chicago Girds for Big Battle over Its Skyline."

47b Following *Chicago* manuscript format

Title page.   About halfway down the title page, center the full title of your project and your name. Unless otherwise instructed, at the bottom of the page also list the course name, the instructor's name, and the date submitted. Do not type a number on this page. Check to see if your instructor has a preference on whether to count the title page as part of the text (if so, the first text page will be page 2) or as part of the frontmatter (if so, the first text page will be page 1).

Margins and spacing.   Leave one-inch margins at the top, bottom, and sides of your pages. Double-space the entire text, including block quotations, notes, and bibliography.

Page numbers.   Number all pages (except the title page) in the upper right-hand corner. Also use a short title or your name before page numbers.

Long quotations.   For a long quotation, indent one-half inch (or five spaces) from the left margin and do not use quotation marks. *Chicago* defines a long quotation as one hundred words or eight lines, though you may set off shorter quotes for emphasis (39a).

Headings.   *Chicago* style allows, but does not require, headings. Many students and instructors find them helpful.

Visuals.   Visuals (photographs, drawings, charts, graphs, and tables) should be placed as near as possible to the relevant text. (See 15b for guidelines on incorporating visuals into your text.) Tables should be labeled *Table*, numbered, and captioned. All other visuals should be labeled *Figure* (abbreviated *Fig.*), numbered, and captioned. Remember to refer to each visual in your text, pointing out how it contributes to the point(s) you are making.

Notes.   Notes can be footnotes (each one appearing at the bottom of the page on which its citation appears) or endnotes (in a list on a separate page at the end of the text). (Check your instructor's preference.) Indent the first line of each note one-half inch and

begin with a number, a period, and one space before the first word. All remaining lines of the entry are flush with the left margin. Single-space footnotes and endnotes, with a double space between each entry.

Use superscript numbers (1) to mark citations in the text. Place the superscript number for each note just after the relevant quotation, sentence, clause, or phrase. Type the number after any punctuation mark except the dash, and do not leave a space before the superscript. Number citations sequentially throughout the text. When you use signal phrases to introduce source material, note that *Chicago* style requires you to use the present tense (*citing Bebout's studies, Meier points out . . .*).

IN THE TEXT

Sweig argues that Castro and Che Guevara were not the only key players in the Cuban Revolution of the late 1950s.[19]

IN THE FIRST NOTE REFERRING TO THE SOURCE

19. Julia Sweig, *Inside the Cuban Revolution* (Cambridge, MA: Harvard University Press, 2002), 9.

After giving complete information the first time you cite a work, shorten additional references to that work: list only the author's last name, a comma, a short version of the title, a comma, and the page number. If you refer to the same source cited in the previous note, include only the author's last name and the page number.

IN FIRST AND SUBSEQUENT NOTES

19. Julia Sweig, *Inside the Cuban Revolution* (Cambridge, MA: Harvard University Press, 2002), 9.

20. Sweig, 13.

21. Ferguson, "Comfort of Being Sad," 63.

22. Sweig, *Cuban Revolution*, 21.

Bibliography.   Begin the list of sources on a separate page after the main text and any endnotes. Continue numbering the pages consecutively. Center the title *Bibliography* (without underlining,

italics, or quotation marks) one inch below the top of the page. Double-space, and then begin each entry at the left margin. Indent the second and subsequent lines of each entry one-half inch, or five spaces.

List sources alphabetically by authors' last names or by the first major word in the title if the author is unknown. See p. 332 for an example of a *Chicago*-style bibliography.

In the bibliographic entry, include the same information as in the first note for that source, but omit the page reference. Give the first author's last name first, followed by a comma and the first name; separate the main elements of the entry with periods rather than commas; and do not enclose the publication information for books in parentheses.

IN THE BIBLIOGRAPHY

Sweig, Julia. *Inside the Cuban Revolution*. Cambridge, MA: Harvard University Press, 2002.

47c Creating *Chicago* notes and bibliographic entries

The following examples demonstrate how to format both notes and bibliographic entries according to *Chicago* style. The note, which is numbered, appears first; the bibliographic entry, which is not numbered, appears below the note.

Print and digital books

The note for a book typically includes five elements: author's name, title and subtitle, city of publication and publisher, year, and page number(s) or electronic locator information for the information in the note. The bibliographic entry usually includes all these elements but the page number (and does include a URL or other locator if the book is digitally published), but it is styled differently: commas separate major elements of a note, but a bibliographic entry uses periods.

1. ONE AUTHOR

1. Nell Irvin Painter, *The History of White People* (New York: W. W. Norton, 2010), 119.

Painter, Nell Irvin. *The History of White People*. New York: W. W. Norton, 2010.

2. MULTIPLE AUTHORS

2. Margaret Macmillan and Richard Holbrooke, *Paris 1919: Six Months That Changed the World* (New York: Random House, 2003), 384.

Macmillan, Margaret, and Richard Holbrooke. *Paris 1919: Six Months That Changed the World*. New York: Random House, 2003.

With four or more authors, you may give the first-listed author followed by *et al.* in the note. In the bibliography, list all the authors' names.

2. Stephen J. Blank et al., *Conflict, Culture, and History: Regional Dimensions* (Miami: University Press of the Pacific, 2002), 276.

Blank, Stephen J., Lawrence E. Grinter, Karl P. Magyar, Lewis B. Ware, and Bynum E. Weathers. *Conflict, Culture, and History: Regional Dimensions*. Miami: University Press of the Pacific, 2002.

3. ORGANIZATION AS AUTHOR

3. World Intellectual Property Organization, *Intellectual Property Profile of the Least Developed Countries* (Geneva: World Intellectual Property Organization, 2002), 43.

World Intellectual Property Organization. *Intellectual Property Profile of the Least Developed Countries*. Geneva: World Intellectual Property Organization, 2002.

4. UNKNOWN AUTHOR

4. *Broad Stripes and Bright Stars* (Kansas City, MO: Andrews McMeel, 2002), 10.

Broad Stripes and Bright Stars. Kansas City, MO: Andrews McMeel, 2002.

5. ONLINE BOOK

5. Dorothy Richardson, *Long Day: The Story of a New York Working Girl, as Told by Herself* (1906; UMDL Texts, 2010), 159, http://quod.lib .umich.edu/cgi/t/text/text-idx?c=moa;idno=AFS7156.0001.001.

Richardson, Dorothy. *Long Day: The Story of a New York Working Girl, as Told by Herself*. 1906. UMDL Texts, 2010. http://quod.lib.umich.edu /cgi/t/text/text-idx?c=moa;idno=AFS7156.0001.001.

6. ELECTRONIC BOOK (E-BOOK)

6. Manal M. Omar, *Barefoot in Baghdad* (Naperville, IL: Sourcebooks, 2010), chap. 4, Kindle.

Omar, Manal M. *Barefoot in Baghdad*. Naperville, IL: Sourcebooks, 2010. Kindle.

7. EDITED BOOK WITH NO AUTHOR

7. James H. Fetzer, ed., *The Great Zapruder Film Hoax: Deceit and Deception in the Death of JFK* (Chicago: Open Court, 2003), 56.

Fetzer, James H., ed. *The Great Zapruder Film Hoax: Deceit and Deception in the Death of JFK*. Chicago: Open Court, 2003.

8. EDITED BOOK WITH AUTHOR

8. Leopold von Ranke, *The Theory and Practice of History*, ed. Georg G. Iggers (New York: Routledge, 2010), 135.

von Ranke, Leopold. *The Theory and Practice of History*. Edited by Georg G. Iggers. New York: Routledge, 2010.

9. SELECTION IN AN ANTHOLOGY OR CHAPTER IN A BOOK WITH AN EDITOR

9. Denise Little, "Born in Blood," in *Alternate Gettysburgs*, ed. Brian Thomsen and Martin H. Greenberg (New York: Berkley Publishing Group, 2002), 245.

Give the inclusive page numbers of the selection or chapter in the bibliographic entry.

Little, Denise. "Born in Blood." In *Alternate Gettysburgs*. Edited by Brian Thomsen and Martin H. Greenberg, 242–55. New York: Berkley Publishing Group, 2002.

10. INTRODUCTION, PREFACE, FOREWORD, OR AFTERWORD

10. Robert B. Reich, introduction to *Making Work Pay: America after Welfare,* ed. Robert Kuttner (New York: New Press, 2002), xvi.

Reich, Robert B. Introduction to *Making Work Pay: America after Welfare,* vii–xvii. Edited by Robert Kuttner. New York: New Press, 2002.

11. TRANSLATION

11. Suetonius, *The Twelve Caesars,* trans. Robert Graves (London: Penguin Classics, 1989), 202.

Suetonius. *The Twelve Caesars.* Translated by Robert Graves. London: Penguin Classics, 1989.

12. EDITION OTHER THAN THE FIRST

12. Dee Brown, *Bury My Heart at Wounded Knee: An Indian History of the American West,* 4th ed. (New York: Owl Books, 2007), 12.

Brown, Dee. *Bury My Heart at Wounded Knee: An Indian History of the American West,* 4th ed. New York: Owl Books, 2007.

13. MULTIVOLUME WORK

13. John Watson, *Annals of Philadelphia and Pennsylvania in the Olden Time,* vol. 2 (Washington, DC: Ross & Perry, 2003), 514.

Watson, John. *Annals of Philadelphia and Pennsylvania in the Olden Time.* Vol. 2. Washington, DC: Ross & Perry, 2003.

14. REFERENCE WORK. In a note, use *s.v.,* the abbreviation for the Latin *sub verbo* ("under the word"), to help your reader find the entry. Do not list reference works such as encyclopedias or dictionaries in your bibliography.

14. *Encyclopedia Britannica,* s.v. "carpetbagger."

15. WORK WITH A TITLE WITHIN THE TITLE. Use quotation marks around any title within a book title.

15. John A. Alford, *A Companion to "Piers Plowman"* (Berkeley: University of California Press, 1988), 195.

Alford, John A. *A Companion to "Piers Plowman."* Berkeley: University of California Press, 1988.

16. SACRED TEXT. Do not include sacred texts in the bibliography.

> 16. Luke 18:24–25 (New International Version).

> 16. Qur'an 7:40–41.

17. SOURCE QUOTED IN ANOTHER SOURCE. Identify both the original and the secondary source.

> 17. Frank D. Millet, "The Filipino Leaders," *Harper's Weekly*, March 11, 1899, quoted in Richard Slotkin, *Gunfighter Nation: The Myth of the Frontier in Twentieth-Century America* (New York: HarperCollins, 1992), 110.

> Millet, Frank D. "The Filipino Leaders." *Harper's Weekly*, March 11, 1899. Quoted in Richard Slotkin, *Gunfighter Nation: The Myth of the Frontier in Twentieth-Century America* (New York: HarperCollins, 1992), 110.

Print and digital periodicals

The note for an article in a periodical typically includes the author's name, the article title, and the periodical title. The format for other information, including the volume and issue numbers (if any) and the date of publication, as well as the page number(s) to which the note refers, varies according to the type of periodical and whether you consulted it in print, on the web, or in a database. In a bibliographic entry for a journal or magazine article from a database or a print periodical, also give the inclusive page numbers.

 Checklist

Citing Sources without Models in *Chicago* Style

To cite a source for which you cannot find a model, collect as much information as you can find—about the creator, title, date of creation or update, and location of the source—with the goal of helping your readers find the source for themselves, if possible. Then look at the models in this section to see which one most closely matches the type of source you are using.

In an academic writing project, before citing an electronic source for which you have no model, also be sure to ask your instructor's advice.

18. ARTICLE IN A PRINT JOURNAL

> 18. Karin Lützen, "The Female World: Viewed from Denmark," *Journal of Women's History* 12, no. 3 (2000): 36.

Lützen, Karin. "The Female World: Viewed from Denmark." *Journal of Women's History* 12, no. 3 (2000): 34–38.

19. ARTICLE IN AN ONLINE JOURNAL. Give the DOI, preceded by *https://doi.org/*. If there is no DOI, include the article URL. If page numbers are provided, include them as well.

> 19. Jeffrey J. Schott, "America, Europe, and the New Trade Order," *Business and Politics* 11, no. 3 (2009), https://doi.org/10.2202/1469-3569.1263.

Schott, Jeffrey J. "America, Europe, and the New Trade Order." *Business and Politics* 11, no. 3 (2009). https://doi.org/10.2202/1469-3569.1263.

20. JOURNAL ARTICLE FROM A DATABASE. For basic information on citing a periodical article from a database in *Chicago* style, see the source map on pp. 322–23.

> 20. W. Trent Foley and Nicholas J. Higham, "Bede on the Britons," *Early Medieval Europe* 17, no. 2 (2009): 157, https://doi.org/10.1111/j.1468-0254.2009.00258.x.

Foley, W. Trent, and Nicholas J. Higham. "Bede on the Britons." *Early Medieval Europe* 17, no. 2 (2009): 154–85. https://doi.org/10.1111/j.1468-0254.2009.00258.x.

21. ARTICLE IN A PRINT MAGAZINE

> 21. Terry McDermott, "The Mastermind: Khalid Sheikh Mohammed and the Making of 9/11," *New Yorker*, September 13, 2010, 42.

McDermott, Terry. "The Mastermind: Khalid Sheikh Mohammed and the Making of 9/11." *New Yorker*, September 13, 2010, 38–51.

22. ARTICLE IN AN ONLINE MAGAZINE

> 22. Tracy Clark-Flory, "Educating Women Saves Kids' Lives," *Salon*, September 17, 2010, http://www.salon.com/life/broadsheet/2010/09/17/education_women/index.html.

Clark-Flory, Tracy. "Educating Women Saves Kids' Lives." *Salon*, September 17, 2010. http://www.salon.com/life/broadsheet/2010/09/17/education_women/index.html.

23. MAGAZINE ARTICLE FROM A DATABASE

23. Sami Yousafzai and Ron Moreau, "Twisting Arms in Afghanistan," *Newsweek*, November 9, 2009, 8, Academic Search Premier.

Yousafzai, Sami, and Ron Moreau. "Twisting Arms in Afghanistan." *Newsweek*, November 9, 2009. 8. Academic Search Premier.

24. ARTICLE IN A NEWSPAPER. Do not include page numbers for a newspaper article, but you may include the section, if any.

24. Caroline E. Mayer, "Wireless Industry to Adopt Voluntary Standards," *Washington Post*, September 9, 2003, sec. E.

Mayer, Caroline E. "Wireless Industry to Adopt Voluntary Standards." *Washington Post*, September 9, 2003, sec. E.

If you provide complete documentation of a newspaper article in a note, you may not need to include it in the bibliography. Check your instructor's preference.

25. ARTICLE IN AN ONLINE NEWSPAPER

25. Andrew C. Revkin, "Arctic Melt Unnerves the Experts," *New York Times*, October 2, 2007, http://www.nytimes.com/2007/10/02/science/earth/02arct.html.

Revkin, Andrew C. "Arctic Melt Unnerves the Experts." *New York Times*, October 2, 2007. http://www.nytimes.com/2007/10/02/science/earth/02arct.html.

26. NEWSPAPER ARTICLE FROM A DATABASE

26. Demetria Irwin, "A Hatchet, Not a Scalpel, for NYC Budget Cuts," *New York Amsterdam News*, November 13, 2008, Academic Search Premier.

Irwin, Demetria. "A Hatchet, Not a Scalpel, for NYC Budget Cuts." *New York Amsterdam News*, November 13, 2008. Academic Search Premier.

1. **Author.** In a note, list the author(s) first name first. In the bibliographic entry, list the first author last name first, comma, first name; list other authors first name first.

2. **Article title.** Enclose the title and subtitle (if any) in quotation marks, and capitalize major words. In the notes section, put a comma before and after the title. In the bibliography, put a period before and after.

3. **Periodical title.** Italicize the title and subtitle, and capitalize all major words. For a magazine or newspaper, follow with a comma.

4. **Volume and issue numbers (for journals) and date.** For journals, follow the title with the volume number, a comma, the abbreviation *no.*, and the issue number; enclose the publication year in parentheses and follow with a comma (in a note) or with a period (in a bibliography), or with a colon when page numbers follow. For other periodicals, give the month and year or month, day, and year, not in parentheses, followed by a comma.

5. **Page numbers.** In a note, give the page where the information is found. In the bibliographic entry, give the page range.

6. **Retrieval information.** Provide the article's DOI, if one is given, the name of the database, or a "stable or persistent" URL for the article in the database. Because you provide stable retrieval information, you do not need to identify the electronic format of the work (i.e., PDF, as in the example shown here). End with a period.

Citations for the journal article on p. 323 would look like this:

ENDNOTE

1. Elizabeth Tucker, "Changing Concepts of Childhood: Children's Folklore Scholarship since the Late Nineteenth Century," *Journal of American Folklore* 125, no. 498 (2012): 399, http://www.jstor.org /stable/10.5406/jamerfolk.125.498.0389.

BIBLIOGRAPHIC ENTRY

Tucker Elizabeth. "Changing Concepts of Childhood: Children's Folklore Scholarship since the Late Nineteenth Century." *Journal of American Folklore* 125, no. 498 (2012): 389–410. http://www.jstor.org /stable/10.5406/jamerfolk.125.498.0389.

③ **Periodical Title**   ④ **Volume and Issue Numbers and Date**

Changing Concepts of Childhood: Children's Folklore Scholarship since the Late Nineteenth Century
Author(s): Elizabeth Tucker
Source: *The Journal of American Folklore*, Vol. 125, No. 498 (Fall 2012), pp. 389–410
Published by: University of Illinois Press on behalf of American Folklore Society
Stable URL: http://www.jstor.org/stable/10.5406/jamerfolk.125.498.0389

⑥ **Retrieval Information**   ⑤ **Page Numbers**

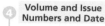

ELIZABETH TUCKER

① **Author**

Changing Concepts of Childhood: Children's Folklore Scholarship since the Late Nineteenth Century

This essay examines children's folklore scholarship from the late nineteenth century to the present, tracing key concepts from the Gilded Age to the contemporary era. These concepts reflect significant social, cultural, political, and scientific changes. From the "savage child" to the "secret-keeping child," the "magic-making child," the "cerebral child," the "taboo-breaking child," the "monstrous child," and others, scholarly representations of young people have close connections to the eras in which they developed. Nineteenth-century children's folklore scholarship relied on evolutionism; now evolutionary biology provides a basis for children's folklore research, so we have re-entered fam"

② **Article Title and Subtitle**

SINCE 1977, WHEN THE American Folklore Society decided to form a new section for scholars interested in young people's traditions, I have belonged to the Children's Folklore Section. It has been a joy to contribute to this dynamic organization, which has significantly influenced children's folklore scholarship and children's book authors' focus on folk tradition. This essay examines children's folklore scholarship from the late nineteenth century to the present, tracing key concepts from the Gilded Age to the contemporary era in the English language. These concepts reflect significant social, cultural, political, and scientific changes that have occurred since William Wells Newell, the first secretary of the American Folklore Society and the first editor of the *Journal of American Folklore*, published *Games and Songs of American Children* in 1883. They also reveal some very interesting commonalities. Those of us who pursue children's folklore scholarship today may consider ourselves to be light years away from nineteenth-century scholars' research but may find, when reading nineteenth-century works, that we have stayed fairly close to our scholarly "home base."

Before examining concepts of childhood that folklorists have developed, I will offer a working definition of this life stage and briefly explain the beginning of childhood studies. I will also summarize the Children's Folklore Section's work during the past thirty-four years. According to the *Oxford English Dictionary*, childhood consists of "the state or stage of life of a child; the time during which one is a child; the time from birth to puberty" (2011). Scholars of childhood tend to draw a line between childhood and adolescence, which begins at puberty and follows pre-adolescence. The folklore

ELIZABETH TUCKER is Professor of English at Binghamton University

Journal of American Folklore 125(498):389–410
Copyright © 2012 by the Board of Trustees of the University of Illinois

323

27. BOOK REVIEW. After the information about the book under review, give publication information for the appropriate kind of source (see models 18–26).

> 27. Arnold Relman, "Health Care: The Disquieting Truth," review of *Tracking Medicine: A Researcher's Quest to Understand Health Care,* by John E. Wennberg, *New York Review of Books* 57, no. 14 (2010), 45.

> Relman, Arnold. "Health Care: The Disquieting Truth." Review of *Tracking Medicine: A Researcher's Quest to Understand Health Care,* by John E. Wennberg. *New York Review of Books* 57, no. 14 (2010), 45–48.

Online sources

In general, include the author (if given); the title of a work from a website (in quotation marks); the name of the site (in italics, if the site is an online publication, but otherwise neither italicized nor in quotation marks); the sponsor of the site, if different from the name of the site or name of the author; the date of publication or most recent update; and a URL. If the online source does not indicate when it was published or last modified, or if your instructor requests an access date, place it before the URL.

For basic information on citing works from websites in *Chicago* style, see the source map on pp. 326–27.

28. WEBSITE. For clarity, you may add the word *website* in parentheses after the title.

> 28. Rutgers School of Arts and Sciences, Rutgers Oral History Archive (website), 2010, http://oralhistory.rutgers.edu/.

> Rutgers School of Arts and Sciences. Rutgers Oral History Archive (website). 2010. http://oralhistory.rutgers.edu/.

29. WORK FROM A WEBSITE

> 29. Rose Cohen, "My First Job," Remembering the 1911 Triangle Factory Fire, Cornell University ILR School, accessed October 13, 2017, http://trianglefire.ilr.cornell.edu/primary/testimonials/ootss_rosecohen.html.

> Cohen, Rose. "My First Job." Remembering the 1911 Triangle Factory Fire. Cornell University ILR School. Accessed October 13, 2017. http://trianglefire.ilr.cornell.edu/primary/testimonials/ootss _rosecohen.html.

30. BLOG (WEB LOG) POST. Treat a blog post as a short work from a website (see model 29).

30. Jai Arjun Singh, "On the Road in the USSR," *Jabberwock* (blog), November 29, 2007, http://jaiarjun.blogspot.com/2007/11/on-road-in -ussr.html.

Chicago recommends that blog posts appear in the notes section only, not in the bibliography, unless the blog is cited frequently. Check your instructor's preference. A bibliography reference to an entire blog would look like this:

Singh, Jai Arjun. *Jabberwock* (blog). http://jaiarjun.blogspot.com/.

31. EMAIL AND OTHER PERSONAL COMMUNICATIONS. Cite email messages and other personal communications, such as letters and telephone calls, in the text or in a note only, not in the bibliography.

31. Kareem Adas, email message to author, February 11, 2013.

32. PODCAST. Treat a podcast as a short work from a website (see model 29) and give as much of the following information as you can find: the author or speaker, the title or a description of the podcast, the date of posting, the title of the site, the site sponsor (if different from the author or site name), the type of podcast or file format, the time stamp, and the URL.

32. Toyin Falola, "Creativity and Decolonization: Nigerian Cultures and African Epistemologies," Episode 96, November 17, 2015, in *Africa Past and Present*, African Online Digital Library, podcast, MP3 audio, 43:44, http://afripod.aodl.org/2015/11/afripod-96/.

Falola, Toyin. "Creativity and Decolonization: Nigerian Cultures and African Epistemologies." Episode 96, November 17, 2015. *Africa Past and Present*. African Online Digital Library. Podcast, MP3 audio, 43:44. http://afripod.aodl.org/2015/11/afripod-96/.

33. ONLINE AUDIO OR VIDEO. Treat an online audio or video source as a short work from a website (see model 29). If the source is downloadable, give the medium or file format before the URL (see model 32).

33. Alyssa Katz, "Did the Mortgage Crisis Kill the American Dream?" YouTube video, 4:32, posted by NYCRadio, June 24, 2009, http://www.youtube.com/watch?v=uivtwjwd_Qw.

Katz, Alyssa. "Did the Mortgage Crisis Kill the American Dream?" YouTube video, 4:32. Posted by NYCRadio. June 24, 2009. http://www.youtube.com/watch?v=uivtwjwd_Qw.

CHICAGO SOURCE MAP: Works from Websites

① Author. In a note, list the author(s) first name first. In a bibliographic entry, list the first author last name first, comma, first name; list additional authors first name first. Note that the host may serve as the author.

② Document title. Enclose the title in quotation marks, and capitalize all major words. In a note, put a comma before and after the title. In the bibliography, put a period before and after.

③ Title of website. Capitalize all major words. If the site's title is analogous to a book or periodical title, italicize it. In the notes section, put a comma after the title. In the bibliography, put a period after the title.

④ Sponsor of site. If the sponsor is the same as the author or site title, you may omit it. End with a comma (in the note) or a period (in the bibliographic entry).

⑤ Date of publication or last modification. If a time stamp is given, include it. If no date is available, include your date of access (with the word *accessed*). End with a comma (in the note) or a period (in the bibliographic entry).

⑥ Retrieval information. Give the URL for the website. If you are required to include a date of access, put the word *accessed* and the date in parentheses after the URL. End with a period.

Citations for the website on p. 327 would look like this:

ENDNOTE

1. Rebecca Edwards, "The Populist Party," 1896: The Presidential Campaign: Cartoons & Commentary, Vassar College, 2000, http://projects .vassar.edu/1896/populists.html.

BIBLIOGRAPHIC ENTRY

Edwards, Rebecca. "The Populist Party." 1896: The Presidential Campaign: Cartoons & Commentary. Vassar College. 2000. http://projects.vassar .edu/1896/populists.html.

The Populist Party **2** Document Title

The Rise of Populism
The People's Party (or Populist Party, as it was widely known) was much younger than the Democratic and Republican Parties, which had been founded before the Civil War. Agricultural areas in the West and South had been hit by economic depression years before industrial areas. In the 1880s, as drought hit the wheat-growing areas of the Great Plains and prices for Southern cotton sunk to new lows, many tenant farmers fell into deep debt. This exacerbated long-held grievances against railroads, lenders, grain-elevator owners, and others with whom farmers did business. By the early 1890s, as the depression worsened, some industrial workers shared these farm families' views on labor and the trusts.

In 1890 Populists won control of the Kansas state legislature, and Kansan **William Peffer** became the party's first U.S. Senator. Peffer, with his long white beard, was a humorous figure to many Eastern journalists and politicians, who saw little evidence of Populism in their states and often treated the party as a joke. Nonetheless, Western and Southern Populists gained support rapidly. In 1892 the national party was officially founded through a merger of the Farmers' Alliance and the Knights of Labor. In that year the Populist presidential candidate, James B. Weaver, won over one million votes. Between 1892 and 1896, however, the party failed to make further gains, in part because of fraud, intimidation, and violence by Southern Democrats.

By 1896 the Populist organization was in even more turmoil than that of Democrats. Two main factions had appear... organi... "fused... third p...

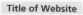 **3** Title of Website

Homepage

© 2000, Rebecca Edwards, Vassar College

5 Date of Publication   **4** Sponsor of Site

1 Author

Other sources

34. PUBLISHED OR BROADCAST INTERVIEW

> 34. Nina Totenberg, interview by Charlie Rose, *The Charlie Rose Show*, PBS, June 29, 2010.

> Totenberg, Nina. Interview by Charlie Rose. *The Charlie Rose Show*. PBS, June 29, 2010.

Interviews you conduct are considered personal communications (see model 31).

35. VIDEO OR DVD. Include both the date of the original release and the date of release for the format you are citing.

> 35. *American History X*, directed by Tony Kaye (1998; Los Angeles: New Line Studios, 2002), DVD.

> Kaye, Tony, dir. *American History X*. 1998; Los Angeles: New Line Studios, 2002. DVD.

36. SOUND RECORDING

> 36. Paul Robeson, *The Collector's Paul Robeson*, recorded 1959, Monitor MCD-61580, 1989, compact disc.

> Robeson, Paul. *The Collector's Paul Robeson*. Recorded 1959. Monitor MCD-61580, 1989, compact disc.

37. WORK OF ART. Begin with the artist's name and the title of the work. If you viewed the work in person, give the date the work was created, the medium, and the name of the place where you saw it.

> 37. Mary Cassatt, *The Child's Bath*, 1893, oil on canvas, The Art Institute of Chicago, Chicago, IL.

> Cassatt, Mary. *The Child's Bath*. 1893. Oil on canvas. The Art Institute of Chicago, Chicago, IL.

If you refer to a reproduction, give the publication information.

> 37. Mary Cassatt, *The Child's Bath*, 1893, oil on canvas, *Art Access*, The Art Institute of Chicago, accessed October 13, 2017, http://www.artic.edu/aic/collections/exhibitions/Impressionism/Cassatt.

Cassatt, Mary. *The Child's Bath*. 1893. Oil on canvas. *Art Access*. The Art
   Institute of Chicago. Accessed October 13, 2017. http://www.artic
   .edu/aic/collections/exhibitions/Impressionism/Cassatt.

38. PAMPHLET, REPORT, OR BROCHURE. Information about the author
or publisher may not be readily available, but give enough informa-
tion to identify your source.

   38. Jamie McCarthy, *Who Is David Irving?* (San Antonio, TX:
   Holocaust History Project, 1998).

   McCarthy, Jamie. *Who Is David Irving?* San Antonio, TX: Holocaust History
      Project, 1998.

39. GOVERNMENT DOCUMENT

   39. U.S. House Committee on Ways and Means, *Report on Trade
   Mission to Sub-Saharan Africa*, 108th Cong., 1st sess. (Washington, DC:
   Government Printing Office, 2003), 28.

   U.S. House Committee on Ways and Means. *Report on Trade Mission to Sub-
      Saharan Africa*. 108th Cong., 1st sess. Washington, DC: Government
      Printing Office, 2003.

47d A sample student research essay, *Chicago* style

On the following pages are excerpts from an essay by Amanda
Rinder that conforms to the *Chicago* guidelines described in this
chapter. The digital resources for this book include her complete
project. (See the inside back cover for more details.)

First page of
body text is p. 2

Paper refers
to each figure
by number

Thesis
introduced

Double-spaced
text

Source
cited using
superscript
numeral

Figure caption
includes
number, short
title, and
source

Rinder 2

Only one city has the "Big Shoulders" described by Carl
Sandburg: Chicago (fig. 1). So renowned are its skyscrapers and
celebrated building style that an entire school of architecture is
named for Chicago. Presently, however, the place that Frank Sinatra
called "my kind of town" is beginning to lose sight of exactly what
kind of town it is. Many of the buildings that give Chicago its
distinctive character are being torn down in order to make room for
new growth. Both preserving the classics and encouraging new
creation are important; the combination of these elements gives
Chicago architecture its unique flavor. Witold Rybczynski, a professor
of urbanism, told Tracie Rozhon of the *New York Times*, "Of all the
cities we can think of . . . we associate Chicago with new things,
with building new. Combining that with preservation is a difficult
task, a tricky thing. It's hard to find the middle ground in Chicago."[1]
Yet finding a middle ground is essential if the city is to retain
the original character that sets it apart from the rest. In order to

Fig. 1. Chicago skyline, circa 1940s. (Postcard courtesy of Minnie
Dangburg.)

Annotations indicate effective choices or *Chicago*-style formatting.

Rinder 9

Notes

1. Tracie Rozhon, "Chicago Girds for Big Battle over Its Skyline," *New York Times*, November 12, 2000, Academic Search Premier.

Newspaper article in database

2. David Garrard Lowe, *Lost Chicago* (New York: Watson-Guptill Publications, 2000), 123.

Print book

3. *Columbia Encyclopedia*, 6th ed. (2000), s.v. "Louis Sullivan."

4. Daniel Bluestone, *Constructing Chicago* (New Haven: Yale University Press, 1991), 105.

5. Alan J. Shannon, "When Will It End?" *Chicago Tribune*, September 11, 1987, quoted in Karen J. Dilibert, *From Landmark to Landfill* (Chicago: Chicago Architectural Foundation, 2000), 11.

Indirect source

6. Steve Kerch, "Landmark Decisions," *Chicago Tribune*, March 18, 1990, sec. 16.

7. John W. Stamper, *Chicago's North Michigan Avenue* (Chicago: University of Chicago Press, 1991), 215.

8. Alf Siewers, "Success Spoiling the Magnificent Mile?" *Chicago Sun-Times*, April 9, 1995.

9. Paul Gapp, "McCarthy Building Puts Landmark Law on a Collision Course with Developers," *Chicago Tribune*, April 20, 1986, quoted in Karen J. Dilibert, *From Landmark to Landfill* (Chicago: Chicago Architectural Foundation, 2000), 4.

10. Gapp, quoted in Dilibert, 4.

Reference to previous source

11. Rozhon, "Chicago Girds for Big Battle."

12. Kerch, "Landmark Decisions."

Second reference to source

13. Robert Bruegmann, *The Architects and the City* (Chicago: University of Chicago Press, 1997), 443.

Rinder 10

Bibliography
starts on new
page

Print book

Pamphlet

Newspaper
article

Article from
database

Bibliography
entries use
hanging indent
and are not
numbered

Bibliography

Bluestone, Daniel. *Constructing Chicago*. New Haven: Yale University Press, 1991.

Bruegmann, Robert. *The Architects and the City*. Chicago: University of Chicago Press, 1997.

Dilibert, Karen J. *From Landmark to Landfill*. Chicago: Chicago Architectural Foundation, 2000.

Kerch, Steve. "Landmark Decisions." *Chicago Tribune*, March 18, 1990, sec. 16.

Lowe, David Garrard. *Lost Chicago*. New York: Watson-Guptill Publications, 2000.

Rozhon, Tracie. "Chicago Girds for Big Battle over Its Skyline." *New York Times*, November 12, 2000. Academic Search Premier.

Siewers, Alf. "Success Spoiling the Magnificent Mile?" *Chicago Sun-Times*, April 9, 1995.

Stamper, John W. *Chicago's North Michigan Avenue*. Chicago: University of Chicago Press, 1991.

48 CSE Style

Writers in the physical sciences, the life sciences, and mathematics often use the documentation style set forth by the Council of Science Editors (CSE). Guidelines for citing print sources can be found in *Scientific Style and Format: The CSE Manual for Authors, Editors, and Publishers*, Eighth Edition (2014).

48a Following CSE manuscript format

Title page. Center the title of your paper. Beneath it, center your name. Include other relevant information, such as the course name and number, the instructor's name, and the date submitted.

Margins and spacing. Leave standard margins at the top and bottom and on both sides of each page. Double-space the text and the references list.

Page numbers. Type a short version of the paper's title and the page number in the upper right-hand corner of each page. Omit the page number on the title page and number the first page of text as page 2.

Abstract. CSE style frequently calls for a one-paragraph abstract. The abstract should be on a separate page, right after the title page, with the title *Abstract* centered one inch from the top of the page.

Headings. Use headings when possible to help readers quickly find the contents of a section of the paper.

Tables and figures. Tables and figures must be labeled *Table* or *Figure* and numbered separately, one sequence for tables and one for figures. Give each table and figure a short, informative title. Be sure to introduce each table and figure in your text, and comment on its significance.

List of references. Start the list of references on a new page at the end of the essay, and continue to number the pages consecutively. Center the title *References* one inch from the top of the page, and double-space before beginning the first entry.

48b Creating CSE in-text citations

In CSE style, citations within an essay follow one of three formats.

- The *citation-sequence format* calls for a superscript number or a number in parentheses after any mention of a source. The sources are numbered in the order they appear. Each number refers to the same source every time it is used. The first source mentioned in the paper is numbered *1*, the second source is numbered *2*, and so on.
- The *citation-name format* also calls for a superscript number or a number in parentheses after any mention of a source. The numbers are added after the list of references is completed and alphabetized, so that the source numbered *1* is alphabetically first in the list of references, *2* is alphabetically second, and so on.
- The *name-year format* calls for the last name of the author and the year of publication in parentheses after any mention of a source. If the last name appears in a signal phrase, the name-year format allows for giving only the year of publication in parentheses.

Before deciding which system to use, ask your instructor's preference.

1. IN-TEXT CITATION USING CITATION-SEQUENCE OR CITATION-NAME FORMAT

VonBergen[12] provides the most complete discussion of this phenomenon.

For the citation-sequence and citation-name formats, you would use the same superscript ([12]) for each subsequent citation of this work by VonBergen.

2. IN-TEXT CITATION USING NAME-YEAR FORMAT

VonBergen (2003) provides the most complete discussion of this phenomenon.

Hussar's two earlier studies of juvenile obesity (1995, 1999) examined only children with diabetes.

The classic examples of such investigations (Morrow 1968; Bridger et al. 1971; Franklin and Wayson 1972) still shape the assumptions of current studies.

48c Creating a CSE list of references

The citations in the text of an essay correspond to items on a list titled *References*, which starts on a new page at the end of the essay. Continue to number the pages consecutively, center the title *References* one inch from the top of the page, and double-space before beginning the first entry. Start each entry flush left and indent subsequent lines one-quarter inch.

The order of the entries depends on which format you follow:

- **Citation-sequence format:** number and list the references in the order the references are first cited in the text.
- **Citation-name format:** list and number the references in alphabetical order.
- **Name-year format:** list the references, unnumbered, in alphabetical order.

In the following examples, you will see that both the citation-sequence and citation-name formats call for listing the date after the publisher's name in references for books and after the periodical name in references for articles. The name-year format calls for listing the date immediately after the author's name in any kind of reference.

CSE style also specifies the treatment and placement of the following basic elements in the list of references:

- **Author.** List all authors last name first, and use only initials for first and middle names. Do not place a comma after the author's last name, and do not place periods after or spaces between the initials. Use a period after the last initial of the last author listed.
- **Title.** Do not italicize titles and subtitles of books and titles of periodicals. Do not enclose titles of articles in quotation marks. For books and articles, capitalize only the first word of the title and any proper nouns or proper adjectives. Abbreviate and capitalize all major words in a periodical title.

As you refer to these examples, pay attention to how publication information (publishers for books, details about periodicals for articles) and other specific elements are styled and punctuated.

Books

1. ONE AUTHOR

CITATION-SEQUENCE AND CITATION-NAME

1. Buchanan M. Nexus: small worlds and the groundbreaking theory of networks. New York (NY): Norton; 2003.

NAME-YEAR

Buchanan M. 2003. Nexus: small worlds and the groundbreaking theory of networks. New York (NY): Norton.

2. TWO OR MORE AUTHORS

CITATION-SEQUENCE AND CITATION-NAME

2. Wojciechowski BW, Rice NM. Experimental methods in kinetic studies. 2nd ed. St. Louis (MO): Elsevier Science; 2003.

DIRECTORY TO CSE STYLE

CSE style for references

NAME-YEAR

Wojciechowski BW, Rice NM. 2003. Experimental methods in kinetic studies. 2nd ed. St. Louis (MO): Elsevier Science.

3. ORGANIZATION AS AUTHOR

CITATION-SEQUENCE AND CITATION-NAME

3. World Health Organization. The world health report 2002: reducing risks, promoting healthy life. Geneva (Switzerland): The Organization; 2002.

Place the organization's abbreviation at the beginning of the name-year entry, and use the abbreviation in the corresponding in-text citation. Alphabetize the entry by the first word of the full name, not by the abbreviation.

NAME-YEAR

[WHO] World Health Organization. 2002. The world health report 2002: reducing risks, promoting healthy life. Geneva (Switzerland): The Organization.

4. BOOK PREPARED BY EDITOR(S)

CITATION-SEQUENCE AND CITATION-NAME

4. Torrence ME, Isaacson RE, editors. Microbial food safety in animal agriculture: current topics. Ames (IA): Iowa State University Press; 2003.

NAME-YEAR

Torrence ME, Isaacson RE, editors. 2003. Microbial safety in animal agriculture: current topics. Ames (IA): Iowa State University Press.

5. SECTION OF A BOOK WITH AN EDITOR

CITATION-SEQUENCE AND CITATION-NAME

5. Kawamura A. Plankton. In: Perrin MF, Wursig B, Thewissen JGM, editors. Encyclopedia of marine mammals. San Diego (CA): Academic Press; 2002. p. 939–942.

NAME-YEAR

Kawamura A. 2002. Plankton. In: Perrin MF, Wursig B, Thewissen JGM, editors. Encyclopedia of marine mammals. San Diego (CA): Academic Press. p. 939–942.

6. CHAPTER OF A BOOK

CITATION-SEQUENCE AND CITATION-NAME

6. Honigsbaum M. The fever trail: in search of the cure for malaria. New York (NY): Picador; 2003. Chapter 2, The cure; p. 19–38.

NAME-YEAR

Honigsbaum M. 2003. The fever trail: in search of the cure for malaria. New York (NY): Picador. Chapter 2, The cure; p. 19–38.

7. PAPER OR ABSTRACT IN CONFERENCE PROCEEDINGS

CITATION-SEQUENCE AND CITATION-NAME

7. Gutierrez AP. Integrating biological and environmental factors in crop system models [abstract]. In: Integrated Biological Systems Conference; 2003 Apr 14–16; San Antonio, TX. Beaumont (TX): Agroeconomics Research Group; 2003. p. 14–15.

NAME-YEAR

Gutierrez AP. 2003. Integrating biological and environmental factors in crop system models [abstract]. In: Integrated Biological Systems Conference; 2003 Apr 14–16; San Antonio, TX. Beaumont (TX): Agroeconomics Research Group. p. 14–15.

Periodicals

Provide volume and issue numbers for journals. For magazines, include the month and year or the month, day, and year. For newspaper articles, include the section designation and column number, if any, and the date. For all periodicals, give inclusive page numbers. For rules on abbreviating journal titles, consult the CSE manual or ask an instructor.

8. ARTICLE IN A JOURNAL

CITATION-SEQUENCE AND CITATION-NAME

8. Mahmud K, Vance ML. Human growth hormone and aging. New Engl J Med. 2003;348(2):2256–2257.

NAME-YEAR

Mahmud K, Vance ML. 2003. Human growth hormone and aging. New Engl J Med. 348(2):2256–2257.

9. ARTICLE IN A WEEKLY JOURNAL

CITATION-SEQUENCE AND CITATION-NAME

9. Holden C. Future brightening for depression treatments. Science. 2003 Oct 31:810–813.

NAME-YEAR

Holden C. 2003. Future brightening for depression treatments. Science. Oct 31:810–813.

10. ARTICLE IN A MAGAZINE

CITATION-SEQUENCE AND CITATION-NAME

10. Livio M. Moving right along: the accelerating universe holds secrets to dark energy, the Big Bang, and the ultimate beauty of nature. Astronomy. 2002 Jul:34–39.

NAME-YEAR

Livio M. 2002 Jul. Moving right along: the accelerating universe holds secrets to dark energy, the Big Bang, and the ultimate beauty of nature. Astronomy. 34–39.

11. ARTICLE IN A NEWSPAPER

CITATION-SEQUENCE AND CITATION-NAME

11. Kolata G. Bone diagnosis gives new data but no answers. New York Times (National Ed.). 2003 Sep 28;Sect. 1:1 (col. 1).

Kolata G. 2003 Sep 28. Bone diagnosis gives new data but no answers. New York Times (National Ed.). Sect. 1:1 (col. 1).

Digital sources

These examples use the citation-sequence or citation-name system. To adapt them to the name-year system, delete the note number and place the update date immediately after the author's name.

The basic entry for most sources accessed through the Internet should include the following elements:

- **Author.** Give the author's name, if available, last name first, followed by the initial(s) and a period.
- **Title.** For book, journal, and article titles, follow the style for print materials. For all other types of electronic material, reproduce the title that appears on the screen.
- **Description.** Identify sources such as images, infographics, podcasts, videos, blogs, and social media posts with descriptive words in brackets: *[infographic]*, *[video]*, *[podcast, episode 12]*.
- **Place of publication.** For online books and websites, include the place of publication as you would for print sources.
- **Publisher.** For material other than journal articles from websites and online databases, include the individual or organization that produces or sponsors the site. If no publisher can be determined, use the words *publisher unknown* in brackets.
- **Dates.** Cite three important dates if possible: the date that the publication was placed on the Internet or the copyright date; the latest date of any update or revision; and the date the publication was accessed by you.
- **Page, document, volume, and issue numbers.** When citing a portion of a larger work or site, list the inclusive page numbers or document numbers of the specific item being cited. For journals or journal articles, include volume and issue numbers. If exact page

numbers are not available, include in brackets the approximate
length in computer screens, paragraphs, or bytes: [2 screens], [10
paragraphs], [332K bytes].

- **Address.** Include the URL or other electronic address, followed by a
period.

12. MATERIAL FROM AN ONLINE DATABASE

12. Shilts E. Water wanderers. Can Geographic. 2002 [accessed
2010 Jan 27];122(3):72–77. Academic Search Premier. http://www
.ebscohost.com/ Document No.: 6626534.

13. ARTICLE IN AN ONLINE JOURNAL

13. Perez P, Calonge TM. Yeast protein kinase C. J Biochem. 2002 Oct
[accessed 2008 Nov 3];132(4):513–517. http://edpex104.bcasj.or.jp
/jb-pdf/132-4/jb132-4-513.pdf.

14. ARTICLE IN AN ONLINE NEWSPAPER

14. Brody JE. Reasons, and remedies, for morning sickness.
New York Times Online. 2004 Apr 27 [accessed 2009 Apr 30].
http://www.nytimes.com/2009/04/27/health/27BROD.html.

15. ONLINE BOOK

15. Patrick TS, Allison JR, Krakow GA. Protected plants of Georgia. Social
Circle (GA): Georgia Department of Natural Resources; c1995 [accessed
2010 Dec 3]. http://www.georgiawildlife.com/content/displaycontent
.asp?txtDocument=89&txtPage=9.

To cite a portion of an online book, give the name of the part after
the publication information: *Chapter 6, Encouraging germination.*
See model 6.

16. WEBSITE

> 16. Geology and public policy. Boulder (CO): Geological Society
> of America; c2010 [updated 2010 Jun 3; accessed 2010 Sep 19].
> http://www.geosociety.org/geopolicy.htm.

17. GOVERNMENT WEBSITE

> 17. Health disparities: reducing health disparities in cancer. Atlanta
> (GA): Centers for Disease Control and Prevention (US); 2010 [updated
> 2010 Apr 5; accessed 2010 May 1]. http://www.cdc.gov/cancer
> /healthdisparities/basic_info/disparities.htm.

48d A sample student writing project, CSE style

The following excerpt from a literature review by Joanna Hays conforms to the name-year format in the CSE guidelines described in this chapter. The digital resources for this book include her complete project. (See the inside back cover for more details.)

Niemann-Pick Disease 2

Overview

Niemann-Pick Disease (NP) occurs in patients with deficient
acid sphingomyelinase (ASM) activity as well as with the lysosomal
accumulation of sphingomyelin. It is an autosomal recessive disorder
(Levran et al. 1991). As recently as 1991, researchers had classified
two major phenotypes: Type A and Type B (Levran et al. 1991). In
more recent studies several more phenotypes have been identified,
including Types C and D. Each type of NP has distinct characteristics
and effects on the patient. NP is distributed worldwide, but is closely
associated with Ashkenazi Jewish descendants. Niemann-Pick Disease
is relevant to the molecular world today because of advances being
made in the ability to identify mutations, to trace ancestry where the
mutation may have originated, and to counsel patients with a high
potential of carrying the disease. Genetic counseling primarily consists
of confirmation of the particular disease and calculation of the
possible future reappearance in the same gene line (Brock 1974). The
following discussion will summarize the identification of mutations
causing the various forms of NP, the distribution of NP, as well as new
genotypes and phenotypes that are correlated with NP.

Mutations Causing NP

Levran et al. (1991) inform readers of the frequent identification
of missense mutations in the gene associated with Ashkenazi Jewish
persons afflicted by Type A and Type B NP. This paper identifies the
mutations associated with NP and the beginning of many molecular
techniques to develop diagnoses. Greer et al. (1998) identify a new
mutation that is specifically identified to be the cause of Type D. NP
in various forms is closely associated with the founder effect caused
by a couple married in the early 1700s in what is now Nova Scotia.
Simonaro et al. (2002) discusses the distribution of Type B NP as well
as new phenotypes and genotypes. All three of these papers identify

Niemann-Pick Disease 9

References

Brock DJH. 1974. Prenatal diagnosis and genetic counseling. J Clin Pathol. 27(8 Suppl):150–155.

Greer WL, Ridell DC, Gillan TL, Girouard GS, Sparrow SM, Byers DM, Dobson MJ, Neumann PE. 1998. The Nova Scotia (type D) form of Niemann-Pick disease is caused by a $G_{3097} \rightarrow T$ transversion in NPC1. Am J Hum Genet. 63(1):52–54.

Levran O, Desnick RJ, Schuchman EH. 1991. Niemann-Pick disease: a frequent missense mutation in the acid sphingomyelinase gene of Ashkenazi Jewish type A and B patients. P Natl Acad Sci. 88(9):3748–3752.

Simonaro CM, Desnick RJ, McGovern MM, Wasserstein MP, Schuchman EH. 2002. The demographics and distribution of type B Niemann-Pick disease: novel mutations lead to new genotype/phenotype correlations. Am J Hum Genet. 71(6):1413–1419.

Glossary of Usage

Conventions of usage might be called the "good manners" of discourse. And just as manners vary from culture to culture and time to time, so do conventions of usage. Matters of usage, like other language choices you must make, depend on what your purpose is and on what is appropriate for a particular audience at a particular time.

a, an Use *a* with a word that begins with a consonant (*a book*), a consonant sound such as "y" or "w" (*a euphoric moment, a one-sided match*), or a sounded *h* (*a hemisphere*). Use *an* with a word that begins with a vowel (*an umbrella*), a vowel sound (*an X-ray*), or a silent *h* (*an honor*).

accept, except The verb *accept* means "receive" or "agree to." *Except* is usually a preposition that means "aside from" or "excluding." *All the plaintiffs except Mr. Kim decided to accept the settlement.*

advice, advise The noun *advice* means "opinion" or "suggestion"; the verb *advise* means "offer advice." *Doctors advise everyone not to smoke, but many people ignore the advice.*

affect, effect As a verb, *affect* means "influence" or "move the emotions of"; as a noun, it means "emotions" or "feelings." *Effect* is a noun meaning "result"; less commonly, it is a verb meaning "bring about." *The storm affected a large area. Its effects included widespread power failures. The drug effected a major change in the patient's affect.*

aggravate The formal meaning is "make worse." *Having another mouth to feed aggravated their poverty.* In academic and professional writing, avoid using *aggravate* to mean "irritate" or "annoy."

all ready, already *All ready* means "fully prepared." *Already* means "previously." *We were all ready for Lucy's party when we learned that she had already left.*

all right, alright Avoid the spelling *alright*.

all together, altogether *All together* means "all in a group" or "gathered in one place." *Altogether* means "completely" or "everything considered." *When the board members were all together, their mutual distrust was altogether obvious.*

allude, elude *Allude* means "refer indirectly." *Elude* means "avoid" or "escape from." *The candidate did not even allude to her opponent. The suspect eluded the police for several days.*

allusion, illusion An *allusion* is an indirect reference. An *illusion* is a false or misleading appearance. *The speaker's allusion to the Bible created an illusion of piety.*

a lot Avoid the spelling *alot.*

already See *all ready, already.*

alright See *all right, alright.*

altogether See *all together, altogether.*

among, between In referring to two things or people, use *between.* In referring to three or more, use *among. The relationship between the twins is different from that among the other three children.*

amount, number Use *amount* with quantities you cannot count; use *number* for quantities you can count. *A small number of volunteers cleared a large amount of brush.*

an See *a, an.*

and/or Avoid this term except in business or legal writing. Instead of *fat and/or protein,* write *fat, protein, or both.*

any body, anybody, any one, anyone *Anybody* and *anyone* are pronouns meaning "any person." *Anyone* [or *anybody*] *would enjoy this film. Any body* is an adjective modifying a noun. *Any body of water has its own ecology. Any one* is two adjectives or a pronoun modified by an adjective. *Customers could buy only two sale items at any one time. The winner could choose any one of the prizes.*

anyplace In academic and professional discourse, use *anywhere* instead.

anyway, anyways In writing, use *anyway,* not *anyways.*

apt, liable, likely *Likely to* means "probably will," and *apt to* means "inclines or tends to." In many instances, they are interchangeable. *Liable* often carries a more negative sense and is also a legal term meaning "obligated" or "responsible."

as Avoid sentences in which it is not clear if *as* means "when" or "because." For example, does *Carl left town as his father was*

arriving mean "at the same time as his father was arriving" or "because his father was arriving"?

as, as if, like In academic and professional writing, use *as* or *as if* instead of *like* to introduce a clause. *The dog howled <u>as if</u>* [not *like*] *it were in pain. She did <u>as</u>* [not *like*] *I suggested.*

assure, ensure, insure *Assure* means "convince" or "promise"; its direct object is usually a person or persons. *She <u>assured</u> voters she would not raise taxes. Ensure* and *insure* both mean "make certain," but *insure* usually refers specifically to protection against financial loss. *When the city rationed water to <u>ensure</u> that the supply would last, the Browns could no longer afford to <u>insure</u> their car-wash business.*

as to Do not use *as to* as a substitute for *about. Karen was unsure <u>about</u>* [not *as to*] *Bruce's intentions.*

at, where See *where.*

awhile, a while Always use *a while* after a preposition such as *for, in,* or *after. We drove <u>awhile</u> and then stopped for <u>a while</u>.*

bad, badly Use *bad* after a linking verb such as *be, feel,* or *seem.* Use *badly* to modify an action verb, an adjective, or another verb. *The hostess felt <u>bad</u> because the dinner was <u>badly</u> prepared.*

bare, bear Use *bare* to mean "uncovered" and *bear* to refer to the animal or to mean "carry" or "endure": *The walls were <u>bare</u>. The emptiness was hard to <u>bear</u>.*

because of, due to Use *due to* when the effect, stated as a noun, appears before the verb *be. His illness was <u>due to</u> malnutrition.* (*Illness*, a noun, is the effect.) Use *because of* when the effect is stated as a clause. *He was sick <u>because of</u> malnutrition.* (*He was sick*, a clause, is the effect.)

being as, being that In academic or professional writing, use *because* or *since* instead of these expressions. *<u>Because</u>* [not *being as*] *Romeo killed Tybalt, he was banished to Padua.*

beside, besides *Beside* is a preposition meaning "next to." *Besides* can be a preposition meaning "other than" or an adverb meaning "in addition." *No one <u>besides</u> Francesca would sit <u>beside</u> him.*

between See *among, between.*

brake, break *Brake* means "to stop" and also refers to a stopping mechanism: *Check the <u>brakes</u>. Break* means "fracture" or an interruption: *The coffee <u>break</u> was too short.*

breath, breathe *Breath* is a noun; *breathe,* a verb. "*Breathe,*" said the nurse, so June took a deep *breath*.

bring, take Use *bring* when an object is moved from a farther to a nearer place; use *take* when the opposite is true. *Take the box to the post office; bring back my mail.*

but that, but what Avoid using these as substitutes for *that* in expressions of doubt. *Hercule Poirot never doubted that* [not *but that*] *he would solve the case.*

but yet Do not use these words together. *He is strong but* [not *but yet*] *gentle.*

can, may *Can* refers to ability and *may* to possibility or permission. *Since I can ski the slalom well, I may win the race.*

can't hardly *Hardly* has a negative meaning; therefore, *can't hardly* is a double negative. This expression is commonly used in some varieties of English but is not used in academic English. *Tim can* [not *can't*] *hardly wait.*

can't help but This expression is not used in academic English. Use *I can't help going* rather than *I can't help but go.*

censor, censure *Censor* means "remove that which is considered offensive." *Censure* means "formally reprimand." *The newspaper censored stories that offended advertisers. The legislature censured the official for misconduct.*

compare to, compare with *Compare to* means "regard as similar." *Jamie compared the loss to a kick in the head. Compare with* means "examine to find differences or similarities." *Compare Tim Burton's films with David Lynch's.*

complement, compliment *Complement* means "go well with." *Compliment* means "praise." *Guests complimented her on how her earrings complemented her gown.*

comprise, compose *Comprise* means "contain." *Compose* means "make up." *The class comprises twenty students. Twenty students compose the class.*

conscience, conscious *Conscience* means "a sense of right and wrong." *Conscious* means "awake" or "aware." *Lisa was conscious of a guilty conscience.*

consensus of opinion Use *consensus* instead of this redundant phrase. *The family consensus was to sell the old house.*

consequently, subsequently *Consequently* means "as a result"; *subsequently* means "then." *He quit, and subsequently his wife lost her job; consequently, they had to sell their house.*

continual, continuous *Continual* means "repeated at regular or frequent intervals." *Continuous* means "continuing or connected without a break." *The damage done by continuous erosion was increased by the continual storms.*

could of *Have*, not *of*, should follow *could, would, should,* or *might*. *We could have [not of] invited them.*

criteria, criterion *Criterion* means "standard of judgment" or "necessary qualification." *Criteria* is the plural form. *Image is the wrong criterion for choosing a president.*

data *Data* is the plural form of the Latin word *datum*, meaning "fact." Although *data* is used informally as either singular or plural, in academic or professional writing, treat *data* as plural. *These data indicate that fewer people are smoking.*

different from, different than *Different from* is generally preferred in academic and professional writing, although both of these phrases are widely used. *Her lab results were no different from [not than] his.*

discreet, discrete *Discreet* means "tactful" or "prudent." *Discrete* means "separate" or "distinct." *The leader's discreet efforts kept all the discrete factions unified.*

disinterested, uninterested *Disinterested* means "unbiased." *Uninterested* means "indifferent." *Finding disinterested jurors was difficult. She was uninterested in the verdict.*

distinct, distinctive *Distinct* means "separate" or "well defined." *Distinctive* means "characteristic." *Germany includes many distinct regions, each with a distinctive accent.*

doesn't, don't *Doesn't* is the contraction for *does not*. Use it with *he, she, it,* and singular nouns. *Don't* stands for *do not*; use it with *I, you, we, they,* and plural nouns.

due to See *because of, due to*.

each other, one another Use *each other* in sentences involving two subjects and *one another* in sentences involving more than two.

effect See *affect, effect.*

elicit, illicit The verb *elicit* means "draw out." The adjective *illicit* means "illegal." *The police elicited from the criminal the names of others involved in illicit activities.*

elude See *allude, elude.*

emigrate from, immigrate to *Emigrate from* means "move away from one's country." *Immigrate to* means "move to another country." *We emigrated from Norway in 1999. We immigrated to the United States.*

ensure See *assure, ensure, insure.*

enthused, enthusiastic Use *enthusiastic* rather than *enthused* in academic and professional writing.

equally as good Replace this redundant phrase with *equally good* or *as good.*

every day, everyday *Everyday* is an adjective meaning "ordinary." *Every day* is an adjective and a noun, meaning "each day." *I wore everyday clothes almost every day.*

every one, everyone *Everyone* is a pronoun. *Every one* is an adjective and a pronoun, referring to each member of a group. *Because he began after everyone else, David could not finish every one of the problems.*

except See *accept, except.*

explicit, implicit *Explicit* means "directly or openly expressed." *Implicit* means "indirectly expressed or implied." *The explicit message of the ad urged consumers to buy the product, while the implicit message promised popularity if they did so.*

farther, further *Farther* refers to physical distance. *How much farther is it to Munich? Further* refers to time or degree. *I want to avoid further delays.*

fewer, less Use *fewer* with nouns that can be counted. Use *less* with general amounts that you cannot count. *The world needs fewer bombs and less hostility.*

finalize *Finalize* is a pretentious way of saying "end" or "make final." *We closed [not finalized] the deal.*

firstly, secondly, etc. *First, second,* etc., are more common in U.S. English.

flaunt, flout *Flaunt* means to "show off." *Flout* means to "mock" or "scorn." *The drug dealers flouted authority by flaunting their wealth.*

former, latter *Former* refers to the first and *latter* to the second of two things previously mentioned. *Kathy and Anna are athletes; the former plays tennis, and the latter runs.*

further See *farther, further.*

good, well *Good* is an adjective and should not be used as a substitute for the adverb *well. Gabriel is a good host who cooks well.*

good and *Good and* is colloquial for "very"; avoid it in academic and professional writing.

hanged, hung *Hanged* refers to executions; *hung* is used for all other meanings.

hardly See *can't hardly.*

herself, himself, myself, yourself Do not use these reflexive pronouns as subjects or as objects unless they are necessary. *Jane and I [not myself] agree. They invited John and me [not myself].*

he/she, his/her Better solutions for avoiding sexist language are to write out *he or she,* to eliminate pronouns entirely, or to make the subject plural. Instead of writing *Everyone should carry his/her driver's license,* try *Drivers should carry their licenses* or *People should carry their driver's licenses.*

himself See *herself, himself, myself, yourself.*

hisself Use *himself* instead in academic or professional writing.

hopefully *Hopefully* is often used informally to mean "it is hoped," but its formal meaning is "with hope." *Sam watched the roulette wheel hopefully [not Hopefully, Sam will win].*

hung See *hanged, hung.*

illicit See *elicit, illicit.*

illusion See *allusion, illusion.*

immigrate to See *emigrate from, immigrate to*.

impact Some readers object to the colloquial use of *impact* or *impact on* as a verb meaning "affect." *Population control may <u>reduce</u> [not impact] world hunger*.

implicit See *explicit, implicit*.

imply, infer To *imply* is to suggest indirectly. To *infer* is to guess or conclude on the basis of indirect suggestion. *The note <u>implied</u> they were planning a small wedding; we <u>inferred</u> we would not be invited*.

inside of, outside of Use *inside* and *outside* instead. *The class regularly met <u>outside</u> [not outside of] the building*.

insure See *assure, ensure, insure*.

interact, interface *Interact* is a vague word meaning "do something that somehow involves another person." *Interface* is computer jargon; when used as a verb, it means "discuss" or "communicate." Avoid both verbs in academic and professional writing.

irregardless, regardless *Irregardless* is a double negative. Use *regardless*.

is when, is where These vague expressions are often incorrectly used in definitions. *Schizophrenia <u>is a psychotic condition in which</u> [not is when or is where] a person withdraws from reality*.

its, it's *Its* is the possessive form of *it*. *It's* is a contraction for *it is* or *it has*. *<u>It's</u> important to observe the rat before it eats <u>its</u> meal*.

kind, sort, type These singular nouns should be modified with *this* or *that*, not *these* or *those*, and followed by other singular nouns, not plural nouns. *Wear <u>this kind</u> of dress [not those kind of dresses]*.

kind of, sort of In formal writing, avoid these colloquialisms. *Amy was somewhat [not kind of] tired*.

know, no Use *know* to mean "understand." *No* is the opposite of *yes*.

later, latter *Later* means "after some time." *Latter* refers to the second of two items named. *Juan and Chad won all their early matches, but the <u>latter</u> was injured <u>later</u> in the season*.

latter See *former, latter* and *later, latter*.

lay, lie *Lay* means "place" or "put." Its main forms are *lay, laid, laid*. It generally has a direct object, specifying what has been placed. *She <u>laid</u> her books on the desk*. *Lie* means "recline" or "be

positioned" and does not take a direct object. Its main forms are *lie, lay, lain. She lay awake until two.*

leave, let *Leave* means "go away." *Let* means "allow." *Leave alone* and *let alone* are interchangeable. *Let me leave now, and leave [or let] me alone from now on!*

lend, loan In academic and professional writing, do not use *loan* as a verb; use *lend* instead. *Please lend me your pen so that I may fill out this application for a loan.*

less See *fewer, less.*

let See *leave, let.*

liable See *apt, liable, likely.*

lie See *lay, lie.*

like See *as, as if, like.*

likely See *apt, liable, likely.*

literally *Literally* means "actually" or "exactly as stated." Use it to stress the truth of a statement that might otherwise be understood as figurative. Do not use *literally* as an intensifier in a figurative statement. *Mirna was literally at the edge of her seat* may be accurate, but *Mirna is so hungry that she could literally eat a horse* is not.

loan See *lend, loan.*

loose, lose *Lose* is a verb meaning "misplace." *Loose* is an adjective that means "not securely attached." *Sew on that loose button before you lose it.*

lots, lots of Avoid these informal expressions meaning "much" or "many" in academic or professional discourse.

man, mankind Replace these terms with *people, humans, humankind, men and women,* or similar wording.

may See *can, may.*

may be, maybe *May be* is a verb phrase. *Maybe* is an adverb that means "perhaps." *He may be the head of the organization, but maybe someone else would handle a crisis better.*

media *Media* is the plural form of the noun *medium* and takes a plural verb in formal contexts. *The media are [not is] obsessed with scandals.*

might of See *could of.*

moral, morale A *moral* is a succinct lesson. *The moral of the story is that generosity is rewarded. Morale* means "spirit" or "mood." *Office morale was low.*

myself See *herself, himself, myself, yourself.*

no See *know, no.*

nor, or Use *either* with *or* and *neither* with *nor.*

number See *amount, number.*

off, of Use *off* without *of. The spaghetti slipped off* [not *off of*] *the plate.*

OK, O.K., okay All are acceptable spellings, but avoid the term in academic and professional discourse.

on account of Use this substitute for *because of* sparingly or not at all.

one another See *each other, one another.*

or See *nor, or.*

outside of See *inside of, outside of.*

owing to the fact that Avoid this and other wordy expressions for *because.*

passed, past Use *passed* to mean "went by" or "received a passing grade": *The marching band passed the reviewing stand.* Use *past* to refer to a time before the present: *Historians study the past.*

per In formal writing, use the Latin *per* only in standard technical phrases such as *miles per hour.* Otherwise, find English equivalents. *As mentioned in* [not *As per*] *the latest report, the country's average daily food consumption is only 2,000 calories.*

percent, percentage Use *percent* with a specific number; use *percentage* with an adjective such as *large* or *small. Last year, 80 percent of the members were female. A large percentage of the members are women.*

plenty *Plenty* means "enough" or "a great abundance." *They told us America was a land of plenty.* Colloquially, it is used to mean "very," a usage you should avoid in academic and professional writing. *He was very* [not *plenty*] *tired.*

plus *Plus* means "in addition to." *Your salary plus mine will cover our expenses.* In academic writing, do not use *plus* to mean "besides" or "moreover." *That dress does not fit me. Besides* [not *Plus*], *it is the wrong color.*

precede, proceed *Precede* means "come before"; *proceed* means "go forward." *Despite the storm that* precede *the ceremony, the wedding* proceeded *on schedule.*

pretty Except in informal situations, avoid using *pretty* as a substitute for "rather," "somewhat," or "quite." *Bill was* quite [not *pretty*] *disagreeable.*

principal, principle When used as a noun, *principal* refers to a head official or an amount of money; when used as an adjective, it means "most significant." *Principle* means "fundamental law or belief." *Albert went to the* principal *and defended himself with the* principle *of free speech.*

proceed See *precede, proceed.*

quotation, quote *Quote* is a verb, and *quotation* is a noun. *He* quoted *the president, and the* quotation [not *quote*] *was preserved in history books.*

raise, rise *Raise* means "lift" or "move upward." (Referring to children, it means "bring up.") It takes a direct object; someone raises something. *The guests* raised *their glasses to toast. Rise* means "go upward." It does not take a direct object; something rises by itself. *She saw the steam* rise *from the pan.*

rarely ever Use *rarely* by itself, or use *hardly ever. When we were poor, we* rarely *went to the movies.*

real, really *Real* is an adjective, and *really* is an adverb. Do not substitute *real* for *really*. In academic and professional writing, do not use *real* or *really* to mean "very." *The old man walked* very [not *real* or *really*] *slowly.*

reason is because Use either *the reason is that* or *because*—not both. *The* reason *the copier stopped* is that [not *is because*] *the paper jammed.*

reason why Avoid this expression in formal writing. *The* reason [not *reason why*] *this book is short is market demand.*

regardless See *irregardless, regardless.*

respectfully, respectively *Respectfully* means "with respect." *Respectively* means "in the order given." *Karen and David are,* respectively, *a juggler and an acrobat. The children treated their grandparents* respectfully.

rise See *raise, rise.*

set, sit *Set* usually means "put" or "place" and takes a direct object. *Sit* refers to taking a seat and does not take an object. *Set your cup on the table, and sit down.*

should of See *could of.*

since Be careful not to use *since* ambiguously. In *Since I broke my leg, I've stayed home,* the word *since* might be understood to mean either "because" or "ever since."

sit See *set, sit.*

so In academic and professional writing, avoid using *so* alone to mean "very." Instead, follow *so* with *that* to show how the intensified condition leads to a result. *Aaron was so tired that he fell asleep at the wheel.*

someplace Use *somewhere* instead in academic and professional writing.

some time, sometime, sometimes *Some time* refers to a length of time. *Please leave me some time to dress. Sometime* means "at some indefinite later time." *Sometime I will take you to London. Sometimes* means "occasionally." *Sometimes I eat sushi.*

sort See *kind, sort, type.*

sort of See *kind of, sort of.*

stationary, stationery *Stationary* means "standing still"; *stationery* means "writing paper." *When the bus was stationary, Pat took out stationery and wrote a note.*

subsequently See *consequently, subsequently.*

supposed to, used to Be careful to include the final *-d* in these expressions. *He is supposed to attend.*

sure, surely Avoid using *sure* as an intensifier. Instead, use *certainly. I was certainly glad to see you.*

take See *bring, take.*

than, then Use *than* in comparative statements. *The cat was bigger than the dog.* Use *then* when referring to a sequence of events. *I won, and then I cried.*

that, which A clause beginning with *that* singles out the item being described. *The book that is on the table is a good one* specifies

the book on the table as opposed to some other book. A clause beginning with *which* may or may not single out the item, although some writers use *which* clauses only to add more information about an item being described. *The book, which is on the table, is a good one* contains a *which* clause between the commas. The clause simply adds extra, nonessential information about the book; it does not specify which book.

theirselves Use *themselves* instead in academic and professional writing.

then See *than, then*.

thorough, threw, through *Thorough* means "complete": *After a thorough inspection, the restaurant reopened*. *Threw* is the past tense of *throw*, and *through* means "in one side and out the other": *He threw the ball through a window*.

to, too, two *To* generally shows direction. *Too* means "also." *Two* is the number. *We, too, are going to the meeting in two hours*. Avoid using *to* after *where*. *Where are you flying* [not *flying to*]?

two See *to, too, two*.

type See *kind, sort, type*.

uninterested See *disinterested, uninterested*.

unique Some people argue that *unique* means "one and only" and object to usage that suggests it means merely "unusual." In formal writing, avoid constructions such as *quite unique*.

used to See *supposed to, used to*.

very Avoid using *very* to intensify a weak adjective or adverb; instead, replace the adjective or adverb with a stronger, more precise, or more colorful word. Instead of *very nice*, for example, use *kind, warm, sensitive, endearing*, or *friendly*.

way, ways When referring to distance, use *way*. *Graduation was a long way* [not *ways*] *off*.

well See *good, well*.

where In formal writing, use *where* alone, not with words such as *at* and *to*. *Where are you going* [not *going to*]?

which See *that, which*.

who, whom In formal writing, use *who* if the word is the subject of the clause and *whom* if the word is the object of the clause. *Monica, <u>who</u> smokes incessantly, is my godmother.* (*Who* is the subject of the clause; the verb is *smokes*.) *Monica, <u>whom</u> I saw last winter, lives in Tucson.* (*Whom* is the object of the verb *saw*.) Because *whom* can seem excessively formal, some writers rephrase sentences to avoid it.

who's, whose *Who's* is a contraction for *who is* or *who has*. *<u>Who's</u> on the patio? Whose* is a possessive form. *<u>Whose</u> sculpture is in the garden? <u>Whose</u> is on the patio?*

would of See *could of.*

yet See *but yet.*

your, you're *Your* shows possession. *Bring <u>your</u> sleeping bag along. You're* is the contraction for *you are*. *<u>You're</u> in the wrong sleeping bag.*

yourself See *herself, himself, myself, yourself.*

Index

with Glossary of Terms

Words in blue are followed by a definition. **Boldface** terms in definitions are themselves defined elsewhere in this index.

regular verb, 118 A **verb** that
forms the **past tense** and past
participle by adding *-d* or *-ed* to the
base form (*care, cared, cared; look,
looked, looked*).

subject The **noun** or **pronoun** and
related words that indicate who or
what a **sentence** is about. The simple
subject is the noun or pronoun:

transition A word or **phrase** that signals a progression from one **sentence** or part of a sentence to another.

transitive verb, 127, 157 A **verb** that acts on an **object**: *I posted my review online.*

U

V

verb, 118–32 A word or **phrase**, essential to a **sentence**, that expresses the action of a sentence or

For Multilingual Writers

 Look for the "Multilingual" icon to find advice of special interest to international students and others whose home language is not English.

- Adapting genre structures (10d)
- Building verb phrases (21b)
- Using infinitives and gerunds (21c)
- Using conditional sentences appropriately (21i)
- Understanding count and noncount nouns (22a)
- Using determiners (22b)
- Using articles (22c)
- Choosing the right preposition (27a)
- Using two-word verbs idiomatically (27b)

Boxed Tips for Multilingual Writers

Revision Symbols

Numbers in bold refer to sections of this book.

abbr	abbreviation **42a**	para	paraphrase **15a**
ad	adjective/adverb **24**	pass	inappropriate passive **21g, 34b**
agr	agreement **23, 26b**	ref	unclear pronoun reference **26c**
awk	awkward		
cap	capitalization **41**	run-on	run-on (fused) sentence **28**
case	case **26a**	sexist	sexist language **18b, 26b**
cliché	cliché **20d**	shift	shift **34**
com	incomplete comparison **30d**	slang	slang **20a**
concl	weak conclusion	sp	spelling
cs	comma splice **28**	sum	summarize **15a**
def	define	trans	transition
dm	dangling modifier **25c**	verb	verb form **21**
doc	documentation **45–48**	vs	verb sequence **21f**
emph	emphasis unclear	vt	verb tense **21e–f**
ex	example needed	wc	word choice **20**
frag	sentence fragment **29**	wrdy	wordy **32**
fs	fused sentence **28**	wv	weak verb **32d**
hyph	hyphen **44**	ww	wrong word **20b**
inc	incomplete construction **30**	. ? !	period, question mark, exclamation point **37**
it	italics **43**		
jarg	jargon **20a**	,	comma **35**
lc	lower case **41**	;	semicolon **36**
lv	language variety **19**	'	apostrophe **38**
mix	mixed construction **30, 34**	" "	quotation marks **39**
mm	misplaced modifier **25a**	( ) [ ] —	parentheses, brackets, dash **40a–c**
ms	manuscript form **45c, 46b, 47b, 48a**	: / …	colon, slash, ellipses **40d–f**
no ,	no comma **35i**	^	insert
num	number **42b**	∽	transpose
¶	paragraph	⌒	close up
//	faulty parallelism **33**	X	delete

390